Mary is for Everyone

In memory of Martin Gillett KCSG (1902–1980)
the Founder of the Ecumenical Society
of the Blessed Virgin Mary
and of
Léon-Joseph Cardinal Suenens (1906–1996)
its Patron and Supporter

Mary is for Everyone

Papers on Mary and Ecumenism
given at International Congresses of the
Ecumenical Society of the Blessed Virgin Mary
at Winchester (1991), Norwich (1994),
and Bristol (1996),
and a Conference at Dromantine, Newry (1995)

edited by

William McLoughlin OSM
and
Jill Pinnock

with a Foreword by

Michael Nazir-Ali, Bishop of Rochester

First published in 1997

Gracewing
Fowler Wright Books
2 Southern Avenue, Leominster
Herefordshire HR6 0QF

© The Ecumenical Society of the Blessed Virgin Mary 1997

The right of the editors and contributors to be identified as the authors of this work has been asserted in accordance with the Copyright, Designs and Patents Act 1988.

ISBN 0 85244 429 X

Typeset in Palatino by Jill Pinnock

Printed by Cromwell Press
Broughton Gifford
Wiltshire SN12 8PH

Contents

Notes on Contributors   vii
Foreword by Bishop Michael Nazir-Ali   xi
Acknowledgements   xii
Preface   xiii

Mary in Scripture

1   Behold your Mother: reflections on John 19.25–27   2
    John McHugh
2   Did Mary remain a virgin?   15
    William J. Bridcut

Mary in systematic theology

3   A systematic theology of Mary   22
    Edward Yarnold SJ
4   Feminist theology: a view of Mary   32
    Ann Loades
5   The Marian church: Hans Urs von Balthasar   41
    and the ordination of women
    Paul McPartlan
6   The Blessed Virgin Mary in the Protestant tradition   56
    David Butler
7   Mary's spiritual maternity   68
    Arthur Burton Calkins
8   The Blessed Virgin in depth psychology: a theological   86
    appraisal
    Donald Dawe

Mary and the unity of the churches

9   Five ecumenical heroes (Mercier, Halifax, Willebrands,   102
    Ramsey, Suenens)
    Alberic Stacpoole OSB
10 Corporate reunion – dream or nightmare? the legacy of   116
    Malines
    Bernard Barlow OSM
11 The Malines Conversations: a significant milestone   128
    in the history of Anglican-Roman Catholic dialogue
    Roger Greenacre

12   The meaning of the Malines Conversations for today   146
     Pierre Parré

13   Mary – Servant of the Word: towards   157
     convergence in ecclesiology
     David Carter

14   Mary, Mother of the Lord, sign of grace, faith and   171
     holiness: reflections on the Methodist–Roman Catholic
     joint statement
     John Newton

15   Letters of Paul VI and John Paul II on the Virgin Mary: 181
     the evolution of a dialogue
     Mary Ann DeTrana

16   The Melkite Church – unity with diversity   195
     David J. White

17   Catholic-Orthodox relations in the patriarchate of Antioch 208
     Archbishop Isidore Battikha

Mary and spirituality

18   A personal approach to Marian spirituality: a Lutheran   220
     perspective
     Anita J. Baly

19   Julian of Norwich and the Blessed Virgin Mary   236
     John P. H. Clark

20   Mary, Mary, quite contrary: a meditation on Mary   251
     in natural religion and psychology
     Emma Shackle

21   Mary, intercessor on our behalf, one with us   266
     in the communion of saints, and witness to
     what we may become in Christ: a personal
     ecumenical journey
     Ross Mackenzie

22   Why should he send his Mother? some reflections on   274
     Marian apparitions
     Richard Rutt

23   Apparitions of our Lady   285
     Michael O'Carroll CSSp

Mary in literature

24   The Blessed Virgin Mary in some modern poets   294
     Gordon S. Wakefield

Notes on Contributors

Anita J. Baly, PhD, writes from the perspective of the Lutheran tradition; she lectures at Mount St Mary's College, Emmitsburg MD USA.

The Revd Fr Bernard Barlow OSM recently completed and defended his PhD research on the topic of 'The Malines Conversations'; he is now serving as Prior-Provincial of the English Province of Servite Friars, a Roman Catholic religious order.

H E Archbishop Isidore Battikha is Melkite–Greek Catholic Archbishop of Pelusium, and Patriarchal Vicar in Damascus of His Beatitude Maximos V Hakim, Melkite Patriarch of Antioch, Alexandria and Jerusalem.

The Revd William J. Bridcut, an Evangelical member of the Church of Ireland, is Superintendent of the Irish Church Missions, and a longstanding and respected member of the Dublin branch of ESBVM.

The Revd David Butler MA BSc contributes from within the Methodist tradition; he lectures in Church History at The Queen's College, Birmingham. He is presently researching the life of Bishop Richard Challoner, and is author of *Methodists and Papists* and *Dying to be One*.

The Revd Arthur Burton Calkins STD is a priest of the Roman Catholic diocese of New Orleans, USA, presently serving as an official in the Pontifical Commission *Ecclesia Dei* in Rome.

David Carter MA MLitt was formerly Head of Religious Studies at Wilson's School, Wallington, Surrey, and is Chairman of the London branch of ESBVM; he is a Methodist member of the Roman Catholic – Methodist Theological Dialogue in England and Wales and of the British Methodist – Roman Catholic committee which produced *Mary, Mother of the Lord: sign of grace, faith and holiness*.

The Revd John P.H. Clark DD contributes from within the Anglican tradition; he is Vicar of Chevington, Northumberland, and an expert on the 14th-century English Mystic, Julian of Norwich.

The Revd Donald G. Dawe ThD is now Robert L. Dabney Professor of Systematic Theology, Emeritus, at Union Theological Seminary, Richmond VA, USA, and a frequent Presbyterian contributor at ESBVM Congresses.

Mary Ann DeTrana MA is President and a founder-member of the American Chapter of ESBVM, and has contributed to several past Congresses. She is a member of the Orthodox Church in America, and leads retreats for Orthodox clergy wives.

The Revd Canon Roger Greenacre ChLJ MA, an Anglican priest, is Canon Precentor of Chichester Cathedral and a member of the Council of ESBVM. He worked for ten years in France, and is an Oblate of the Abbey of Notre Dame du Bec: in 1966 he was a main speaker at the twelfth International Mariological Congress at Czestochowa.

Ann Loades BA PhD (Durham) **MA** (McMaster) writes as an Anglican; she is Professor of Divinity in the Department of Theology, University of Durham, England.

The Revd Dr Ross Mackenzie, sometime Professor of Church History, Union Theological Seminary, Richmond VA and formerly Pastor of the First Presbyterian Church, Gainesville FL, is now Director of the Department of Religion at Chautauqua Institution, Western New York.

The Very Revd Canon John McHugh DD, formerly Lecturer on New Testament at Ushaw College and Durham University, and English member of the Pontifical Biblical Commission, is author of *The Mother of Jesus in the New Testament* (1978), and is presently engaged in research on St John's Gospel.

The Revd Paul McPartlan MA STD DPhil is a priest of the Archdiocese of Westminster, formerly a Research Fellow of St Edmund's College, Cambridge and now Lecturer in Systematic Theology at Heythrop College, University of London. Dr McPartlan is a well-known published writer and speaker on ecclesiology and ecumenism.

The Revd John Newton MA PhD DLitt, sometime President of the Methodist Conference and Moderator of the Free Church Federal Council (1989), is a patron of the ESBVM, and has been a significant contributor to and supporter of the Society's endeavours in the field of ecumenism.

M L'Abbé Pierre Parré MA is ecumenical officer for Cardinal Danneels, Archbishop of Malines–Brussels and co-chairman of the Belgian ARC; he helped organise the celebrations to mark the 1996 Malines Conversations anniversary.

The Revd Fr Michael O'Carroll DD is an internationally-renowned Mariologist and ecumenist whose extensive writings include his celebrated Mariological encyclopaedia *Theotokos*; he holds both earned (Fribourg) and honorary (Maynooth) doctorates. He was the first chairman of the Dublin branch of ESBVM, and is engaged in research on the authorised biography of Bartholomew I, Ecumenical patriarch of Constantinople.

The Revd Richard Rutt CBE MA DLitt, sometime Anglican Bishop of Taejon, Korea and Bishop of Leicester, contributes now from within the Roman Catholic tradition.

Emma Shackle MA MLitt (Oxon) MPhil (London) is Lecturer and Tutor in Psychology at Plater College, Oxford, specialising in the psychology of religion. She is Chair of the Catholic Psychology Group.

The Revd Fr Alberic Stacpoole OSB MC MA DPhil FRHistS is a monk of Ampleforth, formerly Senior Tutor at St Benet's Hall, Oxford, and currently serving in the Benedictine parish of Leyland. He was General Secretary of ESBVM from 1980 – 1994, and has often contributed to the published writings of the Society.

The Revd Gordon S. Wakefield DD MA MLitt was formerly Principal of the ecumenical theological seminary, The Queen's College, Birmingham. A distinguished Methodist, he is a much respected ecumenist, and a patron of the Society.

The Revd David J. White JChLJ MA FIL, sometime Rector of Lapford, Devon, is now ordained to serve as a priest of the Melkite–Greek Catholic Patriarchate of Antioch, and of the Patriarchal Eparchy of Alexandria.

The Revd Fr Edward Yarnold SJ DD is University Research Lecturer and Tutor in Theology at the University of Oxford, and formerly Master of Campion Hall, Oxford. He is internationally renowned as a writer and speaker, and has served the ESBVM both as Associate General Secretary and, since 1994, as Hon. General Secretary.

Foreword

Over the past few years I have been heartened to see a growth, in the West, of the understanding of icons and their use. There are, of course, many icons of the Virgin with Child. They are popular because they are about a very basic aspect of Christian belief. God has revealed himself in human form, and to do so he has used the weak but obedient humanity of Mary. Many of these icons show the Child in Mary's lap, or playing with her as children do with their mothers.

It is noteworthy that the earliest icons and mosaics always show Mary *with* the Child. She is significant because of him. The Slavonic Icon of the Mother of God of the Sign – *Znamenaya* – (referring to Isaiah 7.14) is different. Here the Child is not in the Virgin's lap, or in her arms: he is in her *womb*. Mary was carefully prepared for her high calling by the light of the Eternal Word about to become incarnate through her.

Christ was not only in her womb but in her heart. At the time of his birth, and throughout his life, Mary had the Gospel in her heart (Luke 2.19, 51). She is, therefore, the first Christian, and her faith challenges us today.

It is right to teach the truth, as John Betjeman puts it,

> That God was Man in Palestine,
> And lives today in bread and wine.

It is right to put the Christian story in its historical and social context. But this should lead to personal commitment and to inner transformation. These, in turn, should lead to making a difference in the world. When Mary realised that she was to be the mother of the Messiah, she knew that this would scatter the proud, upset the mighty, exalt the humble and feed the hungry (Luke 1.51–53). The coming of the Messiah into our hearts should lead to a similar revolution.

I welcome and commend this collection of papers concerning the Virgin Mary. My hope and prayer is that through them we may once again discover Mary's proper place in the life of the Church.

+Michael Roffen:
Easter 1997

Acknowledgements

The Editors wish to express their appreciation for editorial assistance from Fr Edward Yarnold SJ and Mr David Carter; for assistance in the preparation of material to Mr David G. Saul and Mr Frank O'Brien, and for information on icons to Mrs Mariamna Fortounatto.

'Jesus and his Mother', from *Collected Poems* by Thom Gunn. Copyright © 1994 by Thom Gunn. Reprinted by permission of Farrar, Straus & Giroux, Inc. and of Faber and Faber Ltd.

The cover picture is reproduced by kind permission of the Federation of Provinces of the Friar Servants of Mary of Italy and Spain.

Preface

Pope John Paul II's stated intention, in his 1987 encyclical *Redemptoris Mater*, was to promote a renewed ecumenical dialogue focused on the Virgin Mary: he explained that

> the circumstance which now moves me to take up this subject once more is the prospect of the year 2000, now drawing near, in which the Bi-millennial Jubilee of the birth of Jesus Christ at the same time directs our gaze towards his Mother (*RM* 3).

However one calculates the Thousand Days countdown to the Jubilee, whether according to the French–American reckoning or according to Greenwich's, the transferred celebration of the Solemnity of the Most Holy Annunciation from the usual date of 25 March (which this year fell during the Christian West's Holy Week) to the observance of it at the beginning of those thousand days, helps us to direct our gaze as the Pope suggested a decade ago.

Days and decades, millennia and anniversaries shape the human interest, and as we ponder the close of this second millennium, we might cast our mind back to the drawing to a close of the first. In the second half of the tenth century an observable, intense and lively interest in, and increased attention to, the Blessed Virgin Mary and her cult emerged in England. It found expression less in theological discussion of Marian doctrine, and more notably in the Marian dedications and rededications of the monastic reforms focused on Winchester among other centres, where monastic preaching actively encouraged the laity to venerate the Virgin. Perhaps it is not too contrived to see a parallel in England in the second half of the twentieth century, as the second millennium draws to a close, in which we have seen a similar intense and lively interest in Mary emerging, more certainly seeking to advance theological discussion of her cult, but also to promote a devotion that could truly recognise Mary as for everyone.

A major participant in this has been the Society now marking its 30th anniversary of foundation, when on 28 April 1967, at an informal meeting held at the Charing Cross Hotel in London, a society with an express dedication to the Blessed Virgin Mary and based on a strict ecumenical parity came into being, to be known as the Ecumenical Society of the Blessed Virgin Mary. The Society's establishment was due to the vision and effort of H.M. Gillett, known to all as Martin. In 1966 he had attended the two days of celebrations marking the 40th anniversary of the famed Malines Conversations, and, in the course of his own personal 'Malines Conversations' with other participants, was led to discuss plans for a new force in the efforts for Christian Unity. Names later to have celebrated status in the annals of ecumenism aligned themselves to his cause. To name them all is a task already well done in other published works of the ESBVM and elsewhere in this volume, but perhaps it is not invidious to mention Léon-Joseph Cardinal Suenens, to whose memory this volume of our collected Congress papers is dedicated, and whose first encouragement to promote the idea in England sent Martin on a pilgrimage of love that had first been awakened, he told Miss Veronica O'Brien at the Malines anniversary, by the frequency of the church dedications to Mary that he had noted as a boy in North Hampshire – that same area of influence at the end of the first millennium when intensity of devotion to the Virgin was expressed in a rise in Marian dedications. What came of that pilgrimage was Martin's inspirational role as Founder of a movement dedicated to the Blessed Virgin Mary, which brings together Christians of different traditions to examine her role in the Church, and which laid the foundations of a new force in ecumenism that at its inception was felt, even by its ardent supporters, to have a less than sanguine future.

With thoughts of a thousand years being but a day, and realising that 30 years more have passed since the Malines anniversary of 1966 that looked back, but also gave rise to a fresh ecumenical inspiration whose 30th anniversary we now mark, the Ecumenical Society of the Blessed Virgin Mary now offers a collection of its Congress papers to a readership that has expressed impatience for their coming. The publication of this selection of papers in some measure echoes the struggle of the ecumenical movement to include all. It is only a selection because a number of the papers have not, despite best efforts, come into the hands of the editors. Those not included do not appear for a range of reasons. Rather like the ecumenical movement itself, the journey to this publishing moment spans years. In fact, these papers are the product of International Congresses at Winchester (1991), Norwich (1994) and Bristol (1996), along with the Dromantine Conference (1995). In the course of years some papers, no doubt possessing rich content of truth and insight, were lost or lost sight of, having been spirited away. This was a matter of regret to the editors because it considerably delayed publication, and occasions an apology to those whose work did not appear for this reason. Some were thought by their authors, in the event of the Society's failure to publish speedily, to have been overtaken by time, and in one illustrious case the author provided his own response to his own earlier paper, which now appears in one inclusion. Some were missed due to the usual failure of good intentions on the part of authors to furnish us with texts of their papers at the time of the Congresses or even after reminders subsequent thereto. Despite the regrettable omissions, however, there is a range included that reflects the interests and preoccupations of an ecumenical society that contributes from a commanding and respected position. It would be a great encouragement to the work of the ESBVM if the appearance of these papers encouraged new contributors to the ecumenical exchange in regard to the Blessed Virgin Mary, especially if the representation of all traditions could be strengthened thereby.

Editors might be forgiven for fearing the charge of lack of rigour in exercise of editorial power in allowing a weakness or uneven quality in what is included in a collection. In this the ESBVM avails itself of a defence that is derived from its very *raison d'être*, namely, to promote ecumenical devotion, and the study, at various levels, of the place of the Blessed Virgin Mary in the Church, under Christ. The 24 papers we are able to publish reflect the title of the collection, which could very well have been Martin Gillett's own motto, encapsulating as it does what the ESBVM is for and about. That title itself was inspired by that of another work that was published by Fr Graham Leonard, former Bishop of London, a founder member of ESBVM. His title was *The Gospel is for Everyone*, which also goes to the heart of the ESBVM. To be allowed to hear and to have the right to have preached the good news, Christians know there can be no cause of division among us. Instead of her being a cause of such, the ESBVM seeks to show that Mary does not divide but brings together, when we properly understand the role of Mary in the work of salvation. The Gospel and Mary, who are both then for everyone, convey to us a belief in God's love of and caring for everyone too.

To come then to an anniversary year so readily seems to express a conclusion when in fact the task is still so very much alive and needing still more effort. Indeed, begging for forgiveness for plagiarising another's brilliant line, to make an end is to make a beginning, for the end is where we start from. The continuing efforts of the local branches of the ESBVM, a celebratory Conference in July of this year (1997) and preparations for the XIIth International Congress of the ESBVM in August 1998 indicate the constancy to purpose that the Society seeks to continue to pursue. Constancy to purpose must not go unacknowledged, and what better moment to think of some distinguished members of our Society? Since 1978 our International Congresses have been guided skilfully by our Associate General Secretary, Mr Joe Farrelly KSG. In 1980 he took over from Martin Gillett, with uncanny similarity to the same, that inspirational and tenacious animating role that guaranteed his promise to the Founder to ensure that the ESBVM should not be allowed to die. In this his 80th year, we wish Joe sincere thanks for his indefatigable services to the ESBVM, and we acknowledge also the unsung and unseen but definitely unstinting support in those services of his beloved wife Anne. We also owe a debt of gratitude to our Hon

General Secretary, the Revd Dr Edward Yarnold SJ, whose involvement in the ESBVM since its earliest days and since 1994 in his presiding role, has added a distinction to its efforts that have been enhanced and enriched by his very great gifts so generously and humbly shared with us. Finally, an inevitably inadequate word of thanks to Mrs Jill Pinnock, the ESBVM's Publications Secretary and co-editor of this volume. It is appropriate that an expression of gratitude for her service to our Society should appear in a volume on which she has lavished so much care and skill, and that we hope will reach not only the readership of the ESBVM's membership list through the Newsletter, which itself displays her outstanding editorial excellence and devotion to the Society's need to communicate well its contributors' efforts, but also those outside the ESBVM who benefit from and deeply appreciate its published work of recent years. The Society is indebted to her and yet again to a hidden resource in the support of her dear husband, Fr Geoffrey Pinnock. In an ecumenical society such as ours, that experiences and reflects the tensions and pressures that come from the constantly changing world of ecumenical pilgrimage, we have been well served by these good servants of the Blessed Virgin Mary, and we give thanks for them.

The ESBVM has journeyed far already in its 30 years of existence, and with the help and generosity of many – some famous and acknowledged, many less well-known and sadly not so easily acknowledged as they should be – has learnt an important way of advancing. It is clear there is no profit in merely rearranging the pieces on a doctrinal chessboard to achieve a supposed success, but there is gain in seeking to discover the meaning of the doctrine that occasions division by appropriately praying one's way into the religious experience of what is expressed in it. The Spirit will use this experience to bring followers of the Virgin's Son together even if the way we struggle to express truth is unequal to the task. The experience of prayer gathered together with Mary as in Acts 1.14 enables us to experience division as the scandal and stupidity it is. The Ecumenical Society of the Blessed Virgin Mary exists to advance the study at various levels of the place of the Blessed Virgin Mary in the Church, under Christ, and of related theological questions, and in the light of such study to promote ecumenical devotion. We thank God for what the ESBVM has done already, and ask that the Blessed Virgin Mary may keep us close to her Son as we respond to her urging to do whatever he tells us.

7 April 1997
Solemnity of the Most Holy Annunciation of the Lord
W.M. McLoughlin OSM
Priory of St Philip Benizi, Begbroke, Oxford.

Mary
in
Scripture

1

Behold your Mother
Reflections on John 19.25–27

John McHugh

Twenty years ago, at our first International Conference in Coloma College in 1971, I read a paper on the Mother of Jesus in the Gospel according to John, the content of which was published four years later in the book entitled *The Mother of Jesus in the New Testament*.[1] Twenty years later, I am still willing to defend the conclusion I advanced there, but I now want to rewrite the arguments, and to reach the conclusion by a somewhat different route.

Among the principal problems facing anyone who reads the New Testament is the relationship between the first three Gospels and that of St John. One way of resolving it is to affirm that John's is not a historical record of the life of Jesus, but only a symbolic and theological interpretation of that life. Though this is, in my view, too simplistic a solution, I would readily agree that the primary purpose of the Fourth Gospel is to present a symbolic and theological interpretation of Jesus' life; I would add, however, that most of its symbolism and interpretation is intended to elucidate the deepest meaning of events or sayings related in the Synoptic tradition. I propose to re-examine the passage in John 19.25–27 in the light of this theory.

> Standing by the cross of Jesus were his mother, and his mother's sister, Mary the wife of Clopas, and Mary Magdalene. When Jesus saw his mother, and the disciple whom he loved standing near, he said to his mother, 'Woman, behold, your son!' Then he said to the disciple, 'Behold, your mother!' And from that hour the disciple took her to his own home (John 19.25–27 in the Revised Standard Version).

When one compares this passage with the parallel scene in the Synoptics, three problems arise. First, if Mary the mother of Jesus was in fact present, and stood beside the cross, why is it that neither Matthew nor Mark mentions the fact? More significantly still, why does Luke not record it? When we remember the prominent role that he assigns to Mary in his Infancy Gospel, and the quite unexpected reference to her presence in the Upper Room after the Ascension (Acts 1.14), can we really accept that if she had been present at the crucifixion, Luke would not have known of it? He appears to be very well informed about (and possibly by) 'the women who had followed along with Jesus from Galilee' (cf. Luke 8.2–3; 23.49, 55–56; and 24.10). A second, though in comparison a minor, problem is that Matthew (27.55), Mark (15.40) and Luke (23.49) all affirm that the women present on Calvary stood 'at a distance', whereas John (19.25) says they stood 'beside the cross'.[2] Thirdly, there is some difficulty in correlating the lists of names given by the Synoptics and by John; they certainly seem *prima facie* to be distinctly different.

These problems are, of course, far from new. In fact, they are nearly two thousand years old, and the classical solution has always been that the Fourth Gospel was written by John the son of Zebedee, that this same John is the disciple mentioned in this passage, and that in this very scene he (or his editor) assures the reader that he was truly present on Calvary. The assertion in John 19.35 cannot be lightly overlooked, much less dismissed as historically worthless, for nowhere else in the Gospels is there so solemn a claim that a particular fact is being guaranteed by the word of an eye-witness. In itself, this verse declares only that someone who stood beside the cross is vouching for the fact that blood and water flowed from Jesus' side; but if that is true, it is surely reasonable to infer that the other events related in John 19, including the episode about Jesus' mother, are also based ultimately on the testimony of that same person, whether or not this witness was himself the disciple referred to in verses 25–27.

But the problem remains; indeed, the difficulty is only aggravated. If Mary was in fact present on Calvary, why does St Luke, of all people, not record the fact, particularly in the light of his inclusion of Simeon's prophecy that 'A sword shall pass through your own soul' (Luke 2.35)? For those who accept the historical trustworthiness both of Luke and of John, this is a most serious dilemma, and it is regrettable that the most common reaction is silence.

Twenty years ago, I myself took refuge in silence, for I was baffled. I was very conscious that even if the writer of the Fourth Gospel was not John the son of Zebedee, John 19.35 still contains a claim that the written account rests on the testimony of an eye-witness. At the same time, I could offer no explanation for the silence of the Synoptics. It would have been easy to say that much of the account in John was not meant to be factual, but only interpretative and merely symbolic; but what prevented me from adopting this view was that, quite apart from the affirmation in John 19.35, I could find no symbolic role for three of the women mentioned, namely, 'his mother's sister, Mary the wife of Clopas, and Mary Magdalen'. The naming of these women, in these terms, plus 19.35, seemed to me to turn the balance of probability against the theory that this episode represented a purely symbolic story unconnected with observed historical fact. On balance, I was convinced that the writer who penned the account of the crucifixion in John intended to assert that his account was trustworthy, and the simplest and most satisfactory way forward was to take him at his word and to accept the historicity of the scene as described in the Fourth Gospel.

Today, I want to put before you some further reflections which may, I hope, take us a little deeper into the thought of the Gospel according to John. And for the sake of clarity, let me state my thesis as clearly as I can. I do not now think that the Blessed Virgin Mary was physically present at the crucifixion, but I firmly believe that the scene in the Fourth Gospel which portrays her as personally present is *therefore* of even greater significance when we seek to assess the role and function of Mary in the work of redemption and in the Church.

I. Who were the women at the crucifixion?

According to the Synoptics the following women were present at the crucifixion:

i)	Mary Magdalen, according to Matthew, Mark and Luke;
ii)	Mary the mother of James (and Joses), according to Matthew, Mark and Luke;
iii)	according to Matthew, the mother of the sons of Zebedee (27.56);
iv)	according to Mark, Salome (15.40);[3]
v)	according to Luke, Joanna, the wife of Herod's steward (24.10; cf. 8.3).

In fact, Luke does not, in his account of the death of Jesus, mention any of them by name, but in 24.10 he speaks of Mary Magdalen, Joanna and Mary the mother of James. However, his phrase 'the women who had followed him from Galilee' (23.49, cf. 55, and 8.3) is both clear enough to identify the group, and vague enough to permit us to include among them the three women mentioned under iii, iv, and v. Note that all three Synoptics give pride of place to Mary Magdalen, and that all mention by name Mary the mother of James and Joseph [Joses]. The reason that the Synoptics mention these names becomes clear immediately: the women who are the witnesses of Jesus' death and burial, are also the first witnesses of the empty tomb.

Let me next present, without proof, the pattern of relationships within the Holy Family which I have argued for in my book. I suggest that the relationships were as shown in the following diagram: that is to say, Mary the mother of James and Joseph [Joses], who is certainly the 'other

Mary' mentioned in Matt. 27.61 (cf. Mark 15.47), was Joseph's sister, and
therefore the sister-in-law of the Blessed Virgin.[4]

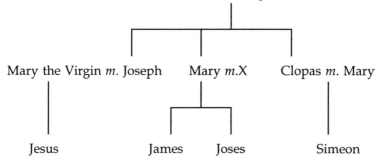

In the light of the above pattern of relationships, we may therefore
translate and gloss John 19.25 as follows: 'There stood beside the cross of
Jesus (1) his mother, and (2) his mother's sister-in-law [that is, Mary the
mother of James and Joseph], (3) Mary the wife of Clopas, and (4) Mary
Magdalen.' I have here translated the Greek word ἀδελφη not as 'sister'
but as 'sister-in-law', because it is almost unthinkable that the mother of
Jesus had a sister who was also called Mary. There is no reason why the
word should not be interpreted as meaning 'sister-in-law', for Greek at
this period does not have a specific term for such a legal relationship;
when a woman married, she became a member of her husband's family,
and thereby the 'sister' of all within that family. 'Mary the mother of
James and Joseph' is therefore here identified as 'his mother's sister-in-
law'. In that case, John lists for us two of the principal Synoptic witnesses
of the burial and of the empty tomb, namely, Mary the mother of James,
and Mary Magdalen. Mary the wife of Clopas is also, by marriage, a
relative of the Lord.

John therefore names three women who were unusually close to Jesus
throughout his earthly life, Mary Magdalen, and two others who were
members of his family. More significantly, these two aunts (one by
marriage) were mothers respectively of James and of Simeon, who were
successively leaders, 'presidents' or 'bishops' of the church of Jerusalem.[5]
According to Eusebius (2.23), James was put to death at Easter AD 62,
and his cousin Simeon was elected to succeed him (3.10.22), a position he
held until his own martyrdom under Trajan i.e. between AD 98 and 117
(3.32).[6] If Simeon was indeed bishop in Jerusalem at the time the Fourth
Gospel was being composed, this would be ample reason for recalling
that his mother had been present at the crucifixion.

With these ideas in mind, I now wish to suggest how the writer who
composed the Fourth Gospel took these basic facts, and pondered them,

and then skilfully incorporated them into his new interpretation of the story of the crucifixion.

II. 'There stood beside the Cross of Jesus his mother'

In the Synoptic Gospels, the women present on Calvary are there as witnesses of the death and burial of Jesus (Matt. 27.56, 61 = Mark 15.40–41, 47 = Luke 23.49, 55–56), and of the empty tomb (Matt. 28.1 = Mark 16.1 = Luke 24.1–11, especially v. 10). In the Fourth Gospel, they have a different role.

Let us suppose that the evangelist took from the common Church tradition the names of two women, namely, Mary Magdalen and Mary the mother of James, and added to them, from Jerusalem tradition, the name of Mary, the wife of Clopas. Then, instead of following the Synoptic tradition and writing that 'they stood afar off', or 'at a distance', he settled on a novel interpretation: he would present these women as standing 'close beside' the cross, thus stressing their courage and fidelity in following Jesus not merely to Jerusalem but even to Golgotha. The word used for 'beside' is of importance, for this is the only instance in the entire New Testament where this Greek preposition παρά, when used with the dative case, is followed by a noun denoting not a person but a thing. Perhaps it can best be rendered into English as 'beside the Cross' (with a capital C). The meaning is therefore, by metonymy, 'beside the Crucified'.

This verse, however, affirms that not only these women, but the mother of Jesus also stood close beside the Cross, and we must ask why. Some (notably C. H. Dodd) think that the meaning of the scene is now lost and beyond recovery,[7] but one symbolic interpretation has been widely published, and may be cited in the words of Rudolf Bultmann, its foremost protagonist.

> Doubtless this scene, which in face of the Synoptic tradition can make no claim to historicity, has a symbolic meaning. The mother of Jesus, who tarries by the cross, represents Jewish Christianity that overcomes the offence of the cross. The beloved disciple represents Gentile Christianity, which is charged to honour the former as its mother from whom it has come, even as Jewish Christianity is charged to recognize itself as 'at home' within Gentile Christianity, i.e. included in the membership of the one great fellowship of the Church. And these directions sound out from the cross: i.e. they are the commands of the 'exalted' Jesus.[8]

Now though I can see excellent reasons for affirming that the mother of Jesus, being a Jewess, and a member of the Christian fellowship (Acts 1.14), may represent Jewish Christianity, I can see no ground for affirming that the beloved disciple represents Gentile Christianity.

Indeed, his presence and his privileged position at the Supper (cf. John 13.25) would imply rather the opposite. Admittedly, the Fourth Gospel does not present the Last Supper as a Passover meal (which it certainly is in the Synoptics), because John wishes to identify the moment of Jesus' death with the sacrificing of the Passover Lamb (cf. John 19.31, 36); had he identified the Supper with the Passover meal, the disciple would of necessity have had to be either by race a Jew or by circumcision a member of the fellowship of Israel (cf. Exod. 12.43–49; Num. 9.14). But even if in the Fourth Gospel the Supper is not presented as a Passover meal, Bultmann's suggestion that the disciple beside the Cross stands for Gentile, as distinct from Jewish, Christianity is far from convincing, for there is no positive evidence in the text to support it.

But let us examine whether some genuine symbolism is not hidden in the term 'mother of Jesus'.

i) Could this term be intended to imply that she is that eschatological Daughter of Zion referred to by the prophets, so that John is here taking up the theme so skilfully used by Luke in Luke 1 – 2? Luke presented Mary, the young maiden, as the personification of the Daughter of Zion at the moment of the virginal conception (compare Luke 1.28 with Zeph. 3.14; Zech. 9.9 and Joel 2.21).[9]

In John's Gospel, however, the only occurrence of the term 'Daughter of Zion' is at 12.15:

Fear not, daughter of Zion;
behold, your king is coming.

Here it is the Jewish crowds which represent the Daughter of Zion, greeting their king at his entry into Jerusalem. John cannot therefore easily use the same motif, 'Daughter of Zion', with reference to the mother of Jesus standing beside the Cross, unless, of course, we see the little group beside the Cross as the faithful remnant of the Daughter of Zion. That much is possible, but there is no positive indication in the Johannine Passion narrative to suggest that the evangelist had that concept in mind.

ii) Could the term 'mother of Jesus' be intended to imply 'mother of the Messiah'? Many centuries earlier, in the kingdom of Judah, the queen mother had an official status, but there is no evidence that this was a live concept in New Testament times.[10] Certainly, there was no role in contemporary Jewish expectation for the mother of the warrior-king, the new Davidic Messiah.

In fact, the evangelist is neither interested in nor sympathetic to this expectation. C.H. Dodd writes:

As for the title 'Messiah' itself, I have already observed that no other New Testament writer shows himself so fully aware of the Jewish ideas associated with it[11] as does the Fourth Evangelist. He develops his teaching, in part, by way of opposition to such ideas ... That the Messiah is Son of David, he appears to set aside (like Mark) as at best irrelevant to the true Christian doctrine of the Messiah.[12]

In other words, there is no role in the Fourth Gospel, and particularly not at the foot of the Cross, for Mary as mother of the Messiah in the contemporary Jewish understanding of that term. On the other hand, the evangelist might have welcomed the idea of describing her as mother of the Christ (or Messiah) in the Christian sense of that term, i.e. as the mother of God's Anointed (in a spiritual sense: cf. John 20.31); but his preferred term is simply 'the mother of Jesus'.

iii) *Stabat mater dolorosa*. Since around 1300, in the Latin West, the classical interpretation of the scene at the Cross has been that Mary shared to the full in the sufferings of her Son. Could it be that the Fourth Gospel itself means to present her as the mother of the Suffering Servant portrayed in Isaiah 53?

There is little doubt that the idea of Jesus as Servant of the Lord is present to the mind of the evangelist (cf. John 1.29, 35, and 12.38), but there is nothing in the Old or New Testament to suggest a role for the mother of this Servant. Hence, whatever later Latin tradition may have done with the interpretation of this scene, and however legitimately, and however profitable this may have been for Christian piety, I am not convinced that the *primary* idea of the evangelist as he composed this scene was to assert that the mother of Jesus shared in the *suffering* of her Son. Note the double emphasis, on the words 'primary' and 'suffering'.

For it cannot be too frequently stressed that in John, the crucifixion is not (as in Paul and the Synoptics) the time and place of Jesus' humiliation. Indeed, John's characteristic term for this event is exactly the opposite; for John, the crucifixion is the time and place of Jesus' *exaltation*. This is assuredly, seen from our standpoint, the moment of his most painful suffering; but it is most significant that nowhere in John's Gospel is Jesus ever said 'to suffer', nor is the noun 'suffering' ever used with reference to him. From the standpoint of the evangelist, precisely because of the intensity of the suffering, the crucifixion was the very 'hour' of Jesus' greatest triumph, the ultimate manifestation of his love. 'Jesus knowing that his hour had come to pass over out of this world to the Father, having loved his own who were in the world, loved them to the end' (John 13.1). The theme of the expiation of evil by suffering voluntarily undertaken on behalf of others is exactly the message of Isaiah 53.

Hence Jesus' last word before his departure from this world is 'It is accomplished!' (John 19.30). If we compare this with Jesus' final cry according to Matthew (27.46) and Mark (15.34), 'My God, my God, why hast thou forsaken me?', it becomes luminously clear that the expression in John is a cry of victory: everything is now accomplished. I suggest therefore that the evangelist is concerned not to stress the suffering of the mother of Jesus, but rather to represent her, and the other women, as witnessing and therefore sharing, by reason of their enduring faith, in the *triumph* of Jesus. Perhaps the most accurate artistic representation of this same motif is to be found in the *Pietà* of Michelangelo, where one sees both compassion and sorrow, but also dignity, and even a noble serenity, in the features of the mother. Indeed, if anyone wants a Latin liturgical title for the scene in John, I would suggest, in preference to *Mater dolorosa*, the words *Alma Redemptoris Mater*, 'Dear Mother of the Redeemer'.

iv) For John's primary intention was to show the mother of the Lord as the exemplar of faith. The evangelist first introduced her, in chapter 2, as one who, before Jesus had worked a single sign, could say to the servants at Cana, 'Do whatever he tells you' (2.5).

And because her faith was not then, never had been, based on the evidence of 'signs and wonders' (contrast 2.11 and 4.48), it endured to the last. Perhaps that is why John never uses her proper name, Mary; she is presented only as 'the mother of Jesus', both at Cana and on Calvary. She is seen only in her relationship to Jesus, maybe because John has in mind a tradition that she freely consented, through faith, to whatever destiny God might call her, and so became the mother of Jesus,[13] and followed him to the end. Luke's 'Behold the servant of the Lord' (Luke 1.38) is then faultlessly reflected in John's 'Behold your mother!' (John 19.27).

This interpretation, I believe, provides a satisfactory explanation of the scene in 19.25–27. The mother of Jesus is then represented in the Fourth Gospel as the prototype and exemplar of faith, the first to believe totally and unconditionally, and therefore the one who remains faithful to the end. This interpretation would give a wholly satisfactory sense to the words of Jesus to the disciple, 'Behold your mother'. In other words, I am suggesting that if we look thoughtfully at the Fourth Gospel, Mary is, by reason of her faith, presented at the end as mother of the disciple whom Jesus loved, that is, as Mother of the Christian Church, and only implicitly (there is not a word about it) as a *mater dolorosa* grieving over the death of her son.[14]

v) Can we go further? 'There stood beside the Crucified his mother ...' A tradition going back as far as Irenaeus explains this by comparing Mary with Eve (*advocata Evae*), presenting her as fulfilling the prophecy about the woman in Gen. 3.15, sharing in the triumph of Jesus, the New

Adam. Again, though I do not in any way wish to deny the applicability of this comparison, I am not (yet!) fully convinced that the Fourth Gospel wishes to present Jesus as the Second Adam; but I think it is certainly possible, when we remember the Gospel's interest in Genesis, and especially the line 'In the place where he was crucified there was a garden' (John 19.41; cf. Rev. 22.2). In that case, the mother of Jesus standing beside the tree of the Cross would truly be, in the intention of the evangelist, a Second Eve, sharing in the triumph of the Second Adam, on the day when he by embracing the tree of death changed it into the tree of life, and so reopened to all the gates of Paradise.

III. John's vision of the Cross in the New Jerusalem

It is not in the least surprising that many Christians are disturbed when they hear scholars questioning tenets which they have always taken to be fundamental to their faith, particularly when these questions concern matters that are central in the life of our Lord Jesus Christ. Some remarks on this point may therefore serve to bring this paper to a rounded conclusion.

I would certainly maintain that the four Gospels are true and trustworthy records of the life and teaching of Jesus Christ; but this does not mean that the Gospels are records compiled according to the conventions of positivist nineteenth-century scholarship, in which the cool and impartial, but observant and accurate, recording of facts was seen as the ideal to strive for. Our four Gospels were not written in the universities of nineteenth-century Europe for the benefit of scholars eager to know all the facts about Jesus of Nazareth, to enable them to assess calmly and coolly the claims he is alleged to have made. On the contrary, the four Gospels come from the Eastern Mediterranean, and from the first great epoch of the Roman Empire, and were composed according to the standards and conventions of that era. Above all, they were written not dispassionately, but with a burning faith and a passionate conviction that the generation just past had witnessed the bodily appearance on earth, in Palestine, of the very Son of God, who had permitted himself to be tried like a criminal, to be reviled and crucified, and who had then risen to life from the tomb. It is surely reasonable to ask whether anyone who honestly believed such a story to be true could ever relate it in a cool and disinterested manner.

Nor must we forget that these four Gospels, judged even as literature, are quite evidently written by persons of extraordinarily high intelligence. Consequently, we should not readily suspect these writers of misleading their readers when a reasonable explanation of some apparent problem is to hand.

Over the last three centuries, there has been uninterrupted debate among Christians on what belief in the inspiration of the Bible entails.[15] Successive generations have struggled to find a formula which would preserve a doctrine of divine inspiration without obliging a believer to hold that this divine inspiration guarantees the historical exactitude of every statement made in the Bible. The Second Vatican Council has, I believe, found a balanced and satisfactory formula, in its declaration that 'the books of Scripture teach certainly, faithfully and without error the truth that God for our salvation willed to be recorded in Holy Writ'.[16] 'The truth recorded' is certainly intended to embrace certain historical events, such as the fact of an Exodus from Egypt, and of the Babylonian Exile, and narratives about the life, teaching and suffering of Jesus. On the other hand, the Council's statement is carefully worded. Assuredly it does not mean that when Holy Scripture narrates historical events 'certainly, faithfully and without error', its narratives are like a transcript or tape-recording of a broadcast 'from our own correspondent in Jerusalem'. Such a view of biblical inerrancy is really claiming that Holy Scripture provides a record analogous to one which a television camera crew might have compiled of (say) Jesus' last days in Jerusalem, and postulating also that this alone would represent 'true history'.

Many a painting provides a more faithful likeness than a photograph, and many a novel gives a more accurate record of a period than a formal history. I am therefore deeply grateful to Fr Edward Yarnold for calling our attention to the famous Isenheim altar-piece by Matthias Grünewald (1460–1528), now in the Unterlinden Museum at Colmar in Alsace. It is deservedly regarded as one of the greatest masterpieces depicting the crucifixion, and there beside the Cross, with a lamb beside him, and with his finger pointing to Jesus Crucified, stands – John the Baptist! And Mary too. I think we can all accept that it was perfectly legitimate for the artist to include, in this thoughtful representation of Calvary, John the Baptist and even his little lamb. Karl Barth worked for almost fifty years with a copy of it hanging over his desk.[17] May we not allow an evangelist also the freedom to include, in his word-picture of the scene on Calvary, the mother of Jesus?

Let me therefore end by making a suggestion about the way in which the evangelist may have been inspired to compose this scene. Suppose that, according to the tradition recorded in the Synoptics, Mary Magdalen, and Mary the mother of James, and certain others, did in fact witness the crucifixion, though only from a distance. Whether Jewish convention would have allowed women to approach so close to so gruesome an execution is very debatable, and one very attractive suggestion, recently put forward, is that they might have watched from the city wall, perhaps a hundred yards away.[18]

In the Synoptics, these women are presented as witnesses to the death and burial of Jesus, and to the discovery of an empty tomb. But in the community for which John's Gospel was written, there was no further need of witnesses to testify that Jesus truly died and truly rose. Indeed, granted that Jesus was truly Lord and God (John 20.28), the Cross itself was of necessity the place of his earthly exaltation (12.31–32). The author of the Fourth Gospel therefore gave the women a different role. It was as if he wished to paint in words a holy icon of the Crucifixion as the place and time of Jesus' victory.

Instead of presenting the holy women as witnesses of the death and of the empty tomb, he depicts them as model disciples, faithful to Jesus to the end (as they clearly were). Hence in John they are no longer depicted as 'watching from a distance' (Matt. 27.55 = Mark 15.40 = Luke 23.49); they 'stand beside the Cross' (John 19.25). Where Matthew and Mark list them in the order of their importance as witnesses, with Mary Magdalen (who was not a relative) in the first place, and in second place Mary the mother of James, John arranges the names in a different order. John's order is: Mary the mother of James, first bishop in Jerusalem; then Mary the wife of Clopas and mother of Simeon, successor to James in the church of Jerusalem; and finally Mary Magdalen. Thus John is here composing the scene of a faithful group, representative of the primitive church of Jerusalem, standing beside the Crucified.

What was the motive for including the mother of Jesus in this scene? In Luke, Mary is presented as one who believes without question in the word of God (Luke 1.38 and 45; 11.28; cf. 2.19, 51). I suggest that John shared this belief (compare 2.5, 'Do whatever he tells you'), and presented it pictorially in its ultimate logical development. In John's vision, the icon of Jesus' exaltation and the picture of the infant Church of Jerusalem would not have been complete if it had not included the mother of Jesus. Mary *had* to be represented at the moment when 'all was accomplished' and 'Jesus breathed his last and bequeathed the Spirit' (John 19.29, 30),[19] as had every believer who shares in the victory of the Cross. If Mary Magdalen represents all those disciples (mainly Jewish) who followed Jesus during his earthly life, and Mary the mother of James represents the next generation of believers (mainly Jewish but open to Gentiles), and Mary the wife of Clopas and mother of Simeon represents the generation after that, what is the significance of 'the disciple whom Jesus loved'? I suggest that he represents all those who follow Jesus, Jew and Gentile alike, with no distinction between them. The doctrine that the evangelist is here proposing may therefore be summarized in this manner. Jesus from the Cross, exalted in glory, asks all his disciples, whether Jewish or Gentile, to look to Mary as their mother, and to recognize all that they owe to the faithful souls in Israel; and from that hour the truly faithful follower of Jesus, taking her 'for his own', accepts that 'salvation is of the Jews' (John 4.22).

Notes

1 London (Darton, Longman and Todd) and New York (Doubleday), 1975.
2 In Luke 23.49, some editors of a Synopsis (Huck–Lietzmann, Boismard–Lamouille, but not Aland) italicize the words 'his acquaintances ... stood at a distance' as a quotation of Ps. 38.12 (RSV).
3 Many commentators identify Salome with the mother of the sons of Zebedee, and it is quite possible, but of no relevance for the present argument.
4 For the full supporting arguments, see *The Mother of Jesus in the New Testament*, pp. 234–54.
5 'After the martyrdom of James the Just on the same charge as the Lord, his uncle's child Simeon, the son of Clopas, is next made bishop. He was put forward by everyone, he being yet another cousin of the Lord.' (Hegesippus, who flourished around AD 160–180, wrote five books of *Memoirs*, from which this text is cited by Eusebius, in his *History of the Church*, 4.22).
6 Traditionally, in AD 106, and at the age of 120.
7 Thus, for example, *The Interpretation of the Fourth Gospel* (Cambridge University Press 1954) p. 428. 'The episode of the Mother and the Beloved Disciple (xix 26–27) is peculiar to the Fourth Gospel. Whatever its motive, it does not seem to be dictated by the Johannine theology. It may belong to a special form of the tradition. [Footnote:] Attempts to give a symbolic meaning are in general singularly unconvincing. If a "tendency" is present it seems more likely to have something to do with claims made for the Church at Ephesus for the enigmatic "Beloved Disciple" than with theology.'
8 *The Gospel of John* (Oxford, Blackwell, 1971), p. 673.
9 For a fuller statement of the argument see *The Mother of Jesus in the New Testament*, pp. 37–52.
10 R. de Vaux, *Ancient Israel: Its Life and Institutions* (London, Darton, Longman and Todd, 1961), pp. 117–119. cf. 1 Kings 2.19 (Bathsheba); 15.13 (Maakah); 2 Kings 11.1 (Athaliah).
11 Among 'the Jewish ideas associated with it' is, of course, that of a military leader who would lead a nationalist insurrection against any foreign occupying power and drive it by force of arms from the land, to establish an independent Jewish empire. See, for example, the *Psalms of Solomon*, Ps. 17.
12 *The Interpretation of the Fourth Gospel* (Cambridge University Press 1954), p. 228.
13 There is a little more detail in *The Mother of Jesus in the New Testament*, pp. 128–9.
14 The commonly heard objection, voiced by many after the Second Vatican Council, that Mary, being a member of the Church, cannot logically be called also Mother of the Church, is found equivalently in Bultmann, *The Gospel of John*, p. 673, n. 5. 'That the Mother of Jesus represents the Church is an impossible assertion; the Church on the contrary is the Mother of believers

and the Bride of Christ!' Yet Bultmann himself is here using the term 'Church' as if it excluded Jesus Christ, the Head of the body, and seems momentarily to have forgotten that the term is polyvalent, and is regularly used to denote Christian disciples, followers of Christ. Why, then, should Mary, the earthly mother of Jesus, not be called in this sense the Mother of the Church?

15 I say 'three centuries' in order to place the start of this debate with the publication of John Locke's *The Reasonableness of Christianity as Delivered in the Scriptures* (London 1695), and John Toland's *Christianity not Mysterious* (London 1696).

16 In its *Decree on Divine Revelation*, 11.

17 See E. Busch, *Karl Barth: His life from letters and autobiographical texts* (London, SCM Press, 1976), pp. 116 and 408. The painting provides the frontispiece of the book.

18 The suggestion is by H. Riesner, in *Bibel und Kirche* 40 (1985), p. 24. I owe this reference to J. Gnilka, 'Jesus von Nazareth: Botschaft und Geschichte', in *Herders Theologischer Kommentar zum Neuen Testament*, Supplementband III (1990), p. 313.

19 Only the double rendering can do justice to the meaning of the Greek.

(This paper, delivered at the ESBVM Conference at Dromantine College, Newry, Co. Down, in October 1995, is the revised text of a paper given at the ESBVM Congress at Winchester in August 1991)

2

Did Mary remain a virgin?

William J. Bridcut

The words of Jesus to his mother Mary and to his disciple John, 'Woman, behold your son', 'Son, behold your mother', are said to constitute the strongest argument against the idea that Mary gave birth to and reared other children besides Jesus.[1] How could Jesus be so insulting as to entrust his mother to John if Mary had other children?

But no matter what interpretation we put on the 'brothers' and 'sisters' of Jesus which we read about in the Gospels, there is a difficulty if Mary is entrusted to a man who was not called 'brother'. The difficulty is admittedly greater if the 'brothers' and 'sisters' of Jesus were children of Mary, but there is still a difficulty. John, the disciple whom Jesus loved, and who was probably a cousin of Jesus, is not called 'brother' and yet the Lord's mother is given into his hands.

Different answers are given by those who believe that Mary had other children: John was close to Jesus and was fairly prosperous and had influential friends[2] or that the 'brothers' and 'sisters' were married and so were less able to give Mary a home. These reasons are given when it is felt that Mary stayed with John for the remainder of her life. But we are not told that.[3] It is possible that Jesus simply wished to spare his mother the agony of watching him die and spare himself watching her, and so he asked John to take her away from the scene of crucifixion. This is borne out in Acts 1, where after the resurrection the mother of Jesus is yet again linked with the Lord's brothers.[4]

Marcion, the prominent second century heretic, had used the Lord's question, 'Who is my mother and who are my brothers?' in an effort to prove that Christ was not really human. Tertullian replied[5] and he wrote as if there were no other view than that the brothers and sisters of Jesus were children of Joseph and Mary. Writing at the end of the second century, Tertullian shows not the slightest sign of consciousness that he is going against an established tradition in favour of the perpetual virginity of Mary.[6] Origen, the third-century Alexandrian theologian contradicted Tertullian, but he did not say that Tertullian was going against the teaching of others. Origen merely argues that his own view is admissible.[7] Even Hilary of Poitiers who, in the middle of the fourth century in his *Commentary on Matthew* is the first resolutely to uphold Mary's eternal virginity, has to defend it against numerous people who appeal against this doctrine to the text of Matthew's Gospel and as a result reject this new 'spiritual doctrine' as it was called.[8]

As time passed, those who quoted Scripture in the hope of showing that Mary did not remain a virgin after the birth of Jesus were treated as people who did not understand, even though they might be able to read.[9] It is, however, to the Scriptures that we must turn.

The Scriptures

At the end of the first chapter of Matthew's Gospel we read that Joseph took Mary as his wife but did not know her *until* she had borne a son.

Matthew makes it clear that Joseph did not have sexual relations with Mary *before* the birth of Jesus. Matthew felt it necessary to say this for he knew that everyone would assume that Mary and Joseph would have a normal sexual relationship. If this is the case, then Matthew will assume that his readers will understand that Joseph and Mary lived together as a normal married couple apart from the period before our Lord's birth.

In the Greek, the verb 'to know' is in the imperfect tense, 'he used not to' or 'he was not knowing her until', and implies that the previously abstained from action later took place.[10] Matthew writes like one who knew that the 'brothers' mentioned later on[11] were Mary's children, but did not want to say so explicitly at this point. If Matthew knew that Mary remained a virgin, he would have made it clear that Jesus was her *only* child. Instead, he uses an expression which suggests that Joseph and Mary had normal sexual relations after the birth of Jesus.

In the first chapter of Luke's Gospel the angel informs Mary that she will have a son, and Mary asks, 'How can this be, since I have no husband?' These words are said to show that Mary had taken a vow of virginity. But the picture of Mary in Luke's Gospel is that of a normal Jewish girl looking forward to marriage. Indeed, she had already entered the process of Jewish marriage. We have no evidence from this period that Jewish betrothed women ever took such a vow, and without more information the people for whom Luke was writing would not see such a vow at this place. Mary was wondering how she could conceive immediately or in the near future since she was still in the betrothed period and had not yet been sexually united to Joseph.

In Luke 2, Jesus is described as Mary's *first*born son. If there were no other children, why did Luke not speak of Mary's *only* son? We ask this because Luke is not slow to speak of an only child. In two incidents in the Gospels, the raising of Jairus' daughter and the healing of the demon-possessed boy whom the disciples could not cure, Luke speaks of an only child, while Matthew and Mark, who record the same incidents, do not.[12] Luke is also the only Evangelist to record the story of the widow of Nain who had an only son.[13] So Luke, who is not slow to speak of an only child, does not describe Jesus in this way.

Why did Luke not say that Elizabeth gave birth to her *first*born? Had he done so, and later written about John the Baptist's 'brothers' we would assume that Elizabeth had other children even though, unlike Mary, she was well on in years.

Matthew 12. 46–50 and Mark 3. 31–35

In these places we read of Jesus teaching in a house when Mary and his brothers come along and a message is sent into the house, 'Your mother and your brothers are outside asking for you'. Jesus replied, 'Who are my mother and my brothers?' And looking at his listeners he said, 'Here are my mother and my brothers! Whoever does the will of God is my brother and sister and mother.'

In speaking like this the Lord Jesus is saying that there are closer bonds than those of blood, and his words have force only if the spiritual relationship he speaks about is seen to be as close as *the closest* of family ties. Our Lord's words would fall flat if he said what could mean, 'Whoever does God's will is my cousin'. The words lose their wonderful meaning if the contrast is not with Mary and the brothers related *by blood* to each other and to Jesus on the one hand and those who do God's will on the other.

But notice what Jesus says, 'Whoever does God's will is my *sister*'. There is no mention of sisters waiting outside the house.[14] Commentators give different reasons as to why 'sister' is *introduced*, but can we not say that Jesus would not have said 'sister' unless he had uterine sisters? Jesus is drawing attention to a spiritual relationship closer than the closest of family ties; he would not therefore *introduce* 'sister' unless 'sister' described the closest natural brother-sister relationship.

Matthew 13.54–58 and Mark 6.1–6

Here we are told that Jesus in his last recorded visit to a synagogue was teaching as though he were a qualified rabbi who also displayed powers. When Jesus came into his own country, the people were astonished, saying, 'Where did this man get all this? What is the wisdom given to him? What mighty works are wrought by his hands! Is not this the carpenter (or the son of the carpenter), the son of Mary and brother of James and Joses and Judas and Simon, and are not his sisters here with us?' And they took offence at him.

Jesus is no longer a familiar face around Nazareth, but he is recognised and the recognition is confirmed by those who know close relatives. The people say that Jesus cannot be what he seems since they know who he is, and they speak of brothers and sisters to show that he was quite ordinary. The people who felt that they knew his background said that since he came from an ordinary village family he had no right to set himself up as the Messiah from God. It can be hurtful to see someone from the same humble background promoted above us and resentment can set in. In this case they say of Jesus, 'We know his origin: he cannot be the Christ.'

The local people were also amazed at the wisdom of Jesus and at his ability to perform mighty works and they wondered how he came to have such power. 'Who would ever think that a carpenter could teach so well? Who would ever think that Mary's son could do such wonderful things?'

So the people of Nazareth speak of Jesus as coming from an ordinary family in order to put him in his place and also as part of their expression of amazement. The carpenter and Mary and brothers and sisters are mentioned to put him down and also because what they saw and heard was so different from what they would have expected.

But if the 'brothers' and 'sisters' were merely cousins, a relationship which others could claim, then there would be *no surprise* at any difference. People express surprise only when they see blood brothers who are different from each other. There is no surprise at cousins being different.

When the crowd says in effect, 'He is only ordinary', the 'put down' loses its savour of scandal if it is not meant that the brothers and sisters are other children of Mary.

Some other points

The ecumenical study *Mary in the New Testament* says that the normal meaning of the Greek *adelphos* is 'blood-brother' and adds, 'Clearly it is later church tradition that has led many to argue for the broad translation.' The note in the Roman Catholic *New American Bible* on 'brother' and 'sister' in Mark 6. 3 reads, 'The question of meaning here would not have arisen but for the faith of the church in Mary's perpetual virginity'.[15]

If the Gospel writers believed that the perpetual virginity of Mary was something which Christians down the ages should celebrate, we would have to say that they were careless writers. No inspired writer speaks of Mary as a virgin after the birth of Jesus.

But would it not be *fitting* for the Son of God to be the only child born to Mary and that Mary should not have sexual relations with Joseph? To discuss this we need to try and place ourselves in the position of Mary and Joseph.

Mary and Joseph were religious Jews pledged to be married. Marriage would have been seen as a duty and children as a blessing. It was revealed to both of them that the Messiah would be conceived in a miraculous way and born of Mary. They knew that the baby would grow up to be greater than Moses or David, but Mary's Magnificat leads us to think that her mind turned to the stories of other miraculous births such as those of Isaac, Samson and Samuel, for her song is very like the song of Hannah, Samuel's mother.

Mary and Joseph would have seen the boy Jesus as very special but still a boy who would benefit from being reared in a normal household with other children. We can imagine Joseph and Mary being *willing* to abstain from doing what would bring other children into the world if they felt, or if God revealed, that this would be the right way to proceed. But Mary was not barren or old like Sarah or Elizabeth, and the great prophets Moses and Samuel and David were brought up along with brothers and sisters. Is it not likely then that Mary and Joseph felt it right to have other children?

Once we are open to the possibility that Mary could have had other children, the mention of the brothers of Jesus living with his mother and associated with her on different occasions presents little problem. Nor will we be embarrassed by words in Psalm 69, a psalm quoted more than once in the New Testament as applying to the Christ:[16] 'I have become a stranger to my brothers, an alien to my own mother's sons.'[17]

Notes

1 This is the argument of Hilary of Poitiers (*c.* 315–368), Ambrose of Milan (*c.* 339–397), Epiphanius (*c.* 315–403), Bishop J.B. Lightfoot (1828–1889), Archbishop J.A.F. Gregg of Armagh (1873–1961).
2 John 18.15–16.
3 John Wenham, *Easter Enigma* (Exeter 1984), p. 138.
4 Acts 1.14.
5 *Against Marcion* 4.19; *On the Flesh of Christ* 7; *On the Veiling of Virgins* 6; *On Monogamy* 8.
6 We find a similar unconsciousness in other places. In one of three apocryphal writings attributed to James, James whose father is presumably Joseph, is said to be a physical brother to Jesus as well as a spiritual brother (2 *Apoc. Jas.* 50.8–23; 51.19–22). This writing is said to date from the first half of the second

century. A later copy of it, deposited late fourth century, was discovered in 1946 near Nag Hammadi in upper Egypt.

In another Nag Hammadi Gnostic text, *The Book of Thomas the Contender*, Jesus says to Thomas, 'You are my twin ... you will be called my brother'(138.7–11). This apparently spiritualizes an alleged physical kinship. See article by James A. Brashler in *Anchor Bible Dictionary* III. 820.

7   See J.B. Mayor's *Commentary on James* p. x, and article 'Brethren of the Lord' in Hastings' *Dictionary of the Bible* I. 320. Origen took the view that the 'brothers' of Jesus were children of Joseph by an earlier marriage.

8   See 'The Virgin Birth in the Theology of the Ancient Church', Hans Von Campenhausen, *Studies in Historical Theology 2* (SCM 1964), p. 72. Hilary also held that the 'brothers' of the Lord were sons of Joseph.

9   Jerome, *Against Helvidius* 2.

10   *Dictionary of Jesus and the Gospels* (Leicester 1992), p. 71.

11   Matthew 12.46, 13.55.

12   Luke 8.42; Matthew 9.18; Mark 5.23 and Luke 9.38; Matthew 17.15; Mark 9.17.

13   Luke 7.12.

14   'Sisters' is added by a few MSS but see *A Textual Commentary on the Greek New Testament*, B.M. Metzger on Mark 3.32.

15   *Mary in the New Testament* ed. Raymond E. Brown et al. (London 1978). *The New American Bible* (Catholic Bible Publishers, Wichita, Kansas 1988).

16   On verse 4: John 15.25; on verse 9: John 2.17, Romans 15.3; on verses 22 and 23: Romans 11.9–10; on verse 25: Acts 1.20.

17   Psalm 69.8.

(This paper was given at the ESBVM Conference at
Dromantine College, Newry, Co. Down,
in October 1995)

Mary
in
systematic
theology

3

Towards a systematic theology
of Mary

Edward Yarnold SJ

As systematic theology is a term which is often used but rarely explained, I shall begin by offering my definition of the term. By 'theology' I mean the attempt to expound the meaning of Christian revelation with the aid of the insights of the theologian's age and culture, and in the light of that age's aspirations and problems. In this sense theology is different from biblical exegesis or dogmatic history, both of which are the investigation of what authors meant in their own age and context. Theology asks after the truth and value as well as the meaning of a doctrine. Theology is *systematic* when it treats doctrines not as a series of separate propositions, but weaves them together into a pattern. St Thomas's *Summa* is a well-known example.

In systematic theology you have to choose which point you are going to begin from. One procedure would be to start from traditional doctrines and interpret them in the light of the thought and problems of our own time and place. This method could be called *dogmatic*. A second method would involve starting from scripture and, by reflecting on it, reaching theological conclusions. You could call this the *biblical* method. A third option would be to start with human experience and aspirations, and show how revealed Christian truth corresponds to them. This method, which is that used by Tillich and Karl Rahner (though not, I think, applied by them to Mary), one might call *anthropological*. I shall apply in turn each of these three methods to the theological understanding of the Blessed Virgin Mary.

I. A dogmatic theology of Mary

A complete dogmatic theology of Mary would probably begin with the doctrine of Mary as the Mother of God, and involve the investigation not only of the meaning of the incarnation, but also of motherhood. One would then consider the implications of the further doctrine that Mary exercised this motherhood as a virgin. But, as the title of this paper indicates, I am not attempting to construct a complete systematic theology of Mary but to contribute some thoughts on the subject. I shall therefore in this section confine myself to the two characteristic Roman

Catholic Marian doctrines, the Immaculate Conception and the Assumption. The first of these doctrines affirms that Mary was redeemed in a unique way in that her redemption was preventive rather than remedial, so that she was preserved from original sin from the first moment of her human existence, a preservation which came about through an anticipated effect of the saving work of her Son. The second doctrine asserts that when Mary departed from this life, she was at once received body and soul into glory; the pious belief that she was exempt from death is not affirmed in the 1950 definition, and not many theologians can be found now who maintain it.

That is what the doctrines *mean*. But the dogmatic theologian must also ask the question, What is their *function*? C.S. Lewis asked this question of the doctrine of the fall, answering that its function was to assert that God is good and that all moral evil comes not from God but from our misuse of the gift of free will; to draw any other conclusions from the doctrine, such as that we are punished for the sins of our ancestors, is to misunderstand doctrine's function.[1] What then is the function of the two Marian dogmas?

The function of the dogma of the Immaculate Conception can be explained in several ways. I suggest that its function is to show that God's saving work in the Incarnation, and the incarnate life, of the Son came about through human freedom – a freedom which is itself the achievement of God's own action. God does not force his redemption on us; but the more human freedom is involved, the *more*, and not the less, is God's sovereign power at work. The Reformers insisted that Christ alone can save – *solus Christus, soli Deo gloria*. The Catholic tradition can subscribe to this insight, provided that the 'alone' means not that human beings are inert recipients of God's grace, but that all comes from God's grace, including human co-operation.[2] Accordingly, in preparation for the Incarnation God prepares a creature who in her freedom will say Yes to God's plan from the bottom of her heart. At a secondary level the dogma tells us about the way in which God's grace works in all of us: Mary is the type or model of the Church. Karl Rahner gives a similar explanation, which he believes should be acceptable to Protestants as well as Catholics.[3] ARCIC I also undertook to explain the function of the Marian dogmas – 'the truth that these two dogmas are designed to affirm':

> The affirmation of the Roman Catholic Church that Mary was conceived without original sin [i.e. the dogma of the Immaculate Conception] is based on recognition of her unique role within the mystery of the Incarnation. By being thus prepared to be the mother of our Redeemer, she also becomes a sign that the salvation won by Christ was operative among all mankind before his birth.[4]

The function of the doctrine of the Assumption, I suggest, is to show that the glory into which Mary has been received as the consequence of the grace by which she lived is not a salvation from the effects of a body which imprisons the spirit, but the glorification of her whole embodied human existence; and secondarily that this destiny manifested in Mary is one to which we are all called. Again Rahner gives a similar, ecumenically acceptable explanation.[5] ARCIC however identifies a different function of the doctrine:

> The affirmation that her glory in heaven involves full participation in the fruits of salvation [i.e. the dogma of the Assumption] expresses and reinforces our faith that the life of the world to come has already broken into the life of our world.[6]

II. A biblical systematic theology of Mary

Throughout Christian history the biblical method has been applied to the implications of the fact affirmed in all the Gospels, that Mary was the mother of the Saviour, the Son of God, the Lord. The debate started by Nestorius concerning the title *Theotokos* (God-bearer, Mother of God) is the best known example. Our own times have also witnessed considerable debate concerning the meaning of Mary's virginal motherhood. I do not intend to pursue these points further here, but will instead consider the other bases in the New Testament for a biblical systematic theology of Mary, investigating in turn Luke, John and Paul.

Luke sees Mary as the mother of the 'Son of God' (1.35). Whether he took this title of Jesus, which is placed on Gabriel's lips, to imply simply messiahship or an eternal deity is not our concern here The same question can be asked of the other form of words that Luke uses to describe Mary's unique role, namely 'the mother of my Lord', a form of address ascribed to Elizabeth (1.43). But what can be said with certainty is that it is characteristic of Luke that he shows an interest in the qualities with which Mary was endowed so that she could fulfil her vocation as mother of the Son of God.

First of all, Mary is the woman who *obeys*. Her words of assent, 'I am the handmaid of the Lord; let it be to me according to your word' (1.38), express obedience to God's will, an attitude reaffirmed in the Magnificat when she speaks of 'the low estate of his handmaiden' (1.48). But Luke implies that this obedience is grounded on a more fundamental virtue, the *faith* by which she believes God's word before obeying it. He contrasts Mary's faith systematically with the lack of faith shown by Zechariah, who is punished, Gabriel says, 'because you did not believe my words, which will be fulfilled in their time'(1.20).

Mary, on the other hand, is 'blessed' (*makaria*) because she 'believed that there would be a fulfilment of what was spoken to her from the Lord' (1.45).

Luke reaffirms this understanding of Mary's blessedness in two other places. The first is in an incident which is also recorded in the first two synoptic Gospels, when Jesus is told that his mother and brothers are looking for him. His reply is that all who hear the word of God and do it are his mother and brothers (8.21). Luke makes two significant changes in the version of the saying given in Mark and Matthew, where Jesus says 'Whoever does the will of God [Matt. of my Father in heaven]' etc (Mark 3.35; Matt. 12.50). i) In accordance with Luke's theology of Mary's faith, he changes 'will' to 'word' (resulting in an awkward use of the verb 'do' (*poiein*) with 'word' instead of 'will' as the object; ii) 'hearing' is added to 'doing' God's word.

Jesus' words are often interpreted as a rejection or renunciation of his mother and brothers. Whether or not this is the correct understanding of the passage in Matthew and Mark, it cannot be so in Luke, for Jesus' words must be taken in conjunction with Elizabeth's acclamation in praise of Mary: 'Blessed is she who believed that there would be a fulfilment of what had been spoken to her by the Lord.' In the third Gospel, at least, Jesus' words must mean that the faith which he is commending as a possibility for every disciple is precisely the faith which is characteristic of his Mother.

The second place in which this quality of Mary is reaffirmed is found in Luke alone. In reply to the woman who cries out: 'Blessed is the womb which bore you ...', Jesus replies: 'Blessed rather are those who hear the word of God and keep it' (11.27–28). The interpretation demanded of this passage is the same as for the one previously considered. The foundation of Mary's blessedness is her faith, i.e. her hearing and keeping of God's word; but this is a blessedness in which others can share.

There are two earlier passages in which Luke shows an interest in Mary's faith not simply as an abstract principle, but in its practical psychological implications. On two occasions, after the visit of the shepherds and after the finding in the temple, he emphasises Mary's reflection on what she has heard. After the shepherds had reported the angel's message, 'Mary kept all these words, pondering them in her heart' (2.19). After Jesus had spoken of his need to be in his Father's house, 'his mother kept all the words in her heart' (2.51). Luke's choice of expressions in these two passages is subtle and significant. He uses the term *rhēma* (saying) rather than *logos* (idea), presumably because he reserves the latter term for a word spoken directly to Mary by God. Again the verb used in chapter 2 for the 'keeping' of what is spoken (compounds of *tērein: suntērein* and *diatērein*) is different from the verb chosen in 11.28, *phulassein*. Accordingly in chapter 11 keeping God's word appears to mean obeying it; in chapter 2 keeping the words means cherishing their memory.[7] Faith in God's word and obedience require us to ponder on the indications coming our way which help us to discover what God is saying to us. Mary is the believing and obedient woman because she is the contemplative woman.

In the Syriac tradition Mary's motherhood is seen to spring from her faith: she conceives the Word in her womb through receiving the word through her ear.[8] An interest in Mary's psychology is important for another reason, though it is a reason Luke no more than hints at. Mary's motherhood was not only biological (though this was the emphasis that was placed on the term *Theotokos*, God-bearer, in fifth-century controversy). Greek icons more commonly give her the title *Mētēr Theou* (Mother of God); for motherhood is only just beginning when the biological function of conception is completed. Jesus, being a true human being, experienced psychological development as well as bodily growth. Mary needed to be the believing and contemplative woman because she had to help her Son to grow not only in physical stature but also in wisdom and grace before God and mankind (Luke 2.52; cf. 2.40).

There is another aspect of this obedient faith. It involves servanthood and humility – virtues which are precisely Mary's point of openness to God's power. It would be wrong to interpret the Magnificat as proclaiming that God's exaltation comes as a *compensation* for humility; in the light of our Lord's words about the necessity to become like little children to receive the Kingdom, it seems nearer the truth to suggest that Mary's littleness is her potentiality for receiving God's power.

In emphasising Mary's faith in all these ways, Luke sets her, as we have seen, among the other disciples of her Son. We see her there again after the Ascension in Acts 1.14 among the apostles and women praying in the upper room. But Luke also emphasises her uniqueness. Elizabeth, and in some MSS Gabriel also, hails her as 'blessed among women'.[9] She is 'graced' (*kecharitomenē*, 1.28); she has found 'favour' (*charis*) with God (1.30). The Holy Spirit comes upon her; the power of the most High overshadows her (1.35).[10] The Mighty One has done great things for her (1.51).

Luke shows an interest in another aspect of Mary's psychology which she possessed in common with the rest of the human race: like her Son she was tempted. This seems to me the most plausible interpretation of Simeon's prophecy that a sword would pierce her soul (2.35): Catholic tradition has understood these words to refer to the sword of sorrow; popular art even depicted her as the *Mater Dolorosa* with seven swords fixed in her heart; but the text does not support this interpretation. If for the time being we set aside the part of v.35 which speaks of the sword, Simeon's prophecy concerns the way in which Jesus is set for the fall and rising of many in Israel, so that the thoughts of hearts may be revealed. If the saying about the sword refers to Mary's sorrows, it interrupts the sense of the rest of the passage; recognition of this fact causes the saying commonly to be printed as a parenthesis.[11] This device is only possible if the force of 'also' (*kai*) is ignored: 'and your own soul *also* a sword shall pierce'. The point of the 'also' is that the piercing of Mary's soul is an *instance* of the way Jesus will provoke falling and rising and will reveal thoughts, not an *interruption* to the statement. The sword has the same function as the sword in Hebrews 4.12, which pierces to the division of soul and spirit, and discerns the thoughts of the heart.[12] I conclude then that the point of Simeon's prophecy is that Mary, like all the human race, will be tempted through her Son, though, as Hebrews affirms (4.15), temptation does not necessarily imply sin. She will find Jesus provokes temptation in the sense of a trial, a crisis of decision which is an opportunity for spiritual growth.

One would expect then to find that Luke's interest in Mary's psychology would lead him to give at least one instance of such a temptation or point of decision. Perhaps he saw Mary's reaction (a dozen verses later) on finding Jesus in the temple an example of such a crisis. Although both Mary and Joseph are said to be 'astonished', it is only his mother who rebukes Jesus: 'Son, why have you treated us so? Behold, your father and I have been looking for you anxiously' (2.48).[13]

To systematise Luke's theology of Mary, one could say that she is uniquely prepared by God to be the Mother of the Saviour. Her qualities however of obedient and humble faith do not put her apart from the rest of the human race, but are the paradigm for all Christian holiness. For all Christians it is true that God prepares them by his grace for the task to which he calls them, and which must be accepted in obedient, contemplative faith. Moreover we should attach due weight to the fact that Luke accords these truths about Mary an important place in his proclamation of the good news. For him, therefore, the Gospel is not only about the life, death and resurrection of Jesus Christ, but also about the effect of these saving mysteries on human lives, and about the cooperation which God empowers human beings to make to the process of redemption. This last point fits in with Luke's theology of the Holy Spirit. While his Gospel emphasises the power of the Holy Spirit which worked through Jesus, his second work, Acts, is composed as a parallel to the Gospel in order to show that same Spirit working in and through the Church.

The Mariology of *John* and *Paul* must be treated more briefly. In the Fourth Gospel Mary is not mentioned in the great incarnational prelude narrating how the Word became flesh; but she features prominently in two pivotal episodes, Cana and the cross. In both episodes she is addressed as 'Woman'. Some commentators suggest that underlying the superficial meaning of 'madam', there is a reference to the 'Woman' of Genesis 2 and 3.[14] We would thus have an anticipation of the patristic doctrine of Mary as the second Eve, 'the mother of all living beings' (3.20), the one whose progeny is set at enmity with the serpent (3.15). Just as in the synoptic Gospels Jesus appears at first sight to set his mother at a distance from himself, so too he does at Cana. But even here the distancing is only apparent, for it is at the instance of Mary's faith – 'Do whatever he tells you' (2.5) – that Jesus performs the first sign which reveals his glory (2.11). On Calvary Mary as the Woman stands for the Church, the mother of the disciples represented by John.[15] The same message is contained in the Apocalypse in the vision of the woman who is not only the mother of the Messiah, the one 'who is to shepherd all the nations with a rod of iron' (Rev. 12.5), but also stands for the Church, with whose remaining offspring the serpent makes war (12.17), as the woman in childbirth stands for Zion in Isaiah 66.7–8 and Micah 4.10. In the Johannine writings therefore the mother of Jesus is both the woman of faith and the figure of the Church.

In Galatians 4.4 Mary is again the 'woman', who is the point of insertion of God's Son into the human race and the number of those under the law, so that God might redeem those under the law and make them his sons and daughters.

III. An anthropological theology of Mary

The logic of the anthropological method is to observe human needs and aspirations, and then to show that these aspirations are fulfilled by Mary's place in the economy of salvation under her Son. The argument recalls the traditional scholastic justification of belief in Mary's Immaculate Conception, derived from the British monk Eadmer, St Anselm's disciple: *Potuit, decuit, ergo fecit* (God could do it, it was fitting, therefore God did it).[16] It also resembles Paul Tillich's method of 'correlation', which consists in first analysing the needs of fallen human nature, and then showing that they are met by the New Being in Christ Jesus. Karl Rahner's method is also anthropological, though it works differently. While for Tillich Christ is the answer to human aspirations, for Rahner the aspiration itself is already an experience of Christ.

One would begin then phenomenologically by inviting the reader to recognise certain human aspirations in his or her own experience: the aspiration that we may experience grace and salvation working within us – 'God is within you both to will and to work for his good pleasure'

(Phil. 2.13); that we may believe that our own life and history as a whole has a meaning; that we may see that grace triumphs over evil; that we may have an assurance of the continuance after death of the truest part of ourselves, which includes the body as well as the soul; that we may enjoy a continuing relationship with those dear to us who have died. The fulfilment of these aspirations is of course ultimately contained for us in the risen Christ, our head; but there is an added reassurance in seeing them fulfilled in one who is not the head, not God made a human being, but one who is part of the body like ourselves, needing redemption like ourselves, human only and not God, and indeed female not male. In the grace bestowed on the highly favoured one we see God's grace which prepares us and works in each of us for the unique task for which he has made us. In Mary's *fiat* given in the fullness of time to open the way for the coming of God's Son to identify himself with his creation, we see God's plan working through cosmic evolution.[17] In Mary's preservation from sin we see the same triumph of grace over sin which can be operative for us. In Mary's bodily assumption into heaven we see the affirmation of the eternal value of the body as well as of the soul. In her continuing intercession for us in heaven we see affirmed the continuing care of the departed in heaven for those who were close to them on earth. In Mary's holiness we are given the paradigm of redemption operative in the human nature of a woman.

IV. Mary and the One Mediator

In these three attempts to sketch in turn a dogmatic, a biblical and an anthropological systematic theology of Mary we have not yet faced the problem of the apparent conflict between Mariology and Christology. Can there be a Mariology at all without diminishing the one thing necessary, our faith in Jesus Christ?

In a proper Mariology there can be no conflict with Christology for two reasons. First, from first to last Mariology shows Mary's dependence on Jesus Christ. As Dante put it, she is daughter of her Son. Her uniqueness rests on her unique faith, and all faith is ultimately faith in him, and is the gift of grace which comes from him. Her grace and her mission were for the sake of his work. For this reason the point has often been made, e.g. by Newman, that the correct understanding of Mary leads to a correct understanding of her Son. In the words of the Response for the Annunciation addressed to her in the old breviary antiphon, 'Singlehanded you have put an end to all heresies'.[18]

Secondly, Mariology must be understood according to the hierarchy of truths, according to which, in the words of the Vatican II *Decree on Ecumenism*, truths 'vary in their relationship to the foundation of the

Christian faith' (n. 11). That is to say, every dogmatic truth must be explicitly or implicitly Christological, and the more explicit this reference to Christ is, the more central its importance. This truth has an application on the existential as well as the *logical* level. It is not just that all dogmas have an implicit logical dependence on Christology. All dogmas are *existentially* subordinate to Christology. In our *lived* faith Christ must be more important than Mary. And this I believe can be, and usually is, true even of people whose favourite prayer is the Rosary, whose instinct is to place their needs before Mary, and whose favourite devotion is the lighting of candles before Our Lady's statue in church.

Notes

1   *The Problem of Pain* (London 1940), ch. 5.
2   The same relationship between God's sovereign action and the creature's co-operation is apparent in other areas of doctrine. The doctrine of the incarnation implies that the fact that Jesus Christ is fully human is not inconsistent with the fact that he is fully divine. Again, the doctrine of biblical inspiration combines belief in the Holy Spirit's authorship of Scripture with belief that the biblical books were composed by the normal, historically and socially influenced process of literary composition. cf. P Schoonenberg, *The Christ*, ch. 1, 'God or Man: a False Dilemma' (London 1972).
3   *Theological Investigations* XVIII (London 1984), p. 50: 'If it is recalled that Mary also is redeemed by Christ – that is, she is in need of redemption and this need is among the permanent existentials of her existence – then the normal infralapsarian human being and Mary are not really distinguished because of a difference in a period of time at the beginning of existence, but because Mary receives the offer of grace to her freedom in virtue of her predestination to be the mother of Jesus and consequently as an offer efficaciously prevailing and as such also perceptible in salvation history. A Protestant theology of pure grace, efficacious as such, should not really find this distinction offensive. The dogma of the Immaculate Conception does not necessarily imply that the beginning of grace for her is different in a temporal sense from what it is for us, who likewise do not receive grace for salvation as a permanent existential of our freedom for the first time only in baptism.'
4   *Final Report. Authority.* II, n. 30.
5   ibid. pp. 50–51: 'For the content of the doctrine of the Assumption does not imply that Mary's "bodily" assumption into heaven is a privilege granted (apart from Jesus) to her alone ... If today, as against a Platonizing interpretation of the "separation of body and soul" at death, we may certainly hold that every human being acquires his risen body at death, "at that very moment" (in so far as terms relating to time make sense in this respect), a view often maintained in Protestant theology and quite legitimate with the aid of a little justifiable demythologizing, then this dogma does not refer to

something granted to Mary alone, but to what belongs generally to all who are saved, while appropriate to her in a special way in virtue of her function in salvation history and consequently more clearly understood in the Church's sense of faith than it is in other human beings.'

6   *Authority* II, n. 30.

7   The New RSV has 'treasured' at 2.19 and 2.51, 'obey' at 11.28.

8   cf. Sebastian Brock, 'Mary in the Syriac Tradition', in *Mary's Place in Christian Dialogue*, ed. A. Stacpoole (London 1982), pp. 182–191.

9   *Eulogēmenē*, not *makaria* here; the same verb is applied to the blessedness of the fruit of her womb.

10 The verb 'overshadow' (*episkiazein*) suggests the *shekinah* (God's visible presence among his Chosen People) by its sound as well as its meaning.

11 The New RSV adopts a different device, changing the order of the clauses, so that the statement about the sword occurs at the end of the prophecy.

12 However the vocabulary is different. For 'sword' Luke has *romphaia*, Hebrews *machaira*; for 'thoughts' Luke has *dialogismoi*, Hebrews *enthumēseis* and *ennoiai*.

13 I gladly acknowledge a debt here to J. McHugh, *The Mother of Jesus in the New Testament* (London 1975), pp. 104–112, though his conclusion differs a little from my own.

14 See for example R. Russell's commentary on John in *A New Catholic Commentary on Holy Scripture* (London 1969), pp. 1041, 1071.

15 John McHugh's paper at the conference explored this point at great depth

16 cf. A. Stacpoole, 'The English Tradition of the Doctrine of the Immaculate Conception', in *Mary's Place in Christian Dialogue*, esp. p. 231.

17 Thus Mary is a symbol for 'green' theology!

18 *'Cunctas haereses sola interemisti.'*

(This paper was given at the ESBVM Congress at Winchester in July 1991)

4

Feminist theology: a view of Mary

Ann Loades

It seems to me that Mary is a significant symbol in the ecumenical context.[1] This is for the simple reason that whatever it is that is symbolized by her has been and remains central to the vitality of Christianity in many parts of the world, though some are still vigorous in their protest that this is the case.[2] A relatively new feature of ecumenical dialogue, however, is the contribution made by women to it, and some of them are alert to feminist theological concerns. So long as these women continue to make the effort to participate in Christian institutions or societies, their voices are bound, one hopes, to make a difference to the way theology is done, and how it comes out. And it can require a considerable effort to stay, in the face of reproaches that one is betraying other women and their needs by so doing, since there exists some justifiable criticism of what the Christian tradition has had and still does have on offer for women.

Much depends on whether one thinks that a tradition is or can be alive enough to change for the better – it is not change just for the sake of it. And there are signs of hope, as for instance in *Marialis Cultus (To honour Mary)* of 1974. So in paragraph 34 Pope Paul VI maintains:

> Devotion to the Blessed Virgin must also pay close attention to certain findings of the human sciences. This will help to eliminate one of the causes of the difficulties experienced in devotion to the Mother of the Lord, namely, the discrepancy existing between some aspects of this devotion and modern anthropological discoveries and the profound changes which have occurred in the psycho-sociological field in which modern man lives and works. The picture of the Blessed Virgin presented in a certain type of devotional literature cannot easily be reconciled with today's life style, especially with the way women live today. In the home, women's equality and co-responsibility with man in the running of the family are being justly recognized by laws and the evolution of customs. In the sphere of politics women have in many countries gained a position in public life equal to that of men. In the social field women are at work in a whole range of different employments, getting further away every day from the restricted surroundings of the home. In the cultural field new possibilities are opening up for women in scientific research and intellectual activities.

In some ways, one might say that the papal sketch needs to be more sharply drawn. For instance, it needs to advert clearly to the massive double work burden most women have always carried, inside their homes in 'unpaid' work and outside their homes in paid employment, necessary if their families are not to fall into poverty. In societies where the family is still the economic unit, at least half of the so-called Third World's food is produced by women, including their work at the heavy agricultural labour involved. In so-called First-World cultures women can suffer in different ways if restricted to the 'private' as distinct from the public and political realms, reinforced by suburban housing patterns; and, as we know, home can be hell for other reasons. What could the symbolization of Mary have to do with all this? Not simply, one hopes, what another papal document *Redemptoris Mater (Mother of the Redeemer)* calls 'limitless fidelity and tireless devotion to work',[3] since these are not unambiguously praiseworthy qualities in many contexts.

Marialis Cultus goes on to point up Mary as a disciple (para 35) which in the Gospels at least (as distinct from other parts of the New Testament) even for women has little to do with domesticity. The women associated with Jesus of Nazareth are an unconventional group, to put it mildly. Paragraph 36 of *Marialis Cultus* also comments that:

> It should be considered quite normal for succeeding generations of Christians in differing socio-cultural contexts to have expressed their sentiments about the Mother of Jesus in a way and manner which reflected their own age.

And further:

> When the Church considers the long history of Marian devotion she rejoices at the continuity of the element of cult which it shows, but she does not bind herself to any particular expression of an individual cultural epoch or to the particular anthropological ideas underlying such expressions. The Church understands that certain outward religious expressions, while perfectly valid in themselves, may be less suitable to men and women of different ages and cultures.

Various scriptural reflections follow, which offer us a Mary taken into dialogue with God, giving her active and responsible consent to what was to happen, a woman of courageous choice, a woman who proclaims God's vindication of those who need it, who survived poverty, flight and exile, who presumably brought her family through it, but was far from being exclusively concerned with her own family (any more than were other women in the Gospels, we might add).

We need not minimize the difficulties men as well as women may have with traditions about Mary. For instance, *Under the heel of Mary*[4] is a fascinating but sorry story about Marianism, which includes reference to Mary as 'exterminator of all heresies', as a symbol for cold war warriors and for some of those who promoted the dogma of the Assumption, as well as 'Our Lady of National Security'. And Mary of the

Magnificat may be an uncomfortable figure of a different kind for a church producing an indigenous theology in South America (liberation theology), requiring primarily liberation from the thugs and torturers of that continent, but also from possibly inappropriate hierarchical structures in the Church itself. For women, in the first instance, but also for men, if we are to be serious about humanly inclusive theology, we need to think about feminist theology and Mary as a significant figure in the tradition. As it happens, the 1986 conference papers included one from Donal Flanagan,[5] 'Mary: some problems in ambivalence' which he concluded by asking: 'Are we then doomed to choose between an ecclesiastical Mary unrelated to twentieth-century woman and a theory of woman, feminism, which has no place for the greatest woman who ever lived?' He held out the possibility that 'these rock-hard certainties which now clash so destructively will slowly mature towards a constructive ambivalence and through that stage to a new vision'. Only a few years later, we may have arrived at that stage of 'constructive ambivalence', with even some elements of the new vision in the sight-lines, which is what feminist theology in the end is all about, assuming that to be feminist and to be a feminist theologian is not a contradiction in terms, of course.

One fundamental problem highlighted by feminist theology is the gap between the *proclamation* of full personhood for women (associated in some parts of the tradition with the 'new Eve–Mary') and the *practice* of associating them with the 'old Eve'. On the one hand, male-and-female together 'image' God (Gen. 1); and Galatians signals that in the Christian community one abandons supposed privileges of race, social status and sex. Some of this has been conveyed by the symbol of Mary as a symbol of honour for women, not just for Mary, in the sense that honour for one is honour for all those like her. A woman who will quiz an archangel, give her (rapturous? enthusiastic?) assent, or agreement to the divine spirit working within her, risk scandal and single parenthood is, one might think, something of a risk-taker, and by no means a model of submission, subordination and passivity. To hail her (in Traherne's version, in the Ecumenical Office of the Ecumenical Society of the Blessed Virgin Mary) as 'Daughter of the Eternal Father, Mother of the Eternal Son, Spouse of the Eternal Spirit, Tabernacle of the most glorious Trinity' is at one level absurdly extravagant, but in so far as women have been allied with her, Mary is thus a symbol of affirmation for them. Even so hostile a critic of the tradition as Mary Daly acknowledges that very problematical dogmas, such as the Immaculate Conception, *can* signal to women the negation of the myth of feminine evil, that is, the association of women with the sacred and the good. And the Assumption too can represent a categorical 'no' to the peculiar association of women with sin-flesh-matter[6] in the context of a religion which proclaims incarnation but which is sometimes anti-incarnational, anti-sacramental, and in which grace may be treated as a denial of the creature instead of its blessing. The Assumption helps to redress the balance in a dramatic way, giving some sense to Cornelius Ernst's remark that 'grace is not faceless'[7] that is, the face can be female as well as male.

The trouble is, that women have all too consistently been allied with the old Eve, rather than with the new one, and this has been done by undercutting the ideal of whole personhood. This can be illustrated in the first instance by attending to an example given by Nelle Morton in her book, *The Journey is Home*.[8] In one of her essays, she describes a sculpture in wood outside a church building, a sculpture on the theme of vocation taken from 1 Cor. 10.31, 'Whether therefore ye eat, or drink, or whatsoever ye do, do all to the glory of God'. The sculpture shows thirty individual forms representing nineteen different kinds of work. Only seven of the thirty figures are women, represented as nursing a baby, on knees scrubbing a floor, serving a man seated at table, assisting a male doctor, feeding chickens, pounding a typewriter, and teaching children. All these figures represent tasks that arguably need doing, but it is absurd to associate that necessity with women alone, and absurd to exclude them from connection with the other twenty-three figures representing nineteen kinds of work. It needs little imagination to think out the likely roles of the male figures in the sculpture. The point is that as well as at one level honouring women and teaching them new aspirations, the Christian tradition has also undercut that honour and aspiration by teaching women a disabling gender construction, and this is why it has by no means always fostered whole personhood in women. Not surprisingly, it is now regarded as one of the sources of 'sexism', that is, the belief that persons are superior or inferior to one another on the basis of their sex.

It might be better to refer to the problem as gender-stereotyping. For we can distinguish between 'sex' and 'gender' in the following way. Sex has to do with basic biological differences which develop in a human embryo at about the sixth week of development. 'Gender' refers to what a particular society makes of relationships between males and females, and no society lives free of gender constructs in all their astonishing variability. What one can do at the least is to attend to them and evaluate them, especially as these are conveyed by religious symbols, as realities which may help us to lay hold of or be laid hold of by realities beyond those which we see or think about. The object is not to obliterate differences, but to value them appropriately, and this need not mean that all those associated with males or masculinity are put at the top of some hierarchy of value, with those associated with females or femininity put at the bottom. It can be argued that notwithstanding some of the meanings associated with the symbol of Mary, the dominant gender construction of Christian culture for women has been that they are passive, dependent, bodily, emotional, weak, peculiarly responsible for evil and sin, are childlike in the worst senses, and bear the image of God only derivatively. Men, on the other hand, are active, independent, intelligent, brave, strong, good, bear the image of God in their own right, and are of course godlike. Males are always more godlike than females could ever be, even when the latter try religiously sanctioned experiments of trying to approximate to males.[9]

To claim that 'in the whole of human instinct and understanding it is the masculine which is associated with giving and the feminine with receiving' (to cite the words of one of the patrons of the Ecumenical Society of the Blessed Virgin Mary) is as intolerable and bad for men as it is dishonest about women. Human beings each need to give and receive from one another in as open and reciprocal way as they can. Women who internalize the dominant gender construction have to engage in a very painful process of giving it up. As with the tasks represented by the sculpture, and giving and receiving, so passivity, dependence, bodiliness, emotion, acknowledging weakness etc. are arguably as important aspects of being human as being active, independent, intelligent, brave, strong and so on, and it is damaging to associate these possibilities primarily with one sex rather than another, regardless of time, place and circumstance. Yet it is probably harder to give up playing Cinderella, Snow White or Sleeping Beauty, than to give up playing Prince Charming, since this involves taking responsibility for oneself, rather than continuing with the symptoms of what is sometimes called co-dependence: low self-esteem, an inability to take care of oneself, wasting time thinking about what other people want, deluding oneself into thinking oneself responsible for its delivery, and that whatever goes wrong is one's personal responsibility to put right. Women, like men, need boundaries, permeable indeed, but secure, knowing what they think and feel from the inside, which is part of what feminist praxis is about. Once the boundaries are found, women can move through the limitations set for them by those who may not have their interests at heart.

One illustration of how this could work, drawing on the symbol of Mary, was given in a recent essay by Lavinia Byrne,[10] a good example of someone who wants to make constructive use of some of the paradoxes of the tradition. The paradoxes are well set out by Peter Canisius in the sixteenth century:[11]

> A virgin not sterile, but fertile; married to a man, but made fruitful by God; bearing a son, but knowing not a man; forever inviolate, yet not deprived of

progeny. A virgin pregnant but incorrupt, and intact even in childbirth. A virgin before marriage and in marriage, a pregnant virgin, a virgin giving suck, a perpetual virgin. A virgin without concupiscence conceiving the saviour. A virgin bearing a child in the womb without hardship, giving birth to God without pain.

Lavinia Byrne must, as with others dealing with the legacy of the symbol, be both selective, and a translator, re-interpreter of the tradition, because Mary, as in the quotation from Canisius, is otherwise an impossible ideal for women. To be true to her tradition, she has to allow 'virginity' and 'motherhood' both to stand as reality, but *also* use them as metaphor for the experience of all women. Virginity as metaphor is about separation, and motherhood as metaphor is about integration.

> A woman who holds both of these in balance demonstrates the sanctifying power of differentiation. She is both apart from and part of the human condition. The virgin is the reserved figure who does not define herself in terms of her relationships with men. She is autonomous. The mother, meanwhile, is essentially in relationship. The virgin is barren through choice or misfortune. Her energy is inner-directed. The mother is fecund. She is creative of life and ongoing nurture.

Then she argues that women are entitled to space both in the domestic context and in the public domain, but 'space' means something different in each place, as it were. First, where some women are free to make vows of chastity, we are reminded that all women should be free to refuse men access to them. Second, space in the public domain means that 'women are entitled to the freedom to engage with and be part of all the creative, nurturing processes with which we organize human reality'. Women should be allowed to differentiate, enabled to experience desires they do not ordinarily give themselves credit for, and to exercise choices society is reluctant to admit.

Quite a different example of constructive reinterpretation can be found in the work of two Latin American religious, Ivone Gebara and Maria Clara Bingemer, in their *Mary, Mother of God, mother of the poor*.[12] Although the book attempts a near-impossible task of exercising a method of interpretation alien to those who constructed Roman Catholic dogmas about Mary in relation to those dogmas, the main thrust of the book is intelligible enough, and makes clear why those concerned with women's lives will associate Mary with them in so far as they can, in order to mobilize for change. It is not simply, though it is essential in the Latin American context, that whereas to invading Spaniards Mary represented the triumph of conquest, to the despairing Indians lamenting the destruction of their religion and culture she represented the promise of a new life.[13] It is also that women across national boundaries are becoming alert to their predicament, in the words of the UN in 1980, that 'Women constitute half the world's population, perform nearly two-thirds of its work hours, receive one-tenth of the world's income, and own less than one-hundredth of the world's property'. Central to their predicament is that they are poor not because they bear children, but because they also have to do most of the work in raising them. Women experience in an acute form the conflict between the public-economic and the domestic which simply does not allow for support for the next generation, of the fragile and of the aging, and sentimentality about Mary should in no circumstances render their plight worse.

This is certainly not the intention of the authors of this book. For them, above all, Mary is one who 'lives in God', who expresses or embodies an unlimited yearning for life. She participates wholly and fully in the glory of the living God, rescued from humiliation, but has to do with saving life in the here and now. So the authors write that life is such a tough battle, that the relationship with Mary, she who is 'alive in God', full of affection and power, is direct. It is connected to people's immediate and vital needs, 'since the life of the poor unfolds basically at this level'.[14] So too Anne Carr, in *Transforming Grace*[15] writes of Mary as the poor one in whom God does great things:

> Mary as virgin and mother need not be understood as an impossible double bind, an inimitable ideal, but as a central Christian symbol that signifies autonomy *and* relationship, strength *and* tenderness, struggle *and* victory, God's power *and* human agency – not in competition but co-operation; Mary *is* a utopian figure, a mystery. Her intimate place in the Christian pattern enables us to imagine a healed, reconciled, finally transformed world.

These writers are all alert to some of the dangers associated with the symbol of Mary, including idealized femininity from a male viewpoint, and Mary as 'mother' of the Church strengthening the religious and cultural foundations of androcentrism which has not attended to women, heard their voices, or been humanly inclusive in a consistent way in its institutions or its theology. James Mackey has shrewdly pointed out[16] (referring to the book by Ivone Gebara and Maria Clara Bingemer) that images, metaphors and symbols are based on some actual state of affairs from which the range of significance is extended to bring to light a greater range of actual or possible experience. The authors quoted in this essay are engaged in that process of extension. But, as Mackey goes on:

> Virginity, as an image or symbol, has its basis in a genital sexual state, and it symbolizes closedness, if anything at all, certainly not openness; and the failure so far to realize any possibilities whatsoever. It forces imagery beyond the range of intelligibility to suggest otherwise; and it borders on the perverse to choose the virgin rather than the married woman as a symbol of fidelity.

Be that as it may (and Peter Brown for one shows us how in the fourth century, for instance, virginal integrity represented sacralized culture, and literacy)[17] Mackey makes effectively some of the points women have been making about the use and abuse of the symbol to keep women in their place, particularly within the Church, though he, like others, remains hopeful that our symbols of divine, effective and saving power can have a transforming impact on us. We need a renewed vision of goodness, to be given and to gain access to it, in both Church and society, a new sense of co-inherence between women and men, so that each actualizes the dignity and worth of the other, and the symbol of Mary may help us to achieve this. Preoccupation with the symbol may also help us not to attend to one central issue for the tradition, however, that is, its failure to take seriously a point made from time to time. We may pick up the point in some words of Elaine Storkey's, where she writes that:

> there is nothing demeaning in the notion of Mary bearing her own Saviour. It is not an assertion of the supremacy of maleness or the arrogance of patriarchy. It is simply a statement of the humility of a non-gendered God who was prepared to come in human, sexual form.[18]

The crucial phrase is 'the humility of a non-gendered God', for the main goal of feminist theology is a humanly inclusive theology, and the hope and necessity that we can envision the mystery of God in gender-inclusive ways. As Elizabeth Johnson properly insists[19] this is not a matter of adding a female-related or feminine dimension to a God imaged as male or masculine, but the claim that the female and feminine can of and by itself image God, *in as full and in as limited a way* as God is imaged by the male and masculine. Both sexes and genders are as capable or incapable of imaging the mystery of God. In Elizabeth Johnson's reflections on Mary as symbol, therefore, she retrieves the creativity and caring intrinsic to good mothering; compassion as primordially divine; saving and protective power; the immanence and living presence of God – Gerard Manley Hopkins' 'Wild air, world mothering air'. We might add what Hannah Arendt in her political philosophy called natality, the capacity for new beginnings, so closely related to the capacity for forgiveness.[20] For Elizabeth Johnson, ways of referring to the mystery of God which could be received within a believing community include maternity with its nurturing and warmth; unbounded compassion; power that protects, heals and liberates; all-embracing immanence; and recreative energy.

Mary then is one way of referring to the mystery of God, but that she does, or in so far as she does, should not be allowed to shift our focus from this central task, and unless it is achieved, it is at least arguable that the future vitality of the tradition is at stake. Concentrating on the symbol of Mary to the exclusion of this task will not save it, or at least, it may not be as good as it could be, for men as well as women.

Notes

1   See also Ann Loades, 'The Virgin Mary and the feminist quest' in Janet Martin Soskice (ed), *After Eve* (Collins, 1990), pp. 156–178 (a paper for the Ecumenical Society of the Blessed Virgin Mary and other similar groups).

2   D. Wright (ed), *Chosen by God: Mary in evangelical perspective* (Marshall Pickering, 1989) provides some recent examples.

3   *Redemptoris Mater*, para 46.

4   N. Perry and L. Echeverria, *Under the heel of Mary* (Routledge, 1988).

5   Donal Flanagan, 'Mary: some problems in ambivalence' in A. Stacpoole (ed), *Mary and the Churches* (Columba, 1987), pp. 73–84.

6   See the references in the paper listed in note 1 above.

7   C. Ernst, *Multiple Echo* (Darton, Longman & Todd, 1979), p. 124.

8   Nelle Morton, *The journey is home* (Beacon, 1985), pp. 21–22.

9   See, for instance, Averil Cameron, 'Virginity as metaphor: women and the rhetoric of early Christianity' in A. Cameron (ed), *History as text: the writing of ancient history* (Duckworth, 1989), pp. 181–205; Elizabeth Castelli, 'Virginity and its meaning for women's sexuality in early Christianity' in *Journal of Feminist Studies in Religion* 2:1 (1986), pp. 61–88.

10 Lavinia Byrne, 'Apart from or a part of: the place of celibacy' in Alison Joseph (ed), *Through the devil's gateway* (SPCK, 1990).

11 I. MacLean, *The Renaissance notion of women* (CUP, 1980), p. 29.

12 Ivone Gebara and Maria Clara Bingemer, (trans P. Berryman), *Mary, Mother of God, mother of the poor* (Burns & Oates, 1989).

13 Patricia Harrington, 'Mother of death, mother of rebirth: the Mexican Virgin of Guadelupe' *Journal of the American Academy of Religion* 56:1 (1988), pp. 25–50

14 Gebara and Bingemer, pp. 23, 119, 126.

15 Anne Carr, *Transforming Grace* (Harper & Row, 1988), p. 193.

16 J. Mackey, 'The use and abuse of Mary in Roman Catholicism' in R. Holloway (ed), *Who needs feminism?* (SPCK, 1991), pp. 99–116.

17 Peter Brown, *The body and society* (Faber 1989), especially pp. 259–284..

18 Elaine Storkey, 'The significance of Mary for feminist theology' in D. Wright (ed), op. cit. (note 2), pp. 184–199, especially p. 198.

19 Elizabeth Johnson, 'Mary and the image of God' and 'Reconstructing a theology of Mary' in Doris Donnelly (ed), *Mary: woman of Nazareth* (Paulist, 1989), pp. 25–68 and 69–91. See also Elizabeth Johnson, 'The incomprehensibility of God and the image of God male and female' in Joann Wolski Conn, *Women's spirituality* (Paulist, 1986), pp. 243–260.

20 Hannah Arendt, *The human condition* (Doubleday, 1958), pp. 10–11 and 221–222.

*(This paper was given at the ESBVM Congress at Winchester
in July 1991 and was first published in* The Way *34:2 1994
under the title* 'On Mary: Constructive Ambivalence')

5

The Marian Church:
Hans Urs von Balthasar
and the ordination of women

Paul McPartlan

In the first half of the seventeenth century, there was a remarkable Bishop of Belley in France, called Jean-Pierre Camus (1584–1652). As well as being a prolific writer, with two hundred books to his credit, he was renowned for his preaching. He used to refer to preachers as 'the breasts of the Church'. Put into context this vivid image becomes very understandable. Camus was the eldest in a family of twenty-one children. The feeding of his younger siblings must have been a constant activity in the family. He would surely have had a strong sense of how a mother nourishes her baby at the breast and would naturally have drawn on this in his preaching.

To understand the theology of Hans Urs von Balthasar, we must recognise a very strong female influence upon his life, in the form of Adrienne von Speyr. In 1984, von Balthasar stated that it would be mistaken to try and separate his theology from that of Adrienne. One commentator has gone further. 'There is ample evidence,' he says, 'that not only von Balthasar's Marian theology but – even more deeply – his personality structure, his habits of the heart and his intellectual framework as well have been influenced and co-shaped by Adrienne von Speyr.'[1] Von Balthasar met Adrienne in 1940. Let us briefly survey his life up to this decisive point.

He was born in 1905 in Lucerne, Switzerland, and he grew up with a passion for literature, philosophy and music. A brilliant and cultured student, his deep faith led him to a doctorate examining the treatment of theological topics, especially the so-called Last Things, in modern German literature. As he was completing his doctorate, he went on retreat and was transfixed by something he had never bargained for, a call from God to leave everything and go where He would lead. He likened the experience to being struck by lightning.[2]

He duly gained his doctorate and entered the Jesuits, but was deeply unsatisfied with the intellectual fare put before him. He described his two years of philosophy as 'languishing in the desert of neo-scholasticism', and the great benefit of his four years of theology was not the lectures, which he found terribly boring, but the encounter with Henri de Lubac, living in the same house, who showed him 'the way beyond the scholastic stuff', as he called it, 'to the Fathers of the Church'.[3]

De Lubac 'was able to pass his younger friend an "ambience", a so-to-speak Catholic atmosphere in which he [von Balthasar] could live and think creatively'.[4] At that time, de Lubac was composing his famous book, *Catholicism*. Its influence on Balthasar can be gauged from the fact that he translated it into German in 1943 and again in 1970, calling it the 'basic book' of theology,[5] 'a major breakthrough'.[6] Like de Lubac, von Balthasar was named as a cardinal late in life, though unlike de Lubac he died suddenly (on 26 June 1988) just before actually receiving the red hat. Enigmatic to the end, we might say.

De Lubac's vibrant theology equipped the Church for a mission to the whole of humanity, with a message for every heart.[7] Under its influence, it is not surprising that, when the choice came in 1940, von Balthasar opted for pastoral work as university chaplain in Basel, instead of academic work, lecturing at the Gregorian University in Rome. It was envisaged that he and three others might establish an ecumenical institute in Rome. It would seem that this idea did not particularly excite him. There is perhaps an indication why in a later comment about what he called 'the almost inevitable pattern of ecumenical dialogues, whereby the papacy, the very epitome of the question of ministry, is put to the end of the discussion'; 'a blind eye is turned', he says, 'to the one office that can finally banish the abstractness of all other agreements and is able to give them their proper ecclesiological concreteness'.[8]

To those Catholics as well as non-Catholics who would regard the papal prerogatives and, likewise, the Marian dogmas defined in the last hundred and fifty years as an irritating modern accretion, von Balthasar responds with a vision of their interrelated timeliness and absolute necessity for the Church's understanding of herself and her mission. He is refreshingly frank about all of this and refuses to let Mary and Peter be marginalised. Moreover, he speaks of them in a way that is all his own, with a unique subtlety and persuasiveness, that combines Catholic conviction with great humanity.

Lest we should mistakenly imagine someone strident and unapproachable, let us realise that he regards the whole business of definitions as rather 'eccentric', in the literal sense. Peter's central role, carried on in his successors, is to shepherd a flock receptive to God's gifts and purposes. The whole Church, himself included, has the Marian stamp of active receptivity. However, because there is sin in the world and resistance to God, law, definition and judgement become necessary, and it is Peter's calling to exercise them, as and when necessary, stepping out to do so from his more habitual activity of encouraging and building up. Tending the flock involves judgement, he says. '[L]aw is elicited from within the *communio* of love by the existence of sin in the world': 'Peter must be concerned with the position of the sinner who stands outside the Marian centre of love'. His office is rooted 'in the divine sovereignty and in the office of Judge that Christ, the Redeemer of the world, received from his Father'.

> 'Jesus' sovereignty and judicial authority ... may be described as 'eccentric' only because in the relationship between God and the truly redeemed, who have received the 'spirit of sonship' and can boldly call God 'Abba, Father', abstract law is absorbed back into love's intimacy.' (*Office*, p. 209)

What is first and last is the intimacy of love. Charismatic ministries of all sorts arise and interact in the Church. Von Balthasar's ecclesiology has a seething sense of life about it, as we shall see. He understands Christ as the focal point of a 'constellation' of followers (cf. *Office*, pp. 136ff., 308ff.), shimmering with many lights. But all is enveloped in love, regulated by love and absorbed back into love's intimacy.

The only one who is perfect in love is Mary (cf. *Office*, p. 313). All others, including Peter and his successors, are faltering learners. How the Petrine ministry should be exercised in the *communio* of love is a question which will never receive a final answer. If the pope must act with compassion, so the Church must have compassion on him. As he must act always from the imperative of love, so he must be embraced with love by the Church. Only in this way will he and we together learn and grow. Let us note the care of the following words.

> [W]e hold that it is the special duty of the pastoral office, following the Twelve and Peter, to lead the faithful to the highest level of their own faith. And it must be said that there is the element of *risk*, both in existing faith and in being led to a deeper faith. Every believer takes the risk of faith ... Since the measure of personal risk where faith is concerned varies greatly among individual Christians, the pastoral office is faced with an equally great risk in trying to anticipate what degree of risk Christian people as a whole are willing to take for their faith ... (*Office*, pp. 240–241).

So, 'Peter too must be continually learning; he must not think that he can carry out his office in isolation'.

> Revelation is entrusted to the whole Church, and all, under the leadership of Peter, are to preserve it, interpret it and produce a living exposition of it. And since the office of Peter is borne by fallible human beings, it needs everyone's watchful but loving cooperation so that the exercise of this office may be characterized by the degree of 'in-fallibility' that belongs to it. More precisely, this means that a pope can exercise his office fruitfully for all only if he is *recognised* and loved in a truly ecclesial way, even in the midst of *paraklesis* or dispute.

Those who 'fail to love the office ... automatically drop out of the communion of the Church, whose concrete unity is created by the Holy Spirit of love': 'what has to be corrected is always enveloped in love' (*Office*, pp. 314–316).

Time and again we come back to love, which unites the 'constellation of Christ'. We have already seen something of Mary and Peter within the constellation and there are many other figures to locate also, but let us return to 1940, and ask who was the utterly remarkable woman that the new university chaplain met in Basel.

Born in 1902, three years older than von Balthasar, Adrienne von Speyr was a physician, one of the first women doctors in Switzerland. She was a Protestant, whose first husband had been professor of history in the university. They had two children. Two years after his sudden death, she married his successor as professor of history in Basel. When she met von Balthasar, she was still grieving over the death of her first husband and felt unable to say the Lord's Prayer. He explains their dramatic encounter:

> When I showed her that the expression *Thy will be done* does not mean that we offer God what we are able to do ourselves, but rather that we offer him our willingness to let what he does take over our lives and move us anywhere at will, it was as though I had inadvertently touched a light switch that at one flick turned on all the lights in the hall. Adrienne seemed to be freed from the claims of restraint and was carried away on a flood of prayer as though a dam had burst.'[9]

Adrienne became a Catholic on November 1 in that same year, and von Balthasar remained her spiritual director until her death in 1967. What a humbling role it must have been! At first, he had to instruct her and initiate her into the mysteries of Christ, but she was already having mystical experiences of all kinds, visions, ecstasies, bilocations. She was clairvoyant and had the gift of healing. Then from 1944 to 1960, she dictated to him her insights into the scriptures for twenty to thirty minutes each afternoon. She would read the verse, close her eyes, pause and then speak swiftly and continuously. He would copy it all out and arrange it for publication. The fruit of the intense years of dictation, 1944 to 1948, was no less than thirty-five books. To the end, he regarded the publication of her works as probably the most important achievement of his life.

With regard to himself, he says: '[she] pointed out the fulfilling way from Ignatius to John, and thus laid the foundation for most of what has been published by me since 1940'.[10] Indeed St John the Evangelist stands over von Balthasar's work as a great patron. With Adrienne, he quickly founded the *Johannesgemeinschaft*, the Community of John, and the *Johannesverlag*, a publishing house for all of their writings. His utter dedication to the Community led to his conflict with the Jesuits, who would not allow it to be established within the framework of their own organisation and who would not accept one of their members committing himself for evermore to one specific apostolate. So, with great regret, von Balthasar left the Jesuits in 1950, though still a priest and still profoundly marked by the Ignatian drive to combine contemplation and action and find God in all things. Apparently, St Ignatius of Loyola appeared frequently to Adrienne![11] Von Balthasar went on giving the *Spiritual Exercises* of St Ignatius for the rest of his life and wanted his Community to live an Ignatian spirituality in the midst of the world, but he himself went rather into the wilderness (as did de Lubac in the same year, 1950, though for different reasons). He was never offered a Chair in Theology. He spent six years in Zurich and then returned to Basel in 1956, where he lived with Adrienne and her husband until her death in 1967. Only gradually thereafter was he rehabilitated into the Catholic theological world and his unique contribution recognised. In the meantime, of course, the Second Vatican Council had taken place, from 1962–5, entirely without his participation.

It has been said that one way of seeing their relationship is 'to attribute the creative insights to Adrienne, and to Balthasar the filtering of these insights through the theological tradition of the Church'.[12] The insights are many. I quote from John O'Donnell's list: 'Christ's descent into hell as his solidarity with the abandoned, Jesus' Sonship as obedience to the point of powerless identification with the Godforsaken, faith as Marian womb-like receptivity, virginity as spiritual fruitfulness for the world, personhood as unique sending from God, the vicarious representative character of prayer and suffering in the Church [and] the bodiliness of Christian existence'.[13]

By imagining von Balthasar, the man of brilliant intellect, being given these insights from Adrienne, the woman without theological training, who had received them directly from God in prayer, we may perhaps understand better his conviction that the life of faith is essentially a *feminine* one of active receptivity to God's gifts, and that women are most attuned to God's gifts and most integrated, so to speak, in their bodily living out of spiritual truths. The poor man, we may almost hear him say, has to cope with a tension between actual masculinity and spiritual femininity, and will always be inherently more fragile. Not only was Adrienne telling him of the prerogatives of femininity, she was profoundly impressing these mysteries upon him existentially.

Adrienne's main scriptural dictations to von Balthasar were her commentaries on John's Gospel, his Letters and his Apocalypse. She surely influenced Balthasar's unique interpretation of John's Gospel as a study of the relation between 'love' and 'office' in the Church, a study culminating in 'a huge, subtly complex fugue' (*Office*, p. 160). As we look at how he sees the fourth Gospel, we may note, first of all, that Balthasar does ecclesiology not with abstract notions, like 'love' and 'office', but around concrete figures, 'real symbols' (cf. *Office*, p. 146), as he calls them, in this case, John and Peter, respectively. Balthasar says that it seems almost as if the writer of the fourth Gospel foresaw the isolation which might befall the principle of office in the church, for example on the basis of the famous Petrine text in Matthew's Gospel, and that he acted to forestall this by interweaving Peter and John, office and love, in a way that bonds them much more closely than the traditional pairing of Peter and Paul (*Office*, p. 161).

Let us follow his account. First, Balthasar understands John to be the unnamed companion of Andrew, two disciples of John the Baptist, who points out Jesus, the Lamb of God, to them. This means that John is called before Peter, who appears on the scene the next day, when Andrew goes to fetch his brother (John 1.37–39). At the Last Supper, it is John, the Beloved, who is close to Jesus, resting on his breast, so much so that Peter refers to *him* to question the Lord about who will betray him (13.23–24). As Jesus goes on trial, it is John who enters the court of the High Priest along with him, while Peter stays outside the door until John has a word with the maid to bring him in (18.15–16). At the Cross, it is John who is present with Mary, and Peter who is missing (*Office*, p. 160, n. 26).

Nevertheless, John has already shown Peter being singled out for a distinct role. As soon as Jesus meets him, he changes his name from Simon to Peter (John 1.42; cf. *Office*, pp. 142, 149, 223), though John will continue to call him 'Simon Peter', as if there is a transition between the two which Peter must stumblingly work through. When the crucial questioning of the Twelve takes place after Jesus' teaching on the Eucharist (in John 6) and his abandonment by many of his disciples, it is Simon Peter who professes their faith in him (6.66–71). There is the drama of Simon Peter wanting to follow Jesus and claiming he will lay down his life for him, and being told that he will in fact deny the Lord three times (13.37–38), and we hear then how it happens (18.15–27). But, says Balthasar, Peter makes these impetuous claims because he is aware that something exceptional has been assigned to him (cf. *Office*, p.150).

The fugue between Peter and John, between office and love, begins in earnest in John's portrayal of Easter Sunday. Apparently, Balthasar would conclude his retreats for students in the 1940s with an account of the finale of John's Gospel so expressive and urgent that some still remember it today.[14] Peter and John run together to the tomb. The eagerness of pure love arrives first (cf. *Office*, p. 160, n. 26), while office, charged with shepherding not only the saints but also the sinners, proceeds more slowly (p. 329). Love *looks* in, but yields his place to office to *enter* first (cf. p. 160, n. 26; p. 293). Office verifies the facts, the emptiness, the cloth and the napkin, then on the strength of this guarantee, love enters, sees and believes (John 20.3–8).

When Jesus then appears to the disciples by the Sea of Tiberias, Peter is three times questioned by Jesus about his love. Balthasar sees great significance in that Jesus thrice calls him 'Simon, Son of John'. At this point, he says, John is being acknowledged as the one whose love grounds the office Peter is to assume, while he is also being stripped of his prerogative of the greater love, because Peter is being asked for a love more than that of the others, including John. Love is being taken from the realm of personal devotion in John and put into the realm of public witness in Peter. John is not being rejected, because this witness will speak for all, including him, but he is retiring from the spotlight into a position from which he will constantly support with his love the office which Peter now properly assumes (cf. *Office*, pp. 222–223).

The hidden but decisive task which John now assumes is indicated by the dialogue between Jesus and Peter. Jesus has just indicated that Peter will be taken and put to death, in a final act of witness glorifying God, and then Peter asks about John who is following behind. 'If he is to remain until I come', says Jesus, 'what is that to you?' (John 21.20–23). 'The Church of love will "remain" until the Lord comes again, but how and where, only the Lord knows'.[15] All that Peter, the servant, needs to know is that his task has been given him personally by the Lord with the all-embracing summons: 'Follow me' (John 21.22).

At the outset, we spoke of Mary and Peter, now we have spoken of John and Peter. How does von Balthasar view the trio? He regards Mary and Peter as the primary symbols of the Church's life and activity. The entire Church is both Marian and Petrine (cf. *Office*, p. 205), but these two can so easily become polarised. John is the one who has 'the mediating role that prevents the Church from falling into two separate parts' (*Office*, p. 224, cf. pp. 145, 294). Mary and Peter never actually encounter each other in the Gospels; it is John who unites them and mediates each to the other. To Peter, he mediates the all-embracing reality of Marian love which grounds Peter's office, and, to Mary, at the foot of the Cross, he mediates the presence of Peter who, there and then, receives the Marian Church into his care. John lives on primarily in those saints 'who have, as it were, an unofficial ecclesiastical mission and whose authenticity can be recognised by the fact that they always represent the link between the Marian and the Petrine in the Church, supporting both, even when this seems to lead nowhere' (*Office*, p. 225). St Catherine of Siena, who strove to bring the pope back to Rome from Avignon would be a good example, as would also, of course, be St Ignatius of Loyola (cf. p. 257).

Balthasar fits the Avignon exile into a survey of the immense saga of the freeing of the Church from the state, a freedom which was only finally secured by the definition of papal prerogatives at the First Vatican Council. The Christian Roman emperors had the power to summon important Church councils, but their influence also tended to propagate heresy. Popes had to stand up to them, sometimes encouraged by outstanding figures such as Ambrose, who insisted that the emperor was 'in the Church, and not above it' (*Office*, p. 254). Periodically the Church plunged back into subservience, not least when Pope Leo III crowned Charlemagne in 800, and humiliation, as at the time of Avignon and the Great Schism (1378–1417). Some sought a solution by making a general council and not the pope the supreme authority in the Church, but such conciliarism tended to cut bishops loose into groupings of one sort or another, often determined by nationalistic considerations, as in Gallicanism (cf. p. 215–216), with resultant fragmentation of the Church and subjection of the fragments once again to civil power and manipulation.

Ultimately, and perhaps paradoxically, it must be recognised that 'the freedom of the Church is guaranteed solely by the papacy', whose proper function is to defend all the constituent local churches from the power of the state (cf. *Office*, pp. 269, 276). Vatican I succeeded in stating this once and for all by pope and bishops together, and it was then the task of Vatican II to integrate the papal office into the fabric of the episcopate and, indeed, of the Church as a whole. What also, providentially, happened at the time of Vatican I was that the Church was itself stripped of the scandalous vestiges of statehood, by the loss of the Papal states (cf. p. 257), and freed to live by purely spiritual credentials, the unfolding story of which continues into our own day.

In the mighty upheaval of the mid-19th century, several inter-related truths came into focus. At the start of the letter to the Ephesians, Paul blesses God for having chosen us in Christ before the foundation of the world to be holy and unblemished before him' (Eph. 1.4). We are such, of course, as members of the Church, and, later, with bridal imagery, Paul adds that Christ has in fact loved the Church and given himself up for her, cleansing and sanctifying her so as to take her 'holy and unblemished' to himself (5.25–27). The Fathers loved to contemplate this pre-existing and spotless bride, who seems not to have had a particular face, but rather to have hovered after the fashion of a Gnostic *aeon* (cf. *Office*, p. 192). At the same time, certain Fathers explored another track deriving also from Paul. If the Church is the bride of Christ and if Christ is the new Adam (cf. Rom. 5), then the Church is the new Eve, born from the side of Christ on the Cross as Eve was taken from the side of Adam while he slept. Moreover, when Irenaeus focused specifically on the obedience of Mary as that which counteracted the disobedience of Eve, then the Church suddenly assumed the face of Mary (cf. *Office*, pp. 196–199).

The early middle ages saw the final decline of the faceless pure Church and the danger that the Church would disintegrate into 'mediocrity and ultimately into sociology' (*Office*, p. 202). What preserved the sense of holiness and mystery was increasing adherence to Mary as the real and historical focal point of that pure Church, the spotless personification of what the historical community is called to be, the archetype of the fullness of grace (cf. p. 201).

In the 1850s, Pope Pius IX sent a widespread enquiry out to the Church to gauge what was believed by the faithful regarding the Virgin Mary, and the response came back that the *sensus fidelium* was that the Church had 'an "unblemished", real and personal centre in the person of the Mother of the Lord' (*Office*, p. 212). Accordingly, he defined the dogma of the Immaculate Conception in 1854. Nearly a century later, Pope Pius XII sent out an even more detailed questionnaire to ask the faithful about Mary's Assumption and received a resounding request back to define what was believed by the Catholic faithful on all sides, namely that Mary is now body and soul in heaven, again as the anticipation of the fulfilment which awaits the whole Church, and that the marriage of the Lamb has already been consummated in the core of the Church (cf. p. 241).

What is striking in both cases is that the Pope was simply making explicit what was already believed. The indefectibility of the whole Church in matters of faith is what is primary. The infallibility of the college of bishops and ultimately of the pope himself are functions of that basic reality (cf. *Office*, pp. 125, 215), and eccentric functions at that, in Balthasar's terminology (cf. pp. 213, 220). At the First Vatican Council, the urgency of the task in hand led the fathers to take first what in fact was the eleventh of fifteen chapters in the draft text on the Church. This was the chapter on papal primacy and infallibility and, in context, it followed chapter 9, which was entirely about the prior indefectibility of the whole Church (cf. p. 219). The plan was to move on to those other areas later, but war broke out between France and Prussia the day after the decree on the pope was promulgated in 1870 and the Council was prematurely ended (cf. p. 214), unfortunately leaving this decree standing alone.

The net result, however, was that, within the space of twenty years or so, decisive *ecclesial* prerogatives of Mary and Peter, respectively, had been defined; namely that in Mary the unblemished Church has an historical beginning and centre and that in Peter the faith of the unblemished Church has an historical judge and voice. Balthasar says simply that Mary and Peter 'belong together' as reference points for the Catholic consciousness of belief, that is, for the *sensus fidelium* (cf. *Office*, p. 213).

Of course, there is a vital difference between the two. Balthasar says of Mary's bodily Assumption that it enables the 'integral and ever-present reality of [the] genuine personal centre' of the Church (*Office*, p. 212). I take this to mean that, as Christ's bodily Ascension releases him from the physical particularity of being in only one place on this earth at a given time, so the same is true, *mutatis mutandis,* for Mary. As Christ is now free to be everywhere and in all as God's gift, so Mary is free to be everywhere and in all as the principle of active receptivity of that gift.[16] She, uniquely, needs no particular fleshing out, because she is in *all.* However, Peter *does* need a regular new fleshing out in the person of each successive pope. So, too, do all the others whom Balthasar locates in the constellation of Christ, John, as we have seen, but also Paul and James (cf. *Office*, pp. 308–312), all of whom are 'prototypes ... forming the Church throughout history' (p. 148).

Vatican II duly followed up these tumultuous ecclesial definitions in its Dogmatic Constitution on the Church, *Lumen Gentium (LG)*, which integrated both the pope and Mary into the fabric of the Church as a whole. In chapter 3, it specifically endorsed the teaching of Vatican I on the primacy and infallibility of the pope and undertook to set it in the context of the ministry of the bishops as a whole to 'direct the house of the living God' (*LG* 18). Then, in the final chapter 8, it said of Mary that 'in the most Blessed Virgin the Church has already reached that perfection whereby she exists without spot or wrinkle (Eph. 5.27)' (*LG* 65): 'the Mother of Jesus in the glory which she possesses in body and soul in heaven is the image and beginning of the Church as it is to be perfected in the world to come'. 'Likewise she shines forth on earth, until the day of the Lord shall come (cf. 2 Peter 3.10), a sign of certain hope and comfort to the pilgrim People of God' (*LG* 68).

The femininity of Mary, the actively receptive one, marks the whole Church and each Christian soul. Balthasar believes that ministry has a fundamentally *masculine* quality, but he insists that this is rooted in the Church's femininity and does not somehow by-pass it. Such a vision, he maintains, avoids 'a twofold danger':

first, that the Church might become a self-sufficient entity, interposing herself as an 'intermediary' between the believer and Christ, whereas she is primarily an open womb and teaches mankind, in her and with her, to be similarly open; and secondly, that the clergy might equate their paternal role with the divine paternal role of God instead of recognising that their exercise of authority is pure service, the pure communication of the authority that belongs solely to God' (*Office*, p. 185).

John O'Donnell expresses Balthasar's vivid sexual imagery as follows.

'[The Church of love] is most fully realised in Mary ... Within this Church of love is inserted the institutional Church symbolised in the figure of Peter ... The institutional Church is masculine. This is the Church governed by the ordained pastors whose task is to represent Christ before the community. In Balthasar's opinion Christ is masculine because he represents the Father's will to the world. Just as the man gives his seed in sexual intercourse, so Christ sows the seed of the Word and is a total outpouring of himself for his bride, the Church. The ordained members of the community, those who receive the office of representing Christ in the community, represent Christ in his masculine function. But the ordained are first and foremost baptised Christians. As the baptised they are feminine, they are receptive of Christ's grace, they must imitate Marian openness to the Word. Hence Peter has a subordinate role in regard to Mary. As regards authority Mary stands under Peter. But as regards the essence of the Church, Peter must be inserted within the Marian Church. His institutional authority has no sense apart from the Church of love. In this sense, Balthasar would argue that in no way does woman have less in the Church. For woman represents the essence of what it means to be Church.[17]

Balthasar's Marian and Petrine terminology has passed into the official documents of the Catholic Church in recent times, indicating that it is his thought that is particularly driving the Church's understanding of sexuality in relation to witness and ministry in the Church. The *Catechism of the Catholic Church (CCC)* clearly echoes Balthasar when it talks about the purpose of ministry in the following terms.

The Church's structure [i.e. its being gathered around an ordained ministry] is totally ordered to the holiness of Christ's members ... Mary goes before us all in the holiness that is the Church's mystery as 'the bride without spot or wrinkle'. This is why the 'Marian' dimension of the Church precedes the 'Petrine' (*CCC* 773).

In fact, at this point, the *Catechism* is quoting Pope John Paul in his 1988 Apostolic Letter on the dignity of women, entitled *Mulieris Dignitatem (MD)*. Popes rarely quote modern theologians in such texts, but the present Pope did not hesitate to quote Balthasar: Mary is 'Queen of the Apostles without any pretensions to apostolic powers: she has other and greater powers' (*MD* 27, note 55). Those words indicate both the unity and the distinction between the two dimensions or profiles of the Church, the Marian and the Petrine; the link is both 'profound and complementary' says the Pope.[18]

Max Thurian summarises and develops the Pope's words when he says that: 'It is to this Marian profile of the Church that we should look to discover in depth the role of women in the Church and her possible ministry.' 'It is absolutely necessary' he says 'to preserve and develop in the Church, which is a mother, the characteristic of femininity which is of her essence'. 'To confer the ministerial priesthood on women would contradict their proper nature and the specific gifts which they possess.' Striving to define those gifts, he says: 'The ministry of woman is characterized by spiritual motherhood: gifts of acceptance, spiritual discernment, counselling, etc. The contemplative life and the spiritual combat of intercession are also among the specific gifts of the Christian woman who can be led to exercise a true ministry of leadership in the heart of the Church.'[19]

However, an American woman, Joyce Little, views spiritual motherhood more widely and sees the potential for a female lead in the lay apostolate: 'it is', she says, 'the specific female role of Mary and the Church to bear Christ into the world...the female role of making salvation a reality in the whole of creation is essential'. Thus, she maintains that women are specifically equipped to fulfil 'the special obligation of the laity', which, 'as Vatican II pointed out, is the renewal of the temporal order'.[20]

This brings us back to the ethos of Balthasar's Community of John, to consecrate the world. Interestingly, it is only the female branch of the Community that has ever flourished. Given that the lay apostolate is a field far from fully developed, Balthasar would wish us to see the unique potential of women for performing that vital task rather than the duties of priesthood.

Pope John Paul chose the Feast of Pentecost, 1994, for his most recent and most firm statement about the ordination of women, saying that 'the Church has no authority whatsoever to confer priestly ordination on women'.[21] He was emphatically restating the judgement delivered in 1976 by the lengthy Vatican document *Inter Insignores (II)*.[22] There it was said not just that 'the Church, in fidelity to the example of the Lord does not consider herself authorised to admit women to priestly ordination', but also that this position 'can be of help in deepening understanding of the respective roles of men and of women' (*II*, Introduction).

The document claims not a conclusive argument for the ordination of men only, but simply a 'profound fittingness' for this arrangement (*II* 5). It recalls the nuptial imagery which runs all through the scriptural account of God's covenant with humanity. The final form of this image is the marriage of Christ and the Church, but its roots are in the one and only fundamental distinction between human beings which God inscribed in creation itself, namely the difference between man and woman (*II* 5; cf. Gen. 1.27). There is something primordial in this distinction. 'Christ himself was and remains a man', it says, and a Church which considers that the priest acts *in persona Christi* must consider only men for this role (*II* 5). The Galatians text which rejects distinction between male and female in Christ (Gal. 3.28) refers not to ministry but to baptised membership of his body, within which the richness of this distinction can be explored (cf. *II* 5, 6).

What, then, is to be the role of women? It is sometimes said that, since it was women who first saw the risen Lord and took the first paschal message to the apostles, they themselves, especially Mary of Magdala, surely qualify as apostles along with the men and thus that women should be ordained. But it is clear that these women were *not* counted as apostles; rather their task, as the Declaration says, was 'to prepare [the Apostles themselves] to become the official witnesses to the Resurrection' (*II* 2, cf. 3). Here, perhaps, in the same incidents, but differently viewed, lies a key to true feminine ministry, that of anchoring the Church's public witness in deep faith. The Declaration concludes by stressing that 'the greatest in the Kingdom of Heaven are not the ministers but the saints', which perhaps points towards women as particularly apt exponents of the fundamental qualities of discipleship. Women, it says have a great mission 'for the rediscovery by believers of the true face of the Church' (*II* 6). It is, I think, von Balthasar who can particularly help us to unpack that statement.

We have just recalled the act of creation, noting that God established the distinction between male and female in that act and deducing that this distinction is primordial, a distinction ripe for use by God in the fullness of time to express, with nuptial imagery, his relationship with his creation, as von Balthasar has described. However, it is interesting to note that this view, with its apparent coherence, is open to quite a radical critique. The critique comes from an eminent Orthodox theologian and bishop, John Zizioulas, Metropolitan of Pergamon.[23]

Zizioulas draws strongly on the Cappadocian Fathers and points out that one of them, Gregory of Nyssa, proposed that the famous Genesis text actually speaks of the creation of humanity in terms of *two* acts.[24] A precise translation says: 'God created man in his own image; in the image of God he created him [the *first* creative act]; male and female he created them [the *second* creative act]' (Gen. 1.27). Respecting the subtle precision of this text, Gregory of Nyssa deduced that the distinction between male and female is not primordial but secondary, instituted by God because he foresaw that humanity would sin and therefore be subject to death and therefore need to procreate in order to survive. When sin is driven out, when death is no more and God's Kingdom is fully established, presumably we shall then move beyond this distinction. Jesus himself suggests as much, when he says to the Sadducees trying to trap him with the story of the seven brothers who successively married the same woman that, 'In the resurrection they neither marry nor are given in marriage, but are as the angels in heaven' (Matt. 22.30).

If, then, the Eucharist is a foretaste of that *heavenly* life and state of existence, is the heavenly Christ still *masculine* in some sense, and is masculinity as we know it now in our *fallen* state essential to the eucharistic *imaging* of Christ in the midst of the saints in the heavenly Jerusalem? Zizioulas considers that such are the issues that need to be investigated. Even if the heavenly Christ is masculine, his is nevertheless not a *procreative* masculinity. Balthasar's use of the imagery of sexual activity for the relationship between God and creation or between Christ and the Church is thus open to serious objection.

In recent times, Catholic teaching against the ordination of women has particularly drawn on the theology of von Balthasar. However, as Zizioulas indicates, there are questions to be asked of this theology. It is to be hoped that a vigorous and constructive Catholic–Orthodox dialogue may cast valuable light on this much debated issue.[25]

Notes

1   Johann Roten, 'The Two Halves of the Moon', in David L. Schindler (ed.), *Hans Urs von Balthasar. His Life and Work* (Communio Books, Ignatius, San Francisco, 1991; hereafter, *Life and Work*), p. 66.

2   cf. Peter Henrici, 'Hans Urs von Balthasar: A Sketch of His Life', in *Life and Work*, p. 11.

3   ibid. pp. 12–13.

4   Medard Kehl, 'Hans Urs von Balthasar: A Portrait', in Medard Kehl and Werner Loser (eds.), *The Von Balthasar Reader* (Crossroad, New York, 1982; hereafter, *Reader*), p. 31.

5   cf. ibid. p. 7.

6   Von Balthasar, *The Theology of Henri de Lubac* (Communio Books, Ignatius, San Francisco, 1991), p. 35.

7   cf. my books, *The Eucharist Makes the Church. Henri de Lubac and John Zizioulas in Dialogue* (T & T Clark, Edinburgh, 1993), particularly chapters 1 and 2; and *Sacrament of Salvation. An Introduction to Eucharistic Ecclesiology* (T & T Clark, Edinburgh, 1995), chapters 4 and 5.

8   Von Balthasar, *The Office of Peter and the Structure of the Church* (Ignatius, San Francisco, 1986; hereafter, *Office*), pp. 124–125.

9   Von Balthasar, *A First Glance at Adrienne von Speyr* (Ignatius, San Francisco, 1981), p. 31; quoted by Roten in *Life and Work*, p. 67.

10 Quoted in *Reader*, p. 42.

11 cf. Roten in *Life and Work*, p. 71, n. 23.

12 John O'Donnell, *Hans Urs von Balthasar* (Geoffrey Chapman, London 1992), p. 5.

13 ibid. p. 5; cf. Roten in *Life and Work*, pp. 76–78.

14 cf. Henrici in *Life and Work*, p. 42.

15 Quoted by Henrici in *Life and Work*, p. 42.

16 Balthasar was influenced, via de Lubac, by Teilhard de Chardin's Mariology, a bold aspect of which was Teilhard's application not just to Christ but also to *Mary* of the Ephesians passage: *descendit et ascendit ut impleret omnia* (Eph. 4.9–10); cf my book, *The Eucharist Makes the Church*, p. 64, and also my pamphlet, *'Mary for Teilhard and de Lubac'* (ESBVM, 1987).

17 O'Donnell, *Hans Urs von Balthasar*, p. 120.

18 cf. *Osservatore Romano* (English edition), 24/3/93, p. 8.

19 ibid. p. 8.

20 *Osservatore Romano* (English edition), 14/4/93, p. 6.

21 Pope John Paul II, Apostolic Letter, *Ordinatio Sacerdotalis*, 4.

22 Declaration on the Admission of Women to the Ministerial Priesthood, issued by the Congregation for the Doctrine of the Faith on 15 October 1976. Introduction.

23 cf. my book, *The Eucharist Makes The Church. Henri de Lubac and John Zizioulas in Dialogue*. For what follows, I draw gratefully upon personal discussions with Zizioulas.

24 cf. Gregory of Nyssa, *De hominis opificio* ('On the Formation of Man'), 16 (*PG* 44, 177–185).

25 cf. my article, 'Mary and Catholic–Orthodox Dialogue', *The Month 29* (1996), pp. 476–484.

(This paper was given at the ESBVM Congress at Norwich in July 1994)

6

The Blessed Virgin Mary
in the Protestant tradition

David Butler

One major enjoyment of an English summer is the series of international cricket matches which are played out on the major county grounds. If I cannot afford the money or the time to be at Edgbaston or Lords there is the possibility of watching or listening. The commentary on colour television is I think not all that good and adds little to the enjoyment of the match; in fact it is best to turn off the sound completely. The commentary on the radio on the other hand is excellent, critical and informed in the best sense. Hence my ideal is to listen to the commentary on Radio 4 while watching the action in colour on television. In a curious sense it is better than being there.

What connection has this with the Blessed Virgin Mary? By analogy, I want to suggest that there is here a comparison to be made between the Catholic view of Mary and the Protestant view. The Catholic seems to Protestants to be wholly in technicolour with no commentary, or at least if there is commentary, it is highly uncritical, with little reference to the Scriptures as they have been interpreted in the Protestant tradition. The Protestant seems to the Catholic to have been concerned only with commentary, usually being a totally biblical and a totally critical commentary with no regard for the history of the Church down the centuries, nor for the worship life of the Church which is its very life-blood. At this point the Catholic is able to suggest that the Protestant *Scriptura Sola* has been very selective as offering a criterion of what is preached since there is more about the Virgin Mary in the Bible than there is about the Holy Eucharist or the Lord's Supper. I have verified this by doing a rough count of verses concerning the Virgin Mary and the institution of the Eucharist:

    i) Concerning the Virgin Mary: **129 vv.** (Matt. 1.6; 1.18–25; 2.11; 2.13–15; 2.19–21; 12.46–50; Mark 3.31–35; Luke 1.26–38; 1.39–57; 2.1–51; 8.19–21; John 2.1–12; 19.25–27; Acts 1.14; Gal. 4.4)

    ii) Concerning the Institution of the Eucharist: **29 vv.** (Matt. 26.26–9; Mark 14.22–25; Luke 22.14–20; 1 Cor. 11.23–34)

It could be argued that this is very selective and that the Johannine eucharistic passages have not been counted nor have other references to the breaking of bread &c. On the other hand it could equally be argued that other passages belonging traditionally to the Virgin Mary such as Gen. 3, Isa. 7 and Rev. 12 have not been included. A count like this is of course open to all kinds of criticisms, not least that 'more does not mean more important'. However, it does show that those who have been concerned with the main thrust of Scripture have sometimes been very selective in deciding what that main thrust is about.

Before we turn to the work of some of the main Reformers of the Church, we note in passing that in the period before the Reformation there were few who offered protests against Mary or Marian devotion. One of the amazing facts of history is that there are very few disrespectful references to Mary either before or after the Reformation. Perhaps four reasons might be offered for this:

i) The evidence of the Council of Ephesus in AD 431 which defined Mary as the *Theotokos* or Mother of God said something important christologically which could not be combatted without making nonsense of the Incarnation.

ii) Mary is seen in the writings of many authors as the exemplar of faith, the one who said her *fiat mihi* to God at the Annunciation. As an example of faith, she could only be held in reverence, not criticised for the extravagant devotion offered to her by some believers. After all, justification by *faith* became the doctrinal yardstick of the Protestant Reformation.

iii) The pre-eminence of Christmas as a festival over even Easter as a major Christian festival means that Mary still holds the centre stage with her Son at least once a year even within the Protestant tradition.

iv) The use of the Magnificat of Mary in the services of the Book of Common Prayer in the Anglican tradition. This kept the thought of Mary as the one who saw God overturn the presuppositions of humanity in her life of faith.

The earliest negative reference in the Fathers is probably in Tertullian where he counters the acceptance of the perpetual virginity of Mary in *c.* AD 207 (e.g. *Adversus Marcionem* iv.19.12). Tertullian also suggests that Mary was not loyal to her Son at the end of his life:

A woman from the multitude cries out, that blessed was the womb that had borne him, and the breasts which had given him suck. And the Lord answers, Yea rather blessed are they that hear the word of God and keep it: because even before this he had rejected his mother and his brethren, because he prefers those who hear God and obey him. For not even on the present occasion was his mother in attendance on him.

(*Adversus Marcionem* iv.26.13)

John Chrysostom made similar points to Tertullian's in the late fourth century in his homily on John 2.4:

> Verse 4. **Woman, what have I to do with thee? Mine hour is not yet come.**
> For where parents cause no impediment or hindrance in things belonging to God, it is our bounden duty to give way to them, and there is great danger in not doing so; but when they require any thing unseasonably, and cause hindrance in any spiritual matter, it is unsafe to obey. And therefore he answered thus in this place, and again elsewhere, Who is my mother and who are my brethren? because they did not yet think rightly of him; and she who had borne him, claimed, according to the custom of other mothers, to direct him in all things, when she ought to have reverenced and worshipped him.

Until the late thirteenth century the doctrine of Mary's Immaculate Conception was generally denied by the theologians. For example both Anselm in the 11th century and Bernard in the 12th century denied it in their writings. After Duns Scotus in late 13th-century Oxford had written positively about it, it was taken up by his order, the Franciscans, who waged a sort of holy war against the Dominicans who had their representative theologian in Thomas Aquinas. One Franciscan reformer, Bernardino of Siena, in the 15th century suggested in his exaltation of the privileges of Mary that she was in some sense superior to God: 'The blessed Virgin could do more concerning God than God could do concerning himself.' (Sermon 'On the Superadmirable Grace & Glory of the Mother of God'). Bernardino was writing about the humanity of the Virgin that God could not emulate, since God is only able to generate the infinite, the immortal, whereas Mary can generate the finite, the mortal. But the suggestion that Mary could do more than God was hardly justifiable in any sensible theology.

Erasmus (d. 1536) was a little perturbed about the excessive compliments that he found were being paid to Mary in his day. Titles used for the Virgin were often not to be found anywhere in Scripture, such as 'Star of the Sea' and 'Port of Salvation'. The thought that prayers to Mary were particularly efficacious since Jesus would deny his mother nothing were supremely irritating to Erasmus. Yet his most telling piece of anti-Marian writing was an accident, when in his Greek New Testament of 1516 he translated the Greek *'kecharitomenē'* not as *'gratia plena'* but as *'gratiosa'*, i.e. not 'full of grace' but 'being in grace or favour with God'.

In the works of Luther (1483-1546) there is slightly more on the eucharist than on the Virgin, but at least he does discuss her place in the scheme of salvation. His main insistence, as might be guessed, is that Mary should not rob her Son of his foremost place in our redemption:

In their last perils people were led to seek the intercessions of Mary and the saints. They kept repeating these well-known figments: that Mother Mary showed her breasts to her Son, the Son showed his wounds to the Father, and that thus man was saved through the intercession, not of the Son but of the Mother.

(On Genesis 3.13.)

Luther shows himself intensely concerned for the true and complete humanity of Christ as derived from Mary, and protests not only against the Docetists of the early ages but also against the Enthusiasts of his own time for their neglect of the true humanity and divinity of Christ:

Let us go to the child lying in the lap of his mother Mary and to the sacrificial victim suspended on the cross; there we shall readily behold God, and there we shall look into his very heart.

(Commentary on Genesis 19.14)

Hilda Graef offers the thought that Luther's view of Mary is that of a rather pathetic young girl, without intrinsic merit or sanctity. One has to take issue with this in part. It is right as far as the humble and pathetic young girl without merit goes. Listen to Luther as he describes the meaning of 'low estate' in the Magnificat:

This, therefore, is what Mary means: 'God has regarded me, a poor, despised, and lowly maiden, though he might have found a rich, renowned, noble, and mighty queen ... But he let his pure and gracious eyes light on me and used so poor and despised a maiden, in order that no one might glory in his presence, as though we were worthy of this, and that I must acknowledge it all to be pure grace and goodness and not at all my merit or worthiness.'

(Comm Lk 1.48)

But as to her sanctity, Luther seems to accept the idea of her sinlessness as he describes the birth of Christ from Mary:

For this reason her body did not abandon its natural functions which belong to childbirth, except that she gave birth without sin, without shame, without pain, and without injury, just as she had conceived without sin. The curse of Eve, which read: 'In pain you shall bear your children' (Gen. 3.16), did not apply to her. In other respects things happened to her exactly as they happen to any woman giving birth.

(Sermon on the Gospel for Christmas Eve)

Elsewhere the immaculate conception is clearly implied: 'From her he derived everything, except sin, that a child naturally and normally receives from its mother'(*Works* 22. p. 23). At another place he insists that the Immaculate Conception could not be a necessary belief for salvation, even if the pope were to insist upon it. (*Defence & Explanation of the Articles condemned in* Exsurge Domine).

Luther maintains the doctrine of the perpetual virginity of Mary; for example when commenting on John 2.12, 'After this he went down to Capernaum with his mother and his brothers and his disciples', he writes: '... I am inclined to agree with those who declare that "brothers" really means "cousins" here, for Holy Writ and the Jews always call cousins brothers.' He was asked whether Mary had intercourse with Joseph after the birth of Christ and replied:

> The church leaves this and has not decided. Nevertheless, what happened afterwards shows quite strongly that Mary remained a virgin. For after she had perceived that she was the mother of the Son of God, she didn't think she should become the mother of a human child and adhered to this vow.
>
> (*Table Talk.* March 25, 1539)

Luther will have nothing to do with the thought that the Son is vindictive and judgmental while his mother is kind to sinners:

> And St Bernard, who was a pious man otherwise, also said: 'Behold how Christ chides, censures, and condemns the Pharisees so harshly throughout the Gospel, whereas the Virgin Mary is always kind and gentle and never utters an unfriendly word ... Christ is given to scolding and punishing, but Mary has nothing but sweetness and love.' Therefore Christ was generally feared; we fled from him and took refuge with the saints, calling upon Mary and others to deliver us from our distress. We regarded them all as holier than Christ.
>
> (*Works* 22. p. 109)

Luther rejoices that the credal statement 'and was incarnate of the Virgin Mary and was made man' was the cause of genuflection and the removal of hats from ancient times. The implication is that he would like the actions still to be performed during the German Lutheran Mass. But that Mass was a cut-down version of the Roman Mass, so abbreviated that from 1523 it no longer contained the prayer of intercession to the Blessed Virgin Mary. Her prayers were no longer necessary, as her Son had taken his rightful place at the centre of the redemptive act. For 'Hail Mary, full of grace', Luther has substituted 'from his fullness we have all received, grace upon grace'.

Calvin (1509–1564) always insists that Christ should be first in the list of those who are invoked to help us in our search for salvation. Many have been guilty in the past of looking elsewhere than to Christ. They have looked to Mary, to Michael or to Peter, even sometimes asking Mary to bid her Son to do what we request. In his work *On the Canons and Decrees of Trent and their Antidote*, he quotes Ambrosius Catharinus of the Dominicans who suggested that the Mother of Christ sat on Christ's throne to obtain grace for us. Thereby, said Calvin, Christ is divided and half the work of salvation is done by Christ and half by Mary. The fact that Mary is part of the sinful race of Adam is proved from Augustine; that she was herself a sinner is proved from Chrysostom and Ambrose who suspected her of ambition. Commenting on John 2.4, 'Woman, what have I to do with thee?', Calvin writes:

> This saying of Christ openly and manifestly warns men to beware lest, by too superstitiously elevating the honour of the name of mother in the Virgin Mary, they transfer to her what belongs exclusively to God. Christ, therefore, addresses his mother in this manner, in order to lay down a perpetual and general instruction to all ages, that his divine glory must not be obscured by excessive honour paid to his mother. How necessary this warning became, in consequence of the gross and disgraceful superstitions which followed afterwards, is too well known. For Mary has been constituted the Queen of Heaven, the Hope, the Life, and the Salvation of the world; and in short, they in fury and madness proceeded so far that they stripped Christ of his spoils and left him almost naked. (*Commentary on John* 2.4)

Calvin's objection is that Mary is being offered an insult when, being exalted by false praises, she takes from Christ what truly belongs to him. That she should be extolled on the grounds that she is the Mother of Christ and for no other reason seems to be pointless to Calvin, since there are many other things in her that could be extolled. Here perhaps Calvin is thinking of Mary as an example of faith. If Mary is to be praised, says Calvin, she is only to be praised because the Almighty has done great things for her; 'no room is left for the pretended titles, which come from another quarter'. 'Hence we see how widely the Papists differ from her, who idly adorn her with their empty devices, and reckon almost as nothing the benefits which she received from God.' As to whether the passage in Matt. 1.25, 'And knew her not', proves the perpetual virginity of Mary, Calvin is agnostic: 'It is said that Joseph knew her not till she had brought forth her first born son: but this is limited to that very time. What took place afterwards, the historian does not inform us' (*Comm. on Matt.* 1.25). In all Calvin's thinking, of course, the primacy and the initiative is God's. The place of the human, including the place of Mary, is merely that of co-operation with the will of God. The intercession of Mary for us is on this understanding totally excluded.

In the English Reformers, although the 1549 Prayer Book kept many of the feasts of Mary, including the Purification, the Annunciation, the

Visitation, the Conception and Nativity of Mary, the main thrust of Marian understanding is summed up by the 1563 Articles of Religion in Article 22, 'Of Purgatory':

> The Romish Doctrine concerning Purgatory, Pardons, Worshipping and Adoration, as well of Images as of Reliques, and also Invocation of Saints, is a fond thing vainly invented, and grounded upon no warranty of Scripture, but rather repugnant to the Word of God.

Later Anglican writers, however, seem to have been closer to Luther's theology of Mary than to that of Calvin. Francis White, one-time Bishop of Ely, writes in his *Treatise of the Sabbath Day* of 1635 that one Tradition consonant with Scripture is the perpetual Virginity of the Blessed Virgin Mary. Herbert Thorndike in *An Epilogue to the Tragedy of the Church of England* notes three kinds of prayer to the Blessed Virgin Mary and the saints offered by the Church of Rome. The first, of which he gives the example of, 'That we who believe her to be truly the Mother of God, may be helped by her intercession with Thee', he thinks is agreeable with Christianity, as such prayer by Mary is made by one who is part of the mystical Body which consists of both the living and the dead. A third type implies adoration of the Blessed Virgin and this is condemned as idolatrous. A second type is held by Thorndike to be dangerously close to idolatry as when the Virgin is invoked with words such as, 'We beseech thee to hear us', which words are more normally used to God alone. While other Anglicans such as John Cosin and William Clagett object to the worship of Mary, George Hickes acknowledges her perpetual virginity as a part of the early tradition of the undivided Church and urges us to keep her festivals and, like her, to hear the word of God and to keep it.

The main problem for John Wesley (1703–1791) with Catholic devotion to the Blessed Virgin Mary is that she is not merely held in reverence but worshipped. Such worship is gross, palpable idolatry, he says; we can only honour her as the mother of the holy Jesus and a person of eminent piety. Wesley distinguishes in his *A Roman Catechism, with a Reply Thereto*, between *latria* and *doulia* (Q. 46), the former meaning 'worship' and the latter 'reverence', but in his section on the Virgin Mary (Q. 38) he fails to make the distinction between the two. In Nicaea II the distinction was made between 'veneration' and 'adoration', (in the original Greek *'proskunesis'* and *'latreia'*, while confusingly in Latin *'adoratio'* and *'latria'*). One wonders whether the confusion in Wesley and others at this point is not caused by the ambiguous use of *'adoratio'* which looks like 'adoration' and yet is translated 'reverence'. Wesley clearly believed that worship is offered to Mary: 'What is the worship that they give to Mary?'

(Q. 38 in *A Roman Catechism*). He objects to the Catholic faithful applying to Mary as the mediatrix of the gifts bestowed by Jesus and quotes from a book printed in 1685:

> Whatever gifts are bestowed upon us by Jesus, We receive them by the mediation of Mary ... such is the acceptableness of the mother of Jesus to Jesus, that whatsoever is under the verge of her protection may confide in her intercession to Jesus.
>
> (*Contemplations of the Life and Glory of Holy Mary*, pp. 7–9, 14)

He remembers that even a Council, the notorious Council of Constance that burned John Hus in 1415, invoked the Virgin Mary to its aid, while previous Councils had always invoked the Holy Spirit (Q. 40). We read little in the Scriptures of the acts of Mary on earth (clearly Wesley had not noticed the 129 verses), nothing of her bodily Assumption, nor of her being the mother of grace and mercy, the queen and gate of heaven, the advocatrix of sinners, nothing of her power to destroy all heresies, or to be all things to all men. Wesley brings Epiphanius to his aid, who called it an act of impiety when a sect of women offered cakes to the Virgin Mary. He wonders what Epiphanius would have said of the eighteenth century, when not cakes but litanies and prayers are offered to her, in more abundance than prayers to Christ himself. He adds a similar thought in his *Explanatory Notes on the New Testament*, in a comment on Luke 1.28: 'This salutation gives no room for any pretence of paying adoration to the virgin; as having no appearance of a prayer, or of worship offered to her' (*Notes* on Luke 1.28).

In the same *Notes* at Matt. 1.25 he suggests that the perpetual virginity is implied by the Scriptures, since 'he knew her not' could be taken to mean that he did not know her afterwards. The brothers of Jesus described in Matt. 12.46 are in fact cousins, sons of Mary Clopas. A similar thought is found in his *Letter to a Roman Catholic* of 1749 where he makes the perpetual virginity of Mary part of the common creed of Catholics and Protestants.

The horror he feels at the thought of the worship of Mary is seen when he assesses some Catholic figures in his sermon on John Fletcher of Madeley. He compares Fletcher with Gregory Lopez and the Marquis de Renty, all three being examples of Christian perfection in Wesley's eyes. Fletcher, by implication, was better than the two Catholics because he did not fall prey to the idolatry of the Catholics; in particular Wesley means the abominable worship of the Virgin Mary. The religion of Christ has nothing to do with the worship of our Lady of Loreto. The Virgin has no authority over Christ, as Wesley makes clear in his comment on John 2.4:

May we not learn hence, if his mother was rebuked for attempting to direct him in the days of his flesh, how absurd it is to address her as if she had a right to command him on the throne of his glory?

His comment on Mark 3.34 is even more forthright:

In this preference of his true disciples, even to the Virgin Mary, considered merely as his mother after the flesh, he not only shows his high and tender affection for them, but seems designedly to guard against those excessive and idolatrous honours which he foresaw would in after ages be paid to her.

It is of interest that these latter comments are not found in Bengel, Wesley's main source for the *Notes on the New Testament*, but seem to be Wesley's own.

So much for the outline of some traditional historical Protestant reactions to Mary. We need to make three positive comments which may help us to understand mariology better within the Protestant denominations and help us to a more balanced and positive view of Mary and her place in the Church.

I.   Protestants constitute a group of Christians who have had little positively to say about Mary for over 400 years. For example, although Luther preached regularly at the festivals of Mary, by the time of Wesley there are almost no accounts of sermons on Marian themes. In the corpus of 151 written sermons by Wesley, not one has a Marian text. This flight from Mary has slowed down recently and in our lectionaries we are encouraged on the Sunday before Christmas to consider the Annunciation, although carol services and family services might make that difficult. But at least she is there in our readings. But we have even more than 400-odd years to make up because the Tradition of the Catholic Church has moved on. The Catholics have proclaimed the dogmas of the Immaculate Conception and the Assumption, placing those dogmas as I understand them within the context of the saving work of Christ. But they are not understood by Protestants as such because Protestants believe in 'Scripture Alone', or at least they think they do. The place of Tradition within our Churches needs urgent reassessment. Even within my own denomination, Methodism, we have a Tradition, for we believe not only that the Scriptures are the source of our doctrines but we acknowledge the fundamental principles of the historic creeds and the Protestant Reformation, and the *Sermons and Notes on the New Testament* of John Wesley, as defining our beliefs. We are asked, I think, to look at a Tradition that has been around for nearly 2,000 years and one that in a sense can only be lived in if it is to be properly experienced. We have a lot of living in Tradition to get on with.

II.   One way in which we might begin to make progress is by taking the concept of 'reception' really seriously. Protestants need to receive what they already have espoused theologically, in terms of Mary as a type of the true believer, one who offered her 'let it be' to God in faith and thereby becomes an example of how we must act. They need to unpack for themselves the implications of the title offered at Ephesus 431 of *Theotokos,* or Mother of God, for Marian devotion. After all, Protestants acknowledge the fundamental principles of the historic creeds, and the Council of Ephesus 431 safeguards the humanity of Christ. Perhaps this preliminary work, which is devotional as much as it is doctrinal, will enable them to see the value of the definitions of 1854 and 1950. But there is the reverse process that needs to take place too, the 'not I but the grace of God' emphasis of Protestantism that needs to be 'received' on the Catholic side and taken into Marian piety. Both sides have a lot of 'reception' to get on with.

III.   A few years ago I was asked to give a talk on 'Mary and Evangelisation' at the Birmingham (England) branch of the Ecumenical Society of the Blessed Virgin Mary. It felt in prospect like building a house with bricks made without straw, but in retrospect it made sense. For if she is the believer *par excellence*, she will be able to tell us in her life how to be a witness for God. These were the headings I used:

i.   *Style.* Evangelism is often aggressive, with no respect for the individual. Mary's character seems to be non-manipulative, persuasive, a style that gives space to others.

ii.   *Spirituality.* She is an exemplar here; remember Luke 2.19 and 51 where she keeps these things, pondering them in her heart. For evangelism to be true, it needs to offer the content of a full spiritual life to the convert. She is also an example of Christian perfection, one in whom her Son is fully formed.

iii.   *Telling the Story.* One major theme is telling others what God has done for me. Mary tells this in her Magnificat, telling her own story about how she was redeemed through Christ even before her birth.

iv.   *The Whole Church is Responsible.* Mary is the type of the Church in theology. She was there in Acts when the Church began and perhaps her new relationship with the beloved disciple at the cross is a sign of the beginnings of the Church.

v.   *Prevenient Grace.* 'Hail, highly favoured one,' means God was the prime mover in her life of grace. This is what the definition of the Immaculate Conception of 1854 says. When we go out to evangelise, God has already been in the lives of people long before we ring their doorbells.

vi.   *Mary as Disciple.* In John 2.4 we find her co-operating with her Son: 'Do whatever he tells you'; and this is before his twelve disciples believe. In this sense she could be called the first of the believers.

Evangelism/evangelisation is a constant theme in Protestant thinking and action. I suspect that most of us are not very good at it. One reason is that we need our brothers and sisters of the other traditions with their Marian understanding to remind us of these forgotten pieces of Christian faith and experience.

In Britain there has in the last thirty years been something of a sea-change in thinking about Mary within the Protestant tradition. Martin Gillett, a Roman Catholic lay person, dedicated his life from 1967 to the Ecumenical Society of the Blessed Virgin Mary and brought many into the Society from different church backgrounds. John Newton, a former principal of Wesley College at Bristol, described his own involvement with the Society in his recent book *Heart Speaks to Heart*. Newton details his ignorance of Mariology and how his theological tutors would refer him to Giovanni Miegge's *The Virgin Mary*, an Italian Waldensian book on Mary written before Vatican II. He then discusses the impact made upon Protestants by the book of Neville Ward, a Methodist minister, *Five for Sorrow, Ten for Joy*, published in 1971, on the Rosary as a method of devotion. Ward stated that 'in Methodism the silence about the Mother of Jesus is positively deafening', but he noted 'signs of shy but nervous interest in her mysterious being'. Newton became one of the chairs of the Society and learned that Mary was always to be venerated in subordination to her Son and that she could be a bridge between two antagonistic notions of what the Church might be. The Society has done a great deal for ecumenism in Britain and regularly publishes articles about Mary's place in the Catholic, Orthodox and Protestant traditions.

Recently in 1995 the British Committee of the Roman Catholic–Methodist conversations produced a study booklet called *Mary, Mother of the Lord*, in some ways a unique document in attempting a convergence on a very difficult subject. The booklet ranges over Marian doctrine, grace and election, sign of the Church, Mary's 'yes', Mother of God, Immaculate Conception, Virgin Mother, and Assumption. At the end of each section are questions for Catholics and Methodists. Some of these cover crucial questions about Marian understanding; discuss Mary as sign of the doctrine of 'by grace alone'; what does calling Mary 'Mother of God' teach us about Christ himself? what might the Assumption tell us of our hopes for the future in Christ? as Catholics, have you experienced attitudes and devotions to Mary which have undermined the uniqueness of Christ? as Methodists, have you taken seriously enough the Scriptural witness concerning Mary? after your reflection on this document, how much of the prayer called the 'Hail Mary' do you feel able to pray? It is hoped that not only Methodists and Catholics, but other Christians as well, may move further towards a shared understanding.

We began with the colour television switched on but silent while we listened to the test match commentary on Radio 4. As far as the Blessed Virgin Mary is concerned we Protestants have not yet managed to progress to having her in full colour but at least we are beginning to see a black and white picture, which is better than having no picture at all and far superior to just having the sound.

(This paper was given at the ESBVM Congress at Winchester
in July 1991: a version has previously been published
in Liturgical Ministry, Collegeville, Minn. USA.)

7

Mary's spiritual maternity

Arthur Burton Calkins

I. Introduction

From a Catholic perspective the topic of Mary's spiritual maternity is seen as intimately linked with the theme of this Congress, 'Behold Your Mother'. It is a subject at once dear to the hearts of both Catholics and Orthodox and somewhat foreign to those of the Reformed tradition. My aim is to present the basis of this belief from the Roman Catholic perspective according to the directives of the Fathers of the Second Vatican Council in their Decree on Ecumenism 'in such a way and in such terms that our separated brethren can also really understand it'[1] and at the same time in terms of the interrelationship of Scripture, Tradition and the *magisterium* which, according to the same Council Fathers, 'are so connected and associated that one of them cannot stand without the others'.[2] My task is a truly formidable one and in the limits of the time allowed I can only hope to skim the surface of the exceedingly rich content of this topic, inviting those whose interest is stimulated to pursue the indications which I have provided in the footnotes.

While the Church's inchoate belief in Mary's motherhood of all believers reaches back beyond its conscious articulation, the chronicling of this belief provides an interesting instance of the development of doctrine which is thus described in the Dogmatic Constitution *Dei Verbum*:

> The Tradition that comes from the apostles makes progress in the Church, with the help of the Holy Spirit. There is a growth in insight into the realities and words that are being passed on. This comes about in various ways. It comes through the contemplation and study of believers who ponder these things in their hearts (cf. Luke 2.19 and 51). It comes from the intimate sense of spiritual realities which they experience. And it comes from the preaching of those who have received, along with their right of succession in the episcopate, the sure charism of truth. Thus, as the centuries go by, the Church is always advancing towards the plenitude of divine truth, until eventually the words of God are fulfilled in her.[3]

II. Exposition of the doctrine from the *magisterium*

Put very simply, the *magisterium* of the Church teaches the doctrine that as Mother of the Christ, who is 'the head of the body, the Church' (Col.1.18), Mary is also the Mother of the members of that body. Theologically, a distinction is frequently made with regard to the beginning of Mary's spiritual maternity at the time of the Annunciation and its 'promulgation'[4] on Calvary. Father Otto Semmelroth SJ puts it this way:

> When Mary conceived the God-man, she became ontologically the Mother of the Mystical Christ. This element had to receive the addition of moral completion at Christ's sacrifice on the Cross.[5]

Father Wenceslaus Sebastian OFM differentiates these two 'moments' analogously with the Redemption wrought by Christ:

> The Incarnation may be considered as the Redemption in potency or *in actu primo*, and the sacrifice on Calvary, as the Redemption in act, or *in actu secundo*. Mary's co-operation in the production of the supernatural life follows a similar pattern. At the Incarnation, in virtue of her Divine Maternity, she conceives us to the supernatural life, whereas on Calvary she begets us.[6]

Eschewing the distinction between Mary's spiritual maternity *in actu primo* and *in actu secundo* as an unnecessary 'hardening of formulas,' Père Jean-Marie Salgado OMI prefers, following the lead of Pius XII, to speak of Mary's 'double title to motherhood in the supernatural order': her divine maternity and her association with the sacrifice of Calvary.[7]

A. The ontological basis of the spiritual maternity

Let us pursue for a moment what might be called the ontological basis of Mary's spiritual maternity, i.e. the fact that, by virtue of becoming the Mother of Christ, Mary also became the Mother of his members. One of the clearest statements of this foundation, based on the Pauline theology of the Body of Christ, was made by Pope Saint Pius X in his encyclical *Ad Diem Illum* of 2 February 1904:

> For is not Mary the Mother of Christ? She is, therefore, our Mother also. Indeed everyone must believe that Jesus, the Word made Flesh, is also the Saviour of the human race. Now, as the God-Man He acquired a body composed like that of other men, but as the Saviour of our race He had a kind of spiritual and mystical Body, which is the society of those who believe in Christ. 'We, the many, are one body in Christ' (Romans 12.5). But the Virgin conceived the Eternal Son not only that He might be made man by taking His human nature from her, but also that by means of the nature assumed from her He might be the Saviour of men. For this reason the angel said to the shepherds, 'Today in the town of David a Saviour has been born to you, Who

is Christ the Lord' (Luke 2.11). So in one and the same bosom of His most chaste Mother, Christ took to Himself human flesh and at the same time united to Himself the spiritual body built up of those 'who are to believe in Him' (John 17.20). Consequently Mary, bearing in her womb the Saviour, may be said to have borne also all those whose life was contained in the life of the Saviour. All of us, therefore, who are united with Christ and are, as the Apostle says, 'Members of His body, made from His flesh and from His bones' (Ephesians 5.30), have come forth from the womb of Mary as a body united to its head. Hence, in a spiritual and mystical sense, we are called children of Mary, and she is the Mother of us all.[8]

Pope John Paul II likewise acknowledges that this 'service' of Mary to the Church began from the first moment of the conception of Christ. Here is how he put it in Ephesus on 30 November 1979, basing himself on two Fathers and a Doctor of the Church:

> Uttering her '*fiat*,' Mary does not just become Mother of the historical Christ; her gesture sets her as Mother of the total Christ, as 'Mother of the Church.' 'From the moment of the *fiat*' – St Anselm remarks – 'Mary began to bear us all in her womb.' That is why 'the birth of the Head is also the birth of the Body,' St Leo the Great proclaims. On his part, St Ephrem has a very beautiful expression on this subject: Mary, he says, is 'the ground in which the Church was sown'.
>
> In fact, from the moment when the Virgin becomes Mother of the Incarnate Word, the Church is constituted secretly, but perfectly in its germ, in its essence as the Mystical Body: there are present, in fact, the Redeemer and the first of the redeemed. Henceforth incorporation into Christ will involve a filial relationship not only with the heavenly Father, but also with Mary, the earthly Mother of the Son of God.[9]

In Fatima on 12 May 1991 he expressed himself in this way:

> Since she [Mary] gave birth to Christ, the Head of the Mystical Body, she also had to have given birth to all the members of that one Body. Therefore, 'Mary embraces each and every one *in* the Church, and embraces each and every one *through* the Church' (*Redemptoris Mater* 47).[10]

Finally, he wrote thus in his encyclical *Redemptoris Mater* 20:

> If *through faith* Mary became the bearer of the Son given to her by the Father through the power of the Holy Spirit, while preserving her virginity intact, in that same faith *she discovered and accepted the other dimension of motherhood* revealed by Jesus during his messianic mission. One can say that this dimension of motherhood belonged to Mary from the beginning, that is to say from the moment of the conception and birth of her Son. From that time she was 'the one who believed.' But as the messianic mission of her Son grew clearer to her eyes and spirit, she herself as a mother became ever more open *to that new dimension of motherhood* which was to constitute her 'part' beside her Son.[11]

B. The promulgation of Mary's spiritual maternity on Calvary

If the *magisterium* maintains that Mary's motherhood of the members of Christ's Body is implicit in the divine plan from the time of the Incarnation, it has also consistently taught, at least from the time of the pontificate of Benedict XIV (1740–1758),[12] that what John Paul II calls the 'new dimension of Mary's motherhood' was proclaimed by the dying Christ from the cross.[13] Here, for instance, is a statement of the Church's conviction in this regard made by Pope Leo XIII in his encyclical *Adiutricem Populi* of 5 September 1895:

> The mystery of Christ's immense love for us is revealed with dazzling brilliance in the fact that the dying Saviour bequeathed His Mother to His disciple John in the memorable testament: 'Behold thy son'. Now in John as the Church has constantly taught, Christ designated the whole human race, and in the first rank are they who are joined with Him by faith. It is in this sense that St Anselm of Canterbury states: 'What dignity, O Virgin, could be more highly prized than to be the Mother of those to whom Christ deigned to be Father and Brother'.[14]

Let us listen to another formulation of this belief by Pius XII in an allocution which he gave to the Children of Mary on 17 July 1954:

> Jesus Himself from His Cross on high ratified by means of a symbolic and efficacious gift the spiritual motherhood of Mary toward men when He pronounced the memorable words: 'Woman, behold thy son'. He thus entrusted all Christians, in the person of the beloved disciple, to the most Blessed Virgin. The '*Fiat*' of the Incarnation, her collaboration in the work of her Son, the intensity of the sufferings endured during the Passion, and this death of the soul which she experienced on Calvary, had opened the heart of Mary to the universal love of humanity, and the decision of her Divine Son impressed the seal of omnipotence on her motherhood of grace.[15]

We may note that the quotation from Leo XIII seems more ample than that of Pius XII, since the former speaks of Mary's motherhood of the whole human race, but the latter speaks of her motherhood of Christians, though even there Pius speaks of Mary's heart being opened 'to the universal love of humanity'. This problem is not difficult to resolve. Mary's motherhood is intended for all; she is even the mother of non-believers in the sense 'that she is destined to engender them to grace'.[16]

C. Summary

It is not surprising then that the Marian chapter of the Second Vatican Council's Dogmatic Constitution on the Church *Lumen Gentium* presents Mary as the 'mother of Christ and mother of men' (*matrem Christi et matrem hominum*)[17] and cites St Epiphanius's comparison of Mary with Eve, calling the former 'Mother of the living' (*mater viventium*).[18] Its clearest formulation, it seems to me, is the following:

This motherhood of Mary in the order of grace continues uninterruptedly from the consent which she loyally gave at the Annunciation and which she sustained without wavering beneath the cross, until the eternal fulfilment of all the elect. Taken up to heaven she did not lay aside this saving office but by her manifold intercession continues to bring us the gifts of eternal salvation. By her maternal charity, she cares for the brethren of her Son, who still journey on earth surrounded by dangers and difficulties, until they are led into their blessed home.[19]

This teaching was further reconfirmed and given added weight by Paul VI's declaration of Mary as Mother of the Church on 21 November 1964[20] and his solemn Profession of Faith (also known as the Credo of the People of God) made on 30 June 1968.[21] Hence the succinct, but very carefully weighed, treatment of Mary's spiritual maternity in the *Catechism of the Catholic Church* 963–975 solidifies a longstanding magisterial tradition.

III.   The exposition from Tradition

A logical question to ask at this stage is: 'How did the Catholic Church's *magisterium* reach this certitude about Mary's motherhood of the faithful?' The answer, I believe, is to be found in the Church's millenary Tradition. This is not to say that the teaching on the spiritual maternity has sprung full-blown from the sub-apostolic era, but it is to say that we do find major elements of this doctrine appearing at a very early stage and that these continued to develop coherently over the course of the centuries. This is but a verification of the teaching on Divine Revelation of the Second Vatican Council:

The sayings of the Holy Fathers are a witness to the life-giving presence of this Tradition, showing how its riches are poured out in the practice and life of the Church, in her belief and her prayer. By means of the same Tradition the full canon of the sacred books is known to the Church and the holy Scriptures themselves are more thoroughly understood and constantly actualized in the Church. Thus God, who spoke in the past, continues to converse with the spouse of his beloved Son. And the Holy Spirit, through whom the living voice of the Gospel rings out in the Church – and through her in the world – leads believers to the full truth, and makes the Word of Christ dwell in them in all its richness (cf. Col. 3.16).[22]

Here we can only indicate a few salient, but very important texts in support of this doctrine while referring the interested researcher to some of the major historical studies.[23]

A. The spiritual maternity inaugurated at the Incarnation

References to the fact that Mary's spiritual maternity began simultaneously with the Incarnation of the Word may be found scattered throughout the entire patristic period and it is supported by a much firmer tradition than that based on the understanding of John 19.26–27[24] with one very notable exception which we will soon consider. We have already noted that the statement of St Epiphanius (*c.* 315–403) that, in contrast to Eve, Mary is the true 'mother of the living',[25] is cited in *Lumen Gentium* 56, and likewise we have heard Pope John Paul II cite the statements of St Leo the Great that 'the birth of the Head is also the birth of the Body'[26] and of St Ephrem that Mary is 'the ground in which the Church was sown'.[27]

Perhaps one of the most important and influential witnesses of the patristic tradition in this regard is St Augustine who said:

> According to the body, Mary is Mother only of Christ. But in so far as she does the will of God, she is spiritually sister and mother. And thus this unique woman is mother and virgin, not only in spirit but bodily – mother in spirit, not of the Saviour, our Head, of whom rather she is born spiritually, for all who believe in him – and she is one of them – are rightly called sons of the Spouse, but she is really Mother of the members who we are, because she cooperated by charity so that there might be born in the Church believers, of whom he is the Head.[28]

This text is cited in *Lumen Gentium* 53[29] and I think one would not be mistaken in finding an echo of it in *LG* 61 which speaks of the 'wholly singular way' in which Mary 'cooperated by her obedience, faith, hope and burning charity in the work of the Saviour in restoring supernatural life to souls.'[30]

B. The spiritual maternity confirmed by Christ on Calvary

The exception to which I referred above comes from the great Alexandrian exegete Origen (*c.* 185–254). Unlike the other patristic texts which we have considered thus far, his bears an obvious reference to John 19.26–27.

> The Gospels are the first fruits of all Scripture and the Gospel of John is the first of the Gospels. No one can understand the meaning of this Gospel if he has not reclined on the breast of Jesus, if he has not received from Jesus, Mary to be his Mother also ... In fact, every man who has become perfect no longer lives, but Christ lives in him and, because Christ lives in him, it is said of him to Mary: Behold your son Christ.[31]

There are commentators who deny that it is possible to deduce Mary's spiritual maternity as a solid conclusion from this very evocative text.

The underlying logic of Origen, they argue, runs like this: in order to understand the fourth gospel well each one ought to aspire to such perfection that he becomes in effect 'another Christ' about whom Christ himself could say to Mary 'Behold your son', namely, behold Jesus whom you bore, behold another Christ.[32] On the other hand, Father F.M. Braun OP holds that:

> It appears clear that Origen was at least admitting a certain maternity in Mary towards John and those like him ... As inexact as the passage remains, it contains a first indication of the spiritual maternity of Mary.[33]

Father Jean-Marie Salgado OMI, whose magisterial work, *La Maternité Spirituelle de la Très Sainte Vierge Marie*, takes account of all the major treatments on Mary's spiritual maternity until 1990, also maintains that, far from excluding Origen's principal idea of identification with Christ, the doctrine of Mary's universal spiritual maternity is implicitly required by such identification. He further holds that an unprejudiced reading of this text is sufficient to establish the conclusion that perfect and total identification with Christ, according to Origen, requires the acceptance of Mary's spiritual motherhood.[34]

Origen's text seems to have been one of those seeds destined to lie buried in the earth for hundreds of years before beginning to bear fruit. Insofar as we now know it is only with George, Metropolitan of Nicomedia (fl. 880) and contemporary of the Patriarch Photius, that the text of John 19.26–27 is taken up again and recognized as establishing Mary's maternity of the disciples during her lifetime.[35] The theme is movingly developed by Eadmer of Canterbury (1060/64–1141)[36] and with Rupert of Deutz (*c.* 1075–1130), described by Father Ignace de la Potterie SJ as 'the best mediaeval commentator on St. John,'[37] we reach the point of a recognition that Mary's painless parturition of the Son of God in Bethlehem is countered by the great pain with which she was in labour on Calvary in engendering her spiritual children.[38] From the twelfth century onwards the interpretation of John 19.26–27 referring to Mary's spiritual maternity is clearly in possession.[39]

IV.   The exposition from Scripture

From a strictly chronological point of view it would have seemed more sensible for me to begin my treatment with the Scriptures. I have begun instead by sketching the magisterial treatment in order to provide an overview of the Catholic teaching on Mary's spiritual maternity and have then proceeded to explore some of the highlights of the Tradition. I have deliberately done this because of my conviction, shared with the Fathers of the Second Vatican Council, that Scripture, Tradition and the *magisterium* 'are so connected and associated that one of them cannot stand without the others'.[40] Indeed, for Catholics it is the Tradition which provides the context for the reading of Scripture and the *magisterium* which guarantees our understanding of it.[41] This is further illustrated by a statement of the Extraordinary Synod of Bishops of 1985 that:

> the exegesis of the original meaning of Sacred Scripture, most highly recommended by the Council (cf. *DV* 12), cannot be separated from the living tradition of the Church (cf. *DV* 9) *nor from the authentic interpretation of the Magisterium of the Church* (cf. *DV* 10).[42]

I wish to add further that, as a Catholic, I believe that the Holy Spirit is the guide who guarantees the unity of Scripture, Tradition and the *magisterium*. I do not in any way share the presuppositions of those who cooperated in the authorship of *Mary in the New Testament*, a collaborative assessment by Protestant and Roman Catholic scholars, which takes an agnostic position on the historicity of the infancy narratives,[43] finds the first two chapters of Matthew's Gospel agreeing with the first two chapters of Luke's in very few points,[44] does not believe that one New Testament author can be understood from another[45] and largely eschews the acknowledgement that any New Testament text could have been foreshadowed by the Old, even without the human author's specific knowledge.[46]

A. Old Testament context for the spiritual maternity
The biblical research of the last half–century has provided an abundant harvest from which to enter more deeply into the mystery of our Lady's motherhood of the faithful. One of the themes that has emerged with ever greater clarity is that of the 'Virgin Daughter Zion,'[47] a title used by the Second Vatican Council with reference to our Lady.[48] Here is a brief description of the provenance of this designation:

> Among the Semites, a large city, particularly a capital city, was often portrayed as mother and the outlying villages under her protection as daughters. Eventually the word 'daughter' came to be applied to the major city itself, which, in the case of Jerusalem, capital of the Davidic kingdom, also became metonymy for the entire people ... Not only was it an image that crystallized the people's consciousness of their unity; it lent itself beautifully to the covenant theology which was at the heart of Israel's identity as a nation. And it merged with that other feminine image of covenant response, the spouse.[49]

While we cannot enter here into a detailed analysis of texts, we have but to reflect on the references to Daughter Zion in Zephaniah 3.14-15;

Zechariah 9.9, Joel 2.21–23, Lamentations 4.22, Baruch 4.36–37, 5.5 and Isaiah 54.1, 60.4–5 and 66.6–10 to consider this personification of the people Israel as the 'Spouse of Yahweh,' the 'Virgin Israel' and the 'Mother Zion' of whom it is said 'One and all were born in her' (Ps. 87.5). Not a few modern Scripture scholars have found evidence of this theme forming a kind of leitmotif in the first two chapters of Luke's Gospel and an important way of seeing Mary as summing up all the noblest characteristics of Israel.[50] By the same token she may be recognized as the new 'Mother Jerusalem,' the mother of the new people of God.[51] On the basis of their presuppositions, of course, the joint authors of *Mary in the New Testament* are reluctant to recognize any of these Old Testament allusions as possibly applicable to Mary.[52]

B. John 19:26–27

We turn now to consider the last words which Christ addressed to his mother and the beloved disciple, words recorded in John's Gospel in chapter 19, verses 26–27. For hundreds of years, with the exception of Origen, this passage was seen as little more than the provision of a dying son for his mother. Even at the beginning of this century most Catholic exegetes accepted Mary's spiritual maternity as a part of their heritage of faith, but did not think it could be found in the literal sense of the Scriptures.[53] But now after innumerable studies on the unique perspective and symbolism of John's Gospel, there is a general recognition that every detail of this gospel is pregnant with levels of meaning. Owing to this recognition many specialized studies exploring the meaning of Mary's motherhood of the beloved disciple have been produced by both Catholic and Protestant exegetes.[54] Here I can only hope to highlight some of the most important features of this very rich text.

First, we should take note of the fact that several exegetes see the giving of John to Mary and Mary to John as belonging to a literary genre or technical formula found at least four times in John's Gospel and called a 'schema of revelation.'[55] Let us consider Father de la Potterie's explanation:

> If we admit that the evangelist is applying a similar schematic formula to the scene at the foot of the cross (vv. 25–27), then we can say that the two words Jesus addresses to his mother and to the disciple form part of a pattern of revelation. Concretely, then, the dying Jesus *reveals* that his mother (as 'Woman,' with all its biblical resonance), henceforth will also be the mother of the 'disciple.' He, in turn, in representing all of Jesus' 'disciples,' hereafter shall be the son of Jesus' own mother. In other words, Jesus reveals a new dimension to the maternity of Mary, a spiritual dimension, and a new role for the mother of Jesus in the economy of salvation; but at the same time, he reveals that the primary role of the disciple is to be 'son of Mary.'[56]

Secondly, we must reckon with the titles given to the *dramatis personae* in this scene. Without denying that 'Mary and the beloved disciple are individual persons, who have their own personal roles and significance for the mystery of salvation,'[57] it is legitimate to ask why the Fourth Evangelist does not use proper names in this scene. Many argue that the intent is symbolic. Martin Dibelius describes the 'disciple whom Jesus loved' in this way:

> The beloved disciple is the person of faith, who has no need of proof (John 20.8). He is the witness to the mystery of the cross (19.35), and at the foot of the cross he becomes the son of Jesus' mother, thus representing other disciples who, in their relationship with God, have become brothers of Jesus.[58]

Why, then, does Jesus address his Mother as 'Woman'? Throughout the ages various answers have been given.[59] Some point to this as a reference to Genesis 3.15 which implicitly brings up the Eve–Mary antithesis.[60] Feuillet, de la Potterie and others argue, I think quite plausibly, that this is a reference to the 'Daughter of Zion'.[61]

Thirdly, we should notice that

> it is not Mary who is first entrusted to John, but John who is first entrusted to Mary. The accent is placed on the solicitude with which Mary is to surround the disciple, a solicitude to which the disciple is to respond with the tenderness of a son.[62]

'And from that hour the disciple took her to his own home' (John 19.27). Thus the rendition of the usually very dependable Revised Standard Version. 'But,' says Canon McHugh,

> if we take careful notice of John's vocabulary, a more meaningful rendering emerges. In the Fourth Gospel, the verb *lambánō* has two senses. When applied to material things, it means simply 'to take hold of,' 'to pick up,' 'to grasp,' etc. (e.g. 6.11; 12.13; 13.12; 19.23, 40); when applied to immaterial things, it means 'to accept' or 'to welcome,' usually as a gift from God (e.g. his witness, 3.11; his word, 17.8; his Spirit, 14.17; 1 John 2.27). Secondly, the words *eis ta idia*, which certainly can mean 'to one's own home' (in a purely physical sense), can also mean 'among one's own spiritual possessions' (compare John 8.44 and 15.19, in the Greek). The phrase is found in the prologue with this double meaning of 'physical home' and 'spiritual possession,' and in close conjunction with the verb 'to accept or welcome.' 'He came to *what was his own* ... and to all who *accepted* him, he gave the power to become children of God' (John 1.12–13). John 19.27 seems to demand a translation which includes both the purely physical and the deeper, spiritual sense. 'And from that hour the disciple took her into his own home, and

accepted her as his own mother, as part of the spiritual legacy bequeathed to him by his Lord.'[63]

A growing number of exegetes now accepts this interpretation that the meaning of this brief verse is the welcome of Mary by the disciple who is to receive her among his spiritual goods.[64]

Given all that we have already considered, even granting that there may be many who disagree with the interpretation of John 19.26–27 which I have presented, I find the conclusion arrived at by the scholars of the ecumenical task force of the American Lutheran–Catholic dialogue rather amazing. They concede by way of footnote that Roman Catholics would make a distinction between Church teaching on Mary's spiritual motherhood and the teaching of Scripture. 'They may accept the spiritual motherhood of Mary without claiming that it is taught by the Scriptures.'[65]

Catholic scholars willingly grant that the earliest exegesis of John 19.26–27 did not explicitly find therein the doctrine of Mary's spiritual maternity which, as we have seen, was based in the patristic era much more on the implications of the Incarnation. Many, however, do hold that this is an instance of the development of doctrine and a subsequent discovery of the implications contained in this passage from the beginning. They see it neither as a superimposition of an element alien to the original datum nor a denial of the nucleus of that original datum, but an organic development, a deeper awareness of ramifications in the text itself which were gradually brought to light over a period of time under the guidance of the Holy Spirit and authoritatively accepted by the Church.[66]

This position is further solidified by much recent exegesis on the passage about the 'Woman' in Revelation chapter 12.[67] Without denying that the fundamental orientation of this passage may be ecclesiological, may we not also see in this figure the Mother of Jesus? A number of scholars argue that we may.[68] Indeed, Father de la Potterie makes this interesting distinction:

> In the Fourth Gospel, especially at Cana, but also near to the cross, the accent is placed on the individual person of Mary, the Mother of Jesus (it is thus that John names her) but with the ecclesiological resonances which we have tried to echo.
>
> In Revelation 12 the relationship of who Mary personifies is inverse ... In Revelation 12 the accent falls on the Church, but with Mariological resonances. These are two approaches which are complementary, in a constant dialectic between two aspects (individual and collective) of the same mystery, that of the covenant of the daughter of Zion with God.[69]

Briefly, the principal points of interest from our perspective are these: (1) the designation of the term 'Woman'; (2) the reference to the fact that she has other children besides Jesus and (3) the linkage of the spiritual maternity to the mystery of Calvary.[70]

This is magnificently synthesized in the preface of the second Mass of 'Mary at the Foot of the Cross' published in the *Collection of Masses of the Blessed Virgin Mary*:

> In your divine wisdom you planned the redemption of the human race and decreed that the new Eve should stand by the cross of the new Adam: as she became his mother by the power of the Holy Spirit, so, by a new gift of your love, she was to be a partner in his passion, and she who had given him birth without the pains of childbirth was to endure the greatest of pains in bringing forth to new life the family of your Church.[71]

V. Applications by Pope John Paul II

Our present Holy Father, Pope John Paul II, has made the preaching of Mary's spiritual maternity with constant and specific reference to the text of John 19.26–27 a hallmark of his papacy.[72] Perhaps his two most extensive treatments thus far are general audience addresses which he gave on 11 May 1983[73] and on 23 November 1988.[74] Let us consider parts of the catechesis on this point given on that first occasion.

> Asking Mary to treat the beloved disciple as her son, Jesus invites her to accept the sacrifice of his death and, as the price of this acceptance, he invites her to take on a new motherhood. As the Saviour of all mankind, he wants to give Mary's motherhood the greatest range. He therefore chooses John as the symbol of all the disciples whom he loves, and he makes it understood that the gift of his mother is the sign of a special intention of love, with which he embraces all who want to follow him as disciples, that is, all Christians and all men. Besides giving this motherhood an individual form, Jesus manifests the intention to make Mary not merely the mother of his disciples taken as a whole, but of each one of them in particular, as though each were her only son who is taking the place of her Only Son ...
>
> Devotion to Our Lady therefore is not opposed to devotion to her Son. Rather it can be said that by asking the beloved disciple to treat Mary as his mother Jesus founded Marian devotion.[75] John was quick to carry out the will of his Master: from that hour onward the disciple took her into his care, showing her filial affection that corresponded to her motherly affection, thus beginning a relationship of spiritual intimacy that contributed to deepening his relationship with his Master, whose unmistakable traces he found on his mother's face ...[76]

Among hundreds of other variations on this theme – short or lengthy, in homilies, prayers, letters, encyclicals and addresses, always similar, but never the same – he has also devoted sections 20–24 and 44–45 of *Redemptoris Mater* to the topic of Our Lady's spiritual maternity.[77] In that encyclical he developed the concept that the Gospel brings a radically 'new dimension' to every relationship, hence also to motherhood, and, therefore to the motherhood of Mary.[78] One of the personalist arguments developed there which I think is most compelling is the following:

> Of the essence of motherhood is the fact that it concerns the person. Motherhood always establishes a *unique and unrepeatable relationship* between two people: *between mother and child* and *between child and mother*. Even when the same woman is the mother of many children, her personal relationship with each one of them is of the very essence of motherhood. For each child is generated in a unique and unrepeatable way, and this is true both for the mother and for the child. Each child is surrounded in the same way by that maternal love on which are based the child's development and coming to maturity as a human being.
>
> It can be said that motherhood 'in the order of grace' preserves the analogy with what 'in the order of nature' characterizes the union between mother and child. In the light of this fact it becomes easier to understand why in Christ's testament on Golgotha his Mother's new motherhood is expressed in the singular, in reference to one man: 'Behold your son.'[79]

Finally, let us consider the Pope's understanding of *eis ta idia*, taking Mary into the home of one's life. In his homily at Fatima on 13 May 1982, which is a theological as well as pastoral masterpiece, he begins by citing John 19.27, developing first its literal meaning with special reference to Marian sanctuaries like Fatima and then drawing out its 'spiritual sense':

> In all these places that unique testament of the crucified Lord is wonderfully actualized: in them man feels that he is entrusted and confided to Mary; he goes there in order to be with her, as with his Mother; he opens his heart to her and speaks to her about everything: he 'takes her to his own home,' that is to say, he brings her into all his problems, which at times are difficult. His own problems and those of others. The problems of the family, of societies, of nations, and of the whole of humanity.[80]

Just two weeks earlier he developed this same theme with a large group of priests who work with the Focolari Movement (also known as the *Opera di Maria*). This time he drew out the meaning of John 19.27 with particular reference to priests, but I would suggest that it could be applied to all.

> The Gospel text just cited offers us the model for our devotion to Mary. 'And from that hour the disciple took her to his own home' (John 19.27). Can the same be said of us? Do we also welcome Mary into our homes? Indeed, we

should grant her full rights in the home of our lives, of our faith, of our affections, of our commitments, and acknowledge the maternal role that is hers, that is to say, her function as guide, as adviser, as encourager, or even merely as a silent presence which at times may of itself be enough to infuse us with strength and courage.[81]

By way of conclusion I can think of no better words than those spoken by John Paul II on his first return to Poland as Pope on 4 June 1979. He spoke them at the Shrine of the Mother of God at Jasna Góra where, he said, 'One must listen ... in order to hear the beating of the heart of the nation in the heart of the Mother.'[82]

How meaningful for me always have been the words that your Son, born from you, Jesus Christ, the Redeemer of man, spoke from the height of the cross, pointing out John the Evangelist: 'Woman, behold your son!' (John 19.26). In these words I always found the place for every human being and the place for myself.[83]

Abbreviations

AAS	*Acta Apostolicae Sedis* (1909 –).
ASS	*Acta Sanctae Sedis* (1865–1908).
BSFEM	*Etudes Mariales: Bulletin de la Société Française d'Etudes Mariales*, Paris.
CSCO	*Corpus Scriptorum Christianorum Orientalium*, Louvain 1903 –.
CSEL	*Corpus Scriptorum Ecclesiasticorum Latinorum*, Vienna 1866 –.
DV	*Dei Verbum* (Vatican II Dogmatic Constitution on Divine Revelation).
Flannery	Austin Flannery OP, ed., *Vatican Council II: The Conciliar and Post Conciliar Documents* (Gracewing Fowler Wright, Leominster, 1981).
Inseg	*Insegnamenti di Giovanni Paolo II*, I (1978–) (Città del Vaticano, Libreria Editrice Vaticana, 1979–).
LG	*Lumen Gentium* (Vatican II Dogmatic Constitution on the Church).
Maria	Hubert du Manoir SJ (ed.), *Maria: Etudes sur la Sainte Vierge* 8 vols. (Paris, Beauchesne et Ses Fils, 1949–1971).
Mat Spir	*La Maternité Spirituelle de la Très Sainte Vierge Marie* (Città del Vaticano, Libreria Editrice Vaticana 'Studi Tomistici' 36, 1990).
MMC	Ignace de la Potterie SJ, *Mary in the Mystery of the Covenant* trans. Bertrand Buby SM (New York, Alba House, 1992).
MNT	Raymond E. Brown, Karl P. Donfried, Joseph A. Fitzmyer and John Reumann (eds.), *Mary in the New Testament* (Philadelphia, Fortress Press; New York, Paulist Press, 1978).

MSS	*Maria in Sacra Scriptura: Acta Congressus Mariologici-Mariani Anno 1965 in Republica Dominicana Celebrati 5: De Beata Virgine Maria in Evangelio S. Ioannis et in Apocalypsi* (Roma, Pontificia Academia Mariana Internationalis, 1967).
OL	*Our Lady: Papal Teachings*, trans. Daughters of St Paul (Boston, St Paul Editions, 1961).
ORE	*L'Osservatore Romano*, weekly edition in English. First number = cumulative edition number; second number = page.
PG	J.-P. Migne, *Patrologia Graeca*.
PL	J.-P. Migne, *Patrologia Latina*.
Poland	*Pilgrim to Poland* (Boston, St Paul Editions, 1979).
RM	*Redemptoris Mater* Encyclical Letter of Pope John Paul II of 25 March 1987 on the Blessed Virgin Mary in the Life of the Pilgrim Church.
Sebastian	Wenceslaus Sebastian OFM, 'Mary's Spiritual Maternity,' Juniper B. Carol OFM (ed.), *Mariology 2* (Milwaukee, Bruce Publishing Co., 1957) 325–376.
Theotokos	Michael O'Carroll CSSp, *Theotokos: A Theological Encyclopedia of the Blessed Virgin Mary* (Wilmington: Michael Glazier Inc. Dublin, Dominican Publications, 1982).
TPS	*The Pope Speaks*, 1 – (1954 –).
UR	*Unitatis Redintegratio* (Vatican II Decree on Ecumenism) .

Notes

1   *UR* 11 (Flannery 462).
2   *DV* 10 (Flannery 756).
3   *DV* 8 (Flannery 754).
4   cf. Clément Dillenschneider CSSR, *La Mariologie de S. Alphonse de Liguori: Sources et Synthèse Doctrinale* (Fribourg: Studia Friburgensia, 1934) 159.
5   Otto Semmelroth SJ, *Mary, Archetype of the Church* trans. Maria von Eroes and John Devlin (New York: Sheed and Ward, 1963) 132.
6   Sebastian 331.
7   cf. Jean-Marie Salgado OMI, 'La Visitation de la Sainte Vierge Marie: Exercice de sa Maternité Spirituelle,' *Divinitas* 16 (1972) 448–49; *Mat Spir* 192–95.
8   Quoted in Sebastian 350 (also in *OL* 229–30).
9   *Inseg* II 2 (1979) 1289 (*Turkey: Ecumenical Pilgrimage* (Boston: St Paul Editions, 1980) 76–77).
10   *Inseg* XIV 1 (1991) 1217–1218 (*ORE* 1191.5).
11   *RM* 20 (St Paul Editions, 29).
12   cf. his bull *Gloriosae Dominae* of 27 September 1748, *Bullarium Romanum* II (Prati, 1846) 428b (*OL* 2).
13   cf. *Mat Spir* 154–59; Bonaventura Duda OFM, '"Ecce Mater Tua" (Jo. 19, 26–27) in Documentis Romanorum Pontificum,' *MSS* 235–289.
14   *ASS* 28 (1895–1896) 130 (*OL* 168).

14 *ASS* 28 (1895–1896) 130 (*OL* 168).

15 *AAS* 46 (1954) 494; (*OL* 648).

16 Réginald Garrigou-Lagrange OP, *The Mother of the Saviour and Our Interior Life* trans. Bernard J. Kelly CSSp (St Louis, B. Herder Book Company, 1957) p. 167.

17 *LG* 54 (Flannery p. 414).

18 *LG* 57 (Flannery p. 416).

19 *LG* 62 (Flannery pp. 418–419).

20 *AAS* 56 (1964) 1014–1018 (*TPS* 10 (1964–1965) 137–141).

21 *AAS* 60 (1968) 438–439 (Candido Pozo SJ, *The Credo of the People of God: A Theological Commentary* trans. Mark A. Pilon (Chicago, Franciscan Herald Press, 1980) p. 87).

22 *DV* 8 (Flannery pp. 754–755).

23 *Mat Spir* pp. 57–151; Théodore Koehler SM, 'Maternité Spirituelle de Marie,' *Maria* 1.576–589; ibid. 'Maternité Spirituelle, Maternité Mystique,' *Maria* 6.569–597; Sebastian pp. 361–375.

24 cf. Sebastian p. 362.

25 cf. *Theotokos* p. 134.

26 *Sermo 26 in nativitate, PL* 54, 213.

27 *Explanatio Evangelii concordantis*, 4, 15, *CSCO*, 145, 41.

28 *De Sancta Virginitate* c. 6, 6, *CSEL* 41, 239–240 (*Theotokos* p. 254).

29 Flannery p. 414.

30 Flannery p. 418.

31 Greek text in Cipriano Vagaggini OSB, *Maria nelle Opere di Origene* (Roma, Pont. Institutum Orientalium Studiorum 'Orientalia Christiana Analecta' 31, 1962) 177 (Latin text in *PG* 14, 31 A–B): this translation partially adapted from versions given in *Theotokos* pp. 254, 275.

32 cf. Sebastian, p. 373; Bertetto, 'Beata Virgo Maria et testamentum Domini in cruce,' *MSS* 186; Théodore Koehler SM, 'Maternité Spirituelle, Maternité Mystique,' *Maria* 6.582; cf. also Pastor Gutierrez Osorio SI, '"Ecce Mater tua" (John 19.25–27): Maternitas spiritualis Mariae in luce exegeseos SS. Patrum et scriptorum posteriorum,' *MSS* 156; *Theotokos* p. 254.

33 F.M. Braun OP, *Mother of God's People* trans. John Clarke OCD (New York, Alba House, 1967) pp. 99–100.

34 Jean-Marie Salgado OMI, 'La maternité spirituelle de la Sainte Vierge chez les Pères durant les quatre premiers siècles,' *Divinitas* 30 (1986) pp. 58–61; *Mat Spir* pp. 63–65.

35 cf. *PG* 1476–1478; *Mat Spir* pp. 128–129; Sebastian p. 373; *Theotokos* pp. 154–155.

36 *De conceptione Beatae Mariae Virginis PL* 159, 315; cf. Sebastian pp. 373–374.

37 *MMC* p. 212.

38 cf. Deyanira Flores, *La Virgen Maria al Pie de la Cruz (Jn. 19, 25–27) en Ruperto de Deutz* (Roma, Centro de Cultura Mariana, 1993); Sebastian p. 374; *Theotokos* pp. 315–316.

39 cf. Théodore Koehler, 'Les principales interprétations traditionelles de Jn. 19, 25–27 pendant les douze premiers siècles,' *BSFEM* 16 (1959) pp. 119–55; Sebastian p. 372; *Theotokos* p. 255.

40 *DV* 10 (Flannery p. 756).

edition) of 10 December 1985, supplemento, II; *The Extraordinary Synod – 1985* (Boston, St Paul edition, 1986) 49. The italicized section translates *'neque ab authentica interpretatione magisterii Ecclesiae'* which has been inexplicably omitted in both the English and Italian translations, cf. Msgr John F. McCarthy, 'An Assessment of the Recent Extraordinary Synod,' *The Wanderer* 119.11 (13 March 1986) 3. The reference to *DV* 9 is also missing in the English text.

43 *MNT* 12–14.
44 *MNT* 13–14.
45 *MNT* 22–25.
46 *MNT* 29–30.
47 cf. N. Lemmo, 'Maria, "Figlia di Sion", a partire da Lc 1:26–38. Bilancio esegetico dal 1939 al 1982,' *Marianum* 45 (1983) 175–258; *Theotokos* 116–117; *MMC* xxiv–xl and passim; Henri Cazelles PSS, 'Fille de Sion et théologie mariale dans la Bible,' *BSFEM* 21 (1964) 51–71; John McHugh, *The Mother of Jesus in the New Testament* (Garden City, NY, Doubleday & Co. Inc, 1975) 29–52, 438–444.
48 In *LG* 55 Mary is referred to as *praecelsa Filia Sion*.
49 George T. Montague SM, *Our Father, Our Mother: Mary and the Faces of God* (Steubenville, OH, Franciscan University Press, 1990) 103.
50 cf. McHugh 29–52; René Laurentin, *Structure et Théologie de Luc I–II* (Paris, J. Gabalda et Cie, 1964, 4th ed.) 148–163; ibid. *The Truth of Christmas Beyond the Myths: The Gospels of the Infancy of Christ* trans. Michael J. Wrenn and associates (Petersham, MA, St Bede's Publications, 1986) 9, 52–53, 59–60; Max Thurian, *Mary, Mother of All Christians* trans. Neville B. Cryer (New York, Herder & Herder, 1964) 13–19; Lucien Deiss CSSp, *Mary, Daughter of Sion* trans. Barbara T. Blair (Collegeville, MN, The Liturgical Press, 1972) 51–85.
51 cf. *MMC* xxxi–xxxiv, 220–224; Montague 118–127; Koehler, 'Mary's Spiritual Maternity after Vatican II,' 47–51.
52 *MNT* 128–132, 134, 156, 217–218, 285, 289.
53 cf. *Mat Spir* 13–17; Théodore Koehler SM, 'Mary's Spiritual Maternity after the Second Vatican Council,' *Marian Studies* 23 (1972) 44.
54 cf. *MMC* 212.
55 cf. M. de Goedt, 'Un schème de révélation dans le quatrième Evangile,' *New Testament Studies* 8 (1961–62) 142–150; *MMC* 217–218; Ignace de la Potterie SJ, *The Hour of Jesus – The Passion and Resurrection of Jesus According to John: Text and Spirit* trans. Dom Gregory Murray OSB (Middlegreen, Slough, St Paul Publications, 1989) (= *Hour*) 139–146; McHugh 401.
56 *MMC* 218.
57 *MMC* 222.
58 quoted in *MMC* 219.
59 cf. *Theotokos* 373–375.
60 cf. Braun 92.
61 cf. *MMC* 220–222; *Hour* 140–142; André Feuillet PSS, *Jesus and His Mother* trans. Leonard Maluf (Still River, MA, St Bede's Publications, 1984) 125–127; Stefano M. Manelli FFI, *Mariologia Biblica* (Frigento, AV, Casa Mariana Editrice, 1989) 360–365.

Mother trans. Leonard Maluf (Still River, MA, St Bede's Publications, 1984) pp. 125–127; Stefano M. Manelli FFI, *Mariologia Biblica* (Frigento, AV, Casa Mariana Editrice, 1989) pp. 360–365.

62 Deiss p. 194.

63 McHugh p. 378 [in the eighth line of this quotation I have given the reference to John 17.8 rather than to 17.18 which seems to be a typographical error in the book]; cf. also Braun pp. 119–24; Aristide Serra OSM, *Contributi dell'antica letteratura giudaica per l'esegesi di Giovanni 2, 1–12 e 19, 25–27* (Roma, Herder, 1977) pp. 217, 226; *Maria a Cana e presso la croce: saggio di Mariologia Giovannea* (Roma, Centro di Cultura Mariana 'Mater Ecclesiae', 1985) pp. 106–115; *Maria secondo il Vangelo* (Brescia, Editrice Queriniana, 1988) pp. 165–66.

64 *MMC* pp. 226–228; *Hour* pp. 146–151; Manelli pp. 368–371. cf. my book *Totus Tuus: John Paul II's Program of Marian Consecration and Entrustment* (Libertyville, IL, Academy of the Immaculate 'Studies and Texts,' No. 1, 1992) pp. 152–153, 240–248.

65 *MNT* p. 215.

66 cf. *DV* 8.

67 cf. *Theotokos* pp. 375–377.

68 cf. *MMC* p. 257; Braun pp. 153–155.

69 *MMC* p. 263.

70 André Feuillet PSS, *Johannine Studies* trans. Thomas E. Crane (New York, Alba House, 1965) p. 286; *MMC* p. 259.

71 *Collection of Masses of the Blessed Virgin Mary*, Vol. I: *Sacramentary* (New York, Catholic Book Publishing Co, 1992) p. 117; original Latin text in *Collectio Missarum de Beata Maria Virgine* I (Città del Vaticano, Libreria Editrice Vaticana, 1987) p. 49.

72 cf. the index to biblical references and the index to subjects in my book *Totus Tuus*.

73 *Inseg* VI 1 (1983) 1200–02 (*ORE* 784.1).

74 *Inseg* XI 4 (1988) 1635–1638 (*ORE* 1066.1, 16).

75 Père Salgado maintains that this simple but striking affirmation had never been made by the *magisterium* before John Paul II; cf. *Mat Spir* p. 169.

76 *Inseg* VI 1 (1983) 1200–1201 (*ORE* 784.1).

77 cf. Théodore Koehler SM, '"*Redemptoris Mater*" dans la Réflexion Doctrinale sur la Maternité Spirituelle de Marie,' *BSFEM* 50 (1993) pp. 59–84.

78 cf. 20, *Inseg* X 1 (1987) 701 (St Paul edition p. 28).

79 45, *Inseg* X 1 (1987) 734–735 (St Paul edition pp. 63–64).

80 *Inseg* V 2 (1982) 1568, 1578 (*Portugal* p. 73).

81 *Inseg* V 1 (1982) 1370–71 (*ORE* 736.12).

82 *Inseg* II 1 (1979) 1413 (*Poland* p. 103–104).

83 *Inseg* II 1 (1979) 1416–1417 (*Poland* pp. 110–111).

(This paper was given at the ESBVM Congress at Norwich in July 1994)

8

The Blessed Virgin and depth psychology: a theological appraisal

Donald G. Dawe

The advent of modern depth psychology and psychoanalysis has provided one of the most important and controversial means for interpreting the Virgin Mary and her place in the human story. The western world since the Reformation has abounded in polemics between Catholics and Protestants over the place of the Blessed Virgin in the plan of salvation. These arguments about Mary were theological, biblical, and historical in character. With the development of psychoanalytic psychology in the late nineteenth and early twentieth centuries, a new technique was fashioned that promised to disclose how religious beliefs function in the human psyche. Here were new means for interpreting Mary which broke out of the straitjacket of mutual polemics. To comprehend the complexities of devotion to the Blessed Virgin, these psychological interpreters argued, it is necessary to look not just to its historical manifestations, but to how the cult is grounded in the unconscious levels of personality. Psychologists, historians, sociologists, and philosophers of religion have given their accounts of the origins and development of Marian piety in the psychic life of humankind. These investigations have brought both deep fear and high hopes to theologians. The last word has not been spoken on this intriguing subject. However, it is possible to look at its results and evaluate their importance for the new ecumenical approach to Mary on which the church is embarking.

The psychological interpretation of Mary has been argued with varying degrees of sophistication and historical accuracy. But our concern here is not to ferret out misquoted texts or misstated pieties, though there is need for this. It is rather to look at conclusions about Mary and her place in human psychic life that have been reached through depth psychology. There are two major types of findings:

i) Those viewing Marian piety and theology as a block to the actualization of the human self. Mary is a stone of stumbling on the long and arduous road to human fulfilment.

ii) Those viewing Marian piety and theology as a creative means for the actualization of the self. Mary is the sign of hope on the long and arduous road of human fulfilment.

Mary as the stone of stumbling

The modern critique of Marian piety has been given popular expression by Marina Warner, who sees the Blessed Virgin functioning to ensure a passivity in women that allows male dominance. By being both virgin and mother, Mary embodies the submissive role of the chaste ascetic with that of the subservient mother. The cult of the Virgin-Mother leaves women in the double bind situation, in which chastity or fecundity end in submission.[1] Yet males are not free of the power of the Blessed Virgin, the psychological critics argue. Her love entails sexual deprivation and leads to uncritical obedience to authorities in family, state, and church. Although modern Marian piety, such as that at Lourdes and Fatima, is strongly feminine in character, a study by Michael P. Carroll shows that half the reported cases of Marian apparitions were to men. Marian piety, he argues, is a response to repressed sexuality. Eighty percent of those having visions of the Virgin Mary were sexually mature individuals who lacked any obvious sexual partner.[2] William Christian, Guy Swanson, and Ena Campbell see the Virgin Mary as the key to internalization of social control in societies threatened by disorder.[3] The Marian cult has served to reinforce those very aspects of church teaching that have most heavily come under attack in the modern world.[4] These studies of Marian piety establish the link between devotion to the Blessed Virgin and a dependent, immature personality.

The link between Marian piety and inadequate personality development, according to depth psychology, is in the origins of the piety itself. Devotion to the Blessed Virgin is grounded in repressed sexuality and an inadequate or even pathological response to the Oedipal situation. The psychodynamic roots of the Marian cult were identified by Sigmund Freud in his studies of hallucination and sadomasochistic behaviour associated with religion.[5] These psychodynamics have recently been applied in greater detail to Marian piety by Anne Parsons and Michael Carroll.[6]

According to Freud, 'a damned-up libido which cannot in reality be satisfied succeeds, with the help of a regression to old fixations, in finding discharge through the repressed unconscious.'[7] The specific form taken by the blockage of libido is the Oedipal situation in which the child seeks to replace the father as sexual partner of the mother. A realistic resolution of the Oedipal complex is necessary for psychic maturity. However, Marian piety prevents such a resolution. As perpetual virgin, Mary ostensibly overcomes the incestuous desires of males, and as chaste mother, she enables the reproductive role of the female. As Carroll concludes, 'The more a male is characterized by a strong, but repressed, sexual desire for his mother, the more will he be attracted to the Mary cult ... ' Carroll makes a parallel argument for women attached to Marian piety: 'In identifying with Mary, a female can vicariously enjoy an Oedipal fantasy that she herself can never directly experience.'[8]

Even the most convinced devotees of such psychological interpretations of Marian piety admit that psychoanalytical explanations can be 'Just So' stories, 'tailormade to fit the data at hand at all costs.'[9] Carroll argues that there are ways in which the Freudian explanation may be more rigorously related to the data. For the moment, it is not necessary to enter into that argument to move toward a theological appraisal of the Freudian analysis of Marian devotion. Rather it is necessary to identify the fundamental assumptions of these psychological interpretations.

Psychic projection and Marian devotion

The common element in these psychological interpretations of Marian piety is the process of psychic projection. Religious phenomena are, for the Freudian tradition of depth psychology, the projection of psychic conflict onto the mythical plain of the transcendent. However, in this tradition, the transcendent is a null set. It is evidenced only in what Freud called 'the oceanic sense', which is the baseline of consciousness. To deal with the Oedipal conflict through devotion to Mary may bring temporary relief from psychic pain. But it leaves the real conflict unresolved only to reappear in new forms. Marian piety blocks normal development by projecting the Oedipal conflict into the heavenly mythical realm of relationships to a Virgin-Mother.

Religious phenomena are maladaptive because they resolve fundamental personality conflicts by reference to a level of existence that is contentless and powerless. The transcendent is the blank screen upon which inner conflict is projected and given unrealistic resolution. For the Freudian traditions, the technique of psychic projection on to the transcendent is maladaptive because it invokes a level of reality devoid of power and form. The Blessed Virgin, her intercession, her Immaculate Conception, her Bodily Assumption, her spiritual guidance and moral empowerment are not symbolic expressions of a higher level of reality, but the misplaced expression of unresolved psychic conflict. This judgement is the boundary assertion of Freudian psychoanalysis for the interpretations of Marian phenomena. This is the basis for what Robert J. Lifton calls Freud's 'rationalistic-iconoclastic' analysis of religion. Whatever truth has been disclosed about the social and psychological significance of Marian devotion by this approach, it is bounded by its fundamental assumption that the transcendent is a null set.

Logically, there is another option in approaching the psychological analysis of Marian piety. It is to work out the implications of a different boundary assertion about psychic projection. What is the meaning of Marian piety if the transcendent is a realm of meaning and power to which humankind is related? Such a boundary statement leads to an interpretation of Marian devotion that is more consistently phenomenological. Strange as it may seem, the theoretical basis of this second tradition of psychological interpretation of Mary was established by a lapsed and angry son of the Reformed tradition, Carl G. Jung. This is what Lifton calls the 'mythic–hygienic' analysis of religious symbols as the key to the depth of the self and its formation.[10] Its theological implications were elucidated by the Lutheran theologian Friedrich Heiler. It is a tradition that has been explored by Victor White, Vera von der Heydt, Edward Edinger, Gebhard Frei, and has been given historical setting by Erich Neumann.

Jung and the interpretation of Mary

Great care is needed in interpreting what Jung has to say about Mary. As Jung himself realized, his interpretations are open to two misunderstandings, both of which he repudiated. He is not taking an anti-religious stance that seeks to explain away the reality of Marian phenomena by giving them psychological interpretation. Nor is he a crypto-theologian making definitive statements about transcendent reality on the basis of his psychological investigations. His concern is phenomenological. The foundation of his work is empirical, which for him is not limited to mere external behaviour. Rather through the analytic method of depth psychology, the unconscious structures of the self are rendered accessible to study. When Jung speaks of Mary, he is making a psychological delineation of the function of Mary. Jung was open to further theological interpretations of her importance. He had a long supportive relationship with Friedrich Heiler and Victor White, who carried on theological interpretations of Mary in the light of his analysis. But he was clear that theology proceeds from its own sources and norms that lie outside the realm of psychology. A Marian theology may be related to psychological analysis, but it is not identical with it.

Mary, Wisdom, and the self

Jung's approach to Mary is boldly innovative, but has identifiable intellectual roots in the mystical and alchemical traditions of the Middle Ages. The theological traditions in the West have described Mary in historical, exegetical, and theological categories. Mary is the dogmatically defined person to whom believers are related by faith, prayer, and devotion, and from whom certain benefits are obtained. The structure is that of a subject-object relationship. But in the mystical traditions, Mary is so identified with the believer as to be an actor in the drama of the emergence of the self in psychic individuation. In his 'Letter to All the Faithful,' St Francis of Assisi says,

> We are His mothers when we conceive Him in our heart and body by pure love and a clean conscience, and when we bring Him forth by our holy actions, which are to give light and example to others.[11]

This identification was brought into modern thought through the Lutheran mystic Jacob Boehme (1575–1624). Boehme identifies the Virgin Mary with the divine Wisdom (Sophia) at work in the believer. Boehme pictures salvation as the fruit of the marriage of the soul with the Virgin Sophia. The Virgin–Sophia is for him almost a fourth member of the Godhead along with the three persons of the Trinity. 'Wisdom is God's revelation and the Holy Spirit's corporality, the body of the Holy Trinity.'[12]

Boehme is the transitional figure who links Jung to earlier mystical traditions. He provided the warrants for Jung's identification of religious symbols not simply with their historical manifestations but with the underlying structures of the psyche. There is in Boehme's theosophical mysticism a dual identification of Mary as Virgin–Sophia: i) The Virgin is associated with the Godhead and ii) with the inner psychic life of the believer. Mary as the Virgin–Sophia provides a necessary connection between the transcendent and the emerging self of the believer in Jung's thought. It is this identification, given in philosophical and religious terms by Boehme, which is now reaffirmed in psychological terms by Jung. He believes that there is experiential psychological verification for seeing Mary as a vital link in the process of individuation by which the self is formed. For Jung, the transcendent – that which we do not make, shape, or control – is not a null set. It has form and power that are given symbolic expression in Mary.

Jung recognizes that the symbols of divinity and maternity take many forms as they express the archetype of the Great Mother. The Blessed Virgin Mary expresses this archetype in Christendom. But the Great Mother is an archetype expressed in Kali, Demeter, Taizolteotl, and a host of mother goddesses and fertility figures. Jung is not concerned to establish the Blessed Virgin as the only correct expression of the archetype. Rather, he describes how the symbol of the Blessed Virgin in Christianity functions to bring about psychic integration. Jung believes that the Blessed Virgin has not only a legitimate, but a necessary role to play in psychic individuation today. Mary has a uniquely important role in overcoming the affective and spiritual alienation of a male-dominated modernity that is spiritually numb. The cult of the Blessed Virgin is a protest against the patriarchal development of the Judeo-Christian West in which the Great Mother was dethroned and repressed.[13]

Psychic maturity requires the self to be able to deal with the whole range of human experiences, including the powerful forces emerging from the unconscious. The self is able to mature only when the negative and positive, the male and female, the creative and destructive forces at work in human life are owned and integrated. When the symbols of the transcendent – the forces we cannot make, shape, or control – do not contain the full range of human possibilities, both negative and positive, then the emergence of the self is thwarted. Conceptions of the transcendent that do not contain what is symbolized in the Blessed Virgin are unable to integrate the whole gamut of human experience. Such incomplete conceptions of the transcendent lead inevitably to a rationalistic moralistic religion unable to advance psychic wholeness.

Interest in devotion to Mary as the Great Mother was long a concern of Jung and his colleagues who gathered for study and consultation at the Eranos conferences starting in 1933. However, the fullest account of the meaning of Mary was part of his *Answer to Job* (1952).[14] His positive appreciation of Marian devotion included a ringing affirmation of the Dogma of the Bodily Assumption of the Blessed Virgin, made just two years after its definition by Pius XII. Jung was one of the few non-Catholics to have anything good to say about the Dogma of the Assumption. It was a time in which Protestant theologians were in a veritable paroxysm of indignation against the definition. It was widely rejected as biblically unfounded, historically unverified, and theologically heretical.[15] Jung rejected these criticisms as evidence of the rationalism and moralism that have trivialized Protestantism. His critique was aimed not only at the orthodox teachers of Reformed scholasticism, but more particularly at the liberals who then dominated the theological faculties. Jung rejected the rationalistic moralism of the official Swiss Reformed Church embodied in his pastor father. Marian devotion, Jung argued, is a necessary link in the actualization of the divine in human experience. Protestantism was being rendered sterile by her absence.

Mary and the *Answer to Job*

Jung's reflections on Mary are set by his concerns in the *Answer to Job*. This interpretation of Job is the key to a kind of psychological *Heilsgeschichte* in which more and more aspects of existence are integrated by relating them to the divine. The drama of Job is, according to Jung, the unfolding of the implications of a consistent monotheism.

Psychologically viewed, monotheism is not belief in a unitary being apart from the world. It is belief in the possibility of integrating all experience, negative and positive, constructive and destructive, female and male, into a significant whole. Monotheism is the triumph over the dualisms and contradictions that plague human existence. Theologically, these dualisms are enshrined in the moralistic masculine conception of God that dominates much Christianity. The *Answer to Job* investigates the implication of what total integration of human experience by relating it to the divine ground would imply. This integration involves the Virgin Mary as a necessary means of its completion.[16]

For Jung, the cult of the Virgin Mother and the dogma of the Assumption have a vital role to play in the integration of the whole gamut of human possibilities. Through the Virgin Mother it becomes possible to own the generative feminine dimensions of the human psyche as part of the divine. It is the rejection of the Docetic–Gnostic association of the feminine and reproductive with the evil non-spiritual side of life. Without the Blessed Virgin, divinity is associated only with moralistic rational masculinity. A religion that does not honour the archetype of the Great Mother as Christians do in the Blessed Virgin Mary has an incomplete conception of ultimate reality that is unable to integrate experience fully. Put theologically, such a religion is not consistently monotheistic. As Vera von der Heydt concludes in her study of Jung's treatment of the Assumption, 'the incarnation is the descent of spirit–man, thereby spiritualizing matter, earth, woman. The Assumption is the ascent of woman, earth, matter, thereby materializing heaven.'[17]

So wholehearted was Jung's insistence on the importance of the Blessed Virgin for sharing in the divine that he was open to the possibility of seeing Mary as part of a divine quaternity.[18] No matter how contemporary Mariology has avoided any implication of deification in interpreting the Assumption, Jung joined robustly with those pre-Vatican II Roman Catholic theologians who were skirting that possibility as they worked out the implications of such Marian titles as 'Co-Redemptrix' and 'Co-Mediatrix'. Protestant outcries against the deification of Mary were for Jung only further evidence of the obdurate inability of these theologians to deal with the full implications of human psychic wholeness.

> The logical consistence of the papal declaration cannot be suppressed, and it leaves Protestantism with the odium of being nothing but a *man's religion* which allows no metaphysical representation of women.[19]

Their protests expressed the rejection of the feminine, the intuitive, the power of the anima. For Jung, the fixation of Christian theology on the threeness of God in the doctrine of the Trinity was an unfortunate lingering on a symbol of incompleteness.

The theological move

There are evident problems and difficulties as well as valuable insight in Jung's work on the Blessed Virgin. There is much about his interpretation of Mary that post-Vatican II Mariology would seek to correct. There is much about it the feminist theologians would affirm. But for the moment, let us invoke the *epoche*, the temporary suspension of judgment, in order to look at the method Jung utilizes. He realizes that both depth psychology and theology are boundary disciplines. They both investigate the interface between the human psyche and the transcendent.

> It is only through the psyche that we can establish that God acts upon us, but we are unable to distinguish whether these actions emanate from God or from the unconscious ... Both are borderline concepts for transcendental content.[20]

In contrast to analytic psychology, church dogmatics approaches its teachings as metaphysical definitions based on divine revelation. However, Christian doctrines do not describe a divine realm separate from human experience. Dogmatic theology also treats how the divine is related to human reality. Hence all dogmas have a psychological meaning that is open to empirical investigation. As Jung was aware, dogmas are not ideas wilfully invented by theologians. They grow out of the experience by the church of the divine in its redemptive relationship to humankind. Formal theological reflection gives these disclosures of God rational structure. But dogma points to levels of reality not created by our rationality. Hence Jung believes dogmas did not originate in academic discourse, but in dreams and visions.

Psychologically viewed, dogmas are fundamental patterns going back to the beginnings of human consciousness by which we integrate the flood of experiences into a meaningful whole. Without these archetypal patterns, the self would be overwhelmed by the flood of material emerging from the unconscious under the pressure of daily life with its traumas. Dogmas are immediate experiences of the divine made concrete that allow human beings to be related to the divine without being overwhelmed by it. 'Dogma aptly expresses the living process of the unconscious in the form of repentance, sacrifice, and redemption.'[21]

The dogmas of Mary as Virgin Mother express the complex process of psychic individuation. The birth of the Miracle Child is the emergence of the self from its unconscious ground. The Immaculate Conception and the Assumption are the integration of the feminine, intuitive, generative aspects of the psyche into the emerging self. But this is really as far as

Jung was willing to go in his characterization of Marian dogma. For this reason he was often accused by theologians of 'psychologism' – the reduction of theological affirmations to inner-psyche processes. While Jung repeatedly rejected this charge, what theological meaning does his analysis of Mary have?

Friedrich Heiler (1892–1967), a Lutheran theologian and historian of religion, responded theologically to Jung's work on Mary in the Eranos meeting of 1934. In this response he reflects his earlier work on Mary, *Die Gottesmütter* (1931). He saw in Jung the elaboration of his own work as a historian of religion on the worship of the Great Mother and on the Marian piety of Christianity in Germany and its romantic poets.[22] He also perceived in Jung's work the possibilities for an ecumenical dialogue on Mary between Roman Catholics and Protestants in a time when angry polemics were the order of the day. The perspective Heiler brought to Marian questions grew out of a tradition of theology that has been largely overlooked of late. Heiler, Rudolf Otto (1869–1937), and Nathan Söderblom (1866–1933) – Heiler's mentor – stood in the tradition of F.D.E. Schleiermacher in believing that Christian theology must be formed in the context created by the study of human religiousness. Heiler, Otto and Söderblom drew on the growing knowledge of the history of religions available by the early twentieth century to contextualize their theologies, while still holding to their church confessions. In this, they were a contretemps to the crisis theologies of Karl Barth (1886–1968) and Frederick Gogarten (1887–1967), against whom Jung frequently inveighed. These crisis theologians viewed human religiousness as the rejection of revelation. To bring the history of religions into theology, they believed, would hopelessly distort it. Heiler, however, saw Protestant theology developing within the ecumenical context of the Roman Catholic and Eastern churches as well as the wider ecumenism of the other religions. In this context, Mary is not an optional extra grudgingly admitted, but a necessary part of any account of the human relationship with the divine. 'The cult of the Madonna is not a peculiarity of Catholic Christianity or of Christianity in general; it is universally human.'[23]

Jung provided insight into the psychological basis for the universality of Mary as an expression of the Great Mother archetype. For Heiler, this psychological analysis was empirical verification of what mystics had long affirmed. Mary is not only the person who lived long ago and once gave birth to Jesus. Mary was not just once the *Theotokos*, but remains the 'Godbearer' throughout all time and space. Mary is the archetype of every pure soul in whom Christ is born again and again. This universality raises for Heiler the theological question of our attitude toward the phenomenon of the Great Mother outside of Christianity. Should we hold with Tertullian, he asks, that *'Anima naturaliter Christiana'*

– 'the soul is by nature Christian', and be open to the ways in which the non-Christian cults of the Great Mother have enriched and enlarged the Christian understanding of Mary? Or should we follow the critical dictum of Protestantism so evident not only in the past but in his contemporaries, *'Anima naturaliter pagana'* – 'the soul is naturally pagan'? Heiler opts for Tertullian's position. However, he believes we need the critical principle of Protestantism. He does not embrace uncritically all Marian piety or all cults of the Great Mother. His doctrine of creation leads him to affirm the constructive possibilities in the universal phenomenon of the Great Mother. To reject this, he argues, would be to fall into a gnostic-docetic theology, or Manichean dualism. The abundant modern research that has shown the influence of non-Christian goddesses and their cults on Marian devotion do not for Heiler discredit this devotion. Divine grace appropriates and transforms that given in the other religions.

Particularity and universality in Marian piety

For Heiler, the image of Mary in Christendom, what he calls 'the Christian Madonna', is a complex woven of history, theology, legend, and artistic imagination. It has two principal aspects: the dogmatic and the universally human. Theologically, it is necessary to delineate the relationship between these two aspects. In differentiating them, Heiler makes two affirmations. i) 'All non-Christian madonnas are more or less one-sided, fragmentary, distorted, while the Christian Madonna cult is universal, many-sided, harmonious, well-proportioned.' ii) 'Another essential difference is that the Christian Madonna is not a mythical, but a historical, figure. True, she is wreathed about with symbolic legends, but her person is just as indubitably historical as that of Jesus of Nazareth.'[24]

While honouring the universality of the madonna figure, Heiler does not want to reduce Mary to merely the Christian expression of a universal psychic image. For Heiler, the absoluteness of Christianity as the revelation of God becomes evident in the special character of Mary as against all other madonna figures. Yet in turning to the witness to revelation given in Scripture, so little is to be found on which to base the complex reality of the Christian Madonna. Much has come from non-Christian sources. Following the critical principle of Reformation Protestantism, Heiler seeks to discover how Marian theology and piety develop out of the interplay of revelation and folk religion. The key to evaluating this development lies in the doctrine of the Incarnation.

> The Christian Madonna cult – and herein lies the ultimate and crucial difference between it and all non-Christian cults – has its actual centre in the mystery of the Incarnation. All those Christians who have never ceased to affirm the mystery of the Incarnation recognize the need to revere the Lord's mother.[25]

Mary stands so close to her son as to share fully in the graces God bestowed in the Incarnation on him. Her being reflects the very process by which the Incarnation took place. From the doctrine of the Incarnation, Heiler argues, Christians have derived a number of secondary affirmations. These form the basis of the legitimate Marian doctrines. Heiler has a more inclusive list of these than does any other Protestant theologian. At the head of the list is the dogma of Mary as *Theotokos*, to which he has given careful definition.[26] But the list continues with the Immaculate Conception, Mary's Perpetual Virginity, and her bodily Assumption. Heiler accepts these doctrines because he believes them to be correlates of the doctrine of the Incarnation. The list is not fixed. Rather, it points to an area for ecumenical discourse on how Marian teachings relate to the doctrine of the Incarnation. For Heiler, the key to making judgements in this is the formula *'per Mariam ad Jesum'* – 'through Mary to Christ'.

Formal doctrinal definitions touch only part of the Marian phenomenon.

> But to Catholics, Mary is not merely a religious figure of the past, an object of theological speculation; she is always present in their hearts as *Mater Misericordiae*, Mother of Mercy, the universal mother, interceding for mankind, interceding above all for sinners, in the hour of death and judgement.[27]

When attention shifts to this popular piety, the universally human aspects of the veneration of Mary become evident. It is here that Heiler draws most heavily on the psychological interpretations made by Jung. Mary as the mother who understands and makes intercession for her wayward children is a theme not only of Christian piety but of piety throughout the world. However, much popular piety around Mary is open to critical reflection.

In his treatment of Mary's intercession, Heiler's use of the critical principle is evident. In popular piety, Mary intercedes with Christ, who appears as the embodiment of God's stern judgement. It is only because of the intercessions of gentle Mary, the mother who understands, that the bulk of humankind can hope for salvation. Without her, all but the saints would fall before the terrible judgement of her Son. In this vision, some of the most intense and universal of human emotions are expressed. Here the dialectic of justice and mercy, of superego and id, of protection and threat is given dramatic expression and symbolic resolution. The resolution in Mary is one prefigured in the non-Christian madonnas. However, if this drama of redemption is converted literally into a theology that pictures Christ only as judge and Mary as the source of mercy, then it falls into error. This is the truth, Heiler argues, in Luther's critique of medieval Marian devotion. It dishonours Christ if it pictures him only in terms of judgement and not also of mercy. Mary points to the grace of Christ but does not provide the grace herself. The legends of Mary's persistent intercession with her implacable Son are 'an anthropomorphic attempt at a popular embodiment of the polarity and coincidence of divine grace and divine judgement'.[28] The reality of God as both just and merciful is expressed in human terms only as a dialectic. The Marian legends represent the resolution of this dialectic in human experience. However, the dialectic of judgement and grace is already overcome in God. Theology formulates this resolution abstractly in complex patterns of thought. The Marian legends are popular affective means by which men and women may grasp the saving resolution of justice and mercy given by God in Christ. However, when Marian legends absolutize this dialectic, rather than pointing to its resolution, they mislead believers.

In his analysis of Mary's intercession, Heiler identifies a pattern of human life celebrated in Marian devotion – the Immaculate Conception, the Annunciation, the Virgin Birth, her Bodily Assumption, and continuing intercession – as the encounter of the self with the divine in its gracious and its terrifying aspects. In this encounter with the divine, the self is moved toward wholeness by being able to incorporate dimensions of reality embodied in Mary. In this way Mary, the Christian Madonna, is part of the unfolding of the Great Mother archetype that is at work in every time and place in a host of different forms. Dogmatic reflection on Mary illumines those dimensions of her reality unique to Christianity.

Ecumenical possibilities

The interpretation of Mary through depth psychology points to two ecumenical tasks on the pilgrimage toward what Heiler called 'Evangelical Catholicism'.[29]

i) There is need for a psychological and social analysis of the ways in which Mary is being honoured, or, in the case of some churches, being ignored, to determine how this piety and theology affect human renewal. Sharp questions have been raised by feminists and liberation theologies about the ways in which Marian devotion has been utilized for exploitation. The heritage of Marian devotion from the past bears great riches, but also distortions. A piety that deforms affectively and spiritually has no claim to orthodoxy, no matter how venerable its history. At the same time, there is much in the Marian heritage that has been ignored that now speaks to us with fresh vigour. The reinterpretation of the Magnificat as a hymn of liberation for women and for the world represents a contemporary effort by both Catholics and Protestants to find new ways to honour Mary. There is a host of critical and constructive possibilities that await the application of a full-orbed psychological and social analysis of Marian devotion.

Jungian psychology provides a frame of reference that makes this critical analysis fruitful. Jung's psychology is open to the transcendent as a realm of form and meaning to which human life is related. It is able to deal psychologically with the symbols of the divine without reducing them to empty projections.

ii) Heiler has identified the grounds for the ecumenical dialogue on Marian theology. The welter of claims and counter-claims about the meaning of Mary cannot be ignored or negotiated away politically. Rather there is a task of reflection to be carried on by the church as a whole. This task is to be guided by determining how Marian teachings either help or hinder the explication of the central Christian doctrine of Incarnation. Heiler was more open to the traditional Catholic doctrines of Mary than any of his evangelical contemporaries. Yet today an ecumenical dialogue on Mary is under way. This dialogue, as Heiler envisaged it, did not grow out of a list of acceptable and unacceptable doctrines. An ecumenical theology of Mary will emerge out of an openness to new possibilities measured against the touchstone of Incarnation.

Above all else, Mary must be given theological definition because of her inevitable part, not only in the Christian story but in the whole human story. There is a kind of stubborn reality to the presence of Mary that no amount of denial can will away.

> But the Madonna is not only a pleasing image which can at any moment be exchanged for another; she is reality, not only in that remote sense in which everything created can operate as a symbol of eternal divine love, but in the sense of a historical revelation of God, the self-revelation of divine love in space and time ... Like a magnet this one historical personality drew to itself everything that was great, sacred, and beautiful in Christian – and even non-Christian – faith and ethics ... [30]

Notes

1 Marina Warner, *Alone of All Her Sex* (New York, Vintage Books, 1976). This is the theme of the whole book that is set forth in the Prologue, p. xxiv.
2 Michael P. Carroll, 'Visions of the Virgin Mary: The Effect of Family Structures on Marian Apparitions,' *Journal for the Scientific Study of Religion*, 22, 3, pp. 209–212.
3 William A. Christian, Jr., *Apparitions in Late Medieval and Renaissance Spain* (Princeton, Princeton University Press, 1981) and *Local Religion in Sixteenth-Century Spain* (Princeton, Princeton University Press, 1981). Guy Swanson, *Religion and Regime* (Ann Arbor, University of Michigan Press, 1967) and Ena Campbell, 'The Virgin of Guadalupe and the Female Self-Image,' *Mother Worship*, ed. James J. Preston (Chapel Hill, University of North Carolina Press, 1982), pp. 5–24.
4 Victor and Edith Turner, 'Postindustrial Marian Pilgrimage,' *Mother Worship*, pp. 145–171.
5 Sigmund Freud, 'Obsessive Actions and Religious Practice,' *The Complete Psychological Works of Sigmund Freud* (London, The Hogarth Press, 1959), Vol. 9, pp. 15–27. 'A Seventeenth-Century Demonological Analysis,' Vol. 19, pp. 69–105.
6 Parsons, *Mother Worship*, pp. 12–21. Carroll, 'Visions of the Virgin Mary,' pp. 212–219 and Michael P. Carroll, *The Cult of the Virgin Mary* (Princeton, Princeton University Press, 1986), pp. 49–74.
7 Freud, Vol. 19, p. 105.
8 Carroll, 'Visions of the Virgin Mary,' p. 215.
9 ibid. p. 218.
10 Robert Jay Lifton, *The Future of Immortality* (New York, Basic Books, 1987), pp. 12–13.
11 St Francis of Assisi, *His Life and Writings*, trans. Leo Sherley-Price (London, A.R. Mowbray & Sons, 1959), p. 184.
12 Jacob Boehme, *The Way to Christ* (New York, Paulist Press, 1978), p. 9.
13 Erich Neumann, *The Great Mother*, trans. Ralph Manheim (Princeton, Princeton University Press, 1963), p. 531. This book gives the religious historical analysis of the appearance of the Great Mother archetype in many cultures.
14 Carl G. Jung, *Answer to Job*, in *The Collected Works of C.G. Jung*, Vol. 11. *Psychology and Religion: East and West*, 2nd ed., trans. R.F.C. Hull, 1969), pp. 355–470.
15 Donald G. Dawe, 'The Assumption of the Blessed Virgin in Ecumenical Perspective', *The Way*, Supplement 45, Summer 1982, pp. 41–43.
16 Jung, *Answer to Job*, pp. 461–470.
17 Vera von der Heydt, *Prospects for the Soul* (London, Darton, Longman, & Todd, 1976), p. 76.
18 Jung, 'A Psychological Approach to the Dogma of the Trinity', *Psychology and Religion: East and West*, pp. 170–171. Jung does admit that the Definition of the Assumption did not go as far as this. *Answer to Job*, p. 465.
19 Jung, *Answer to Job*, p. 465.
20 ibid. p. 468.

21 Jung, *Psychology and Religion: East and West*, p. 46.
22 Friedrich Heiler, 'The Madonna as Religious Symbol', *The Mystic Vision*, ed. Joseph Campbell; trans. Ralph Manheim (Princeton, Princeton University Press, 1968), pp. 348–374. 'Die Gottesmütter im Glauben und Beten der Jahrhunderte', *Die Gottesmütter*, special issue *Der Hochkirche*, ed. Friedrich Heiler, June–July, 1931, pp. 171–202.
23 Heiler, 'The Madonna as Religious Symbol', p. 51.
24 ibid. pp. 352–353.
25 ibid. p. 354.
26 Heiler, *Die Gottesmütter*, p. 181.
27 Heiler, 'The Madonna as Religious Symbol', p. 360.
28 ibid. p. 363.
29 Heiler, *'Die Gottesmütter'*, p. 202.
30 Heiler, 'The Madonna as Religious Symbol', p. 373.

(This paper was given at the ESBVM Congress at Winchester in July 1991)

Mary
and the
unity of the churches

Five ecumenical heroes:
Mercier, Halifax, Willebrands
Ramsey, Suenens

Alberic Stacpoole OSB

Our much-graced Society, founded after the Second Vatican Council closed in 1965, had a place in the lives of two of these names: Cardinals Suenens and Willebrands were both 'Fathers' of our earlier Congresses. We remember especially Léon-Joseph Suenens at Chichester in 1984, and Jan Willebrands at Winchester in 1991, with affection. Michael Ramsey co-established the first Anglican–Roman Catholic International Commission in 1966, from which our Society called on its members as officers or lecturers, (and one of his successors as Archbishop of Canterbury, Robert Runcie, is one of our Patrons now). So what I have to say is, in its way, background to our own foreground - we have made our small offering to it all.

I. The way to Malines' achievement

Traditionally the beginnings of Christian ecumenism were found in the World Missionary Conference in Edinburgh in 1910, when in a mere ten days some 1355 select delegates began to formulate an ideal of world co-evangelisation. It was agreed that doctrine and church polity should be reserved unconsidered, as being the concern of each church on its own. It is, with hindsight, illuminating to notice the eight prepared subjects, which were these:

i) Conveying the Gospel to all the non-Christian world;
ii) The Church of Christ in the mission field [i.e building new young Churches];
iii) Education in relation to the Christianisation of national life;
iv) The missionary message to non-Christian religions;
v) The preparation of missionaries for their work abroad;
vi) The home base for the missions – its training and economy;
vii) Missions in relation to governments;
viii) Church co-operation and the promotion of unity.

In those ten fertile days of discussion, it became apparent that a continuation committee had to be established with a full-time executive staff. This became the first-ever representative interdenominational organisation to be created. It marks the beginning of serious ecumenism.

Representatives of some 160 missionary societies/boards gave unanimous consent to it.

We should turn next to 1920, to the Lambeth Conference of 252 bishops from all parts of Anglican outreach, distinguished for its *Appeal to All Christian People* for Reunion sent out to the heads of Christian communities throughout the world. It carried much influence. The first such Conference, in 1867, had been presented with a petition signed by 1112 clergy and 44,333 lay communicants, which called for the end of the long separation with the Church of Rome - but the bishops remained silent before it. The third adopted the famous Lambeth Quadrilateral 'as a basis towards home Reunion', the four points being Scripture, Creed, Sacraments, and Historic Episcopate. The 1908 Conference determined that such reunion had to 'include the great Latin Church of the West'. The 1920 *Appeal to All Christian People* set out points for co-operation:

i)   We believe that God wills fellowship ... in an outward, visible and united society, holding one faith ... This is what we mean by the Catholic Church;

ii)   Today we are organised in different groups, each keeping to itself gifts that rightly belong to the whole fellowship;

iii)   The cause of division lies deep in the past – neither simple nor wholly blameworthy;

iv)   The time calls us to new measures, a reunited Catholic Church (under episcopacy), the best instrument for unity and continuity, – unity without absorption, unity in diversity of devotion and life.

What followed, as a direct *fruitio*, was (as now so named) the Malines Conversations of 1921, 1923, 1925 and 1926, led on the Roman Catholic side by Cardinal Désiré Joseph Mercier (b. 1851), who had been Archbishop of Malines and Primate of Belgium since 1906, and had done much for his people during the Great War. He called to Pope Benedict XV's attention the 1920 Appeal, commending that private talks be opened with the separated brethren of the Church. Mercier had a good heart towards those whom he called 'brethren in the Christian faith – brotherly as the corollary of the Fatherhood of God'. But he never quite grasped the Anglican argument, that – as it was put by Archbishop Randall Davidson (1848–1930, Archbishop of Canterbury 1903–28) – the question of the papacy remained 'the great irremovable mountain of difficulty', a corruption of the tenets of primitive Christianity. Nevertheless, the ground rules of inter-church dialogue were laid at Malines, and studied thereafter, bearing fruit in all post-Vatican Council ecumenism.

Mercier was a sound philosopher, educated at Louvain University, becoming a Thomist professor thereafter, in the tradition of Leo XIII's encyclical *Aeterni Patris* (1879). He confronted the scientific positivism of

Mill and Spencer, giving voice to the experimental method and the interplay of faith and reason. He had founded at Louvain a Higher Institute, had written a quartet of books, and in 1894 had launched the *Revue Néoscolastique de Philosophie*. As a prelate, he was devout and ascetical, and a natural organiser. He cared much for the spiritual welfare of clergy and laity alike, but managed to keep his studies going. Rome saw him as ally and champion during the Modernist crisis, but was disturbed at his later ecumenism, as being too unguardedly generous.

The Anglican aspect of the dialogue was led by Charles Lindley Wood, second Viscount Halifax (1839–1934), a disciple of the great scholars of the Oxford Movement such as Pusey, Neale, Liddon and Wilberforce. After Oxford he thought of joining the 'Cowley Fathers' (the Society of St John the Evangelist), a brotherhood of missionary priests founded by R.M. Benson in 1865; and in 1931 he was still making his annual retreat with them. Instead in 1868 he accepted the presidency of the English Church Union and a spate of ecclesiastical arguments that went with it throughout his life. He came to know the Abbé Fernand Portal, a rather lone champion of reunion, in 1890: he and Portal initiated conversations with Rome at a time when Leo XIII had written his Apostolic Letter *Praeclara*, inviting Greeks and Protestants of any complexion to unite with Rome – as more than merely a federation. In his Apostolic Letter of 1895 *Ad Anglos*, Pope Leo heard the call of the English Church Union and gave it encouragement, appointing a commission of study between the two traditions. Alas, and indelicately, the subject of Anglican Orders was immediately confronted – and, as they say, the rest is history. The 1896 bull *Apostolicae Curae*, which condemned the Church of England's orders as 'absolutely null and utterly void', together with the mode of investigation, set ecumenical relations back beyond the worst fear. Halifax and Portal had nothing left to cling to except their friendship. In 1912, after brooding and careful research, Halifax published a fully documented account of *Leo XIII and Anglican Orders*. It took the 1920 Lambeth Appeal to give Halifax enough heart to start again. After Cardinal Mercier's death in 1926, which foreclosed the Malines Conversations, Halifax again published two fully documented reports of those Conversations at Malines (1928-1930). His life's work went unrewarded: as the Lord told us, 'one man sows, another reaps'.

Who initiated those Conversations? Meetings took place with the cognisance of both the Holy See and Lambeth. The two teams which were gathered carried considerable authority. Bishop Charles Gore's advocacy of unity with greater diversity was confronted by Mgr Pierre Batiffol's spirited demonstration of the impossibility of concession. They had to wait for Vatican II's 'hierarchy of values'. From the pen of a monk, Lambert Beauduin, but from the mouth of Mercier, came the most significant advance, entitled *L'Eglise anglicane unie non absorbée*. It was a plan for a Uniate Church of England in communion with Rome. After Mercier's death, his successor, winding up the Talks, suggested that the plan was always with reservations. Cardinal Van Roey's dissociating doubts were mirrored by suggestions in *L'Osservatore Romano* that Mercier's judgement was not always to be trusted: what he had achieved was now eroded, he being dead and so unable to defend his position.

What could not be eroded was the spirit of charity and fellowship that had grown from the outset under the aegis of the Primate of Belgium, till – as later with ARCIC I – it permeated the whole group. The dying Mercier left his pastoral ring to Lord Halifax, and a message *ut unum sint* for Randall Davidson, the Archbishop of Canterbury. Another ring he gave to Dean Armitage Robinson, a member of the Conversations, who bequeathed it to his nephew Dr John Robinson; he on becoming a bishop wore it episcopally until his death on 3 December 1983. Doctrinally the Conversations achieved little, despite the great quality of their theology, beyond an open exchange of views. The time was not ripe.

II. The way to the establishment of the Anglican/Roman Catholic International Commission

A new kind of quasi-professional ecumenism was emerging, with a world-view and a timeless sense of the wholeness of the Church. Bishop Charles Brent, the Canadian leader of the Anglican Faith and Order group, convoked and presided over the first World Conference on Faith and Order at Lausanne in 1927, which represented some 90 Christian churches. It was designed to promote doctrinal unity among these diverse *ecclesiae* which, however, included neither the Roman Catholic Church nor the Russian Orthodox. At once confrontations occurred over sacraments and church history (e.g. the seven Ecumenical Councils of the early centuries). But a start in international co-operative study and accord had been made.

Ten years later, in 1937, 425 delegates to the Life and Work movement gathered in Oxford on the subject 'Church, Community and State', resulting in an eight-volume report, and agreement to work towards the forging of links with the Faith and Order movement, whose members were keen to widen their base. At Edinburgh, a successor to the Lausanne Conference was convoked, and it began to plan what was to be the World Council of Churches, founded eventually after the war, in Amsterdam in 1948. From then on emerged international co-ordinator theologians such as the Dutchman W.A. Visser 't Hooft.

Britain's contribution to this scene was George Bell, Bishop of Chichester 1929–58, chairman of the Anglican Council for Foreign Relations 1945–58 (now Ecumenical Relations), Honorary President of the World Council of Churches, editor of *Documents on Christian Unity*, (OUP, 1924–5), and author of *Christian Unity: the Anglican Position*, (Hodder & Stoughton, 1948).

Rome reacted negatively to these advances. A year after Malines, Pius XI published his encyclical *Mortalium Animos*, 'On fostering true religious unity'. What Rome wrote and Pius XI signed was explicitly exclusive.

> There is but one way in which the unity of Christians may be fostered, and that is by furthering the return to the one true Church of Christ of those who are separated from it; for from that one true Church they have in the past fallen away ... Furthermore, in (it) no man can remain who does not accept, recognise and obey the authority and supremacy of Peter and his legitimate successors.

Such words were of course provocative to other Christian traditions.

It was pleasing then, that the 1930 Lambeth Conference was able to keep alive its policy of 1920; to keep its heart open to the reunion of Christendom. The Conference expressed its 'appreciation of the courage and Christian charity of Cardinal Mercier in arranging the Malines Conversations, unofficial and not fully representative as they were'. Anglicans chose to wait, to persevere in goodwill. On the day that Pius XI died, Archbishop William Temple of York wrote to the Cardinal Secretary of State, asking for unofficial consultation from time to time between Anglican and Roman Catholic theologians and scholars. Bishop Bell then began to encourage Temple to visit Rome directly: '... not leading an Anglican deputation, but as Archbishop of Canterbury, and as yourself ... on your own responsibility.' Temple doubted whether the time was yet ripe.

On the day that Archbishop Temple died, 26 October 1944, Pius XII was writing in his encyclical that the mystical body of Christ and the Catholic Church were coterminous; and that without allegiance to Christ's vicar on earth

> the visible bond of unity [is] broken, the mystical body of the Redeemer is so obscured and disfigured that it becomes impossible for those who are seeking the harbour of eternal salvation to see or discover it. (*MCC* 1943).

By the time that Pope Pius died in 1958, talks between teams of Anglican and Roman Catholic theologians, led by Herbert Waddams, Canon Leonard Prestige of St Paul's and Dr Alec Vidler of Cambridge, had foreshadowed the work of ARCIC I. A group led by Canon Bernard Pawley had stayed a fortnight with the future Paul VI, when he was in

Milan. The Lambeth Conference of 1958 had reported 'welcome signs of an increasing recognition by the Roman authorities of the importance of the Ecumenical Movement'; and delighted in Abbé Couturier's initiative of the joint Universal Week of Prayer for Christian Unity, settled annually for 18–25 January. Bishop George Bell had made a 'necessarily brief, but substantial and sympathetic' visit to Pius XII in the last months of both their lives; both Pope and senior curial officials were disabused of their misconceptions about Anglican ecumenical intentions. Time was ripening.

On 28 October 1958 Pope John XXIII succeeded. Having worked for years in Sofia, Istanbul, Paris, Venice and other *Italia*, living among non-Catholics and non-Christians, Pope John was a natural ecumenist. Announcing the call of the Council, he spoke of 'a friendly and renewed invitation to our *brothers* of the separated *Christian churches* to share with us in this banquet of grace – in this *search* for unity and grace'. Pope John went on, in June 1960, to establish the Secretariat for Promoting Christian Unity (SPCU), under Augustin Cardinal Bea SJ, a Bavarian biblical scholar; and under the secretaryship of Bishop (later Cardinal) Jan Willebrands, a Dutch ecumenical theologian who succeeded Bea in 1969. This body hosted the Observers sent from separated churches to attend all plenary sessions of the Council – a unique event in history. Bishop John Moorman of Ripon, Anglican leader of the Observers, wrote of their playing 'their silent but no less influential part in the *aggiornamento* of the Roman Catholic Church'. At the end of the first session, Willebrands told Moorman: 'You have no idea how much the presence of the Observers here is influencing the work of the Council'. The Fathers had been sensitive to other listening Christians, who brought their own experience of other ways to the dialogue, and who daily shared in the morning Mass in St Peter's nave: their presence changed the atmosphere, bringing another wisdom to it.

Of the two SPCU leaders, Bea came once to England and spoke little English. During and after the Council, it was Willebrands who was ever present to the Church in England; it was he who dealt with Anglican affairs as they developed. His ecumenical awareness grew in the late 1940s, when he was a young president of the *Philosophicum* at Warmond in the diocese of Haarlem, and he was ever accompanied by his *vox clamans* of ecumenism, Fr Frans Thijssen. They both spent much time at the Belgian priory of Chevetogne (with its East–West liturgies), at the J.A. Möhler Institute in Paderborn, and at the Istina centre at Auteuil near Paris. Both were aware of the painful consequences of church division, wanting to bridge gaps between peoples. Forming the Association of St Willibrord from a former apologetic centre directed against Protestantism, they worked for dialogue and witness, through ecumenical study days organised by Willebrands, attended by some 50 priests, religious and layfolk. Willebrands always had more than the directiveness of the scholar, being a priest; he had that pastoral sense we have seen in Pope John, that people are the goal, not systems. In 1952, Willebrands and Thijssen together formed the Catholic Conference for Ecumenical Questions, which leading specialists quickly joined. Thus it was that Willebrands built his own team of Roman Catholic ecumenists, which proved ready to move in and enlighten the Council Fathers.

Mgr Willebrands was already in regular consultation with Augustin Bea SJ by 1960. SPCU under them, once called into being by Pope John, was able to give an institutional structure to those sometimes nebulous or evanescent contacts made between Roman Catholicism and other churches; it gave 'context' and 'memory' to them, and a sense that a programme of advance could be plotted and controlled. It sent its own observers, as of right and necessity, to the WCC 3rd Assembly at New Delhi in 1962. It was extended to include all Orthodox Church affairs. SPCU was given full rank, with power to propose and draft its own schemas, assuming full responsibility for them in the Council. It became evident that SPCU had to remain in being when the Council was closed, as a permanent ecumenical organ. Its department for Eastern Churches was strengthened – notably with Fr Duprey, now Willebrands' successor.

But we should focus on Anglican relations. In December of 1960, after his successful tour to Jerusalem, Beirut and Istanbul, Archbishop Geoffrey Fisher chose to visit Pope John in Rome in his own person – i.e. as Dr Fisher of Lambeth; and the events are oft-told history (heard directly by AJS from both Fisher and his wife Rosamund more than once). This historic visit – the first indeed by any Archbishop of Canterbury since 1397 – broke the ice for Archbishop Michael Ramsey to go to Rome in March 1966.

Let us then turn our attention to the most serious and well-studied of all Archbishops of Canterbury in our time. Arthur Michael Ramsey (1904–88) was Archbishop of Canterbury from 1961 to 1974, during the great years of the foundation of Cardinals Bea and Willebrands' Christian Unity explosion; years of the Vatican Council; years of the steady launch of the Anglican/Roman Catholic International Commission; years of the greatest 20th Century papacy, that of Paul VI; years of journeying by Christian church leaders. Ramsey has been the most travelled Archbishop of Canterbury ever. In 1961 he was elected one of the presidents at the World Council of Churches in New Delhi, where he made a barefoot pilgrimage to Gandhi's memorial before going on to Calcutta's leper work. Besides his many journeys, in 1970 in New York he shared joint lectures with Cardinal Suenens. They repeated this in 1974, and it resulted in a joint book *Come Holy Spirit* (NY 1976).

Ramsey's first major theological work was *The Gospel and the Catholic Church* (still in print). He continued to write as Professor of Divinity at Durham, then successively Regius Professor at Cambridge, Bishop of Durham, and Archbishop of York. In 1961 he was translated to Canterbury. (That news was made public at the moment he was lunching with the monks of Ampleforth, who sang for him *Ad multos annos*). As Archbishop of Canterbury he continued to write, including *Rome and Canterbury* (1964), *God, Christ and the World: A Study in Contemporary Theology* (1969), *The Future of the Christian Church* (1971), with Cardinal Suenens; and *The Charismatic Christ* (1974), about *Godspell, Jesus Christ Superstar,* and the charismatic movement, which Cardinal Suenens had by then done much to bring within Church discipline, through kindness rather than prelacy. Ramsey's last book was entitled *Be Still and Know* (1982).

An Anglo-Catholic himself, he showed great understanding of other traditions and sympathy for them – and, of course, for Roman Catholicism. (One remembers his addresses to young undergraduates at The Old Palace, Oxford, encouraging them to embrace their own). From 1946, when he wrote on the Eastern Orthodox Church, he showed a close interest in Orthodoxy and its prelates, whom he visited as Archbishop of Canterbury – to Athens, Russia, the Balkans... Nor did he miss out attending to the Free Churches at home. Together with his strong belief in a robust but devoted spirituality, he found energy for social issues and the moral law, especially in its sexual ramifications, in Parliament. Withal, Michael Ramsey not only was the great Archbishop of Anglo-Roman ecumenism, but also launched the attempt at reunion with the Methodists in 1969, the failure of which distressed him greatly.

Archbishop Ramsey and Mgr Jan Willebrands first worked together in negotiations leading to the ground-breaking official visit to Rome in March 1966. Affairs reached a dangerous impasse because another department of the Vatican Curia, without consideration of time or juxtaposition, (and this was one of the Bea/Willebrands arguments against Curial conduct), thoughtlessly produced a public document on mixed marriages. Willebrands was quick to make a lightning visit to Lambeth Palace to explain the background of the incident just in time. Ramsey's visit was too important to be knocked off course: it came as a response to the whole Council, but especially to the Decree *Unitatis Redintegratio* on Ecumenism, and especially words from Sec. 13:

> [At the Reformation] many communions, national or denominational, were separated from the Roman See. Among those in which some Catholic traditions and institutions continue to exist, the Anglican Communion occupies a special place.

It was said that Abbot/Bishop Christopher Butler, once an Anglican, had a major hand in those words entering the Decree.

Ramsey visited Rome again after the Council, when the city was once again quiet: 'It was tactful of him', said Willebrands later, in a speech at the Anglican Centre, knowing that such a proposal during the Council would have created complex tensions. He also realised that only a final agreed Council text could be any basis for Anglican dialogue. Reflecting on his visit a year later in 1967, Ramsey remembered the emotions it had stirred; but added that he did not 'underrate the difficulties still to be overcome' - formidable doctrinal differences that give hurt to feelings and consciences, legacies of history's bitterness that leave unhealed wounds. He recorded his gladness at what he saw in the conciliar decrees – the priesthood of the whole Church, beautifully described in *Lumen Gentium*, and with it the bond of unity between the baptised; the plea for forgiveness (both personally papal and within *Unitatis Redintegratio*) and the separated brethren's pardon for 'injuries suffered and grief endured through the long series of dissensions and separations'. He was glad of the further plea that, because of the reality of the divine life among separated Christians, Roman Catholics can be learning from non-Catholics, for their own edification and for their greater understanding of the mystery of Christ and the Church. Ramsey was further pleased with the Decree on Religious Liberty, *Dignitatis Humanae*, wherein is affirmed that the act of faith is of its very nature a free act; and so in matters religious every manner of coercion on the part of man should be excluded.

One sees here an Archbishop of theological depth and penetrating spirituality, who above all others immediately before or after, was fitted to conduct a reunion with Rome after Rome's greatest Council. His 1967 Dublin lecture lodged two *caveats* for Anglicans: modern Marian doctrines, and Petrine/Papal authority as set in apostolic/episcopal colleges. But, he added, *Lumen Gentium* 21–23 gave hearteningly new context to the discussion of infallibility and authority: and indeed such became the material of ARCIC I deliberation.

Michael Ramsey went to Rome on 23–24 March 1966 as a public and solemn act of the Chairman of the Lambeth Conference. On the first night in Rome, the Archbishop formally opened the Anglican Centre in the Palazzo Doria Pamphilj. With characteristic generosity, he showed the Centre to be a return gift:

> The Anglican student is often a debtor to writers within the Roman Catholic Church. This Centre is an attempt to repay that debt by making available the resources of Anglican learning to any who will come and enjoy them.

Pope Paul later responded thus:

> This is the first step in practical ecumenism – to know: to know each other. The distance which separates us should first be diminished by this approach ... Knowledge prepares the way of love, love leads to unity.

What happened in the Sistine Chapel on the morning of 23 March is well recorded. Later, in a quaint third-person mode, Ramsey gave his own account. Suffice it to recall Archbishop Ramsey's initial words of greeting:

> I have come with longing in my heart, which I know to be in your heart also, that we may by our meeting together help in the fulfilment of the prayer of our divine Lord that all his disciples may come to unity in the truth.

He went on thus:

> It is only as the world sees us Christians growing visibly in unity that it will accept through us the divine message of Peace. I would join my voice to the voice of Your Holiness in pleading that the nations agree to abandon weapons of destruction, and to settle their quarrels without war, and to find a sovereignty greater than the sovereignty of each separate State.

Paul VI spoke of rebuilding bridges of esteem and charity ... 'not as strangers and sojourners, but as fellow citizens with the saints, as members of the household of God', and he added, 'surely from heaven St Gregory the Great and St Augustine look down and bless'. Presents were exchanged.

Thus the beginning. The end was this. After the Common Declaration in the Basilica of St Paul's (the English basilica, poignantly used at the canonization of the Forty Martyrs), Pope Paul wanted to find a gesture to express 'the new atmosphere of Christian fellowship'. On the garden steps, Paul embraced Michael Ramsey, and then taking his gold ring from his finger he put it on Ramsey's. Montini had worn that ring all the years of his Milan pastorate. Ramsey, as I have seen and felt, was wearing that ring at Canterbury in May 1982 when another Pope came to Britain: he died, still wearing the ring, on St George's Day, 1988.

III. The way to a wider world during and after the Second Vatican Council

Lord Halifax, who himself died with a Cardinal's ring about him, said in latter days: 'I should die happy if only I could see a meeting between the Archbishop of Canterbury and the Pope.' At the English College, the *Venerabile*, students knelt for a blessing as Ramsey left their College and

Rome. A new ecumenical spirit had begun: symbolic of it is that in the Vatican secret archives, alongside the bull of Excommunication of Elizabeth I is displayed the Common Declaration signed by Pope Paul and Archbishop Ramsey.

In Eastertide 1969, after speculation (not to say struggle), Cardinal Willebrands was officially appointed president of the Unity Secretariat, and soon afterwards Pope Paul made his historic visit to the Geneva headquarters of the World Council of Churches. In their hands ecumenism went forward in an ever more professional manner. Willebrands widened his interests now towards non-Christian religions, notably the Jews – God's initially chosen people, the House of Israel. Born in 1909 and brought up in Bovenkarspel, he studied for the priesthood at Warmond, and was ordained in 1934. He went to Rome to take a doctorate, his subject being 'The illative sense in the thought of John Henry Newman', and returned for three years to Amsterdam, where later Anne Frank and her family, and many other Jews, were to hide from the Nazis as long as they could. Before the Council, Pope John – Angelo Giuseppe Roncalli – had told a Jewish delegation: 'I am Joseph, your brother'. After the Council, Willebrands' Secretariat had developed the implications of the Vatican declaration *Nostrae Aetate* (Relations of the Church to Non-Christian religions) with special attention to the sections referring to the Jewish race and religion. In December 1975, Willebrands – without relinquishing his work for the Unity Secretariat – became Primate of Holland and Archbishop of Utrecht. After giving eight years to the leadership of the Dutch Church, he resumed full duties in Rome at the Secretariat for Promoting Christian Unity, until he reached 80 in 1989, and quietly retired into consultancy. In that year he played 'father' to the ESBVM's Winchester Congress. He presently outlives all.

One whom he has outlived is another of ESBVM's Congress 'fathers', from 1971 present often, and particularly at Chichester, where he both preached in Arundel Cathedral and gave a short paper on the subject of his perennial attention, the Holy Spirit. Cardinal Léon-Joseph Suenens of Malines died on 6 May 1996, aged 91. He was born on 16 July 1904, and when he was not yet four years old his father, a brewer, died. He was educated by the Marist Brothers in Brussels and then at the *Institut Sainte-Marie*, run by diocesan priests. Called to the priesthood, he was sent by the perceptive Cardinal Mercier to study at the Gregorian University in Rome, where he achieved a doctorate in both philosophy and theology with a baccalaureate in canon law. Throughout his time in Rome, he kept up a steady and intimate correspondence with Mercier, who – by then in his last Malines Conversation years – had a lasting influence over him. Ordained in 1927, Suenens studied until 1929, when he returned to his *Institut* in Brussels to teach. For a decade he was at Malines seminary as Professor of Philosophy, teaching pedagogy and the history of philosophy, consolidating his own understanding and influencing the lives of future priests.

In 1940, as Belgium was overrun by the Nazis, he was appointed Vice-Rector of the University of Louvain (now sadly split in two by language, etc.). The Rector was imprisoned by the Nazis, and Suenens, still in his thirties, quietly took on the task, if not the office, for the duration of the war. Among his initiatives was the foundation of the *Institut des Sciences Réligieuses* there – for he had for a while shared the view that the religious education of the laity was never given sufficient attention at university level. On 16 December 1945, Suenens was consecrated (now 'ordained') bishop, and appointed auxiliary to the then aging Cardinal van Roey – he who had eroded the work of Mercier and Halifax. Until he succeeded to the Archdiocese of Malines–Brussels, becoming Primate of Belgium (1961–79), Suenens had a decade to develop the connection between all that he had perceived at the University, and what he saw developing in a rapidly dechristianising world. And so it was said of him in the 1960s that he was 'the single most effective promoter of change within the Roman Catholic Church, after Popes John and Paul'.

Sixteen years as a pastoral auxiliary bishop (1945–61), with time to exercise the lucidity of his literary work, his canon law issues and his connections, was a fair preparation. He minded little that it was not unfairly said of him that 'he won his away matches, but lost those at home'. He was fond of Cardinal Désiré Mercier's phrase: 'Here was someone who dared to concern himself, and with authority, with matters that were none of his business'. He went out beyond Belgium to a wider world, as Mercier had done in tapping the spring stirrings of ecumenism. He became a flag-bearer for the progressives' issues until 1970, when confrontation with Rome began to diminish the influence of his voice. Till then he was taken at his word in describing his position as 'extreme centre'.

During those early episcopal years, the young Suenens discovered the international movement emanating from Dublin, the Legion of Mary. At once he perceived the apostolic potential of such a movement for the laity; so on several occasions he journeyed to the Legion's headquarters in Dublin to confer with Frank Duff and to study the implications of the movement throughout the world. He then wrote a commentary on its promise, *The Theology of the Apostolate of the Legion of Mary*, and later he wrote a biography of one of the Legion's outstanding early members, Edel Quinn. He went on in 1956 to publish *The Gospel to Every Creature*, his own dominant ideas about the pastoral mission of the Church, ideas that he later developed piecemeal into other books – such as *The Nun in the World* (1962), which engendered a strong renewal of apostolic activity among the women's orders. From his interest in the Legion of Mary arose his later interest in the ESBVM. At other times he raised such subjects as celibacy or married priests, priests and laity, population explosion, birth control, nuclear power or weapons, materialism versus oppressed or poverty-stricken people, and generally the developing world. He brought the Church to what was worrying people.

Succeeding to Malines, with a Cardinal's hat in 1962, Suenens changed his interests to ecclesiology: local versus universal church, national versus Rome-orientated church, hierarchy versus laity; and in ecumenism, the truth within other churches. In view of Pope John's health, he was called to deliver/present the encyclical *Pacem in Terris* to the United Nations, assembled on 13 April 1962. When the Council reassembled under Pope Paul, Cardinal Suenens was asked to deliver the eulogy in memory of John XXIII – to his admitted surprise. He compared Pope John to John the Baptist, which of course gave Paul VI the place of Christ: 'he came to give testimony of the light, to bring peace for the world'. Suenens, who with Cardinal Montini had advised Pope John on an early restructuring of the Council in October of the First Session, was asked by Pope Paul to be one of four controlling Moderators thereof, the best of them. He nevertheless made major contributions to *Lumen Gentium* and *Gaudium et Spes* on church life: he pressed for a fuller role for bishops, and for power to be devolved away from the Curia. Afterwards he became the first Cardinal to preach in the cathedrals of both Canterbury and York since the Reformation, and the first to stay at Lambeth Palace since Reginald Pole.

1968 marked the storm over Paul's encyclical *Humanae Vitae* on birth control, which Suenens had begged him not to publish, as it ran against all modern advice and might lose the laity. After long hours of debate, in accord with other enlightened hierarchies, the Belgian bishops decided to stress the place of the individual's decision resulting from an informed conscience. This raised in the mind of Suenens and his like the problem of church government/consultation. In 1968 he wrote his most-read book, *Co-responsibility in the Church Today* (1968) – with laity, religious, deacons, theologians, priests, bishops. He ended: 'The more that the Holy Spirit lives in each one of us ... the more profoundly He will be the Creator-Spirit who renews the face of the earth'. But equally he gave his notorious interview to *Information Catholique*, accusing the Curia of turning pope into emperor, ringed by legalistic mentalities, who all over-centralised, while ignoring the new power of higher education and the structures that this needed. Suenens' attempts to raise Christian consciousness rendered him suspect, a deserted prophet from then on.

Marginalising Suenens in Europe, Pope Paul asked him to lead and 'ground' the forces of charismatic renewal in churches of the USA. His love for the Holy Spirit was able to focus the charismatic movement; he called young people together in mass common prayer, bringing with them the unity of ecumenism at grass-roots level. In Indiana some 25,000 charismatics met for prayer, and as many in arenas in Dublin and Britain. In 1974 he wrote *A New Pentecost?* As Peter Hebblethwaite put it: 'From then on, reform was swallowed up in renewal'. His work in the Spirit was transposed to a new movement, being baptised into Church life, through new liturgies of love and life. Pope Paul saw Suenens as the international chaplain of Roman Catholic charismatics. He in turn began building bridges towards liberation theology, which again met curial disapproval, rebellious as it tended to become. In 1976 he was awarded the Templeton Prize for Religion, worth some £40,000: it was a consolation. Retiring at 75 (as archbishops do) in 1979, Léon-Joseph Suenens settled in Malines, returning to our Lady with his propagation of the Fiat Rosary, and participating in events of the ESBVM. Three books remained to be gathered together: his memoirs in 1991, a semisequel in 1993, and a spiritual portrait of King Baudouin in 1995, with a booklet entitled *De la Vie à la Vie* in 1996; and then decline to death. These last books were very personal, drawing on the privacies of other people's prayerful confidences. For all involved, there is a strong belief in the power of the Holy Spirit directly at work. Enough to say that it is a far cry from early Suenens. Léon-Joseph was completing a spiritual aeneid.

IV. Conclusion

In all brevity, we might ask just two questions:

i) Of these Five Heroes of Ecumenism, who was the most effective? I believe history will show that it was Jan Willebrands, the Dutch Cardinal.

ii) Who then was the greatest man-of-God? Is it impertinent to hold an opinion? I believe biography shows that it was Michael Ramsey, the English Archbishop. Ramsey's biographer was moved to write: 'He died peacefully, still with his sense of glory'. Ramsey's friends decided to procure the great David Kindersley, master of epigraphy, to carve this inscription from St Irenaeus:

+ THE GLORY OF GOD IS THE LIVING MAN +
AND THE LIFE OF MAN IS THE VISION OF GOD

*(This paper was given at the Bristol Congress of ESBVM
in September 1996)*

10

Corporate reunion – a dream or a nightmare? the legacy of Malines

Bernard M. Barlow OSM

Seventy-five years ago, on 6 December 1921, there began a series of meetings or 'Conversations', as they were then called, between a group of Anglicans and a group of Roman Catholics, whose objective it was to begin to 'clear the ground' of some of the many misunderstandings and prejudices which had accumulated throughout the four centuries of history of division since the detachment by King Henry VIII of the Church in England from the Church of Rome. These Conversations began quite unofficially, in the sense that they had no authorization by either church, at the instigation of the second Lord Halifax, and his friend the French Vincentian priest Abbé Fernand Portal. By involving Cardinal Désiré Joseph Mercier, the Archbishop of Malines–Bruxelles, on the Roman side, and because of Lord Halifax's persistence on the Anglican side with the Archbishop of Canterbury, Randall Davidson, these Conversations eventually took on a semi-official status – despite the many reservations by the authorities on either side.

The clear intention of these meetings was to examine the possibility of 'corporate reunion', that is, the coming together of the Roman Catholic Church and the Church of England into that single, unified Church for which Christ prayed. By implication, it was the unspoken and un-discussed alternative to the individual conversions which had been prevalent between the two churches particularly since the Oxford Movement (mainly, but not exclusively, in the direction of the Church of Rome). The English Roman Catholic leadership of the time was not, generally speaking, in favour of corporate reunion, and this had been particularly impressed on Lord Halifax and Abbé Portal during their earlier abortive attempt some twenty-five years previously to initiate inter-church discussions. This first attempt had been circumvented into a single-issue topic about Anglican Orders which ended in Pope Leo XIII's Encyclical *Apostolicae Curae* of 1896 rejecting the validity of those Orders. Cardinal Vaughan in Westminster, and Cardinals Merry del Val and Gasquet in Rome had been instrumental in directing the appeal for open inter-church discussion into a strictly Roman Catholic Commission of Enquiry which led up to the papal condemnation of Anglican Orders.

In the light of their experience with the English Roman Catholics, Lord Halifax and Portal turned to the continental Catholics in the hope of a better response. At their first encounter with Cardinal Mercier, the Belgian prelate asked Halifax why he did not go first to the English hierarchy. Halifax replied that the attitude of mind was not yet favourable in England (*l'états des esprits s'y oppose*). In Halifax's opinion, 'the English Catholics are anxious only for individual conversions and reject any attempt at reunion. Any such attempt is impossible except outside England.'[1] In the light of this explanation, Cardinal Mercier agreed to participate in such a meeting as Halifax and Portal had suggested, making clear that it would be simply private conversations. The Cardinal's motives were summed up later in the 1924 Pastoral Letter to his diocese about the Malines Conversations in which he used the poignant phrase: 'nothing in the world would permit me to allow one of our separated brothers to say that he had knocked on the door of a Roman Catholic bishop and that that bishop had refused to open the door for him.'[2]

Unknown to Halifax and Portal, Mercier had his own particular interest in the proposed meeting with the Anglicans. Cardinal Mercier's interest in reunion was stimulated in the years immediately following the Great War of 1914–18. In December 1919, Mercier went to the United States to thank the American people for their financial contributions to the restoration of many buildings and institutions in Belgium destroyed during the war, and in particular for the re-building of the University Library at Louvain. Mercier was warmly welcomed in the United States, where he was seen as one of the great defenders of the Belgian peoples against the German occupation. Whilst there, he visited and addressed the lower house of Convocation of the American Episcopal Church, then in session. During a speech of thanks, the Cardinal used an expression which immediately caused trouble for him, but one which obviously came from the heart and in response to the sense of fraternity which he had experienced. He told the American Episcopalian bishops: 'I salute you as brothers in the service of common ideals, brothers in the love of freedom – and, let me add – brothers in the Christian Faith.' Cardinal William O'Connell, Archbishop of Boston, was shocked that one of the most prestigious members of the Sacred College should address a group of Protestant bishops and call them 'brothers', and he wrote immediately to Rome complaining about Mercier's speech. Pope Benedict XV was unhappy when it was brought to his attention. On 9 February 1920, on the order of the Pope, Cardinal Merry del Val (then Prefect of the Sacred Congregation), wrote to Cardinal Mercier expressing the astonishment of the Holy See about his statement to the American Episcopalians, and asking for an explanation. In March 1920, Mercier replied to the Pope with a *mémoire* justifying his contacts with the American Episcopalians, and tried to explain that the dissident churches were now being better organized in terms of the Faith and Order movement, and that it was time for Catholics to take more interest in the moves towards reunion. Pope Benedict was not happy with the reply, and in a letter of the following month he expressed his dissatisfaction to Mercier, saying that his explanations were unsatisfactory, and the Belgian Primate was duly reprimanded for his regrettable meeting with the *'pseudo-évêques épiscopaliens'*.

Mercier was not inhibited by this reprimand, and during a visit to Rome in December 1920, he presented a memorandum to Benedict XV on the subject of reunion. He wrote;

> The painful heritage of divisions which the war has inflicted within the souls of men has given birth, at this particular moment in time, to a sincere desire for unity among peoples of different religious confessions. Already, during my voyage to the United States, I became aware of these sentiments, which I believe sincere, on the part of non-catholic theologians ... Your Holiness will perhaps judge that one day a call to the Anglicans, Americans, Russians, Greeks, etc. would be worthy of His apostolic zeal. However, in the meantime, would it not be useful to begin preparing the way for unity? I offer myself to begin such a preparation ... I would like to invite to Malines, in succession, one or two theologians of the main dissident churches, especially the Anglicans and the Orthodox, where, during the space of a few days, I could put them in contact with a catholic theologian of sound doctrine and a loving heart ... My sole desire would be to prepare those loyal souls for whatever solution the Holy See might be disposed to offer at a time and manner of its own choice.[3]

Mercier ended his proposal by asking for permission to embark on this ecumenical enterprise by seeking '... a formal approval by Your Holiness ... for the tranquillity of my own conscience and, if necessary, as a justification'. This memorandum was typical of Mercier's attitude and conception of his position as bishop, seeing himself as co-responsible with the Pope and other Roman Catholic bishops for the totality of the Church and its relationship to the world.

Mercier did not receive any reply from Rome to his memorandum, and actively dropped the matter, but it was in this context that the first letter from Abbé Portal arrived on his desk requesting a meeting with himself and Lord Halifax to discuss the possibility of informal Conversations on reunion between Anglicans and Catholics, particularly in the light of the *Appeal to all Christian People* issued by the Lambeth Conference of 1920.[4] The 252 Anglican Bishops assembled at Lambeth had announced that they would be willing, in the cause of reunion of the

Christian churches, to accept a form of commissioning from the authorities of other churches in order that the ministry of the Anglican clergy might be recognized by others.[5] In fact, this statement was intended principally for the non-Episcopalian churches, because the statement then went on to address those communities which did not possess episcopal structures. However, the Appeal was generous and wide, so all-encompassing in fact that its formulation was capable of being applied also to the Church of Rome. From these beginnings began the series of five meetings known as the Malines Conversations.

The meetings were held in December 1921, March 1923, November 1923, May 1925, and October 1926. The final meeting was simply a winding-up meeting, as, by that time, two of the main participants, Cardinal Mercier and Abbé Portal were dead. The participants at the first two Conversations were Cardinal Mercier, Abbé Portal and Mgr Joseph Van Roey (Mercier's Vicar General in Malines) on the Catholic side, and Lord Halifax, Walter Frere (of the Community of the Resurrection) and J. Armitage Robinson (Dean of Wells) on the Anglican side. At the latter meetings, two French historians, Pierre Batiffol and Hippolyte Hemmer were added to the Catholic side, while the Anglicans added to their number with Bishop Charles Gore and Dr Beresford Kidd from Oxford.

During the fourth of the Conversations, on 20 May 1925, Cardinal Mercier presented an unscheduled paper to the meeting on the possibility of the Church of England being accepted as a Uniate church within the Roman Communion, a prospect which Walter Frere noted: 'all this took our breaths away, especially as it seemed to lead up to a proposal for a Canterbury patriarchate'.[6] This surprise *Mémoire* entitled 'The Church of England, United not Absorbed', which the Cardinal presented, had been prepared by a Belgian Benedictine, Dom Lambert Beauduin, at Cardinal Mercier's request. Mercier had been surprised during the course of the second of their Conversations at how much importance the Anglicans had placed on their historical links with the Apostolic Church, and particularly what type of authority had been granted to St Augustine of Canterbury and his successors by the gifting of the *pallium* by the Pope. Mercier's presentation of the *Mémoire* was, in a sense, an answer to the implicit question which is always present at meetings, namely, how far is the other side prepared to go in order to meet us?

What exactly were the propositions offered by Mercier to the Anglicans?

The first part of the paper contained Beauduin's attempt to show that in the pre-Reformation church in England, ever since the time of St Augustine, the Archbishop of Canterbury had enjoyed a Patriarchal jurisdiction, conferred on him by the Pope by the sign of the pallium. He compared this situation with the Uniate churches of the East, and found a parallel. Therefore, suggested Beauduin, this would be a means of reunion without absorption; the Church of England could come into communion with the Church of Rome and still retain its rite, language, customs, etc., by the recognition by Rome of its Uniate status, and by the acceptance of the pallium from the hand of the Pope by the Archbishop of Canterbury.

The major conclusions reached by Beauduin were as follows:

(a) That there does exist a method or formula for reunion of the two churches which avoids the absorption of one or other of them, and which will safeguard the internal autonomy of each church while at the same time maintaining the unity of the universal Church.

(b) That if ever there was a church which by its origins, history and customs, has the right to concessions regarding autonomy, it is the Church of England.

(c) That the Archbishop of Canterbury would be re-established in his traditional rights as Patriarch of the Anglican Church, after having received the pallium from the Pope. This would give him complete power over the interior organization of the Church of England, such as enjoyed by the Patriarchs of the Uniate East.

(d) That the Latin Code of Canon Law would not be imposed on the Anglican Church just as even now it does not apply to the Oriental Rites.[7]

(e) That the English Church would have its own proper Liturgy, which is, in fact, the old Roman Liturgy of the seventh and eighth centuries.

(f) That the traditional Sees of the English Church would be preserved, and the new Catholic ones, created since 1851 (such as Westminster, Southwark, Portsmouth, etc.) would be suppressed. Evidently, remarks Beauduin, this would be a serious measure, but no more serious than when Pius VII demanded the resignation of all the French bishops and suppression of dioceses in France when he concluded the Concordat with Napoleon.

One can see clearly how the participants were breath-taken at these proposals of the Cardinal Archbishop of Malines–Bruxelles. However, this having been an unexpected presentation by the Cardinal, the participants were not able to discuss the implications of Mercier's *Mémoire*, but went on to discuss the other papers which had been prepared and circulated before the meeting. Dr George Bell, then secretary of Archbishop Randall Davidson and later his biographer, thought that Mercier's *Mémoire* was the more memorable and lasting influence of the Conversations at Malines.[8]

In looking at the Conversations as a whole, there is no doubt that Cardinal Mercier's presentation of the paper 'The Church of England, United not Absorbed' was a courageous attempt to bridge a four-century chasm of division, and to solve the seemingly intractable problem of the 1896 *Apostolicae Curae* declaration of Anglican Orders as 'absolutely null and utterly void'.

For Lord Halifax and Abbé Portal the proposal was a dream solution to the question of reunion between the Church of England and the Church of Rome, one which would give value to and maintain almost intact the heritage of the post-Reformation Church of England, and yet re-unite that church with the mother church of Christianity.

But how far was Cardinal Mercier authorized to offer such a solution, and was there a basis for the historical claims of Canterbury as presented by Beauduin? The idea of a Uniate Church of England had been raised before in 1840 by Ambrose Phillipps de Lisle, a convert to Catholicism in pre-Tractarian times, who was active in ecumenical work for some 35 years. Phillipps de Lisle's idea was slightly different from Beauduin's, but the basic elements were the same.[9] In a letter to Dr John Bloxam on 25 January 1841, Phillipps de Lisle proposed the following; 'You shall lay aside your modern common Prayer, we our Roman Rite, and let the antient (*sic*) rites of Sarum and York resume their Place'. Phillipps proposed that Latin should be the language of the old rites, but that English would be allowed in parish churches. The English clergy would be allowed to retain their wives, and future clergy would also be allowed to marry. The Holy See might sanction the omission of the invocation of the saints from public liturgies, and the church in England would be permitted to make its own decisions regarding the use of images and statues. Phillipps expressed his certainty that 'the Holy See would give every facility for the restoration of catholick (*sic*) unity in England'.[10] However, the premise for Phillipps's projected Uniate church was that the Church of England should expel all Protestants from its midst, and that the remainder (principally the High Church groups) should, with the English Roman Catholics, form a Uniate church such as existed in Eastern Christianity.

This difficulty of the position of the Broad Church and Evangelical membership of the Church of England became a real problem at Malines, for it was clear that none of the Anglican participants at the Conversations represented either of these main strands of Anglican membership, and that not even the High Church group would easily accept Lord Halifax's viewpoint on all the matters under discussion.

On the point of Cardinal Mercier's authorization in presenting the *Mémoire*, it is clear that the Belgian prelate took much of the responsibility on his own shoulders. Before presenting the *Mémoire* at

Malines, Mercier wanted to ensure that Rome was in accord with the principles outlined in the *Mémoire*. He asked Beauduin (who was teaching at the San Anselmo College in Rome) to approach Cardinal Gasparri, the Secretary of State at the Vatican, regarding the matter. Beauduin replied that he thought that the Anglicans had more chance of getting the paper accepted by Rome than the Catholics would. Mercier never went any further with the matter. When he presented the *Mémoire* on 20 May 1925, introducing it as coming from a Roman canonist, he made it quite clear that he was speaking privately and was in no way implicating the Holy See in these opinions. This does not disguise the fact that the contents of the *Mémoire* went further than anything which had ever been proposed before, particularly coming from a personage with as high an office and of such weighty authority as Cardinal Mercier. Nevertheless, Mercier had received a letter dated 30 March 1923 from Cardinal Gasparri in which the Secretary of State had said: 'the Anglicans can rest assured that the Holy See will make all possible concessions in order to facilitate the reunion so desired. Personally, I share the impression that a first reading of the Memorandum had suggested to Your Eminence'. The idea contained in the Memorandum of the second Conversations was that the See of Canterbury should be placed in a position analogous with that of the old Patriarchates, that is, the continuance of their own rites and customs, vernacular in the liturgy, communion under two species, and a married priesthood. So, perhaps Mercier was confident that he was expressing more or less views which would be acceptable at Rome.

Regarding the historical claims made by Beauduin that the Church of England had, historically speaking, acted and been treated by Rome as a Patriarchal church, these were dissected by an historian from Cambridge, Mr Outram Evennet, once the *Mémoire* had been made public. He pointed out that there was a big difference between individual concessions such as a married clergy or communion under both species, and the transformation of the Church of England into a 'Uniate' body preserving its own discipline, ritual and interior government. The Uniate Rites grew up concurrently with the Latin Rite, he noted. Their Rites, customs, discipline and autonomy represent things ancient and catholic; their Orders are unquestioned. No parallel can be drawn between such bodies and the Church of England, whose latter-day liturgy was composed in direct antagonism to the Catholic conception of the Eucharistic Sacrifice. Moreover, the Catholic predecessors of the Church of England never enjoyed the patriarchal self-government of the great Patriarchs of the East.[11] Of interest, however, is that although Mr Evennet criticises Beauduin's historical argument, he passed no judgement on the idea of the *creation* of a Uniate Church of England.

The Conversations proceeded until after the third meeting in November 1923 without any publicity, but unofficial news of them had begun to spread around, not only in Catholic circles, but also among the Anglicans and Methodists. The situation of unofficial discussions regarding something which did not 'officially' exist was especially disturbing to the Archbishop of Canterbury, Randall Davidson, who was by nature a very prudent man. He resolved, therefore, to publish some kind of letter regarding the Conversations at Malines. Davidson, having consulted the Anglican participants, decided that a letter from the Archbishop of Canterbury to the other bishops of the Anglican communion would be the most apt method. The Conversations could be presented as emanating from the general movement towards reunion with the various Churches as an effect of the Lambeth Appeal. The letter was published at Christmas 1923.

Many Roman Catholics in England were greatly upset to find out what had been going on at Malines. The majority of Catholics were still very much of a 'ghetto' mentality, and regarded reunion solely in terms of the complete submission of the other churches to Rome. This concentration of the Catholic Church in England on individual conversions rather than a vision of 'corporate reunion' was one of the reasons which Portal had put forward in favour of approaching continental Catholics rather than the English church hierarchy. The fact, however, that the Anglicans were meeting with 'continental' bishops rather than their own English hierarchy (who had a much more limited outlook as regards ecumenism), might have given the impression that they were being sold out in some manner. This is reflected in an article from the Rome correspondent of *The Times*, published in the edition of 30 December 1923, who remarked rather scathingly on the French and Belgians mixing in English affairs, and suggesting that the Pope should not allow himself to be influenced by such goings-on. Lord Halifax remarked to Portal in a letter of 5 January 1924 that the instigators of this dispatch from Rome were surely Cardinals Merry del Val and Gasquet.[12]

The Archbishop of Westminster during this period of the Conversations at Malines was Francis Cardinal Bourne. His biographer, Ernest Oldmeadow (also editor of the *Tablet*), insists that Cardinal Bourne knew nothing about the Conversations until they were made public in 1924. This assertion is contradicted by what scant documentation remains in the Westminster archives. Bourne was visited twice by Lord Halifax, once in November 1921 and again in November 1922. The Westminster Cardinal certainly knew about the Conversations, although he was not particularly hopeful that any good might come out of them because, as he stated, the Church of England was so divided and Lord Halifax represented only a small minority within that church. The Cardinal's later

Pastoral Letter on the subject of reunion showed a clear good-will towards the Church of England, while not hiding an underlying pessimism about the possible outcome of the Conversations.

The *Tablet*, however, with Oldmeadow as editor, showed no compunction in attacking the whole idea of corporate reunion. The *Universe* and the *Month* joined in the attack sporadically in the English Catholic Press, and the Jesuit French periodical *Etudes* took up the same stance. Among the principal contributors in the anti-Malines campaign was Fr Francis Woodlock SJ, a most consistent opponent of the theory of corporate reunion. Both Halifax and Portal were convinced that Cardinals Merry del Val and Gasquet had a hand in the press campaign against corporate reunion. In support of their suspicion is the fact that the Dominican Order in England (generally supportive of the reunion efforts) were forbidden to publish anything on the subject of reunion without the special permission of the Superior General in Rome. Fr Vincent McNabb OP, the eminent Dominican writer, replied to a letter of Abbé Portal in the following terms:

> You suggest my writing in *Blackfriars* an article on Cardinal Mercier's Pastoral. I would willingly do so, but there are difficulties which perhaps you or His Eminence might help to remove – let me explain.
>
> I have several times already been denounced to Rome for what I have written on the subject of reunion. Indeed both myself and my Dominican brethren in England have been threatened with punishment on account of my writings. I have no great wish to know who is the very energetic person that watches everything I write – whoever he (or she) – for it was once a SHE and not a HE – is, he or she succeeds not merely in misleading himself but in misinforming the authorities in Rome. The last denunciation occurred only a few weeks ago. It was based on my alleged contumacy in having, as they thought, republished in my book *From a Friar's Cell* an article which had already been denounced. But they thought wrongly, because I had not republished the article – the matter was very painful. As an old Irish Catholic my respect for Rome is so congenital and deep seated that I am pained when some ill-informed people send the Sacred Congregations, and even the Cardinal Secretaries of these Congregations – on wild-goose chases.
>
> However the upshot of the matter is that I am not allowed to write anything on reunion unless it is personally approved by the Master General of the Order in Rome.
>
> You will see from this how difficult it is for me to give any written support to what I consider the classical and historical Pastoral of Cardinal Mercier. Perhaps His Eminence could do something in Rome in order to allow at least one (Irish Catholic) theologian to express one side. Perhaps I might be told what I have said that *was wrong*. I am perplexed to know where I am wrong; as I am too loyal a Catholic to hesitate about withdrawing it. I am all the more perplexed because the only alleged mistake I was finally charged

with was to have called 'Rome, the Mother Church of the Church of England'. Yet Wiseman calls Rome the Mother Church of the Lutheran Churches! His Eminence, therefore, might find it possible to do something in Rome towards allowing me to express one view – his own view – on the subject of reunion. Perhaps he could express a wish to me personally, or to the Master General, that I might write on his Pastoral. Otherwise I cannot see that anything can be done.

I hate tittle-tattle and Roman gossip; but someone suggested that one of the chief movers in denouncing me is Dom Langton OSB, chaplain to Cardinal Gasquet ...'[13]

It seems clear that Cardinal Merry del Val used his influence in Rome both as an advisor for those ecclesiastics and lay people in England who were opposed to corporate reunion, and to stem any sort of favourable publicity or views given to the efforts of Halifax and Portal in favour of corporate reunion. The Cardinal was particularly depreciative of the part played by Abbé Portal, declaring him to be a disloyal catholic priest. He encouraged Woodlock and Oldmeadow (in the *Tablet*) and the English and French Jesuits (in the *Month* and *Etudes*) to air their opposition, and, where possible, in silencing favourable opinions (Fr McNabb in *Blackfriars*). The resulting one-sided publicity gave a misleading impression to the general public.

The fears of corporate reunion, as least as it seemed to be presented in the Malines Conversations, were not solely on the Roman Catholic side. The Anglicans too were apprehensive, particularly when the question of the pallium came up during the second meeting, and the idea that this symbol of Roman primacy should be bestowed on the Archbishop of Canterbury by the Pope. This would have been a clear recognition of the authority of the Pope over the whole Church, and this was, and still is, the major stumbling block of Malines and of ARCIC. Archbishop Davidson saw clearly this difficulty when he read the Memorandum from the second Conversation.[14] This was when he pushed to have Bishop Gore included as a member of the third and fourth Conversations, and insisted that the question of the primacy of the Pope should be tackled before any other practical matters of reunion be discussed. It was Dr Gore who, following the fourth Conversation, acknowledged the suppleness of the Roman Catholics on almost all questions of organization, but saw no hope of concessions on any matter of dogma.

Conclusion

We can see from this outline sketch of the Malines Conversations that the idea of 'corporate reunion' was pivotal to the meetings themselves. The idea of these private Conversations as propounded by Halifax and Portal to Cardinal Mercier was essentially to clear the ground for a coming together of the two Churches, and to see if they could dissipate the misunderstandings which had arisen over the centuries of separation. All three of them understood that eventually they should give ground to more 'professional theologians' who would examine in detail the various points of difficulty which had arisen in their 'private Conversations'. They had no expectations of any sort of immediate reunion, and their goal was simply to pave the way.

There is no doubt that when news of the Conversations became public, all sorts of fears and anxieties were stirred up on both Anglican and Roman Catholic sides. For some people the Conversations were a dream come true, and for others they were a nightmare, but both dreams and nightmares have to face up to the cold reality of dawn.

What Halifax, Portal and Mercier initiated at Malines 75 years ago, bore fruit only in 1966 when Archbishop Michael Ramsey and Pope Paul VI laid the foundation of an official theological dialogue between the two churches, the goal of which is specifically the restoration of unity between the two churches. Snatches of both dreams and nightmares always linger on even in the daylight, but time and experience gradually wear down their sharpest edges. The legacy of Malines is that it brought them to the forefront of our lives, even if the daylight takes a long time in coming.

Notes

1   Anselm Bolton, *A Catholic Memorial of Lord Halifax and Cardinal Mercier*, (London, Williams and Norgate, 1935), p. 116.
2   D.J. Mercier, *Oeuvres Pastorales*, 18 January 1924, t. VII, (Louvain, 1929), p. 297.
3   Memorandum of Mercier to Benedict XV, 21 December 1920, Archdiocese of Malines archives, File no. 1.
4   Note: In the postscript of a letter to Cardinal Ceretti dated 25 January, Mercier noted: 'Just today, whether by accident or by providence I don't know, a priest of the Missions, a Lazarist, sent me a copy of a letter which he had received from Cardinal Rampolla on the 9th September 1904. The letter is so much in harmony with the proposal which I have put to the Holy Father for approval, that I cannot restrain myself from telling you all about it.' Letter of Mercier to Ceretti, 25 January 1921, Archdiocese of Malines Archives, File no. 1.
5   *An Appeal to All Christian People*, Conference of Bishops of the Anglican Communion holden at Lambeth Palace July 5 to August 7, 1920, (London, SPCK, 1920), Section V, Report No. 8, pp. 132–161.
6   Walter Frere, *Recollections of Malines*, (London, Centenary Press, 1935), p. 56.

7 *Codex Juris Canonici,* (Vatican, Libreria Editrice Vaticana, 1983), Canon no. 1. This would allow the possibility of having married clergy, as in the Eastern Churches, but under certain strict conditions. It would not allow for married bishops.

8 George K.A. Bell, *Randall Davidson, Archbishop of Canterbury,* 2 vols, (London, Oxford University Press, 1935), vol. 2, p. 1291.

9 Of particular note is the fact that Phillipps also held the opinion that Anglican clergy desirous of reunion with Rome should be advised not to make any advance to Roman Catholic authority, certainly not in England: 'I put them wholly out of the question; it would be most injurious ... to negotiate with them.' Margaret Pawley, *Faith and Family – The Life and Circle of Ambrose Phillipps de Lisle,* (Norwich, The Canterbury Press, 1993), p. 122.

10 Letter of Phillipps to Bloxam of 25 January 1841, published in R.D. Middleton, *Newman and Bloxam – an Oxford Friendship,* (Oxford, University Press, 1947), pp. 102–111.

11 Outram Evennet, *Dublin Review,* no. 186 (1930), p. 246.

12 Letter of Halifax to Portal, 5 January 1924, Portal Papers, Paris.

13 Letter of McNabb to Portal, 18 February 1924, Archdiocese of Malines Archives, File no. 27, B. 2.

14 Note: The Malines Conversations were not the only delicate issue facing Archbishop Davidson at the time. He was trying to steer the revisions of the Book of Common Prayer through Parliament, and at the same time was engaged in unity discussions with the Methodists. In the mind of many Anglicans, the liturgical revisions of the Book of Common Prayer were seen as linked with the Malines Conversations, which was not the case. cf. Bernard Barlow OSM, *A Brother Knocking at the Door – The Malines Conversations 1921–1925,* (Norwich, The Canterbury Press, 1996), pp. 171–177.

(This paper was given at the Bristol Congress of ESBVM in September 1996)

11

The Malines Conversations:
a significant milestone in the history
of Anglican–Roman Catholic dialogue

Roger Greenacre

I. A personal introduction

Let me begin with a personal introduction – three snapshots which go some way to explain my own close interest and passionate involvement in the story I have to recount.

i) After university I did my immediate preparation for ordination at the College of the Resurrection, Mirfield, an Anglican theological college in Yorkshire run by a religious community, the Community of the Resurrection. The church of the Community has two prominent tombs, one each side of the High Altar; the first of Bishop Charles Gore, the Founder, the other of Bishop Walter Frere, Superior of the Community before becoming Bishop of Truro. Both were deeply involved in the Malines Conversations and I am sure that praying every day before that High Altar made Malines part of my life of prayer.

ii) I have in my possession a precious 'secondary relic' of the Conversations, a copy of the collection of Original Documents edited by Lord Halifax, which was published in London and printed in Brussels in 1930. It belonged to Fr Painter, Vicar of Hickleton and Chaplain to Lord Halifax and is inscribed 'To my dearest Friend and fellow conspirator with much affection and gratitude: Shrove Tuesday; Hickleton, March 4, 1930, from H'.

iii) During my time in Paris I had the privilege of getting to know the veteran French Catholic writer, Jean Guitton of the *Académie Française*, still alive today in his 90s. He became a close friend of Paul VI but before that as a young man came to meet Lord Halifax through the Abbé Portal, then Chaplain to the *Ecole Normale Supérieure*, and became a great friend of his. On a visit to York in 1984 (for the celebrations marking the 50th anniversary of Halifax's death) Jean Guitton pulled out from his shirt a silver chain from which depended a shilling. He explained that Lord Halifax had given it to him after showing him the shilling which hung from a chain around his own neck. As a small boy he had been taken by his father to meet the Duke of Wellington. The Duke had given him a shilling when he left and, when he got home, Halifax's father took the shilling from him, bored a hole in it and gave it back to him on a silver chain. It was a moving experience to be present at this scene at York – to realize that I knew a man who knew a man who had met the Iron Duke. All this was possible because the Duke, Lord Halifax and Jean Guitton all lived to a great age.

II. The background to Malines

In the title given for my talk, the Malines Conversations of 1921 – 26 are described as 'A Significant Milestone in the History of Anglican–Roman Catholic Dialogue.' The Conversations therefore need to be set in their historical context and I need first of all to take you (very rapidly) through the pre-history of Malines. The Conversations are often seen as a beginning; that is not, historically speaking correct, but we can understand how later they came to be perceived as such.

I will not, I hope, be accused of bias if I begin the story with a 17th-century Bishop of Chichester, Richard Montagu, an advanced Laudian who was at the giving and receiving end of fierce controversy with the Puritans during the reign of King Charles I. He suggested to Gregorio Panzani, papal envoy to the Court of Charles I, that it would be a good idea to organize bilateral theological conversations between Anglicans and Roman Catholics in France, since he was convinced that one would find there a more serene and irenic climate for theological dialogue than would be possible in England.[1] The reasons for this oft-repeated preference we shall need to examine more closely later; all I need to say at this point is that, since Roman Catholics were being persecuted in the British Isles at that time, Anglicans have no right to complain of any lack of sympathy they encountered then!

Later in the seventeenth century the French Church was dominated by that powerful figure, Bishop Bossuet, 'The Eagle of Meaux'. He was someone Anglicans both feared and admired, whose Gallican principles stirred up echoes of sympathy in many Anglicans. The regard was mutual; Bossuet was largely responsible for the fact that an official letter of gratitude was sent from a Synod of the French clergy at St-Germain to George Bull, Bishop of St Davids, in recognition of his solid and scholarly defence of the Nicene faith.

The eighteenth century for its part was to offer the astonishing spectacle of a correspondence between William Wake, Archbishop of Canterbury since 1716 and for a short time earlier Chaplain to the Ambassador of Charles II in Paris, and two Gallican theologians of the

Sorbonne (the theological faculty of the University of Paris), Du Pin and Girardin, which explored the possibilities of reunion. This dialogue was full of ambiguities, among them the following:

i) Wake was totally isolated in this initiative; nobody else in the Church of England knew what he was up to and none of his fellow bishops was taken into his confidence. All the letters in this correspondence he wrote in his own hand, not daring to entrust them to his secretary. Accordingly he acted with extreme caution, often marked by a touchy nervousness.

ii) Motives on both sides were mixed. Wake started out with the idea that the church in France could be detached from its allegiance to Rome and become an independent national church like the Anglican Church – an *Ecclesia Gallicana* alongside the *Ecclesia Anglicana*. The French theologians for their part started out with the idea of bringing Wake – and any who shared his ideas in the Church of England – back into submission to Rome.

iii) On both sides too, political considerations were powerful. Both Anglicans and Gallicans gave a high profile in the life of national churches to the anointed monarch, and the correspondence took place at a time – the minority of Louis XV and the Regency of Philippe d'Orléans – when there was a lull in the traditional hostility between France and England. It was even suggested that, if the Pope were to prove the only obstacle to an agreement, French troops could march on Rome!

This dialogue had all the weaknesses of a private, and indeed almost conspiratorial, exchange between individuals acting on their own initiative. As Archbishop Henry McAdoo has commented, 'it was forced into a mould essentially élitist, limited and faintly academic'. But that is not his last word, and cannot be mine. 'Those who took part in it', writes Dr McAdoo, 'touched unerringly and with discernment on much of the matter and substance which later conversations ... found it equally necessary to discuss'.[2] Some of those themes were the distinction between fundamentals and *adiaphora* (secondary questions) in doctrine and theology; the necessary balance between unity and diversity; doctrinal agreement on the Eucharist and on Ordination; and the nature of the Roman primacy – with Wake ready to accept a primacy of order and dignity but only within a strongly collegial setting.

But let the last word on this chapter of the history of Anglican – Roman Catholic relations come from Wake's final letter to Du Pin, which the latter never received, for he was to die before it could be delivered.

> May it suffice to have designed something in so great a task; and perhaps to have cast some seeds in the ground which at length will bear manifold fruit.

Meanwhile let us (for this none can deny us) embrace each other as brethren and members of the same mystical body.[3]

We pick up the story again with the 19th-century Oxford Movement, when the Tractarian attempt to rediscover and proclaim the Catholic heritage of the Church of England took on indirectly – and indeed in a way that the earlier Tractarians would not at first have welcomed – an ecumenical dimension. We begin with a somewhat eccentric Roman Catholic who left the Church of England for Rome in 1825, a Leicestershire squire called Ambrose Phillipps de Lisle. His enthusiastic support for the Oxford Movement was found distinctly embarrassing by the Anglican Newman, but he did influence Cardinal Wiseman towards taking a positive rather than a hostile attitude to the Oxford Movement. Phillipps de Lisle was the leading spirit in the foundation of the Association for the Promotion of the Unity of Christendom, (APUC) which encouraged Anglicans, Orthodox and Roman Catholics to take up full membership in order to work, study and pray for unity. It is necessary to evoke – if only very briefly – the existence of this Association in order both to realise that not all the early Anglican–Roman Catholic contacts involved only continental Roman Catholics and also to see why, after the condemnation of the Association, Anglicans once again concentrated their attention on the French connection – or, more strictly, the Franco–Belgian connection.

It is a temptation in this story to cast the participants in the roles of 'goodies' and 'baddies', heroes and villains. It is all too easy to place in the camp of the villains Henry Edward Manning, sometime Archdeacon of Chichester in the Church of England and, later, Archbishop of Westminster and Cardinal, especially as he has suffered from more than one hostile biography. As a convert he became a committed and formidable Ultramontane and was to champion a hardline definition of Papal Infallibility at the First Vatican Council. Though he never forgot his Anglican roots and shocked his successor, a cradle Catholic, by producing from beneath the pillow of his deathbed the manuscript book of prayers of his Anglican wife (who had died while he was still an Anglican), saying that he had used it daily and requesting that it should be put in his coffin, his 1864 publication *The Workings of the Holy Spirit in the Church of England* somewhat belied its title by proclaiming that the Anglican Church was 'the mother of all the intellectual and spiritual aberrations which now cover the face of England'.[4] A little later Manning was able to get a definitive condemnation of the APUC from the Holy Office and to issue a fierce and uncompromising pastoral in 1866. It is not surprising therefore that Anglicans who still wanted to dialogue with Rome should turn to the Continent.

After Newman joined the Roman Catholic Church the leadership of the Tractarian Movement passed to the reluctant hands of the austere and ascetic Dr Pusey. Pusey was not only busy translating and adapting French works of theology and spirituality; he was also visiting convents in France and Belgium in order to deepen his own practical knowledge of the religious life, for the benefit of the new religious communities in the Church of England of which he was the founder or spiritual director. In the course of these visits he became friendly with Mgr Darboy, Archbishop of Paris, and Mgr Dupanloup, Bishop of Orléans, both leaders of the 'Inopportunist' party which was opposing the attempt to define Papal Infallibility at the forthcoming Council, and also with a Belgian Jesuit, Fr Victor de Buck. Pusey was at the time engaged on his vast three-part *Eirenicon* and in it he explicitly evoked the correspondence between Wake and the Sorbonne doctors and praised its positive spirit. Since Mgr Darboy had also received the leading Scottish Tractarian, A.P. Forbes, Bishop of Brechin, this led Fr de Buck to launch the ingenious but unrealistic notion that Forbes should go to the Council as an observer with Pusey as his *peritus*. But Pusey was unimpressed. 'What can we expect', he wrote, 'when they invited the great Greek Church simply to submit? I expect nothing under the present Pope; under a future Pope there may be great changes.'[5] But Pusey, Canon of Christ Church and Regius Professor of Hebrew at Oxford, had had a profound influence on a young Christ Church undergraduate, the Hon. Charles Wood, later to become the second Viscount Halifax.[6] Halifax eventually discovered that his vocation was to remain a layman (and a married layman) but he was to devote all his energies to the promotion of the Catholic Movement within Anglicanism and to the cause of Anglican–Roman Catholic unity.

In the winter of 1884 a fateful meeting took place on the island of Madeira. Halifax was there because of the health of one of his sons; the Abbé Fernand Portal, a French Lazarist (Vincentian) priest, son of a village shoemaker, because of his own health. The two took long walks together along Madeira's aptly named *Caminho novo* (new way) and soon forged a deep, intimate and lasting friendship. At one point Portal urged Halifax to make his submission to Rome but in the end it was Portal who was 'converted' both to a new vision of unity as 'union by convergence' and to a new vocation. 'Oui', he wrote to Halifax, 'vous avez déplacé mon centre de gravité' (you have displaced my centre of gravity). The two friends launched what was to be called *la Campagne Anglo–Romaine*, founded a monthly bulletin, *La Revue Anglo–Romaine*, and tried to enlist the finest minds in both churches and both countries in this attempt to promote Anglican–Roman Catholic unity. The two friends – it was Portal's idea to which an initially reluctant Halifax was brought round – suggested that to get scholars of both churches to sit down together on a basis of equality it would be best to begin the dialogue with a neutral, historical issue, the question of the validity of Anglican Orders 'a question of fact and not of faith' as Portal put it, starting up spirited discussion of the issue by an article he wrote under a pseudonym. There was no initial intention of keeping English Roman Catholics out of the discussion, but the attitude of Cardinal Vaughan, Manning's successor at Westminster, soon moved from reserve to open hostility. 'With the benefit of hindsight', Archbishop McAdoo has written, 'a case can be made for maintaining that the reunion campaign went wrong at the start by a too early introduction of the theme of Orders'.[7] I do not think, however, that it can be disputed that one reason why it went wrong was because it opened a door for those who wanted to stop the dialogue, providing them with an obvious way of doing this by obtaining from Rome a resounding condemnation of the validity of Anglican Orders. A formidable trio of a Cardinal and two future cardinals, Vaughan, Abbot Gasquet and Mgr Merry del Val, worked hard to secure a condemnation. We celebrate the sad centenary of their triumph this year [1996], for it was in September 1896 that Leo XIII issued the bull *Apostolicae Curae*, condemning Anglican Orders as 'absolutely null and utterly void'. Within a month an exultant Cardinal Vaughan made this public appeal to Anglicans: 'Tarry not for Corporate Reunion; it is a dream, and a snare of the evil one'. For Halifax and Portal the blow was heavy and bitter but they refused to lose hope. As Halifax wrote to Portal,

> We tried to do something which God had inspired. We have failed, for the moment; but if it is indeed God's will, then his will shall be accomplished, and if he allows us to be broken, it is only because he means to do the work himself. This is no dream. The matter is as certain as ever it was.[8]

For a long time Halifax and Portal had to lie low – particularly Portal, for he had gained the unrelenting hostility of Merry del Val and was subjected to a number of disciplinary measures. They had to lie low, in fact, for over 24 years before they could really pick up the threads again, and by 1921 Halifax was in his eighties. In that year he crossed the Channel. He and Portal visited the battlefields of the 1914–18 war and then called on Cardinal Mercier, Archbishop of Malines and Primate of Belgium.

III. The Malines Conversations

It used to be thought that it was this personal initiative of Halifax that was the one and only source of the Malines Conversations. In fact there were three sources.

i) The first and most immediate was of course this visit, and Halifax took with him a cautious letter of introduction from the Archbishop of

Canterbury, Dr Randall Davidson, which stressed that 'Lord Halifax does not go in any sense as ambassador or formal representative of the Church of England'.

ii) The second arose from the fact that Cardinal Mercier's courageous stand against the German occupation of Belgium had made him a hero and a symbol of Belgian resistance far beyond the frontiers of his own country. In 1919 he had made a triumphal visit to the USA and in October addressed the General Convention of the Episcopal Church which greeted him with tremendous applause. Towards the end of his speech he said 'I have greeted you as brothers in the service of common ideals, brothers in love of liberty and let me add – as brothers in the Christian faith'. For this he was denounced to Rome by the Cardinal Archbishop of Boston and in 1920 received a letter from Pope Benedict XV, informing him that it was 'regrettable' that he had agreed to meet 'the Episcopalian pseudo-bishops' and 'inadmissible' that he had called them 'brothers in the Christian faith'. Later that year an unrepentant Mercier visited the Pope and not only told him that it was time the Catholic Church began participating in ecumenical conferences but offered to host discussions with Anglican and Orthodox theologians himself.

iii) The third was the Lambeth Conference of 1920 and the famous Encyclical Letter from the Bishops, An Appeal to all Christian People, with which it concluded. This appeal for unity contained one paragraph which seemed to offer a way round the road block created by the bull *Apostolicae Curae*, although it was directed in the first place to the Free Churches and linked with a plea that they would accept an episcopal laying on of hands for their ministers.

> To this end, we who send forth this appeal would say that if the authorities of other Communions should so desire, we are persuaded that, terms of union having been otherwise satisfactorily adjusted, Bishops and clergy of our Communion would willingly accept from these authorities a form of commission or recognition which would commend our ministry to their congregations, as having its place in the one family life.[9]

Can it be denied that gestures of humility in this spirit do more for Christian unity than triumphal blasts of the trumpet?

Copies of the Appeal were sent to the Papal Secretary of State, to Cardinal Bourne, Archbishop of Westminster and to Cardinal Mercier because, as Davidson put it, of 'the great interest which Your Eminence has taken in all that concerns the Christian well-being of Western Europe'. Cardinal Mercier acknowledged this with a telegram to Davidson of prayerful support.

The coming together of these three sources meant that Mercier was open to receive sympathetically all that Halifax and Portal had to suggest. He did hesitate at first, asking why he should take the initiative and not Cardinal Bourne. He was reassured both by indications that Rome would encourage him and also by the arguments of Halifax and Portal that the English Roman Catholic Church was not yet ready to take the initiative. 'If people come and knock at the door of a Catholic bishop', he is reported to have said, 'how can he refuse to open?' This raises two questions – both the historical question of how the initial benevolence of Cardinal Bourne was transformed into active opposition, and also the theological question of how far a bishop's share in the universal mission of the Apostolic College allows him to take initiatives outside his own diocese. The fact was that Cardinal Mercier did respond positively and the first round of Conversations was held in the Archiepiscopal Palace of Malines (Mechelen) in December 1921.

At this point it may be worthwhile stepping back a little to get an overview of the Conversations:

i) There were five **sessions** in all:

> The first from 6 to 8 December, 1921;
> The second from 14 to 15 March, 1923;
> The third from 7 to 8 November, 1923;
> The fourth from 19 to 20 May, 1925;
> The fifth and last (a winding-up operation after the fatal blow of the deaths of Mercier and Portal earlier that year) on 11 and 12 October, 1926.

ii) The **participants** were the following:

> At the **first** (1921) on the Roman Catholic side there were Cardinal Mercier, Mgr van Roey, his Vicar-General and eventual successor, the Abbé Portal; on the Anglican side Lord Halifax, Dr Armitage Robinson, Dean of Wells, and Fr Walter Frere, Superior of the Community of the Resurrection.
>
> At the **second** (March 1923) the same people were present.
>
> At the **third** (November 1923) were added from the Roman Catholic side two French priest historians, Hippolyte Hemmer and Mgr Pierre Batiffol, and from the Anglican side Dr Charles Gore, former Bishop of Oxford, and Dr B.J. Kidd, Warden of Keble College, Oxford.
>
> At the **fourth** (May 1925) the same people were present: Walter Frere was by now Bishop of Truro.
>
> At the **fifth** (1926) only Van Roey, Batiffol and Hemmer were present from the Roman Catholic side, and Halifax, Frere and Kidd on the Anglican side. The meeting had what Halifax's biographer called 'the depressing atmosphere of a liquidation'.[10]

iii) The **subjects** discussed were the following:

At the **first**: The Lambeth Appeal to all Christian People and an explanatory memorandum from Lord Halifax. The agenda therefore was almost exclusively a presentation of Anglican self-understanding with questions and reactions from the Roman Catholic side.

At the **second**: A Memorandum from the Anglicans exploring the idea of legitimate diversity and suggesting some 'characteristic Anglican rites and customs' which should be retained in the case of unity. It was discussion of this item which led Cardinal Mercier to commission the revolutionary paper which was read at the fourth Conversation.

At the **third**: The question of the Roman primacy dominated the agenda, with a paper from Dean Robinson, 'The Position of St Peter in the Primitive Church', and a response to it from Mgr Batiffol. Two papers by Dr Kidd, 'The Petrine Texts, as employed to AD 461', (with a response from Mgr Batiffol) and 'To What Extent was the Papal Authority Repudiated at the Reformation in England', were also discussed.

At the **fourth**: More papers on the Papacy: one from Van Roey on 'The Episcopate and the Papacy from the theological point of view', with a response from Kidd and another from Gore (missing from Lord Halifax's collection) on 'Unity in Diversity'. Gore had been added to the Anglican delegation at the express insistence of Davidson, who heard that Halifax was too favourable to the Roman position, and wanted to add a tougher Anglican in the Liberal Catholic and less Roman tradition. Gore and Batiffol had been indulging in a rather sharp pamphlet controversy: sitting together around the table neither capitulated but, in an atmosphere of dialogue, they did manage to narrow the gap between their respective positions.

It was at this Conversation that Cardinal Mercier launched his bombshell – reading a paper he had commissioned from an unnamed theologian, *L'Eglise anglicane unie non absorbée* – a paper which, as one of the Anglican participants, Dr Frere, remarked 'took our breath away'.

It was only much later that Van Roey revealed that the author of this Mémoire was Dom Lambert Beauduin, a remarkable Belgian Benedictine monk who had been close to Cardinal Mercier both in promoting the Liturgical Movement and also in acting (at considerable risk) as his courier during the German occupation. He was the founder of the Monks of Unity, then at Amay and now at Chevetogne; a single community in which some monks followed the Latin rite and others the Eastern rite within a monastery which contained two churches, one for each rite. Dom Lambert Beauduin managed to forge against himself quite a coalition of enemies and the revelation that he was the author of *L'Eglise anglicane unie non absorbée* was not the least of the factors that led to his being sent into exile from his community and his own country until 1951.

Before I try to draw out some of the lessons from the Malines Conversations and give a more personal comment on them, I think it important to move on. We can only see the true significance of Malines, its strengths and its weaknesses, if we see it not only in the context of what preceded it but also in the context of what followed it.

IV. From Malines to ARCIC

The fifth and final session of the Conversations in October 1926 had, as we have seen, the atmosphere of a liquidation, but worse was to follow. If the first attempt of Halifax and Portal in the 1890s to open the door of dialogue ended with the Vatican slamming the door with the bull *Apostolicae Curae*, this second attempt in the 1920s ended with another door slammed, when Pius XI issued his encyclical *Mortalium Animos* in 1928. This was a general condemnation of the ecumenical movement; it did not specifically mention Malines, and Halifax always maintained that it was aimed more at the meeting of 'Life and Work' at Stockholm in 1925 and the meeting of 'Faith and Order' at Lausanne in 1927 than at the Malines Conversations. On the other hand, its publication was almost immediately followed by an announcement from Rome that there would be no further Conversations at Malines. It also created an extremely difficult situation for Roman Catholic ecumenists, who were obliged to lie low and often found themselves subjected to disciplinary measures. *Mortalium Animos* set out with bleak intransigence the principle that the only way to unity is 'the return to the one true Church of Christ of those who are separated from it'; it also denied that it was permissible to make a distinction between 'fundamental' and 'non-fundamental' articles of the faith – one of the questions that had been explored at Malines.[11] It was not until the Second Vatican Council that Pius XI's assertion was effectively (if implicitly) contradicted, when the *Decree on Ecumenism* taught that 'in Catholic doctrine there exists an order or "hierarchy" of truths, since they vary in their relation to the foundation of the Christian faith.[12]

In the winter of Roman Catholic ecumenism that followed the publication of *Mortalium Animos* Dom Lambert Beauduin and his community at Amay suffered particular hardship. Dom Lambert was exiled from his community and his own country and only allowed to return to it (in its new home at Chevetogne) from a fruitful exile in

France (not exactly Siberia!) in 1951, while the community itself and its review *Irénikon* survived only with great difficulty. But the flame of Roman Catholic ecumenism was not extinguished and two French priests, who actually met each other at Amay, contributed to it powerfully in their different ways. One was Fr Yves Congar, the Dominican theologian disciplined under Pius XII and elevated to the cardinalate by John Paul II, whose pioneer study *Chrétiens désunis* was published in 1937;[13] the other was the Abbé Paul Couturier, an obscure schoolmaster from Lyon, who was the founder (or perhaps, more strictly, the refounder) of the Week of Prayer for Christian Unity. It is also significant that a certain Angelo Roncalli, who was to become Pope John XXIII in 1958 and to announce the summoning of the Second Vatican Council in January 1959, could refer to Dom Lambert as 'my old Belgian friend' and had clearly been influenced by many of his ideas.

The summoning of the Council with its, at first, rather unclear ecumenical orientation, was soon followed up by the establishment of the Secretariat for Christian Unity under the leadership of Cardinal Bea in 1960. Later in that same year the Archbishop of Canterbury, Dr Geoffrey Fisher, paid a call on Pope John in Rome. He was the first Archbishop of Canterbury to visit a Pope since the 14th century and the first ever leader of a non-Roman Catholic communion to do so. This 'first' led in its turn to two more; when the Archbishop appointed an Anglican representative in Rome to study the preparations for the Council and to act in liaison with the Secretariat, and when the Anglican Communion took the lead in accepting an invitation to send official observers to the Council.

Of the texts which were promulgated by the Council one was specifically devoted to Ecumenism, the decree *Unitatis Redintegratio* of November 1964.[14] But others were to have an equally important effect in bringing the Roman Catholic Church, which at first had excluded itself from it, into the mainstream of the Ecumenical Movement; notably its key text, the Dogmatic Constitution on the Church, *Lumen Gentium*. So it was that the then Archbishop of Canterbury, Dr Michael Ramsey, was able, once the Council was concluded, to pay an official visit to Pope Paul VI in Rome in March 1966 and to sign with him a Common Declaration at the Basilica of St Paul-without-the-Walls in order 'to inaugurate between the Roman Catholic Church and the Anglican Communion a serious dialogue which, founded on the Gospels and on the ancient common traditions, may lead to that unity in truth, for which Christ died'.[15]

So in initiating the process which was to lead to the setting up of ARCIC (The Anglican–Roman Catholic International Commission), the Pope and the Archbishop were in one sense re-launching the Malines Conversations. They were in fact doing far more. Where the Conversations at Malines had been unofficial (with attitudes varying from cautious but uncommitted approval to growing uneasiness on the part of the highest authorities in each Communion), had attracted a good deal of hostility from very powerful quarters in both Communions and had a limited membership (both with regard to theological views and nationality), ARCIC was official and international, with members drawn from many countries and reflecting (on both sides) a real theological pluralism, backed by a formal mandate from the highest authorities in each Communion. There was one other striking parallel with Malines. On his deathbed in January 1926 Mercier sent for Lord Halifax and gave him as a memento his episcopal ring (now set in a chalice in York Minster). On 24 March 1966, after the signing of the Common Declaration, Pope Paul VI – in what must surely have been a conscious reference to that scene – took off his own episcopal ring and put it onto the finger of Archbishop Ramsey.

The years between 1966 and 1982 can be seen in retrospect as the high point of Anglican–Roman Catholic relations; it led many on both sides to see this particular dialogue as the most positive and hopeful of all the international bilateral dialogues and allowed some on both sides to imagine that unity could even be envisaged by the end of the century. The immediate consequence of the 1966 Common Declaration was the setting up of a Joint Preparatory Commission, charged with drawing up an inventory of the subjects to be discussed; its work led directly to that of ARCIC, which first met in 1970. The first ARCIC Commission had three main theological issues on its agenda: Eucharistic Doctrine; Ministry and Ordination; and Authority in the Church. Its various agreed statements and elucidations were published separately from 1971 onwards; its *Final Report*, which contained not only these previous texts but a second text on Authority in the Church and an elucidation of the first, together with Preface, Introduction and Conclusion and a number of appendices was published in 1982, earlier in the year that was to see the historic visit of Pope John Paul II to England. The Commission believed that it had reached 'substantial agreement' on the doctrine of the Eucharist and on Ministry and Ordination; on the subject of Authority in the Church the Commission could claim a considerable degree of consensus and convergence which still however left a number of vital problems unresolved. This was not however so much a confession of failure as a call to both Communions to validate and confirm the degree of convergence registered by the Commission and to take 'significant initiatives' that would help to resolve the remaining differences.

The years since 1982 have seen disappointment and even a sense of betrayal (on both sides); there is still, however, a resolve on both sides to persevere with the dialogue, and the work of ARCIC continues, though certainly with a realization that many of the remaining obstacles to unity, some of which have appeared since 1966, will cause the pace of the movement to be slower and progress more difficult. Two principal obstacles can be discerned. On the one hand, there has been the move towards the ordination of women to the priesthood and the episcopate in churches of the Anglican Communion (seen as particularly critical in the case of the 1992 vote of the General Synod of the Church of England), together with the weakening of the bonds of full communion within and between the different Anglican churches and a perceived loss of authority within the Anglican Communion at its highest levels. On the other hand, there has been the fact that, whereas the various Anglican responses to the *Final Report* of ARCIC I (summarized and synthesized by the Lambeth Conference of 1988) were both positive and relatively swift, the long delayed official Roman Response, finally published in 1991, was perceived (and not only by Anglicans) to be very hard-line.[16] Crucially, it judged that ARCIC's claim to have reached 'substantial agreement' on two of the three issues it tackled could not be endorsed by Rome. Both sides therefore had grounds for grievance; both could complain that the goal-posts had been moved. Rome could point to the 'new' and 'grave' obstacle of the ordination of women as priests and bishops; Canterbury could point to the apparent *volte-face* in the Vatican's Responses to the *Final Report* – its requirement of *identity* in doctrine (in content and even in language) rather than *consonance* and its implicit questioning of the approval given by Popes Paul VI and John Paul II to ARCIC's methodology. It is clear therefore, in view of these disappointments and of subsequent sharp exchanges between the Vatican and Lambeth on the subject of women's ordination, that there is now urgent need for the restoration and deepening of mutual *trust* between the two Communions.[17]

V. Towards some tentative conclusions

i) There has already appeared a number of authoritative judgements of the Malines Conversations. We have two public statements of Pope Paul VI on the subject. In 1966 he sent greetings to Cardinal Suenens, Archbishop of Brussels–Malines, on the occasion of the 40th anniversary of the Conversations, and gave this verdict:

> The Conversations mark an epoch in this looking and preparing for the perfect unity of those who believe in Christ. The spirit of openness and Christian brotherhood which characterized them made it possible to approach the delicate, and at times difficult, questions which separate the two Communions, in a common effort towards the establishment of unity in truth and love.

In 1977 Pope Paul welcomed Archbishop Donald Coggan to the Vatican with these words:

> The history of relations between the Catholic Church and the Anglican Communion has been marked by the staunch witness of such men as Charles Brent, Lord Halifax, William Temple and George Bell among Anglicans; and the Abbé Portal, Dom Lambert Beauduin, Cardinal Mercier and Cardinal Bea among the Catholics. The pace of this movement has quickened marvellously in recent years, so that these words of hope 'The Anglican Church united not absorbed' are no longer merely a dream.

From the Anglican side we have a judicious appraisal from Dr Henry McAdoo, former Archbishop of Dublin and Anglican Chairman of ARCIC I:

> Malines marked a new stage in that it became a conference and was therefore an advance in Anglican/Roman Catholic relations. Even if the advance was soon stopped short and no formula of concord or agreed statement on doctrine or policy emerged, it established a measure of formal contact in charity and gave an opportunity to the major themes to surface in the context not of polemic but of dialogue.[18]

ii)   One incontrovertible lesson of Malines is the fundamental importance of deep personal friendships in work for Christian unity. It would not have been possible for Halifax and Portal to have done all that they did without the commitment of a deep and intimate spiritual friendship, into which Mercier was later drawn. Halifax and Portal were to bear testimony to the role of friendship in work for unity at a public meeting in Louvain in November 1925, while, in his Will, Cardinal Mercier gave his own witness in words now justly famous: 'To unite we must love each other, to love each other we must know each other, to know each other we must reach out to meet each other'.[19] In particular, it was through the knowledge that they gained of Halifax's total integrity and deep spirituality that both Portal and (much later) Mercier were converted to a more genuinely ecumenical approach to Anglicans. The role of friendship has not ceased to be vital in our own time; we have only to think – to take but two examples – of the friendship between Paul VI and Michael Ramsey, and of that between Derek Worlock and David Sheppard at Liverpool. The prophetic gestures of Mercier in 1926 and of Pope Paul VI in 1966 were made possible only by deep personal friendship, though their significance was wider and deeper.

iii) Malines marked an important shift (though one that had to wait for over 30 years to gain official approval) in Roman Catholic attitudes to work for unity, the shift from *Unionism* to *Ecumenism*. Unionism is basically the effort to encourage separated Christians (individually or corporately) to 'return' to the communion of the Roman Catholic Church. It demands sympathy, tact and a degree of real understanding of the faith and life of other Christian bodies, but it is still undertaken as a one-way process. If it involves the granting of certain disciplinary and liturgical concessions, they are still only 'concessions'. Genuine ecumenism requires an understanding that conversion and convergence, mutual correction and mutual enrichment, are demanded of all. Some of the Roman Catholic participants at Malines were certainly 'unionist' in their approach; others moved away in the course of the Conversations from a unionist position to a more ecumenical one. On the Anglican side too there was a growing readiness not just to present an Anglican case but to allow oneself to be challenged by the convictions and arguments of one's Roman Catholic partners.

iv) Malines was certainly marked – and its effect in consequence impaired – by a considerable degree of ambivalence. The most basic ambivalence of all was the status of the Conversations themselves. Did the participants speak for anyone but themselves? Did either Rome or Canterbury at any time really approve? It was clear too that the participants were not really representative of their churches, either theologically or nationally. Anglican Evangelicals were in general hostile, as indeed were most Anglicans who were not in some sense Anglo-Catholics, while all the Anglican delegates came from England. It cannot be denied that Cardinal Bourne, Archbishop of Westminster, had legitimate grounds for feeling that he had been misunderstood; he was not (as was at one time supposed) initially hostile, but he became increasingly so as time went on and felt that he was being excluded and kept in the dark. All the Roman Catholic participants were either French or Belgian. Although there were some sympathetic English Roman Catholics (notably among the Dominicans) to compensate for the vociferous hostility of the Jesuit Francis Woodlock and the *Tablet*, at no time did the suggestion that there might be English Roman Catholic participation come to realization. At the time there was great fear of Modernism in the Roman Catholic Church, and many Roman Catholics who wrote and spoke against the Conversations were to a considerable extent motivated by their opposition to Modernism. More directly political considerations also intervened. The British Ambassador in Brussels complained to King George V's Private Secretary, who in turn informed Archbishop Davidson that 'His Majesty is very uneasy about these interviews with Cardinal Mercier'.[20] On the other side, Cardinal Gasquet's humorous but still bitter comment on Cardinal Mercier, 'I might as well go to Belgium and tell Mercier how to solve the Flemish question'[21] reflected on Cardinal Mercier's difficulties over the 'Flemish

Question' and the risk that it could impinge upon the Conversations.

v) Malines tackled a number of themes that have continued to be key issues in Anglican–Roman Catholic dialogue and tackled them in a responsible, sensitive and imaginative way that has had lasting results. One of those themes was that of the Roman Primacy, and at Malines it clearly emerged that it was unreal (even un-evangelical) for Anglicans to posit a primacy of 'honour' unless that honour involved a real degree of spiritual responsibility, spiritual leadership, general superintendence and a care for the well-being of the universal Church. Another theme addressed at Malines was that of the tension between fundamental and secondary truths. It was the issue of unity-in-diversity and the need to have some kind of model which would enable Anglicans to see more clearly what unity with Rome would and would not involve that led Cardinal Mercier to commission from Dom Lambert Beauduin, who was not actually present at any of the Conversations and whose authorship was not divulged until they had ended, his celebrated paper *L'Eglise anglicane, unie non absorbée.*[22] It is easy now to criticize that *mémoire*, which certainly betrayed an inadequate awareness of the full reality of Anglicanism, which leaned too heavily on the 'Uniate' (Eastern Catholic) model, and which contained the less than tactful suggestion (bound to exacerbate feelings once it was made known) that the Roman Catholic hierarchy in England would eventually need to be suppressed; it is even more important to salute its vision and its courage. It can seem premature to draw up such models when doctrinal agreement is still a long way from being complete; it is nonetheless important that Christian communities should be offered such models, since it is fear of compulsory uniformity and of the surrender of cherished traditions and institutions that holds people back from the goal of unity. However great the need for restating the content of Dom Lambert's *mémoire*, the agenda opened up by its title, 'united not absorbed', remains as valid as ever.

vi) Finally, it has to be confessed that it is particularly difficult to give a cool and objective assessment of Malines at the present moment. There are still extremely positive and hopeful signs – of which two examples are the recent encyclical of Pope John Paul II (May 1995) *Ut Unum Sint*, with its courageous and risky invitation to the other churches to enter into dialogue with him on the Roman Primacy, and the fact that, in spite of increasing difficulties at the strictly theological level, good relations and increased practical cooperation are so often to be found at the local level. Against this has to be set the undeniable fact that at the theological level the situation seems to have moved from *convergence* to *divergence*. In these conditions it is extremely difficult to discern the future of the dialogue and agonizingly difficult for those who are distressed, not only by the fact of divergence, but by the weight of responsibility for it which they believe their own church bears, to know where their own duty lies. Do we not perhaps need to recover something of the dogged and unquenchable hope that animated men like Halifax and Portal? *'Un jour on verra que nous avions raison'*.

Notes

1 cf. Anthony Milton, *Catholic and Reformed* (Cambridge, 1995), pp. 355–356.
2 H.R. McAdoo: 'Anglican/Roman Catholic Relations, 1717–1980' in *Rome and the Anglicans*, ed. W. Haase (Berlin and New York, 1982), p. 174.
3 op. cit. p. 157.
4 For this and other unacknowledged quotations in the pages that follow I am indebted to the magisterial work of J.A. Dick, *The Malines Conversations Revisited* (Leuven, 1989).
5 In a letter to Dr. R.F. Littledale, 17 July 1869. cf. H.P. Liddon, *Life of E.B. Pusey DD*, (Longmans, London 1898), vol. IV. p. 181.
6 For the sake of convenience I refer to him throughout as Halifax, even before he succeeded to the title in 1885.
7 *Rome and the Anglicans*, op. cit. p. 183.
8 cf. J.G. Lockhart, *Charles Lindley, Viscount Halifax* (London, 1936), vol. 2, pp. 80–81.
9 The full text of the Appeal has been many times reprinted, e.g. in *The Lambeth Conferences: 1867 – 1948* (London, 1948), pp. 119–124. It can also be found in J.A. Dick, op. cit. Appendix A.
10 J.G. Lockhart: op. cit. vol. 2, p. 332.
11 The full text of *Mortalium Animos* is given by J.A. Dick, op. cit. Appendix G.
12 Chapter II, paragraph 11, cf. Vatican Council II: *The Conciliar and Post Conciliar Documents*, ed. Flannery (Leominster, 1981), p. 462.
13 It was translated into English as *Divided Christendom* (London, 1939).
14 This decree contained a notable and irenic reference to Anglicanism. Speaking of the separated communions of the West, it declares: 'Among those in which Catholic traditions and institutions in part continue to exist, the Anglican Communion occupies a special place' (Chapter III, para 13).
15 cf. e.g. *Anglicans and Roman Catholics: The Search for Unity*, ed. Hill and Yarnold (London, 1994), p. 11.
16 The text of this Response can be found in Hill and Yarnold (op. cit.), pp. 156–166, as can also the critical analysis of it in the comment of the French episcopate, pp. 171–184.
17 cf. Roderick Strange, 'Reflections on a Controversy: Newman and Pusey's "Eirenicon"' in *Pusey Rediscovered* ed. Perry Butler (London, 1983), p. 346: 'At the very least, this controversy is a cautionary tale. It warns us that Agreed Statements ... will count for nothing, *even combined with love, sympathy and friendship*, unless there exists amongst us this deeply-felt, unequivocal trust'.
18 *Rome and the Anglicans*, op. cit. p. 195.

19 Maurice Villain, *Unity: A History and Some Reflections* – EV of *Introduction à l'Oecuménisme* – (London, 1963), p. 262.
20 J.A. Dick, op. cit. p. 144.
21 J.G. Lockhart, op. cit. p. 286. The comment is often attributed to Cardinal Bourne.
22 Original French text in Dick, op. cit. Appendix F. pp. 217–225.

Postscript. Since this lecture was delivered an important commemorative ceremony, at which some significant addresses were delivered, was held at Malines (Mechelen) in August 1996 to mark the 75th anniversary of the opening of the Conversations. An important book has also been published: *A Brother Knocking at the Door* by Bernard Barlow, OSM (London 1996). It has not been possible to introduce references to either of these developments in this text.

*(This paper was given at the ESBVM Conference
at Dromantine College, Newry, in October 1995,
and at the Irish School of Ecumenics in February 1996)*

12

The meaning of the Malines Conversations for today

Pierre Parré

'I placed watchmen on your towers, Jerusalem' (Isaiah 62.6).
'The watchman said: "The morning comes"' (Isaiah 21.12).

The 'morning' of which Isaiah speaks can be interpreted as the dawn of the ecumenical era in the 1920s.

'The Ecumenical Spirit'– a characteristic of the Conversations.

This is the first striking characteristic of the Malines Conversations and those who participated in them. In these years a new, more catholic spirit, emerged. The Malines Group, and other pioneers, shared in it. They helped to break the ice. Their experience had lasting consequences.

What did Halifax, Portal and the others want? They did not hope for a quick resolution of the schism between the Anglican and Roman Catholic Churches. They did not aim at institutional reunion. Rather, they wanted to bring some of their friends from both churches together, in a spirit of friendship and mutual trust, so that they could talk in a good-humoured way. They wanted to be with each other, to be, as Paul puts it in Romans, 'mutually encouraged by each others' faith'. They wanted to listen to each other, to be mutually challenged, 'aglow in the Spirit, rejoicing in hope' (Rom. 12.11–12).

At first, both Portal and Mercier hoped to convert Halifax. However, Halifax's wisdom converted them to the 'ecumenical spirit' and they agreed not to regard him as a 'dissident'. Rather, they saw him as a devout Christian, with many spiritual gifts to share, who could help them in finding new ways ahead. Ecumenism implies a positive attitude to Christians of other traditions, and a larger vision of Christendom. Personal contact broke the ice between the three friends.

The 'ecumenical spirit' opens one's eyes to the particular gifts of each separate tradition. In the 1920s some Christians came to see the question of unity in a new light. Unity could not be achieved by absorption or domination. The new perspective gave due weight to the values of each tradition.

Previously, an attitude of proselytisation was general amongst Christians, together with a lack of due respect for other traditions. In the

1920s, the new ecumenical spirit became more and more widely accepted, though rarely by Roman Catholics. The new attitude brought with it a changed theological and spiritual vision; the whole framework had to be rethought.

Several great theologians had already received such an ecumenical vision. They included Johann Adam Möhler (1796–1838), John Henry Newman (1801–90), Cardinal Mercier (1851–1926) and Metropolitan Andrew Szeptyckyj (1865–1945); Dom Lambert Beauduin, teaching ecclesiology in Rome, Fr Portal and others working with them, had accepted the theological vision of Newman and Möhler. This meant the birth of an ecumenical spirit.

For most Christians, this ecclesiological vision was new. Ecumenism is, in fact, a 'new phenomenon' (this translates Fr Congar's *un fait nouveau*). In the 1920s a new way of thinking developed, the ecumenical way (see Congar's *Dialogue Between Christians*, ET 1966, especially pp. 109–159).

Congar often raises the question of the implications of this new ecumenical attitude. It implies the end of any era of proselytisation. It implies helping all separated churches to converge on the common plenitude that is our calling. It implies seeing this future in terms of the reconciliation and integration of all the riches we have been given separately, remembering that the Church of the future is identical with that founded at Pentecost.

For all Christians and their churches ecumenism is a matter of discerning authentic values wherever they exist. 'Do not quench the Spirit ... test everything; hold fast to that which is good' (1 Thess. 5.19, 21). It involves mature growth towards a common future. In order to reach this maturity, real repentance and changes of attitude are required (see Congar, op. cit. p. 97, 'On the eve of the Amsterdam Assembly', 1947). This was the vision of Möhler, Newman and their disciples, even though they did not formulate it as clearly did Congar later. However, their principles were accepted. The Jesuit Bernard Sesboüé, active in bilateral conversations between Protestants and Roman Catholics, said some time ago that the shape of the Church of the future will be different from the past; it will have to have an 'ecumenical shape'. In *Pour une Théologie de l'Oecuménisme*, (Paris, ed. Cerf, 1990) p. 15, Sesboüé distinguishes two periods in the history of ecumenism:

i)   The ecumenism of love, with a conversion of the heart, and
ii) Doctrinal ecumenism, with a conversion of the intelligence.

He speaks about the necessity of an increasing understanding of our 'divided languages', à propos doctrines which divide or seem to divide us. Sesboüé also argues that Christians in the pew are largely unaware of the progress made in ecumenical research. We must add that many priests and religious are also unaware of it. Sesboüé speaks about the necessity of 'a general conversion of our mentalities and attitudes' among Christians. Many are just not interested. Sesboüé then mentions another step: ecclesial acts of reconciliation, acts which could create 'new conditions, a new milieu'. How can our churches be ready for such acts of reconciliation, even by stages? Our churches will have to find new ways of acting. We should note that the Lambeth Appeal of 1920 was an invitation for such a step. Sesboüé elaborates this on p. 17. He writes: 'Today the status quo becomes an impossible solution'. Still, we think many church leaders have 'Don't rock the boat!' as their motto. Their main purpose is: Save the institution as it now is! We do not know where all these new ideas could lead us.' Instead of *Amicus Plato, magis amica veritas*, it is too often *Amica veritas, sed magis amicus Plato*.

Congar describes the ecumenical spirit thus:

> Ecumenism constitutes a new departure with an essentially universal outlook ... The deeper one's knowledge of the history of Christian divisions, the more one realises how closely they are interconnected, giving rise to one another in a sort of chain reaction in such a way that any endeavour to surmount them must embrace them as a whole.

In the light of this, we will have to review all our separate histories and ecclesial systems and relate them to what is really going on.

Looking at church history, we can see that the errors and divisions of the past have given rise to chain reactions which are tangled up with each other. The ecumenist has to face the entire historical legacy of all the churches and place it in the ecclesiological framework provided by Newman and Möhler. Ramsey and Congar took this approach in the past and Tillard does so today.

Few questions today can be solved piecemeal, in isolation. We now need, in the light of ecumenical principles, to take an overview, engaging simultaneously in a 'serious dialogue based on the Gospel and the ancient common traditions', as called for by Paul VI and Michael Ramsey in their Common Statement in 1966. Today, theologians such as Sesboüé repeat the findings of Ramsey in his *The Gospel and the Catholic Church* of 1936. He wanted to locate the study of church order in terms of the Gospel (ibid. p. 8). I instance one sentence (p. 33):

> A wealth of thought is compressed into this passage (2 Cor. 5.14–17; ... one has died for all; therefore all have died ... those who live might live no longer for themselves ... if anyone is in Christ, he is a new creation). Men are now

to be found identified with Christ's death in such a way that they no longer think of themselves as separate and self–sufficient units, but as centred in Christ who died and rose again ... Christ ... the inclusive head and centre of a new humanity.

Ramsey applies these principles to the Churches and to the 'impasse between two types of Christianity; Catholic tradition and Evangelical tradition' (p. 7). Dom Lialine OSB, (of Amay–Chevetogne) said the same in *Irénikon* in 1936.

Archbishop Ramsey, Sesboüé, John XXIII, Patriarch Athenagoras, the brothers of Taizé, and many others, shared this ecumenical vision and spirit of 'fullness'. Each church has to rediscover values that belong to the Great Living Tradition, but which are better honoured in the life of a mother church than in its own life.

Accepting the ecumenical spirit and principle does not mean averring that one is or may be wrong in belonging to one's own church and in accepting its teaching. It does involve being prepared to put questions differently, in order to set problems in a clearer light, and to advance to reformulations of faith that may overcome earlier objections to them. We have to reformulate in greater depth and clarity, accepting that our partners in dialogue have something to contribute to this process. It will be time-consuming and demand much historical research.

I quote, in simplified form, Congar (op. cit. p. 59). 'I cannot absolutely and completely identify what I now hold with the absolute truth that I profess and which my Church also professes.' Congar cites Berdyaev: 'Ecumenical sincerity presupposes, on the part of every Christian denomination, a sense of its own incompleteness and a striving for completion' (*Ecumenical Review*, Autumn 1948, p. 13). The French philosopher, Etienne Gilson, says the same about the theological systems of Augustine and Aquinas.

> Opponents whose conclusions clash must be given the time to understand themselves better, and to come together again at a point at present indeterminate, but which will certainly lie beyond our present positions.

Gilson was speaking of philosophical research, but Congar applies the idea to theological investigation. Theologians such as the Methodist Newton Flew, who was influential in the Faith and Order Movement, developed similar ideas (cf. Lund, 1952).

So far, we have spoken of doctrine. Practical ecumenism is also necessary. 'Churches Together In England' has encouraged many initiatives and experiments. During the Malines Celebrations in August 1996, Fr Tillard reminded us that ARCIC was convinced, from an early stage, that full communion will only become a possibility if the two churches live together, pray together and act together in a visible way, in *koinonia*. 'We must do the truth together in love' (cf. Tillard's paper, 'How will Communion emerge?').

We can compare the pioneers of Malines with farmers who have found new seeds. They are determined to sow them in their old fields, believing that they will inaugurate a new era in agriculture, with new fruit and new 'leaves for healing' (Ezekiel 47.12).

Impediments to the process of unity

Are the convictions of some churches hindering the movement to full communion? Have these churches really accepted the call to future maturity? Do they leave space for further searching?

We know that the Roman Catholic Church claims, in the *Decree on Ecumenism*, to have 'the fullness of grace and truth entrusted to the Catholic Church' (3) and 'it was to the apostolic college alone, of which Peter is the head, that we believe our Lord entrusted all the blessings of the New Covenant ...' (3). Roman Catholics and Orthodox share similar convictions in such matters. We know what they mean by 'all the blessings' and 'the fullness of grace and truth'. The Roman Catholic Church believes that it is substantially identical with the Church founded by Jesus, and it claims to have preserved a spirit of '*catholicity*' or wholeness, a concept that is wider than that of 'Catholicism'. The Orthodox make similar claims.

These claims mean that these churches believe they have everything that is theoretically necessary to the fullness of churchly life. However, in empirical reality they may need to be reconverted to their principles, and learn to apply them thoroughly. Roman Catholic claims do not negate the statement of John XXIII at the beginning of Vatican II, that 'the substance of the ancient doctrine of the deposit of faith is one thing, and the way in which it is presented is another'. Such representation and its reception by the churches will take much time and energy.

John XXIII's *theologoumenon* reflects the teaching of Newman in the *Essay on the Development of Christian Doctrine*. Newman taught us that many realities in the experience of the Church have not yet become the subject of explicit and clear teaching. We must become good explorers. Many paragraphs in the documents of Vatican II show the necessity of conversion of mind and heart (eg. *Decree on Ecumenism*, 7, 9–12). Ramsey's book, *The Gospel and the Catholic Church* implies the same.

If the churches worked together more ecumenically, we would have more chances to explore these experiences and to grow, through sharing, into greater unity.

Many Christians, albeit still perhaps a minority, have accepted the principles of ecumenism. Church leaders, theologians and educated Christians are especially numerous amongst them. The theological principles involved include the notions of the 'hierarchy of truths' and the distinction between the substance and the historically-conditioned expression of the deposit of faith. We have abandoned simplified, partisan approaches to church history in the interests of more accurate and nuanced views. Today, we are aware that there is no one simple theological system that can give a wholly adequate and definitive expression to all the mysteries of the faith. We are also more aware of our limitations, and of the necessity of a wider vision of church history which shows greater understanding and tolerance. We have to stand back a little to get the whole picture. We are aware of the need to reinterpret Christianity, an awareness that Leo XIII, Pius XI, Mercier, Portal, Beauduin, Ramsey and others all shared. 'We have to recreate the Church' said Portal. This was the motto of his University Group in Paris (see biography by Ladous). Dom Lambert had the same vision, and, by 1909, was working on the Liturgical Movement.

Ecumenism, according to Congar, is this:

> Humbly, laboriously, we have to make the effort to understand specific spiritual milieux. These spiritual worlds have a quality of truth and profundity that eludes our ability to grasp them fully with metaphysical concepts. (Congar, *Dialogue Between Christians*, p. 128).

In the total experience of the Universal Church, there are many spiritual worlds that lie outside of the present experience of existing particular churches and individual Christians (cf. 1 Cor. 13.9, 12: 'our knowledge is imperfect and our prophecy is imperfect ... now we see in a mirror dimly'; more than dimly, indeed; often very obscurely). They also elude our present attempts at definition.

People such as Seraphim of Sarov, Mercier, Bonhoeffer, Ramsey, John XXIII, Athenagoras, de Lubac, Congar, Suenens, Zundel and many other theologians have said that we have to purify ourselves and refine our visions and ways of speaking and thinking. We have to experience real conversion of attitude. We have to formulate some questions more lucidly and effectively.

It is easy to find doctrinal formulae that were or are inadequate. We may instance talk about the renewing of Christ's sacrifice, or a special kind of propitiation in the Eucharist which seems to be different from Christ's unique propitiation. We use naive expressions about the plenitude of jurisdiction confided to Peter. Quite apart from all this, there is much dated and ill-digested theology and preaching in all our churches.

In the last fifty years, ecumenical theology has shown us that, with mutual love and patient research, important questions can be discussed anew and important agreements reached on questions thought earlier to be intractable. We can instance several sets of agreements: the American Lutheran–Roman Catholic Group produced an excellent statement on the Eucharist as sacrifice (1967); ARCIC, working more slowly, produced a similar statement in 1994; the *Groupe des Dombes* has produced a stream of excellent work. Moreover, the Malines papers were extremely rich in insight.

A quick look at some of the protagonists

i)   Lord Halifax: the spirit of ecumenism was very real for him. Already, in Madeira in 1889, he had converted Portal to ecumenism. The Holy Spirit used Halifax as his instrument in converting both Mercier and Portal to the ecumenical spirit. Halifax was the real initiator of the process that led to Malines.

ii)   Portal was a far-seeing prophet. He could already see, in 1900, how far the entire Roman Catholic church had to change. He said – strong words for the times – 'We must refashion the Church'. He became a powerful force for ecumenism, pulling many Catholics, especially from the University of Paris, along in his wake.

iii) Mercier had a transcending vision. At Louvain, he was nicknamed 'the great sympathiser'. (A strange coincidence: in music and acoustics, 'sympathetic' designates a vibration produced in a body by a vibration of exactly the same period in a neighbouring body.) He was always open-minded and generous. His Pastoral Letter of 18 January 1924 shows this clearly.

iv) Dom Lambert Beauduin OSB was also a 'watchman'. He knew the dawn was coming.

The roots of the whole process

The roots of the process go back to Pusey, Keble and Newman. Behind Halifax lies the influence of the Oxford Movement.

The Malines Conversations were the harbinger of a 'new phenomenon: the ecumenical phenomenon' and the sign of a new experience, that of 'the ecumenical spirit'. Congar talks about *le fait oecuménique* as something new in the 1920s. Adrian Hastings gives examples of the new phenomenon when he mentions the first contacts of Archbishop Davidson of Canterbury with Baptist leaders. We can also emphasise J.H. Oldham and John R. Mott as great examples of openness. (See Hastings' *A History of English Christianity* pp. 95–96.)

We should still see the Malines Conversations as paradigmatic, as a signpost forward and as an example of the spirit we should adopt. After 75 years, they still have a meaning for us today, even though many Christians do not yet live in this spirit. In conclusion, the significance of the group involved in the Malines Conversations is that they immersed themselves in the new ecumenical spirit and began a new chapter in church history.

We can now specify and describe **five points of principle** in the method of the Malines team that are still valuable for us today. They are: faith, hope and prayerfulness; radical intellectual honesty; a spirit of freedom; the capacity to discern and follow the signs of the times; and, finally, the promotion of serious scholarship.

   i) **Faith, Hope, Prayer.**

The main driving force behind the group was the faith and hope they received from God the Holy Spirit. Mercier had a great devotion to the Holy Spirit, whom he considered his best friend. He often preached about the Holy Spirit. He wrote a beautiful little prayer to the Spirit, which is still frequently used today in Belgium.

The friendship of Halifax and Portal, from the very beginning in 1889, was one of great spiritual depth. Both were men of great faith, hope and vision. They were prayerful. Their conversation naturally centred on deep spiritual and theological problems.

They often talked and wrote about their spiritual friendship and their mutual joy in it; they extended their friendship to include Frere, Mercier, Robinson and others. When Christians share their thoughts, experiences and visions, they receive great strength. This happened to the Malines Group. They enjoyed being together, praying together and sharing their work. Books on church history often fail to mention the Conversations; however, they were a sign of the times. Much was beginning to change, and we can see them as a key stage in a very important development.

   ii) **Radical intellectual honesty**.

Their frank and honest exchange was the first post-Reformation experiment in theological dialogue between their two churches. Over a period of five years, the two teams were able to talk frankly and responsibly, in a spirit of probity and honesty, and without any outside pressures. Most of them were great scholars, able to transcend the pettiness that sometimes characterises religious institutions. Serious scholarship was essential in such an undertaking.

Both sides prepared for the dialogue by circulating papers beforehand; both received help from other friends. On the Roman Catholic side, Dom Lambert Beauduin and Fr Aloys Janssens, professor of dogmatics at the CICM Fathers' College in Louvain, helped out. Intellectual honesty was the absolute priority for the group: Portal, Mercier and Beauduin repeatedly insisted that they wanted an objective search for the truth. St Albert the Great once wrote about 'the joy of seeking the truth together' (*Libr VIII Politicorum*). They were working in what St Paul calls the love of the truth which saves (2 Thess 2.10).

iii) Spirit of Freedom and independence of mind.

The whole group was able to work in that 'spirit of truth' to which St
John's Gospel so often refers. They showed freedom and independence
of mind, working with that kind of detachment implied in the 'spirit of
poverty' referred to in the Beatitudes. On the Roman Catholic side, this
spirit of independence and detachment owed most to Mercier as leader,
though the patristics scholar Van Roey was also important, as were
Portal, Beauduin, Janssens, and, later, Batiffol and Hemmer. (I suspect
that the Anglican approach was the same.)

Mercier was a philosopher. He had also studied psychology and
psychoanalysis with Prof. Charcot at La Salpêtrière, where he had to
wear lay dress. Mercier was wise and experienced. He had philosophical
contacts all over the world, and particularly fruitful links with the USA.

Mercier did not regard himself as a real dogmatic theologian.
However, in terms of the real sense of the word, 'knowing about God',
he certainly was one. He was an experienced preacher, professor and
writer, capable of offering penetrating observations. He fought
courageously in the First World War to defend human rights and
denounce injustice: he was a light to his people. He was always ready to
take up great causes, having the gifts both of empathy and sympathy. He
showed great talent as an encourager of students and colleagues.

The meetings of the Malines Group were characterised by great
courtesy. Particularly importantly, they could laugh and joke together.
This atmosphere permitted frankness: Mercier was able to tell Gore that
he was 'too obstinate' in his arguments with Batiffol; Gore accepted the
remark and wrote in friendly vein to Mercier after his return home to
England.

Collectively, the group showed considerable wisdom. Régis Ladous,
in his biography *Monsieur Portal et les siens* (Paris, ed. Cerf, 1985), shows
how independently minded Portal and Hemmer were. One can also trace
the connections of Portal with Fr Laberthonnière, a philosopher and
editor of the *Annales de la Philosophie Chrétienne*, and with the Société des
Etudes Réligieuses and its manifesto. Portal's aim was to 'refashion the
Church'. He was ecumenically minded and prized catholicity. Both he
and Hemmer wrote for the same journal *Revue catholique des Eglises*.
Mercier and Beauduin were on the same wavelength. Halifax was also
independently minded, prizing the idea of a 'free church'. Their
harmonious meetings bequeathed a rich heritage to the Universal Church.

iv) The Spirit of the Times. (1910–25).

These fifteen years were a 'time of grace', a *kairos*. The background to
their efforts included the campaign over Anglican Orders (1891–96), the
Edinburgh meeting, the Lambeth Appeal of 1920, and the Appeal of the
Patriarch of Constantinople in 1920. People did not forget that Leo XIII

had once shown some ecumenical leanings. There was great interest in 'catholicity' and a search for its wider realisation. (cf. Fr de Montcheuil, *Aspects de l'Eglise*, Paris, ed Cerf, Lenam Sanctam 18, 1949, ch. 5 and Fr Congar, *Chrétiens en Dialogue*, Paris, Cerf, 1964, passim.)

There was also much good in the new, modern mentality. People sensed an 'inner light' a vision welling up from within that needed to be liberated (cf Ladous, p. 175). Portal did not need to go to China; he found his challenge in his own time and place.

The concept of 'catholicity' is central to this search. It means the affirmation of 'that pluralism which by God's will is integral to history in all the manifold spheres of private and public life', and today signifies 'an interior, qualitative characteristic of the Church' (K. Rahner and H. Vorgrimler, *Concise Theological Dictionary*, Burns and Oates, London, 1965; 'Catholicity', pp. 68–69). 'Everything created by God is good, and nothing is to be rejected if it is received with thanksgiving' (1 Tim 4.4).

The search for the greater wholeness of catholicity was a characteristic of the mind of Newman and the Oxford Movement. Newman had a great desire to promote 'mutual sympathy between estranged communions and alienated hearts' (cf. J. Coulson, 'English Roman Catholics in the XVIII and XIX centuries', in *The Study of Spirituality*, ed. C. Jones, G. Wainwright and E. Yarnold, SPCK 1986, p. 429). He said his goal was not that of immediate conversion, but of changing ways of thinking (cf. W. Ward, *The Life of John Henry Cardinal Newman*, Longmans Green, 1912, Vol.II, p. 55ff): Keble and Pusey shared this vision. The Oxford Movement, with its return to catholicity, to the Church Fathers, to greater independence for the Church and to sacramental principles, paved the way for the birth of the 'ecumenical spirit'.

For Roman Catholics, ultimately, this would mean the end of the traditional spirit of proselytisation, of any simple ecclesiology of return, and of the strategy of uniatism. The ecumenical spirit meant openness and a respectful attitude towards all Christians. In this new style of what was now to be called 'ecumenism', Halifax was a good example and promoter. He was honest and trustworthy, and therefore in a position to influence both Portal and Mercier into catching this spirit. At first, Mercier and Portal had wondered whether Halifax could be converted to their church, but Halifax explained that in the new ecumenical era other considerations were at stake. Through the influence Halifax exerted on them, we can see the importance of their 'ecumenical conversion' – a real sign of the times.

Mercier was able to exercise influence through preaching and writing, especially in his famous, and widely translated Pastoral Letter of 18 January 1924. He helped Dom Beauduin and Dom Bosschaerts in the creation of two Benedictine monasteries dedicated to the work of unity.

Both monasteries encountered terrible difficulties, but finally survived. Today, Chevetogne, Schotenhof, Cockfosters and Turvey are the result of the work of persecuted pioneers. On the Anglican side, even Halifax was not taken very seriously, being seen as an unrealistic dreamer. Most of the pioneers of Malines underwent the same experience as the earliest Christians, as recorded by St Paul in the oldest document of the New Testament, 1 Thess. 1.6: they 'received the word (of God) in much affliction'. Such is often the fate of pioneers.

The influence of Mercier and the other Belgians can easily be seen. Mercier as philosopher and later bishop, influenced many, including Cardinals van Roey and Suenens and a whole group of scholars at Louvain; Thils, Philips, Moeller and Aubert. Mercier also helped in the foundation of Amay–Chevetogne. From these immediate disciples radiated influences that touched many Catholics and scholars, especially in France and Belgium.

v) Theological Work and Scholarship.

The Malines Group produced high-quality scholarship as an integral part of their search for the truth. It is worth reading the summaries of their work, edited by Halifax, and the papers written preparatory to the meetings. Two important books deal with this: John Dick's *The Malines Conversations Revisited* (Leuven UP, Peeters, 1989) and Bernard Barlow OSM, *A Brother Knocking at the Door* (Canterbury Press, 1996). Both contain full bibliographies.

Conclusion.

These pioneers were icebreakers. In one sense, they failed: they made mistakes; they faced very strong opposition; they did not live to see the fruit of their endeavours; many church histories say little about their work. But, considered from another angle, these people were like the 'wise men from the East'. They had seen the stars that would lead them on a new way. They came with new seeds to sow in the old fields. Their methods were imperfect, but the harvest came – after many years.

They were lamps on a lampstand: to some Christians they gave light. Their faith, integrity, scholarship and example have all given hope to many, and many people appreciate their achievement.

On the Roman Catholic side, forty years later, the ecumenical principle was in fact recognised at the Second Vatican Council. So today, we say, 'Keep the faith: fight the good fight!' New things spring forth: the Lord is making highways in our wilderness and rivers in our desert (cf. Isaiah 43).

(This paper is an edited version of that given at the Bristol Congress
of ESBVM in September 1996)

13

Mary – Servant of the Word:
towards convergence in ecclesiology.

David Carter

This paper has been written out of the profound conviction that there is a connection between sound Mariology and sound ecclesiology. Such an assertion has become increasingly commonplace within Catholic theological circles, but has scarcely, as yet, received any exploration within the Reformation theological traditions. The purpose of this paper is to explore the extent to which a Reformed appreciation of the Mother of God can be used to illuminate certain important emphases within Protestant ecclesiology, and yet at the same time can contribute to that ecumenical convergence in ecclesiological understanding that we all, especially in this Society, so much desire.

Central, of course to Protestant theology is the theology of the Living Word of God, uttered in Jesus Christ. The same Risen Christ still addresses his Church in the reading of Scripture, in the word of preaching, and in the rightful 'dividing of the Word of God' in fellowship. It is perhaps strange that Protestant theologians have not given more emphasis to Mary as Servant of the Word, a title that I would propose for reception amongst Protestants who wish to show due respect for Mary in a manner that is entirely warranted by biblical witness. When we first meet Mary in Scripture, it is at the point at which she responds to the angel at the Annunciation, 'Be it to me according to your Word', which is of course, the direct message and Word of God. I have a vivid memory of one Protestant sermon that explored this theme very powerfully. It was preached in the extremely austere French Reformed church in Auxerre in France. I was fifteen at the time and in France on an exchange. Needless to say, I did not follow all the sermon, but I caught enough to realise that it was a powerful and eloquent tribute to the humility and obedience of the Servant of the Word.

Mary, at the Annunciation, shows her attentiveness to, her receptiveness of, and her obedience to the divine Word that comes to her. She manifests her continuity with the prophets of the Old Covenant that come before her and the saints of the New Covenant who are to come after her, and who will find in her obedience a pattern for their own obedience. Mary, of course, is chosen for a special vocation, as Mother of the Incarnate Lord. She is to be responsible for the upbringing of the Word made flesh. She is given, as we are all given, the grace necessary for the particular tasks to which the Lord calls us. In that respect, the 'terms', as it were, of Mary's vocation are analogous to those of every subsequent Christian and her experience is paradigmatic for them; hence her continuing and abiding significance for individual and corporate Christian discipleship. We are all called to receive and assimilate the Word of God. We are all promised the indwelling presence of Christ and his Father. Christ says, 'If a man loves me and obeys my words, my Father and I will come and make our home with him' (John 14.23). St Paul talks of the way in which his apostolic ministry engenders the formation of Christ within his converts, and he talks of himself as 'being in travail until Christ is formed in you' (Galatians 4.19). It is the vocation of every Christian, in a mystical sense, to give birth to the Christ in him or her, the Christ who is waiting to enter their lives in order that he may now serve and love and witness through them. It is part of the mystery of God's love that he entrusts himself to human beings in this way, first to Mary, then, in differing ways, to the rest of his people.

It is, perhaps, in this context that we should examine the Scriptural 'balance' of teaching about Mary. Scripture implicitly warns against making too much or too little of her; it could be argued that it testifies both against Protestant tendencies to ignore her and tendencies in popular Catholic or Orthodox piety to overexalt her. John Newton, in his recent ecumenical autobiography, *Heart Speaks to Heart*, records Raymond George's view that if 'the silence in Methodism concerning the mother of God is deafening', this is because the silence of the New Testament is similarly deafening.[1] With the greatest of respect to Mr George, to whom I, in common with all other British Methodist ecumenists of a younger generation owe so much, I cannot agree. Scripture certainly says little about Mary in terms of sheer numbers of words, but that little is highly significant, as I think modern biblical scholars have shown. What Scripture does, I believe, enable us to do is to locate our Lady carefully as model disciple and exemplar within the total Communion of Saints that follows in her way. Scripture carefully safeguards Mary's importance while ensuring that she is not distanced so far ahead of us, as it were, that we cannot meaningfully relate to her example.

Scripture records Mary's affirmation that 'from henceforth all generations shall call me blessed', (Luke 1.48), but, equally, it records our Lord's warning that Mary is not primarily to be esteemed because she was his physical mother, but rather because she is obedient to the divine will. Thus, 'whoever does God's will, the same is my mother, my brother and my sister' (Mark 3.35). This is not, as might seem at first glance, a 'diminishment' of Mary *per se*; her esteem in the eyes of God and his Church is safeguarded by the fact that she is the pre-eminent doer of the will of God, and this, as we shall see, despite her own questioning and need for growth in understanding. It does remind us that no over-great gulf should be established between Mary and the rest of the faithful. This is a point that a protestant Marian ecclesiology would wish to emphasise. We, too, are called to faithful service of Christ, in which Mary is the first great exemplar.

Obedience to the Word of God was at the centre of Mary's life. We see it at the Annunciation, at the marriage feast at Cana, ('Do whatever he tells you'), and especially in Mary's own devotional life ('And Mary kept all these words in her heart and pondered on them'). The Reformation was faithful to the Marian tradition in making the Word of God the centre of all theological contemplation, and obedience to that Word the criterion of right Christian action. The Reformation should have led to a renewal of authentic Marian piety within the Church, instead of which it led to a sad neglect of her, as the second generation of Reformers took an attitude far more negative than that of their first-generation predecessors.

The Mary who responds to the call of God at the Annunciation should have been for our ancestors, Catholic and Protestant, of the sixteenth century, an inspiration for a reconciling theology and ecclesiology that transcended while including the insights of Reformers and Catholic reformers alike. For it is my belief that there is a 'Protestant' Mary and a 'Catholic' Mary, so to speak. They are not of course two persons, but one pre-eminent disciple, through contemplation of whom 'Protestant' and 'Catholic' insights can be reconciled.

The 'Protestant' Mary, so to speak, hears and obeys the word of grace. She is constituted in her vocation. Her response testifies to the correctness of the Reformation principle of *'sola dei gratia'*. She, granted great grace, points to the action of God in 'regarding the lowliness of his handmaiden'. There is no assertion of her own merit, only wonder at the mighty work of God. This sense of wonder at the totally undeserved grace of God is at the heart of Protestant spirituality and devotion. Isaac Watts, writing of the saints around the throne of God, sings,

> I ask them whence their victory came;
> They, with united breath,
> Ascribe their conquest to the Lamb,
> Their triumph to His death.[2]

The sense of the utterly continuous dependence of the soul on divine grace was at the centre of Wesleyan spirituality. This can be seen in one of Wesley's great hymns on justification and sanctification, now, alas, rarely sung, with its refrain,

> I the chief of sinners am,
> But Jesus died for me.

Significantly, it ends with this verse:

> Jesus, Thou for me hast died,
> And Thou in me shalt live.
> I shall feel Thy death applied,
> I shall Thy life receive;
> Yet, when melted in the flame
> Of love, this shall be all my plea,
> I the chief of sinners am,
> But Jesus died for me.[3]

On the other hand, the Mary who is going to be venerated in Catholic and Orthodox tradition also shows awareness of the significance that her response and life will have, in the providence of God, in the future Communion of Saints of her Son. All generations will call her blessed, and will see in the following of her example the way to bliss. As Charles Wesley puts it in a greatly loved hymn,

> All who read or hear are blessed,
> If Thy plain commands we do.[4]

The hymn, of course refers to the reading of Scripture, but behind the obedient reading of the later Christian and the immediate response of Mary lies the same glad response to the saving Word.

These truths are reinforced as we consider another Marian passage, the concluding verse of the Lukan story of the visit to the Temple. 'And Mary kept all these things in her heart and pondered them'. (Luke 2.51).

Traditional Catholic and Orthodox thought sees in this action of Mary's a foreshadowing of the whole process of tradition in the Church, a process that was defined in the Constitution *Dei Verbum* of Vatican II in these words: 'The Church is always advancing towards the plenitude of divine truth, until, eventually, the words of God are fulfilled in her.' (*Dei Verbum* 8).

Such teaching coheres well with the Johannine promises about the guidance of the Spirit and Paul's grand vision of the developing maturity of the Church in Ephesians 4. It is interesting also in this connection to notice Benjamin Gregory's statement that 'the ideal of the Church was not fully realised in the apostolic times, but is to be realised before the completion of the Church's history'.[5] However, a Reformed reception of this teaching would want to emphasise an aspect of it which could get obscured in the ecclesiology of the pre-Vatican II era. Both Mary's spiritual development, and that of the Church subsequently, take place amidst crisis, struggle, and faithful striving for further understanding. Such were the conditions of Mary's personal pilgrimage and such have been those of the later Pilgrim People of God. They are clearly illustrated within the very story of the visit to the Temple. Mary did not understand her Son's behaviour on that occasion; indeed, she upbraided him for it in no uncertain terms. She had later to ponder what had happened in an attempt to reach a deeper understanding of her Son's vocation and what exactly it entailed. She had to bend her mind and heart in long and prayerful reflection on the words of her Son and the words of Scripture. She had to wrestle for understanding, and seek to set aside preconceived notions. Such processes are involved in all Christian discipleship. It is a constant re-submission of oneself to the word of God in order that the Word may eventually be fulfilled in oneself in all its glory. It involves not just an application of scriptural truth to new situations and problems, but a constant revisiting of scriptural truth in order that the whole of a Christian's life, the whole, indeed, of the Church's life, may be tested and refined in the light of scriptural witness to the 'truth once for all delivered to the saints' (Jude 3). The nature and effect of the guarding in the heart and pondering can be illustrated from Charles Wesley's famous hymn on Scripture,

> When quiet in my house I sit,
> Thy book be my companion still,
> My joy Thy sayings to repeat,
> Talk o'er the records of Thy will,
> And search the oracles divine,
> Till every heartfelt word be mine.[6]

Bishop Klaiber of Germany, in a recent article, explores this Protestant understanding of the constant, creative revisiting of Scripture.[7]

Mary, in her pondering and guarding, sets a model for future disciples, the nature of which is so well described by Wesley. Every Christian is called to be a bearer of the word, a 'Christopher', and so to walk after the example of her who was privileged both to be the bearer of the flesh of the Son of God, and the first bearer within her heart of his words. Mary's transparent and wholehearted reception of the Word is eloquent commentary on the Reformation principle of the sole sufficiency of Scripture. 'O, let me be alone *homo unius libri'*, said Wesley, echoing the Anglican article, 'Holy Scripture containeth all things necessary to salvation'.[8] A Protestant Marian ecclesiology safeguards both the true Catholic emphasis on Mary, model first disciple in the Church, and the Protestant emphasis on the sufficiency of Scripture as the fount and inspiration of true tradition.

The significance of Mary for reformed ecclesiology can best be seen in a contemplation of the scene at the foot of the cross, where Christ commends his mother to John, the Beloved Disciple, and John to his mother. Many modern biblical theologians treat this as the Johannine account of the institution of the Church, which they see as founded, in the Evangelist's understanding, not at Easter or Pentecost, but at the foot of the cross. Several things happen almost simultaneously at the time of the death of the Lord, and they all have profound implications for ecclesiology. Firstly, the Lord commends to the care of each other the two who have been closest to him, his mother and the Beloved Disciple. Then, he cries out that 'It is finished'. His work, consummated in his perfect self-offering on the cross, is now over, and the last act of that work has been the constitution of the fellowship of his Church in the persons of the mother who bore him, and of his most loyal disciple. He then breathes out the Spirit upon them to empower and sustain their fellowship. There is, of course, a later Johannine breathing out of the Spirit recorded at Easter when the apostolic band is empowered for ministry (John 20.21–23), and there is also the later pouring out of the Spirit on all the assembled believers at Pentecost, as recorded in the Lukan writings. But whatever additional strength they may impart to the Church and its leaders, it is quite clear that, for the writer of the Fourth Gospel, Christ first breathes out his spirit for Mary and John as representative of his Church. Finally, water and blood come forth from the side of the Lord, and there is no reason to believe that they are recorded other than because they are symbols of the sacramental life of the Church.

It is interesting to note that, according to John, the Church is first constituted as a fellowship of those who are by the side of Christ, and representative of the many later twos and threes to whom his presence is promised (Matthew 18.20). It is only later that he talks of the institution of the apostolic band (John 20.23) and of a Petrine ministry (John 21.15ff). Neither the Beloved Disciple nor the Mother of the Lord are later referred to as performing any ministry of leadership in the church. They are presented here as faithful laypersons ministering to each other the things that they have drawn from their closeness to Christ. Mary, of course, according to Luke, also appears in the upper room in Acts (1.14), again as model layperson awaiting the coming of the Spirit. The Beloved Disciple is, of course, in later tradition, identified with John the Apostle, but, be that as it may, at this stage he is seen as model disciple rather than leader. The evangelist appears to make the Church as 'family of Jesus', as hearers and doers of the Word, take precedence over the constitution of the apostolate which is created subsequently in order to serve the *koinonia* already established. This coheres very strongly with Lutheran and Wesleyan ecclesiology, both of which see ministry as arising within the existing body of the Church in order to serve the Word rather than as pre-existing it.[9]

Let us now examine and defend these points in the context of a more detailed examination of Johannine theology. Biblical theologians have, in recent years, taken considerable interest in the ecclesiological significance of the Johannine literature. Many have argued that its ecclesiology is that of a gathered church without any distinctive pattern of ministry. All alike in the 'Johannine' church were brothers and sisters, equal disciples, all possessed of the 'anointing' of the Spirit which preserves them in apostolic truth and practice (1 John 2.20), and renders unnecessary a *'magisterium'* in the later 'catholic' sense.

The situation is, however, more complex than that. It is true that there is no mention of eldership or other specific church offices in John, such as one finds in many other places in the New Testament, nor indeed is there the strong emphasis on the disciplinary function of the Church that appears in Matthew. There is, however, in John 21 a clear reference to the establishment of a pastoral 'Petrine' ministry. Some scholars believe that this chapter was added later. Raymond Brown, the American biblical scholar, makes the ingenious suggestion that the addition was made at a point when an originally isolated Johannine church, which had previously lacked ministerial structures, became linked with the wider apostolic church, as the result of an early and apparently successful ecumenical initiative.[10]

That is as maybe. I am certainly not competent to judge the truth of Prof. Brown's ingenious reconstruction. However, I think it suggestive for ecumenical dialogue that the Gospel, as we now have it, sets side by side an account of the foundation of the Church which makes no reference to a ministerial order, and an account of the subsequent creation of a pastoral ministry, which, however, contains interwoven within it an emphasis on the lay 'soul' of the Church. The relationship of Peter, the leader, and the mysterious 'Beloved Disciple' is instructive.

The 'Beloved Disciple' is an intriguing character. He appears five times in the Gospel. Some modern scholars believe he is an idealised character, representing for the 'Johannine' church a model of discipleship that should guide it. He was so close to the Lord that he set an example in spiritual leadership and insight, but not in pastoral ministry or leadership in mission. He is shown first as leaning on the Lord's breast at the Last Supper, a sign of the deep intimacy he enjoyed with Christ

(John 13.23). His role at the Resurrection is especially instructive: he outruns Peter to the tomb (John 20.4). Whether or not this statement preserves a genuine historical reminiscence we cannot now tell, but it is very probable that in it the evangelist sees profound theological significance. John, the model disciple, moves more rapidly in apprehending the truth than Peter, the spokesman of the Twelve and future leader of the Church. He defers to the latter, and Peter enters the tomb first, but fails to draw any clear conclusion from what he sees. John, however, 'saw and believed', the only person to do so in advance of seeing the risen Lord (all the other witnesses in the New Testament believe only after seeing him). The Beloved Disciple is the model disciple and layman. He is without apparent office or special charism in the Church, yet his closeness to the Lord allows him to be first to perceive. It is surely on the basis of the Church's experience of many subsequent 'Johns' following in this tradition, that the later doctrine of the *consensus fidelium* emerges. It is to its 'Johns' that the Church looks for the experimental verification of its faith, and it is only on this 'true experimental religion' that the *magisterium* can erect its dogmatic teaching. It is the Johns of the Church who communicate the true experiential faith within the fellowship. As Charles Wesley teaches,

> The gift which He on one bestows,
> We all delight to prove.[11]

The public articulation of their faith is one of the most vital functions of laypeople in the Church. James Rigg, a great nineteenth-century Wesleyan ecclesiologist, had a high doctrine of the 'Pastoral Office', but, at the same time, he insisted that lay preaching was a key sign of the vitality of the Church.

However, if the Beloved Disciple has great significance in the Johannine understanding of the Christian life, so also does Mary. One Beloved Disciple, in isolation, cannot make a Church, but he and Mary together make the first Church as directly constituted by Christ. Moreover, their relationship may be said, for the evangelist, to represent the model, paradigmatic church, the ideal into which all Christian communities are called to grow.

Interpretations of the exact meaning of the scene at the foot of the cross are legion, and I do not intend to examine them all. At one extreme of interpretation is the view that Jesus was doing no more than to provide for the welfare of his Mother, and maybe, also, his closest friend; in their grief and loneliness they would both need support. Even this interpretation has an ecclesiological significance. Mutual bearing of burdens is at the core of corporate Christian discipleship. But it is unlikely that John, whose work is so packed with symbolism, would have seen the significance of this scene as exhausted by such an interpretation. Very early on in tradition explanations developed which saw Mary as representing the Jewish church, and the Beloved Disciple as representing the Gentile church, now entrusted to each others' fellowship. A little later, Ephrem and Ambrose saw Mary as representing the Church, which, like the symbolic figure of Lady Zion in the Old Testament, brings forth children of whom the first, by adoption, is the Beloved Disciple. Much later comes teaching on the spiritual motherhood of Mary.[12]

I would certainly not reject any of these interpretations, but I would want to add another which I believe to be consistent with the insights of reformed ecclesiology. Mary, like the Beloved Disciple, represents the type of the true disciple. Indeed, it would be possible to say that she represents it more clearly than the elusive figure of the Beloved Disciple. In the story of the marriage feast at Cana, Mary is shown as faithfully expectant that Jesus can work a great miracle that will reveal his messianic status. Jesus, at first, seems to 'fend off' her request on the grounds that his 'hour has not yet come'. Yet such is Mary's trust in him that she expresses, puzzled as she is, her total faith in Christ. 'Do whatever he tells you.' This is the Johannine equivalent of the Lukan 'How can these things be?' followed by 'Be it unto me according to thy Word'. Mary is the type of the faithful, questioning, puzzled pilgrim, who yet trusts totally in the Lord. She has learnt obedience to her Son. Of the Beloved Disciple's pilgrimage we can tell nothing; we know only that he displays extraordinary insight at the empty tomb and that he is privileged to be especially close to the Lord.

In both Mary and John, faith, love and obedience all meet in one response of adoring love to the Saviour. It is probably fanciful to think that Wesley had them especially in mind when he wrote of 'faith that sweetly works by love' yet in their relationship with the Saviour we can see something that renders totally redundant all the sterile reformation controversies about faith and works. There is no faith divorced from love; equally, there is no 'works righteousness'. They both know, 'You have not chosen me, I have chosen you'(John 15.16) and that the only possible response is that of total, adoring love, the glad obedience of free sons and daughters in the Son.

Mary and the Beloved Disciple are entrusted to each other. This, I think, has a vital ecclesiological bearing. Though, certainly, Mary can be seen as a symbol of the Church, the fact that she is entrusted to John is important. The Beloved Disciple has the 'anointing' by which he knows all things, i.e. all things that are necessary to the true well-being of the Church, and it is his duty to care not just for Mary the individual, but for

Mary the Church. Every true follower of Christ bears this responsibility. By our life and our actions, both within the fellowship and in the world, we can help to make the Church, to which we claim allegiance, appear more, or less, credible. The responsibility for the fellowship as such has been particularly well understood within the independent tradition, where the responsibility of every member for the Church has been solemnly expressed in the duty of attendance at the regular church meeting.

It is significant that so much recent ecclesiological discussion has centred on the nature of the local church, the most intense and concrete expression, so to speak, of ecclesial reality, which is paradoxically both complete in itself and yet only fulfilled in total *koinonia* with the rest of the Church across the ages. There are of course different theories as to what exactly constitutes a 'local' church. It is interesting to note that in all traditions it is always a pastoral unit, whether it be, as in Catholic or Orthodox tradition, the diocese as community gathered around its episcopal pastor, or independent congregation gathered around its elected pastor, or Methodist class meeting gathered around its leader. Both the 'independent' concept of the local church and the Methodist class meeting have something vital to say to us here. They represent a particularly sharp focusing of the local church, such as is not easily expressed in a 'catholic' diocese of traditional dimensions.

To return to Mary and John at the foot of the cross: I see them as constituting, in conformity with Christ's promise that 'where two or three are gathered together in my name, there am I'(Matthew 18.20), the first 'local' church, model for every subsequent local church. They are there committed utterly to each other, to care for and to serve each other, and to journey onwards in the Saviour's love. As Charles Wesley puts it,

> Hast Thou not made us one,
> That we might one remain?
> Together travel on
> And bear each other's pain,
> Till all Thy utmost goodness prove,
> And rise renewed in perfect love.' [13]

They are committed at the foot of the cross as the first of all those whom Christ will 'draw to himself' (John 12.32). They stand there as the first members of the Church, the original witnesses of the saving event which constitutes the foundation of the Church Universal. Christ bows his head towards them and breathes out the Spirit which is to join them as one and keep them and all later Christians in fellowship. He cries, 'It is finished' in acknowledgement that the first fruits of his sacrifice have appeared in the founding of his Church and its equipping with the Spirit. John sees the creation of the fellowship as immediately followed by the gift of the Spirit and the sacraments. Everything that is later to characterize the inner worshipping life of the Church is a recapitulation of these events. The Church is constantly sustained by the Spirit. The fellowship of the Church is expressed, strengthened and renewed in the sacramental life of the Church. Charles Wesley puts this well in his hymn, 'See Jesu, Thy disciples see', with its lines,

> Whom now we seek, O may we meet,
> Jesus the crucified

and the clear sacramental reference,

> Cause us the record to receive,
> Speak and the tokens show.[14]

Raymond Brown emphasises the revelatory nature of Christ's committal of Mary and John to each other. 'Here is your son', 'Here is your Mother'. Max Thurian emphasises the way in which they are addressed. Jesus calls Mary not 'mother', but 'woman' because she is now the representative figure in the Church for all time, and no longer just his physical mother The Beloved Disciple is also a representative person.[15] The cross, as Charles Wesley teaches, reveals the full deity of Jesus.

> Faith cries out 'tis he, 'tis he,
> My God that suffers there.[16]

At the same time as the full significance of Christ is revealed, so also is the position of Mary and John as the first members of the Church. Into the pattern of their paradigmatic fellowship, later local churches are called to mature. It is of this model fellowship that Paul talks when he speaks of creation groaning as it awaits the 'revelation of the sons of God' (Romans 8.19). Later on, when the writer to the Ephesians speaks of the eschatological perfection of the Church (Eph. 5.27) he may well have the scene at the foot of the cross in mind. The eschatological perfection of the Church will occur when the full number of the elect is gathered in like mystical fellowship around the cross.

Finally, in connection with this, it is instructive to look at the exact Greek text of the famous final phrase of this passage, 'And thenceforth he took her into his own home' – '*elaben autēn ho mathētēs eis ta idia*'.

The Belgian theologian, Ignace de la Potterie, reminds us that these words imply not just a domestic but a new spiritual relationship. The word *'elaben'* is the past tense of the Greek word 'receive', a word which, in the New Testament, implies close Christian fellowship. It is the word that Paul uses when he commends the reception of Christians from one church to another. It is the word that Jesus uses when he says, 'He who receives me, receives the one who sent me'. In modern ecumenical thought, the concept of reception indicates the assimilation, at a deep level, of the spiritual insights of one Christian church by another, a process that enriches the receiving church without in any way derogating from its own authentic tradition. It is instructive here to remember those patristic texts that see the joining of Mary and John as symbolic of the fellowship of the gentile and Jewish churches. We can see the process of reception as ultimately rooted in the reception of Mary and John by each other in the fellowship of the first 'local' church, where they learnt to receive each other's insight and wisdom in spiritual matters. De la Potterie also emphasises the importance of the phrase *'eis ta idia'* 'to his own', which is, of course used in John 1.4, 'He came to his own' and in John 10.3, where the Good Shepherd is said to 'know his own'. Again, a relationship of great depth and intimacy is implied. [17]

So, in this scene we see the Church constituted as an intimate mutual fellowship. It is constituted by two laypeople, since whatever role the Beloved Disciple may subsequently have played, he is presented here simply as model disciple. We recognise here a complete local church, without as yet any hierarchical ministry, but with a ministry of mutual love and care. According to Johannine theology, at least in this pericope, the mutual caring ministry of laypeople is the first element of the Church to be constituted. However, I am not going to argue from this, as perhaps Quakers or Plymouth Brethren might, that the Church needs no further ministry or structure. John himself goes on in chapter 21 to give his account of the institution of a pastoral Petrine ministry. A ministry of pioneering evangelism and connection of the local churches is vital to the life of the Universal Church, and its development is recorded in later Scripture and tradition.

As a Methodist, I see the pattern that I have claimed as the Johannine one, exemplified, at least in part, in the development of the Methodist revival. The great nineteenth-century Wesleyan theologian, James Rigg, argued that Methodism represented not just a revival of primitive doctrine but also of primitive fellowship. He and other Wesleyans argued that central to authentic Christian community was provision for intimate Christian fellowship through means analogous to those provided in the Methodist class meeting. Wesleyan ecclesiologists argued that such groups were a recurrent feature of the Church during periods of revival from apostolic times down to their own. They did not argue that the class meeting as they knew it was necessarily the best embodiment of such a principle for all time, but they did argue that the Church neglected to provide for something like it at its peril.[18] One can see the class meeting as one of the concrete embodiments resulting from the preaching of the Word. The preached Word leads to the gathering of the people of God. In sacramental life and in class meeting alike, the Word takes root in their lives, effecting a real transformation, such as is spoken of in para 8 of the Vatican II Decree, *Dei Verbum*.

It is worth recording the fact that many of the class leaders of Methodism were women, often subsequently referred to in their obituaries as 'true mothers in Israel'. At a time when the question of women's ministry is being so vigorously debated in the Church, we might find it helpful to reflect on this and to think of Christ saying to them, as he did to Mary, 'Woman, behold your children'. Although they would never have put it this way, we could claim that such women had been configured by the grace of the Spirit to the example of Mary.

My final point is this: to challenge all Christians, Protestant, Catholic and Orthodox, to see in each others' local churches and fellowships the authentic face of the Marian local church, established at the foot of the cross, a paradigm for all later local churches, and to plead for recognition and reception at this level. So often in ecumenism, we have begun with questions of ministry; increasingly, however, it is being emphasised that ecclesial recognition must precede ministerial recognition. I think that when we can recognise the mystery of the Marian local church in each others' communities, then we will be led to a consensus at to what forms of ministry of connection are necessary to link our churches in full and authentic communion. I conclude with a quotation from the Russian Orthodox response to *Baptism, Eucharist and Ministry*, quoted in an article by Dr Anton Houtepen,

> The fundamental ecclesiological problem of unity lies not in an 'ecumenical' recognition of ministry, but in a recognition of the Church in which this ministry is exercised as a 'true Church' confessing the faith of the apostles. This is the essential sign and a prerequisite for the visible unity or restoration of the unity of the Church.[19]

Notes

1   Newton, J.A., *Heart Speaks to Heart*, 1994, p. 87. For an account of the growth
    of Marian devotion in modern British Methodism, see ibid. pp. 85ff.
2   *Hymns and Psalms, a Methodist and Ecumenical Hymn Book*, 1983. 815 v. 3.
3   *Wesley's Hymns*, 1877 edition, 115 v. 3.
4   *Methodist Hymn Book*, 1933 edition, 306, v. 2.
5   Gregory, B., *The Holy Catholic Church*, 1873, p. 17.
6   *Methodist Hymn Book*, op. cit. 310 v. 1.
7   Klaiber, W., 'Interpretation and Development; Consequences and Expressions
    of the Dynamism of Revelation', *One in Christ*, 1994, 2, pp. 152–60.
8   See Articles of Religion No 6 in the Book of Common Prayer.
9   For a good statement of the classical Wesleyan view see Rigg. J.H., *The
    Connexional Economy of Wesleyan Methodism*, 1879, especially pp. 1–23.
    Lutheran systems of ministerial order vary, but are all supposed to subserve
    the transmission of the Word. See also *Sharing in the Apostolic Communion*,
    Interim report of the Anglican–Methodist International Commission, paras
    41–43.
10 For a full account of this thesis see Brown, Raymond, *The Community of the
    Beloved Disciple*, 1979.
11 *Hymns and Psalms*, op. cit. 753, v. 1.
12 For a full range of views see Brown, R. *The Gospel according to St John*, 1982
    edition, pp. 922–27, and de la Potterie, I. *The Hour of Jesus* (English
    translation), 1989, pp. 132–51.
13 *Hymns and Psalms*, op. cit. 374 v. 3.
14 *Hymns and Psalms*, op. cit. 763, vv. 4, 5.
15 Thurian, Max, *Mary, Mother of the Lord, Figure of the Church* (English
    translation), 1963, pp. 145–52.
16 *Methodist Hymn Book*, op. cit. 191, v. 3.
17 De la Potterie, op. cit. pp. 146–51.
18 Rigg, J.H. *Principles of Church Organisation*, 1897, 3rd edition, pp. 11–12;
    Gregory, op. cit. pp. 239ff.
19 *One in Christ* Vol. 25, 1989, p. 219.

*(This paper was given at the ESBVM Congress
at Norwich in July 1994)*

14

Mary, Mother of the Lord
sign of grace, faith and holiness

John Newton

I have recently been reading Shirley Du Boulay's biography of Archbishop Desmond Tutu, that outstanding South African Christian leader. When Desmond was Chaplain at Port Hare University, in Cape Province, he once faced an awkward moment in an inter-denominational student meeting. His biographer describes the incident as follows:

> He once defused a potentially explosive situation when one of the Methodist students objected to invoking the name of the Virgin Mary – a tactless remark in this non-denominational setting. The ensuing silence was broken by a laugh from Tutu: 'You've done away with the whole theory of intercession!'
>
> (Shirley Du Boulay, *Tutu, Voice of the Voiceless*, p. 74)

In other words, in the economy of grace, and in the communion of the faithful on earth and in heaven, we can and do pray for one another; and Mary, far from being excluded from that communion, holds a key place within it.

What that incident also shows is that, even in South Africa, Methodists have been reluctant sometimes to speak of Mary, the Mother of the Lord, and to acknowledge her significance in the life of faith. (I say, 'Even in South Africa ...', because African Christians usually have a strong sense of the Communion of Saints, on earth and in heaven.) But I think that there are signs that Methodist attitudes may be beginning to change. There is a growing awareness of Mary, and less of the crass ignorance about her, as exemplified in the no doubt apocryphal conversation between two Methodists who had just heard a lecture on Christianity and Judaism. They had learnt things they never knew before. After the lecture, one said to the other, 'I didn't know Jesus was a Jew, did you?' 'No', replied the other, 'And isn't it surprising, when you remember his Mother was a Roman Catholic?'

I turn now to the Joint Statement which Methodists and Catholics have recently produced, entitled *Mary, Mother of the Lord: sign of grace, faith and holiness: Towards a shared understanding*. It is a modest document, which does not claim to resolve all differences, and which is written in a most eirenical spirit. Notice the phrase used in the title to describe

Mary. She is a 'sign of grace, faith and holiness'. Each of those three words has a particularly strong resonance within the Methodist tradition, and they provide a most helpful approach for Methodists who want to enter into a deeper understanding of our Lady.

The Statement was published in 1995 jointly by the Methodist Publishing House and the Catholic Truth Society, both of whom, until recently, would probably have found the idea of such joint publication quite anathema. The document, though short – a mere 18 pages – represents a great deal of work. It is the fruit of sustained dialogue and shared study by the members of the British Methodist–Roman Catholic Committee. In a joint Foreword, the two Co-Chairmen, the Revd Dr Richard Jones and Bishop Leo McCartie, express the hope and prayer that we may 'all be inspired by the example of the Mother of our Lord to continue our pilgrimage in discerning and responding to God's will for our Churches'. They also quote a key sentence from the Statement, expressing the conviction that 'It is above all in her personal pilgrimage of faith that Mary is a model for us all'.

Mary is certainly an exemplar of faith and a model of discipleship for each of us in our own Christian pilgrimage. She responds to God's call and offer of grace with complete trust and openness. Her matchless *fiat*, 'Be it unto me according to your word' is a simple, but profound Yes to all that God wills for her. That is the response that every Christian is called to make to God's gracious will, however far short of it we may fall in practice. But Mary is also a pattern of pilgrimage for our churches, as they seek to respond to God's call to fuller unity and deeper mutual understanding.

The Joint Statement is inevitably an interim one. It records honest differences in understanding, and acknowledges areas where we cannot yet register agreement. Yet it is also remarkably positive and conciliatory. It finds common ground in Scripture and the basic Christian Tradition which we share.

It also explores the theology of the Wesleys, in a search for insights which may help Methodists to deepen their understanding and appreciation of Mary, the Mother of the Lord. I think that shows a considerable sensitivity on the part of the Catholic members of the Joint Committee. The truth is that in this area of Marian theology and devotion, Methodists have a great deal to learn. Some leading Methodists have, of course, written with considerable understanding about our Lady: Neville Ward, of blessed memory; Gordon Wakefield; Norman Wallwork; and others. But for most Methodists, it has to be said, Mary does not bulk large in their grasp of the Christian scheme of things. For a minority of Methodists, I suspect, there may be resentment or suspicion of Marian teaching. For the great majority of the Methodist people, however, I do not think it is a matter of being against Mary. It is rather that she has tended to remain marginal to their Christian thought and devotion.

At Christmas and Epiphany, of course, Methodists commemorate Mary. They will say or sing from time to time Mary's Song, Magnificat. They will acknowledge in the Creed that the Lord Jesus was 'born of the Virgin Mary'. In the Eucharistic prayers of the Methodist Service Book, Methodists will give thanks 'For the gift of your Son, Jesus Christ our Lord, for his lowly birth of Mary ...' Yet Mary's place in the whole scheme of salvation, in worship and devotion, is rarely explored in any depth. I have myself often preached on Mary – in Advent, at Christmas, or on Mothering Sunday – but I suspect that, in many Methodist churches, it would be a very rare thing to hear a sermon on our Lady. So I would say to Catholics, 'Be patient with us; be understanding; we have a lot to learn and a long way to go; don't expect us to run before we can walk.'

I turn now to the detailed contents of the Statement. It begins by mentioning the fact that the Ecumenical Society of the Blessed Virgin Mary includes both Methodists and Roman Catholics in its membership, and that is encouraging, because it suggests that sharing in this area of Christian devotion and theology is not confined to scholars, but reaches out across the membership of the two churches. The Statement sees Mary – as the one who cooperates with God in his saving purpose, and in bearing Christ – as a sign of what the Church is meant to do and to be.

> Mary, humble handmaid of the Lord, and yet by God's own election and grace the human mother of our one Lord and Saviour, Jesus Christ, is more widely accepted as a powerful sign or 'icon' of all that we are and can become as the people of God, the Church of Christ.
>
> (*Statement*, p. 3 para. 1)

Like Mary, the Church is called to cooperate with God in his saving purpose for the world, and to bring Christ to birth in the hearts and lives of men and women.

The Introduction then goes on to recognize, quite frankly, the honest differences that exist between Methodists and Catholics in this whole area of theology:

> We acknowledge ... that whereas Catholics affirm the Marian doctrines as part of the development of doctrine, these doctrines are not found in the Methodist tradition, and Methodists in general have not discussed such questions in any great depth. Facing the issues involved is part of the ecumenical challenge.
>
> (*Statement*, p. 3, para. 1)

That is well said, because any Christian unity worthy of the name has to be unity in truth and holiness. We have to face our differences, as this

Statement tries to do. It makes a huge difference, however, whether we approach the sticking points from an embattled position of convinced self-righteousness, or from one of openness to new truth and fuller understanding. It is a sound ecumenical principle that we should try to approach important differences of doctrine from the perspective of the large amount of Christian truth we already hold in common. That is the perspective of John Wesley's celebrated *Letter to a Roman Catholic*, which he published in 1749. Moreover, it is helpful, wherever possible, to try to get behind controversial language in expressions of our belief, and to avoid phrases which come loaded with echoes of 'old, unhappy far-off things, and battles long ago'. It requires effort, of course, but it is part of the essential courtesy of ecumenical dialogue.

The Statement attempts this kind of eirenical approach, for example, in relation to some of the titles given to Mary in traditional Catholic piety: Mother of God, Queen of Heaven, Co-Redemptrix. Now to Methodist ears a title like Co-Redemptrix seems to call in question the unique work of Christ as Saviour and Redeemer. Admittedly, the report states unequivocally:

> We reject any understanding of Mary which detracts from the primacy of God, of Christ and of grace, or which undermines our common Christian faith in Jesus Christ as the one Mediator between God and humanity.

The text then refers to the First Letter to Timothy 2.5–6, with its classic affirmation, 'For there is one God, and there is one mediator between God and men, the man Christ Jesus'. (RSV Catholic Version). At this point, the report might well have quoted the Second Vatican Council's *Lumen Gentium*, the Dogmatic Constitution on the Church:

> The Blessed Virgin and the Church:
>
> We have but one Mediator, as we know from the words of the Apostle: 'For there is one God, and one Mediator between God and men, himself man, Christ Jesus, who gave himself a ransom for all' (1 Tim. 2. 5–6). The maternal duty of Mary toward men in no way obscures or diminishes this unique mediation of Christ, but rather shows its power. For all the saving influences of the Blessed Virgin on men originate, not from some inner necessity, but from the divine pleasure. They flow forth from the superabundance of the merits of Christ, rest on His mediation, depend entirely on it, and draw all their power from it. In no way do they impede the immediate union of the faithful with Christ. Rather, they foster this union.
>
> (W.M. Abbott, ed., *The Documents of Vatican II* (1972), pp. 90–91)

I may seem to be labouring the point, but those words are music to Methodist ears, which have been accustomed to hearing classical

Christian doctrine in the words of Charles Wesley's hymns. The Roman Catholic journalist, Clifford Longley, once defined classical Methodism as 'A choir formed by John Wesley, to sing the hymns of Charles, and to live accordingly'. Methodists sing their faith. So, if they hear Mary described, quite simply and baldly, as 'Co-Redemptrix', they tend to become very concerned for the 'Crown rights of the Redeemer'. They hear an echo in their hearts of Charles's hymns, with lines like:

> Jesus – the name high over all,
> In hell, or earth, or sky!
> Angels and men before it fall
> And devils fear and fly.
>
> (*Hymns & Psalms* 264 v.1)

Or,

> Jesus, lover of my soul ...
> ... Other refuge have I none,
> Hangs my helpless soul on thee ...
> ... Thou, O Christ, art all I want;
> More than all in thee I find ...
>
> (*H. & Pss* 528, vv.1–3)

Or,

> Jesus the good Shepherd is,
> Jesus died the sheep to save;
> He is mine and I am his,
> All I want in him I have:
> Life, and health, and rest and food,
> All the plenitude of God.
>
> (*H. & Pss* 263, v.1)

These, and many other Wesley hymns, speak of the all-sufficiency of Jesus, as Redeemer of all humankind. To hear Mary described as Co-Redemptrix, however that phrase is qualified and expounded, will, I fear, seem to many Methodists to call in question that all-sufficiency. It may well suggest that Mary is not one of the redeemed – as both Catholics and Methodists would confess – but an adjunct Redeemer.

However, if to Methodists Catholics may seem at times to have overstated the case for Mary, it is a fair question for Catholics to ask Methodists, '... is not the Reformed response to some Marian doctrines intimately linked – in some cases – to a rejection of any place for free co-operation under grace with God's saving work in Christ?' (*Statement*, p. 3. para. 2). It has to be said that, although Methodists certainly stand in the Reformed tradition, they are Protestants with a difference. Though John Wesley owed much to Martin Luther's teaching on Justification, and on the sheer unmerited grace of God, he was not content with Luther's summary of the believer's relation to a gracious God: 'Always a sinner, always penitent, always being justified'. Wesley taught that God's grace wrought a real change in the heart and life of the Christian. He urged Methodists to grow in grace, to press on to perfection, to strive for perfect love. It is surely significant that one of Wesley's favourite summaries of the Christian life was taken from St Paul, in Galatians 5.6: 'Faith, working by love'. It was this text which provided the formula of agreement in 1541 at the famous Colloquy of Regensburg, when Catholic and Reformed theologians met and agreed on the fundamental doctrine in the Reformation conflict, justification by grace through faith. Sadly, mistrust had by 1541 gone so far that both sets of church authorities disowned the agreement of the theologians; but the fact remains that concord was achieved. Catholic and Protestant there acknowledged that genuine Christian faith was not a bare intellectual assent, but an active fruitful reality, faith working by love.

Of course, as Ephesians 2.8–9 reminds us, it is 'by grace you have been saved through faith; and this is not your own doing, it is the gift of God – not because of works, lest any man should boast'. Yet, once the grace of forgiveness and new life has been received, it will, as we respond to God and cooperate with his loving purpose, produce goodness as surely as night follows day. 'Faith working by love.' If that is so, as the Statement implies, we may see that what is true of our Christian lives is supremely true of Mary, – that she manifests uniquely that 'free cooperation under grace with God's saving work in Christ'.

The Statement goes on to ask whether 'Methodists respond positively enough to the Scriptural call for all generations to call Mary "blessed"?' (Luke 1.48). I think we must acknowledge that often they do not. Some Protestants, and no doubt Methodists among them, might be inclined to cite another Lukan text, where by implication Mary is referred to as blessed, namely Luke 11.27. The evangelist records that once, hearing Jesus' teaching and approving it, 'a woman in the crowd raised her voice and said to him, "Blessed is the womb that bore you, and the breasts that you sucked!"' In the succeeding verse (28), Jesus replies to this unknown woman, 'Blessed rather are those who hear the word of God and keep it!'

Several comments are in order on that passage. First, Jesus does from time to time give short shrift to people who mouth conventional pious sentiments, and recall them to urgent obedience to the way of the Kingdom. Secondly, it is quite unwarranted to take this word of Jesus as in any way diminishing the role of his mother, for if anyone heard the word of God and kept it, it was she who responded with all her being, 'Be it unto me according to your word'. But thirdly, and despite Jesus' rebuke to the unknown woman, we should, I believe, give full weight to the phrase, 'Blessed is the womb that bore you, and the breasts that you sucked'. I think myself that the joint report might have made more of the fundamental fact of Mary's mothering of our Lord.

Christianity is, after all, the religion of the Word made flesh. Jesus is born of the Spirit of God, but he is also born of Mary, bone of her bone and flesh of her flesh. Having opened herself to the life-giving Spirit of God, she conceives her child. She carries him in her womb, suckles him, nurses him, caresses him and loves him with the unique and irreplaceable love of a mother for her child. Therefore he is Mary's child; so that whoever says Jesus, must also say Mary, for she bore him, shaped him, loved him. We know well how crucial is the mother-child relationship for personal growth and development. 'Mothers are the makers of spirit'. They have, for good or ill, a decisive role in the formation of character. Bishop Lesslie Newbigin, in his autobiography, acknowledges the huge debt he owes to a Christian mother, and no doubt he speaks for many of us when he writes, 'I still live – humanly speaking – by the strength and gentleness of her love'.

All this is highly relevant, in my view, to the one whom the Scripture calls 'blessed'. If we confess that our Lord's humanity was complete and unspoilt – 'tempted in all points as we are, yet without sin' – then that is surely saying something of enormous significance about the mother who bore him, cherished him, and helped so decisively to shape his infancy, youth and manhood.

This line of thinking may help Methodists to realise more fully why Mary is called blessed and to acknowledge her as such. Methodists, and many other Christians, honour John and Charles Wesley. They are both, for example, in the Kalendar of the Church of England, listed in the *Alternative Service Book* among the saints and heroes of the Faith. Methodists, as I say, have long honoured John and Charles. They have taken rather longer to give due veneration to Susanna, the mother of the Wesleys. Yet her Christian influence on her children, especially John, was quite decisive. When John, at the age of six, was pulled out of the burning rectory at Epworth, just before the roof fell in, Susanna wrote in her devotional journal: 'I do mean to be more particularly careful of the soul of this child, whom thou hast so mercifully provided for'. Her faithfulness in that task yielded fruit in John's life and ministry, and Methodists are becoming increasingly conscious of what they owe to her. She has been called, and not unfittingly, 'The Mother of Methodism'.

If, then, with that example of Christian motherhood at the heart of their tradition, Methodists can rise from the lesser to the greater, they may be able to appreciate, with wonder and awe, what the whole Church, indeed the whole world, owes to Mary, the Mother of the Lord.

The Statement (p. 4, para. 5) goes on to make clear that this document is a development from the Committee's previous report on Justification

(1968, revised 1991), which registered agreement that, 'the person who is saved is saved by grace with free consent (in the case of an adult) but not saved by free consent'. First and last, it is God's grace that saves us. But we need to cooperate with God's grace, as Mary supremely did. Here the document cites John Wesley's teaching on Christian Perfection or Scriptural Holiness. Our calling is to be perfect as the Lord our God is perfect; to be entirely sanctified; to be made perfect in love. From a Catholic point of view, this Wesleyan language can be readily and appropriately used of Mary, as someone entirely sanctified and by the grace of God made perfect in love.

I doubt very much whether Methodists have previously thought of linking Wesley's teaching on holiness so directly to the Mother of the Lord. Certainly, I have never done so myself. Yet I think it is a fruitful and helpful approach to our Lady, and though the report only sketches this thought quite briefly in outline, I think it would well repay a fuller and more detailed theological development. Indeed, it might well be an apt subject for a thesis from a Methodist or Catholic research student.

There is a striking sentence in the section of the report entitled 'Grace and Election', which reads: 'Mary is a living proclamation of the mystery of God's grace and a perfect instance of the sovereign power of that grace'. In the mystery of his grace, and in his sovereign freedom, God chooses the poor of this world to confound the mighty, and the weak things of this world to bring to naught the strong. This truth comes out in some of the hymns devoted to our Lady, and it is good to record that, in the latest Methodist hymnbook, *Hymns & Psalms*, there are included for the first time Marian hymns which celebrate this truth. I have already said that Methodists sing their theology. Notice, then, that they now sing, for instance, the carol, 'The angel Gabriel from heaven came', with its praise of Mary:

> For known a blessed Mother thou shalt be,
> All generations laud and honour thee,
> Thy son shall be Immanuel, by seers foretold;
> Most highly favoured lady.
> Gloria!   (*H. & Pss* 87, v.l)

They also sing, 'Hail to the Lord who comes', a hymn of the Presentation:

> Hail to the Lord who comes,
> Comes to his temple gate!
> Not with his angel host,
> Not in his kingly state:
> No shouts proclaim him nigh,
> No crowds his coming wait;

But borne upon the throne
Of Mary's gentle breast,
Watched by her duteous love,
In her fond arms at rest;
Thus to his Father's house
He comes, the heavenly guest.

(H & Pss. 126 vv.1–2)

(cf. 'Born in the night, Mary's child' and 'Lord Jesus Christ, you have come to us ... Mary's Son').

Finally, just a comment on the specifically Marian doctrines of the Immaculate Conception, Mary's perpetual virginity – which, the document points out, John Wesley accepted (p. 13 para. 30) and the Bodily Assumption. The document helpfully points out that in Catholic theology all these doctrines follow from Mary's 'unique calling to be the Mother of God's Son' (p. 10, para. 21). Methodists can accept that unique calling, but it has to be said that the Marian dogmas have played little or no part in our tradition. That is not the end of the matter, however, for I take it to be an ecumenical principle that what is a vital matter of faith to my Christian brother or sister of another tradition, cannot be a matter of indifference to me. I must listen, explore, try to understand.

I am sure there is much work to be done in this field, certainly on the Methodist side, for the Marian doctrines raise many important issues about the interpretation of Scripture; the relation of Scripture and Tradition; the development of doctrine; the nature of authority in the Church; and the difference between fundamentals of the Faith and what are sometimes termed *adiaphora*, lesser matters on which we may make concessions in the interests of peace without prejudice to our own convictions.

I do not want to end on a captious or negative note. I think this is a most useful document, pointing the way ahead for further theological exploration and dialogue. It is good to see our own Society mentioned in the context of Catholic–Methodist Marian discussions. I am sure that the prayer, study, conferences and publications of the Ecumenical Society of the Blessed Virgin Mary have been one factor in opening up greater understanding among separated Christians in this whole dimension of our Faith. I close with some words from the concluding paragraph of the Report, which makes clear how closely related Mary is, in her faith and life, to the obedience of every Christian:

In Mary, we see what great things God can do in a human life freely and fully surrendered and opened to his grace. She sums up the faithful discipleship and perfect holiness to which each of us is called, and embodies in herself the vocation and destiny of the Church. In so many ways, Mary represents what it means to be a truly human being – woman or man – rightly and deeply related to God. The joy which fills Mary's heart should be the hallmark of every Christian, an Easter joy which comes from her risen Son who makes his own joy complete in her (p. 18 para. 42).

(This paper was given at the Bristol Congress of ESBVM
in September 1996)

15

Letters of Paul VI and John Paul II on the Virgin Mary: the evolution of a dialogue

Mary Ann DeTrana

At my very first meeting of the ESBVM in Washington in 1976, I distinctly remember my initial reaction to the paper given by a Catholic. It was, 'That's great, he is saying many of the same things that the Orthodox do about Mary'. And again, over and over at subsequent meetings, I consistently noted similarities. Eventually, I began to have a certain frustration, 'Don't the Catholics know how close they are to the Orthodox in their veneration of Mary?' There were occasional Orthodox papers, but the overriding dialogue, I felt, was between the Catholics and the Protestants. This was natural, because there were often few Orthodox present at the meetings.

Those who are familiar with papers given at meetings over the years are aware of a general progress in understanding between Catholics and Orthodox. It is obvious, if you read, for example, Bishop Kallistos Ware's papers in the order given, that we have made progress, if not in an official way, at least we, as a Society, and certainly as individuals, have, on a certain level, drawn closer together in friendship, and in our understanding for and appreciation of each other's attitudes towards Mary. This is exhibited in the discussion between Fr Yarnold and Bishop Kallistos at the Chichester Congress in 1986.[1]

Finally, in 1987, with the release of Pope John Paul II's encyclical, *Redemptoris Mater*, which contains what some have called 'a private conversation with the Orthodox,' I said to myself, 'At last, the Catholics know how close we are.' Then, the question became, 'Do the Orthodox know that the Catholics know how close we are?'

I then set out, as part of the requirement for a graduate degree, to try to find an answer to my question. My task was to read and to analyse the documents on the Virgin Mary written by Popes Paul VI and John Paul II. Among the documents considered are the two major ones of Pope Paul, *Signum Magnum* (1967), and *Marialis Cultus* (1974), and Pope John Paul's encyclical, *Redemptoris Mater* (1987).

A study of Orthodox publications in English from 1967 to 1988 showed that there was not a single detailed analysis of any of these documents from any Orthodox, official or unofficial, theologian or non-specialist. One may well ask why?

The lack of any formal, written, reply is probably the result of several factors. As Pope John XXIII noted, the Orthodox approach to the Virgin Mary is a liturgical one of veneration and celebration, and there is a consistent reluctance to analyse her role. This resulting lack of a body of systematic Mariology in Orthodox theology makes the production of a theological treatise on her difficult, and for some Orthodox theologians, it seems inappropriate to do so.[2] Another reason may be that Orthodox bishops and theologians do not routinely read papal documents. This does not mean that they are opposed to such efforts, or that they would disagree with them. I talked with Professor John Erickson of St Vladimir's Orthodox Theological Seminary in New York in November of 1988, shortly after he returned from an Inter-Orthodox Theological Consultation in Rhodes, which included both bishops and theologians. He said that most of the participants at that meeting were familiar with *Redemptoris Mater*: 'they generally agreed with its Marian aspects', and were aware of Pope John Paul's attitude towards the Orthodox.[3]

There have been references, of course, to both *Marialis Cultus* and *Redemptoris Mater* in papers given by Orthodox at Marian congresses.[4] The Orthodox theologian from France, Dr Elisabeth Behr-Sigel, remarked favourably about *Redemptoris Mater* in a short article. She agreed with its Marian aspects.[5]

There may be another obvious reason for the lack of Orthodox response, and it rests on the simple fact of the reality of the Orthodox presence in Eastern Europe and in the Middle East, the historical homes of Orthodoxy. Political pressures are no doubt primary in the minds of Orthodox bishops and theologians. In North America, where the Orthodox Churches are, for the first time in centuries, free to govern themselves as they choose, and to speak freely, the efforts to come to grips with jurisdictional disunity among themselves takes precedence over talks about unity with the Roman Church. These practical issues must be considered.

Initially, having found no substantial written response to any of the Marian documents from the Orthodox side, I feared I was set for even more frustration. However, I also noticed, as I read the documents, that there has been a gradual, but steady shift in the focus of these papal writings. Initially, they were written with an inward view towards Catholics only, and then, with the passage of time and the increase in contacts between the Vatican and the heads of other churches, they have an entirely different tone, and are written as if they would be read by all Christians, not only those in the Roman communion. There was also a discernible shift in their orientation, now turning directly toward the

Orthodox Churches. In retrospect its beginning can be seen as early as the end of the Second Vatican Council, with its chapter on Mary in *Lumen Gentium*, and it began in earnest with Paul's *Marialis Cultus*. John Paul's *Redemptoris Mater* completed the transition, and now the Vatican's focus in ecumenical relations, as far as the Virgin Mary is concerned, is directly aimed at the Orthodox Churches.

In order to discover whether the Orthodox were paying attention to Vatican publications in general, I looked at Orthodox publications in the period preceding and during the Second Vatican Council. I discovered that the Orthodox Churches in America were watching the Vatican, and presumably this held true for the other Orthodox Churches as well. As early as 1961 there were short articles in the *St Vladimir's Seminary Quarterly* about the Council. The object of interest in these articles is, not surprisingly, ecclesiology, the papacy and its relationship to the collegiality of bishops, papal jurisdiction and infallibility. The interesting point for our discussion is that in a short article on the Second Session of the Council, Fr John Meyendorff, the Orthodox theologian, does not even mention the debate during that session about the document on Mary.[6]

The Orthodox interest in Vatican publications has continued in the same vein throughout the period I have been studying. There are short notices about the release of a new papal document if it especially pertains to the Orthodox Churches. *Slavorum Apostoli*, for example, in which Pope John Paul II writes about Sts Cyril and Methodius, was simply reported as having been released, followed by a brief summary. None of the articles I found, and they all came directly from the publications of the various Orthodox Churches in America, contained any reaction to them. The tone of the articles in the American Orthodox press, at least, has been friendly and receptive.

It is important to remind ourselves that, for the Orthodox, writing analytical articles about the Mother of God is difficult. It is something which goes against the grain. She is everywhere celebrated in Orthodox liturgy and iconography, but rarely is that celebration analysed, nor is it considered necessary to do so. For example, there are, as far as I have been able to tell, no more than a handful of major articles on Mary in English by Orthodox theologians. In contrast to this, the Marian Library at the University of Dayton holds thousands of articles on Mary, many of which are written by Catholic theologians. On the other hand the countless verses of Marian hymns sung in the yearly liturgical cycle of the Orthodox Churches contrasts dramatically with the comparatively few liturgical hymns to Mary in the Roman Catholic liturgy.

There are regular Marian congresses sponsored by Catholics, but the Orthodox almost never organize meetings around the theme of the

Mother of God. A recent exception was the 1990 Institute at St Vladimir's Orthodox Theological Seminary in New York. The list of topics is again telling about the lack of interest in analysing Mary. The title of the conference was 'The Virgin Mary in Orthodox Liturgy and Spiritual Life.' Notice that it does not say, 'in Orthodox theology.' Of the ten papers given, seven were concerned with Mary in the liturgy, in icons, or in the Scripture readings for the feasts of the Mary. Thus, even in its analysis, the Orthodox theological mind looks to the liturgical veneration of Mary, which is in the form of poetic images, and to iconography, whose purpose is to participate in public worship or private prayer. Nowhere is there an attempt at academic analysis. Vladimir Lossky has said it well, when he asserts:

> It is impossible to separate dogmatic data ... from the data of the Church's cultus, in a theological exposition of the doctrine about the Mother of God. Here dogma should throw light on devotion ... whereas devotion should enrich dogma with the Church's living experience.[7]

We have heard all of this before, but it is important to keep it in mind as we consider the Orthodox response, or lack of it, to these papal documents on Mary.

Now, to the papal documents on Mary. It had been the established practice of Popes for over a hundred years to write short letters in May and October on the Virgin Mary to Catholics. Pope John XXIII did this, and at the beginning of his papacy, Paul VI did also. They usually reminded Catholics to practise traditional Marian devotions such as the Rosary, and to pray for the intercession and protection of Mary. Prayers were to be directed, among other things, for peace, for families, for social and racial justice, for the Catholic Church, and for the success of the Vatican Council. However, the period following the Council and its debate about the place of Mary in Catholic doctrine, saw the beginning of a change.

It will be recalled that the question whether to include the Council's short document on Mary in the long document on the Church was hotly debated, and the vote was very close.[8] The majority prevailed, and the now famous Chapter VIII in *Lumen Gentium* on Mary was the result. This is history, and we are all more or less familiar with its contents. The important thing for our purpose is that for the first time, Roman Catholic Marian documents were looking to the effect they would produce on other Christians.

It can be claimed that since the Second Vatican Council, specifically, with that inclusion of the chapter on Mary in the one on the Church, that the papacy has understood the position of the Mother of God in the

Orthodox Church. In 1949 Fr Georges Florovsky wrote:

> the person of the Blessed Virgin can be properly understood and rightly described only in a Christological setting and context. Mariology is to be but a chapter in the treatise on the Incarnation, never to be extended into an independent 'treatise'.[9]

And again Florovsky:

> Mariology belongs to the very body of Christian doctrine or, if we allow the phrase, to that essential minimum of doctrinal agreement outside which no true unity of faith could even be claimed.[10]

This statement is a paraphrase of that written by Fr Sergius Bulgakov in 1935,[11] and Bulgakov's remark copies that of Cyril of Alexandria.[12]

So it can be said that by starting with the Virgin Mary in seeking to come to a common understanding with the Orthodox at a most fundamental level, the popes have got it right.

With the advantage of hindsight, it is possible to trace the origin and development of a change in papal positions towards the Orthodox. Pope John XXIII was the first Pope in modern times who really knew the Orthodox. His experience of having lived among Orthodox, first in Bulgaria, and then in Turkey and Greece, gave him an appreciation of their veneration of the Virgin Mary. He understood that the place of the Mother of God in the common heritage of the Roman Catholic and the Orthodox Churches could serve as a basis for an understanding between them, in spite of other doctrinal divisions. The time was not ripe for pursuing this idea, even if Pope John's short tenure and the work connected with the planning and convening of the Second Vatican Council had not prevented it.

Pope Paul VI was elected in June 1963, and in December he announced his intention of visiting the Holy Land. In January 1964, Pope Paul VI and Ecumenical Patriarch Athenagoras I met in Jerusalem, the first of many meetings to follow. On 7 December 1965 the mutual anathemas of 1054 were lifted, giving at least a symbolic beginning to a dialogue between Rome and Constantinople. In 1967, things started to change. Pope Paul produced *Signum Magnum*, taking a strikingly different tone, and speaking about the Virgin Mary in ways designed to engage the attention of the Orthodox, beginning with very basic thoughts. He starts with the declaration of the Council of Ephesus (431), which declared the Virgin Mary to be the *Theotokos*. He discusses Mary as the 'New Eve,' fulfilling the Old Covenant and beginning the New, and Mary as a model for the Church, as she is for all Christians. He also speaks of her as a 'sign of unity ... among all Christians.' Most

Protestants would hardly agree with this approach. We can begin to see also, even at this early date in which a papal document on the Virgin Mary includes not only Catholics but 'all Christians,' that the emphasis is more on the Orthodox than on the Protestants, for though Paul VI does speak of Mary in Scripture, and of her faith, the bulk of his discussion would not attract the Protestant reader.

In *Marialis Cultus* in 1974, Paul VI becomes more specific in his focus. While conversing with Roman Catholics about post-Vatican II Mariology, he is now making explicit what he hinted at earlier. Among these are the Immaculate Conception and the Assumption, Mary as the Mother of the Church, Mary as a prototype of the Church and a model of faith, and Mary and the Holy Spirit. He writes about the eschatological implications of Mary's role in the Incarnation and also speaks at length of the importance of the Marian feasts in the liturgical cycle, all of which would appeal to the Orthodox, but not to the Protestant reader.

In October 1978, Karol Wojtyla became the first Slavic Pope. It is likely that he had plans for his encyclical, *Redemptoris Mater*, at the very start of his papacy, for his first major body of work, a trilogy of encyclicals on the Trinity, all contain references to the Virgin Mary. These three extremely long, doctrinal encyclicals supply the background for *Redemptoris Mater*, and in a sense pave the way for it.

In the third of these encyclicals, *Dominum et Vivificantem*, on the Holy Spirit, he writes:

> one of the most important ecclesial events of recent years has been the 16th centenary of the first Council of Constantinople, celebrated simultaneously in Constantinople and Rome on the solemnity of Pentecost in 1981.[13]

He then specifically states his ecumenical intentions:

> The Holy Spirit was then better seen, through a meditation on the mystery of the church, as the one who points out the ways leading to the union of Christians, indeed as the supreme source of this unity.[14]

We begin to see the method which will be employed consistently by this pope throughout these documents. He introduces issues which are intended to draw the attention of the Orthodox reader, either because they are part of a shared heritage of the two churches, or, more importantly, because they constitute areas where there is disagreement or misunderstanding between them.

The Pope has begun at the right place, for, as Meyendorff writes:

> There can be no doubt ... that the really profound reasons for the schism between East and West are of a doctrinal and theological nature, the most important issues being those concerning the Holy Spirit and the nature of the Church.[15]

Having set the stage with this discussion of the Trinity, Pope John Paul begins to introduce themes which will be developed later, and in retrospect, it is possible to see that their emphasis is on the Eastern Churches. He stresses the common ecclesial and conciliar history shared by the Roman Catholic and the Orthodox Churches. For example, in 1981 he marked the 1600th anniversary of the First Council of Constantinople (381) and also the 1550th anniversary of the Council of Ephesus (431) (*A Concilio Constantinopolitano*). The first defined the nature of the Holy Spirit, and the second declared the Virgin Mary *Theotokos*, the Mother of God. His point is that these councils are a common heritage of the Roman Catholic and the Orthodox Churches. But he also mentions the *Filioque*, a matter of disagreement between these churches.

In 1985 he commemorates the eleventh centenary of the evangelizing works of Sts Cyril and Methodius (*Slavorum Apostoli*) and their role in planting the roots of Christianity in Slavic lands. He underscores his own Slavic background, turning the attention of the papacy toward Slavic history.

In 1987, John Paul released *Redemptoris Mater*. It is this document which unequivocally reveals his purpose, to engage the Orthodox Churches in a dialogue focused on the Virgin Mary. It bears discussion in some detail. He begins, as always, with a general and inclusive tone, and, in that sense, he never forgets or ignores the Western churches.

Linking his work with that of the Second Vatican Council, he states his intention:

> the circumstance which now moves me to take up this subject once more is the prospect of the year 2000, now drawing near, in which the Bimillennial Jubilee of the birth of Jesus Christ at the same time directs our gaze towards his Mother (*RM* 3).

The year 1987 was also the twelfth centenary of the Second Ecumenical Council of Nicaea (787), the last Council accepted as Ecumenical by both the Orthodox Churches and by the West. Its main act was to affirm the legitimacy of icons, the memory of which is still kept in the East on the first Sunday of Lent as the 'Sunday of Orthodoxy.' 1988 marked the millennium of the conversion of ancient Rus' to Christianity. The reader is thus prepared for something about relations with Orthodoxy, and about icons.

Beginning now with what can only be called 'signals' which would be recognized by an Orthodox reader, he speaks of Mary as the 'Mother of Christ', and then refers to her as '*Theotokos*'.

He writes of Mary's personal journey and pilgrimage of faith, as if to address members of the Reformed Churches by presenting her as the exemplar of faith. However, as he introduces this theme, the Pope in fact writes as if he were addressing only Catholic or Orthodox readers. He quotes a text of St Ambrose from *Lumen Gentium*, which calls Mary '"a model of the church in the matter of faith, charity and perfect union with Christ"' (*RM* 5). And then he applies to the Virgin the phrase, 'the better part', taken from Luke (10.41), the story of Martha and Mary. This is not the type of exegesis commended by Protestantism; yet this text is used in the gospel reading for three of the four major feasts of Mary in the Orthodox Church (the reading for the feast of the Annunciation is from Luke 1.24–38).

He notes the Vatican Council's assertion that the Mother of God is already the eschatological fulfilment of the Church, when it said, '"In the most holy Virgin the Church has already reached that perfection whereby she exists without spot or wrinkle"' (*RM* 6). However acceptable to Roman Catholics and to the Orthodox, this language is hardly calculated to win new friends among Protestants.[16]

Mary's Immaculate Conception is also addressed by the Pope. She was free, he asserts, 'from the *inheritance* of original sin' [emphasis added]. John Paul may be rephrasing the Roman teaching about Mary's Immaculate Conception to commend it more to the Orthodox, who are far from happy with the Augustinian language of original sin.

In the text from Luke, when Elizabeth speaks to Mary, saying, 'And blessed is she who believed ...' (Luke 1.45) (*RM* 12), John Paul emphasizes Mary's faith, and evidently intends to speak to Protestants in particular, but it would also be immediately recognized by the Orthodox reader as part of the Gospel readings at Matins for all four of the major feasts of Mary.

John Paul now begins to direct his attention to the Orthodox. His tone changes, as well as his subject matter. Previously, he had been careful to link Mary's blessedness with her faith; now he says, 'Knowledge of the mystery of Christ leads us to bless his mother, in the form of special veneration for the *Theotokos*' (*RM* 27). He lists Roman Catholic Marian shrines: Palestine, Rome, Guadalupe, Lourdes, and of course, Jasna Góra (*RM* 29). Now Mary's faith is connected with the unity of the church and even of 'all humanity,' and, by specifically listing Roman Catholic Marian shrines, he has implicitly raised the question of the place of Roman Catholicism in debates about church unity (*RM* 28).

He thus arrives at one of the major themes of this encyclical: the Catholic Church, aware of the urgent need for Christian unity, expressed at the Vatican Council its conviction that Christians must deepen their '"obedience of faith" of which Mary is the first and brightest example'. And secondly, Vatican II noted with joy that 'among the divided brethren there are those who give due honour to the mother of our Lord and

Saviour', mentioning especially Eastern Christians (*LG* 68, 69: *RM* 29).

He contends that in ecumenical dialogues in the West, Christians recognize that 'they must resolve considerable discrepancies of doctrine concerning the mystery and ministry of the Church, and sometimes also concerning the role of Mary in the work of salvation', which the Pope regards as 'two inseparable aspects of the same mystery of salvation' (*RM* 30). But, implying that it is not necessary to resolve these discrepancies concerning Mary in dialogue with the Orthodox, he asserts:

> On the other hand, I wish to emphasize how profoundly the Catholic Church and the Orthodox Church and the ancient churches of the East feel united by love and praise of the Theotokos (*RM* 31).

These words are as striking as the irruption of the chorus into the 'Ode to Joy' in Beethoven's Ninth Symphony: one feels that all the conventions have now been changed. Strongly approving the Eastern churches' veneration of Mary, he recalls that the basic dogmas of the Trinity and Incarnation were defined in councils held in the East. He then pays eloquent tribute to the Orthodox Churches' Christian commitment, their apostolic activity, and their long history of fidelity despite frequent persecution.

He introduces this discussion by first mentioning the liturgical importance of Mary in the Byzantine liturgy. This is important, for Orthodox theology about the Virgin is contained, for the most part, in the vast body of liturgical hymns about her.

Then, taking his cue from the fact that 1987 was the twelfth centenary of the Second Ecumenical Council of Nicaea (787), the last accepted by both Rome and Constantinople, and the Council in which both East and West affirmed the authenticity of the veneration of images in their churches and homes, he begins to write of icons, the area where much of Orthodox theology about the Virgin is contained. There are over 300 different types of icons of her, each expressing aspects of the Orthodox understanding of her role in the Christian life.[17] He names several of these, including references to some which have long histories and great significance to Orthodox believers. Among these is the Vladimir Mother of God, the most well known and one of the most ancient versions of the Lovingkindness image. It is still regarded as the greatest holy treasure of Russia and resides in the Tretiakov Gallery.

In short, John Paul is speaking here not just to Orthodoxy in general, but perhaps to the Russian Orthodox in particular, or – to be more accurate, as he is – to the lands of ancient Rus', i.e. the Ukraine, Byelorussia and Russia itself (*RM* 33). It is in this context that he writes:

Such a wealth of praise, built up by the different forms of the church's great tradition, could help us to hasten the day when the church can begin once more to breathe fully with her 'two lungs,' the East and West (*RM* 34).

If this came about (i.e. if all the Churches of the East which share this veneration of Mary were united with the Catholic West),

it would be an effective aid in furthering the progress of the dialogue already taking place between the Catholic Church and the churches and ecclesial communities of the West (*RM* 34).

He could hardly have said more clearly that he thinks the ecumenical energies of the Catholic Church should be directed first toward full communion with the Orthodox, in the hope that consequently and later, there may be progress in the West.

Pope John Paul now introduces Mary's mediation, and writes of the eschatological importance of Mary and the Church, introducing a discourse on her Assumption. He emphasizes that she can contribute in a special way to the union of the pilgrim Church on earth with the Communion of Saints in heaven precisely because she already enjoys the fullness of the fruits of redemption. So far, this is logical, and would find agreement among the Orthodox[18] (*RM* 40). He does, however, get into an analysis of Mary's mediation, which sounds very strange to Orthodox, who are much happier seeing her within the Communion of Saints.

He concludes with a reference to the territories of Rus', giving a clue as to his intention in continuing to engage in a dialogue with the Orthodox Churches, and specifically, with the Russian Orthodox Church.

Within little more than a year after the publication of *Redemptoris Mater* in March 1987, John Paul issued three other documents which illustrate his Eastward vision.

In December he released the first, marking the twelfth Centenary of the Second Council of Nicaea (787) *(Duodecimum Saeculum)*. It speaks of the legitimacy of revering icons, and of the part played by the Bishop of Rome at that Council in their defence. He also discusses the position of the Bishop of Rome in the reunited Church. He contends that in dialogue between the Catholic and Orthodox Churches, there are available two criteria of doctrine, namely unwritten tradition and the living authority of the teaching Church today, criteria which are not available to participants engaged in ecumenical dialogue with the churches of the Reformation, insofar as the latter stand by the twin principles of 'Scripture alone' and private interpretation of Scripture.

In January of 1988, the second appeared, in which he indirectly speaks to the Russian Orthodox Church, congratulating them on the Millennium of the Baptism of Kievan Rus' *(Euntes in Mundum)* in which he refers to *Redemptoris Mater*, expressing 'the ardent desire to attain full communion with the sister churches of the East'.

The third came in February of 1988 *(Magnum Baptismi Donum)*, a 'Message' written to Ukrainian Catholics for the same occasion. Underlying this document is the sensitive issue of the Eastern Rite Churches in communion with Rome, which would have to be settled to the satisfaction of both the Roman Catholic and the Orthodox Churches before significant progress toward reunion could be made.

We have seen a steady progression in the focus of the Vatican, which has brought the Roman Catholic and the Orthodox Churches face to face, one might say, in their veneration of the Mother of God. As we have noted, the Orthodox response to the documents has been minimal, but that is not to say that Orthodox theologians are unaware of them, or that they disagree with them.

At this point Anglicans or Lutherans, or those whose focus is Geneva rather than Rome or Constantinople, may be feeling a bit exasperated, for none have worked harder at ecumenical progress than they have. It would be perfectly natural to feel, in the spirit of Lewis Carroll's Bellman in *The Hunting of the Snark*, that 'the bowsprit got mixed with the rudder sometimes ... ' and when the wind blew due West, the ship travelled due East! But let us look at this from the whole picture, from the Church in the early centuries.

The first significant split occurred in the fifth century, at the Council of Chalcedon (451). Recent efforts of the Orthodox Churches have been to restore full communion with these Oriental churches (Egypt, Syria, Armenia, India and Ethiopia), not with the Church of Rome. In a recent official agreed statement between these churches, we find this remarkable paragraph:

> Throughout our discussion we have found our common ground in the formula of our common Father, St Cyril of Alexandria ... and in his dictum that 'it is sufficient for the confession of our true and irreproachable faith to say and to confess that the Holy Virgin is *Theotokos* (*Hom.* 15; cf. *Ep.* 39).[19]

The debate between the Orthodox and these Oriental Orthodox Churches was, of course not about the Virgin Mary, but about the nature of Christ. The point is, in the recent agreement between these families of Churches, that the guarantee of Christ's true humanity is to affirm that his mother, a human being, is the Mother of God (*Theotokos*).

This growth in understanding between the Orthodox Churches and the Oriental Orthodox Churches augurs well, especially considering the role played by a mutual understanding about the Virgin Mary.

Little more than a year after he became Pope, John Paul II led the now annual visit of a Catholic delegation to Constantinople on the Feast of St Andrew to '"show the importance the Catholic Church attaches to this dialogue"'. (He refers to the official Catholic–Orthodox dialogue scheduled to begin within a year.) He also called it '"the major event not only of this year but for centuries. We are entering a new phase of our relations."'[20] In an address to the Roman Curia on the same day he said:

> I am convinced that a rearticulation of the ancient eastern and western traditions and the balancing exchange that will result when full communion is found again may be of great importance to heal the division that came about in the West in the sixteenth century.[21]

This is an exceptionally frank statement of his grand ecumenical strategy; but it is also sound ecumenical thinking, for the divisions caused by centuries of disagreements, separation and misunderstanding cannot all be solved at once, and it makes sense to begin first with the one with whom you have a basic understanding. We have seen that John Paul had in his mind, even at this early date, the veneration of the Virgin Mary which is shared by the Roman Catholic and the Orthodox Churches.

As we have noted, there has been no formal response on the part of the Orthodox Churches to any of these documents, which makes a definitive and analytical reply to them difficult. All of the points about the Virgin Mary which have been raised by the two popes have been written about by Orthodox theologians, though none of them are systematic treatises. This dogmatic reticence about the Virgin Mary on the part of Orthodox theologians is, as we have said, related to the reality of the *Theotokos* in the Orthodox Church. It is unlikely that even more specific documents on the Virgin Mary directed to the Orthodox would elicit an official, written response, but of course, one never knows.

Be that as it may, one can see an increased awareness on the part of many Orthodox theologians about what the popes are saying and what they mean about the Virgin Mary. This gives qualified hope for ecumenical progress.

We do not know what progress toward reunion between the churches of the East and the churches of the West will be made in the future, but we can be confident that the will of God will be done in his own time. Our job is to pray that our churches may come to a resolution of the differences among them.

Notes

1 Kallistos Ware and Edward Yarnold, *The Immaculate Conception: A Search for Convergence*, given at the Chichester Congress of the Ecumenical Society of the Blessed Virgin Mary (London, ESBVM, 1987).

2 Vladimir Lossky, 'Panagia', in *The Image and Likeness of God*, (New York, St Vladimir's Seminary Press, 1974), pp. 208–209; originally published in *The Mother of God: a Symposium by members of the Fellowship of St Alban and St Sergius*, ed. E.L. Mascall (Westminster, Dacre Press, 1949), p. 35.

3 Conversation with Dr John Erickson at St Vladimir's Orthodox Theological Seminary, 17 November 1988.

4 See, for example, Kallistos Ware, 'Mary Theotokos in the Orthodox Tradition', *Epiphany Journal*, Winter 1989, pp. 48–59; [republished by ESBVM as an occasional pamphlet, May 1997].

5 'Une théologienne orthodoxe réagit a l'encyclique de Jean-Paul II sur Marie', *Service Orthodoxe de Presse*, 118 (May 1987), 2, quoted by Thomas Ryan in 'Ecumenical Responses to the Papal Encyclical *Redemptoris Mater*', *Ecumenism* no. 87 (September 1987), p. 26.

6 See John Meyendorff, 'Towards the Roman Council', *SVS Quarterly* 5 (1961), pp. 45–47, and 'Vatican II: Definitions or Search for Unity,' *SVS Quarterly* 7 (1963), pp. 164–168; Nicholas Arseniev, 'The Second Vatican Council's *Constitutio de Ecclesia*, *SVS Quarterly* 9 (1965), pp. 16–25.

7 Lossky, p. 196; pp. 24–25.

8 John McHugh, *The Mother of Jesus in the New Testament* (London, Darton, Longman & Todd, 1975), p. xi.

9 Georges Florovsky, 'The Ever-Virgin Mother of God', in *Creation and Redemption: Collected Works*, Vol. III (Belmont, Massachusetts, Nordland Publishing Co., 1976), p. 173; originally published in *The Mother of God*, ed. E. L. Mascall, p. 52.

10 Florovsky, p. 171; Mascall, p. 51.

11 Sergius Bulgakov, 'The Virgin and the Saints in Orthodoxy', *The Orthodox Church* (London, 1935), p. 137.

12 Cited in an agreed statement between the Orthodox and the Oriental Orthodox Churches. See *St Vladimir 's Theological Quarterly* 34 (1990), pp. 78–83.

13 *Dominum et Vivificantem* 3.

14 ibid.

15 John Meyendorff, *The Orthodox Church* (New York, St Vladimir's Seminary Press, 1981), p. 59.

16 For the Orthodox, see, for example, Alexander Schmemann, the eschatological dimension of Mary, 'The first revelation of these "last things" ... is *Mary*' (emphasis in original), in 'Our Lady and the Holy Spirit', *Marian Studies* 23 (1972), p. 76. 'She is ... the "dawn of the mysterious day" of the Kingdom', 'Mary in Eastern Liturgy', *Marian Studies* 19 (1968), p. 82.

17 Mariamna Fortounatto, 'The Veneration of the Mother of God', *Priests and*

People (formerly *The Clergy Review*) 2 (May 1988), p. 145.

18 Among others, Kallistos Ware writes, 'The belief in the Assumption of the Mother of God is best understood in eschatological terms'. See 'The Mother of God in Orthodox Theology and Devotion', *Mary's Place in Christian Dialogue*, ed. Alberic Stacpoole (Wilton, Connecticut, Morehouse–Barlow Co. Inc., 1983), p. 178.

19 See text of final agreement in *St Vladimir's Theological Quarterly* 34 (1990), pp. 78–83. On 23–28 September 1990 the commission met again and produced a 'Second Agreed Statement and Recommendations to the Churches', which contains more precise theological statements and practical recommendations for restoring a formal reunion of these churches (*Sourozh* no. 34, February 1991, pp. 31–37).

20 References quoted by Richard L. Stewart, '"I want to serve Unity": Pope John Paul II and Ecumenism,' *One in Christ* 17:3 (1981), p. 287.

21 ibid.

(This paper was given at the ESBVM Congress at Winchester in July 1991)

16

The Melkite Church – unity with diversity

David J. White

'**Before** 1054 Unity but no Charity. **After** 1054 Charity but no Unity' – words of a retired Melkite archbishop, happily still with us, to stimulate pope and patriarch alike with the wit, wisdom and ecumenical zeal of a Catholic of Byzantine Rite belonging to the Near East, who is impatient for the unity of the Church.

I quote him because his epigrammatic words set my paper to this conference against the background, in part, of a tragedy. The date 1054 may not mean as much as 1066 does to an English person or 1690 to an Irishman, but 1054 is the convenient historical peg used by church historians on which to hang the tragic split between Eastern and Western Christendom. The adjectives 'Catholic' and 'Byzantine', together with that crucial date, introduce me and my paper. My topic and title were chosen for me and I hope to do justice to them, but I have another hope too, and that is to help you to an understanding of the role that the Melkite Church has in the delicate interplay of diversity and unity that both exasperates and inspires so many Christians today. My subject has obvious bearing on the Malines Conversations that we are commemorating during this conference. I am sure there are those present this evening who are well-versed in the Eastern Catholic tradition – to them my contribution will prove merely elementary. But I am equally sure that there are others here to whom all this is new and unknown. After all, lack of knowledge at every level reigns supreme in Western minds about matters Eastern, and I should think the converse is also true. It seems always to have been so. Add to this ignorance the ingredient of suspicion – that great bedevilment of Orthodox and Catholic relationships – together with a dash of indifference and a ghetto mentality for good measure, and there you have a deadly brew which leaves ecumenism precisely where many, many people want it to stay: in the doldrums. So I am very grateful to have the example of my retired archbishop and for his stirring ministry.

Tomorrow the Byzantine Liturgy will be celebrated at Downpatrick, when unity in diversity will be seen and experienced in eucharistic form. You may care to know that the Eastern Churches of today, of all jurisdictions, relate to three liturgical families: the East Syrian, the Antiochene and the Byzantine. The Byzantine is by far the most common and widespread and is used by the Melkites, thus binding them into liturgical unity with so many other Eastern Christians. The Byzantine Liturgy has all along been a vernacular one, and in its Near Eastern homelands is usually sung in Arabic. Hence, tomorrow's celebration will be in English. It is a liturgy of Holy Communion under both kinds and one without the *filioque* clause in the Creed.

A word about nomenclature in the Eastern Churches: it is something of a problem, with many variants, but I would draw your attention to the description 'Greek Catholic' which is often used and which groups together all the Eastern Catholic Churches, thus distinguishing them from the Latin Catholic Church of the West.

I have not provided any resumé of my paper to this conference, and this is for two reasons. First, you may have noticed that when you attend the Liturgy of St John Chrysostom, now more and more common everywhere, it might prove difficult to find a liturgy book. Often enough this is quite deliberate in that worshippers are expected to give prayerful attention to the Liturgy itself and not to a book about it that describes the Liturgy. The injunctions 'Let us attend' 'Be attentive' ring through the Byzantine Rite; so I am fondly hoping you will do the same with this paper of mine this evening.

The other reason is that I intend only to draw your attention to four very important dates in Eastern Christian history which have shaped the Melkite Church. Taken together – and they will not over-tax the memory – the four dates will help you to understand a church that is a living example of diversity in unity – the Melkite Catholic Church.

AD 634: the accepted date for the opening of the Arab invasion of Syria, with its apostolic see of Antioch and its blossoming Christianity; the year when Islam first came up against the flourishing Christian civilizations of the Near East; the year when the Pentarchy – the five patriarchates of Rome, Constantinople, Alexandria, Antioch and Jerusalem – first felt the force of a non-Christian invader with enormous implications for the story of Christianity in that part of the world. By 634 the early Christian Church was organised on a kind of federal basis with fairly flexible groupings covering particular geographical areas and embracing Christians of similar race, language, background and heritage. Those five patriarchates, each with its patriarch as chief bishop, were named after their see cities in an order of precedence first established by the Council of Chalcedon in 451. Each of those cities was a major Christian centre: four of them in the East, with only one, Rome, in the West, and that fact alone points towards the tragedy which was to come. Antioch was the first see to be founded, and that same Antioch maintained its prestige and influence throughout the ensuing centuries as the first see of Peter. It is still so. In the end, however, overriding power was transferred to Constantinople which had grown in importance through its position as the capital of the Byzantine Roman world. The office of Pope, who as Patriarch of the West and Bishop of Rome was recognised as chief bishop of all the patriarchs, and hence first bishop in the Church, called for decisive arbitration everywhere in disputes within the Church, but in matters of jurisdiction each patriarchate jealously guarded its independence in its own area, with the right to appoint its own hierarchy, regulate its own domestic affairs and construct its own liturgies. No one tolerated uninvited intervention in the internal life of another patriarchate. This is still a contentious issue between Rome and the Orthodox.

This, then was the kind of pentarchy which met the onslaught of Islam. The Eastern patriarchates suffered first, of course, but within eighty years the Arab empire had reached the Pyrenees, and the Patriarchate of the West, Rome, felt their presence. Just imagine: only three years after 634, St Sophronius, Patriarch of Jerusalem, was forced to deliver the keys of that city to the Caliph Omar who had come in person to the city gates to receive the submission, and some eighty years later the Arab conquests had created an empire twice the size of the Roman one and ten times that of Napoleon. By that fateful year 634 the Roman Empire had been divided in two for three hundred years, and the Patriarchs of Rome and Constantinople had already begun to eye each other with the distrust and suspicion that were to generate ultimate schism. It was a time when the boundaries of the Patriarchates of Alexandria and Antioch were at their greatest extent; for from its cradle in Jerusalem, Christianity in the East stretched from the borders of Libya in the west as far as India in the east; from the Caucasus Mountains in the north to Yemen and Sinai in the south, with famous names which still resound in the Christian story and which Melkites also claim as their patrimony as shining lights in the early Church.

I think of St Basil the Great (379), Doctor of the Church and the father of Eastern monasticism; of St Gregory of Nazianzus (390), Doctor of the Church and champion of the Holy Trinity; St John Chrysostom, 'of the golden mouth' (407), Doctor of the Church, born in Antioch and one-time Patriarch of Constantinople; St Athanasius (373), Doctor of the Church and Bishop of Alexandria as well as *contra mundum*, with St Cyril of that same city. We could all name many more from that Golden Age who are revered in the calendars of Christendom to this very day, all flourishing in that time of maximum extension of the Faith in the Near East which witnessed also the hammering out of orthodox Christianity.

But it was also a time of dissension within the Church and the alienation of those who rejected the decisions of Ecumenical Councils concerning Christological doctrine which later, in part, gave rise to the

separated Churches of the East. It was the age of the Council of
Chalcedon of 451 and consequently the birthday of the name 'Melkite',
a word coined as a contemptuous nickname by the opponents of the
Chalcedonian definitions and aimed at those who upheld them. Among
those who stood firm to the conciliar teachings was the Emperor in
Constantinople. 'Emperor' is *'malik'* in some Semitic languages, so the
upholders of orthodox faith were dubbed as 'Emperor's men' – Melkites.
It was a nickname that was to spread widely after 451, even to Rome
itself where the popes were known, for long, among other titles, as 'Pope
of the Melkites'. And, would you believe it? there was once a Melkite on
the archiepiscopal throne of Canterbury.

This was St Theodore of Tarsus, whose feast day still falls on 19
September and who reigned in Canterbury from 669 to 690. He was a
scholarly Greek monk from Cilicia in the Patriarchate of Antioch and an
elderly refugee in Rome from Islam, when Pope Vitalian chose him for
far-off England, on the north-western fringe of the known world. In 673
he became the first Archbishop of Canterbury to set a standard of
discipline for the whole church in Britain: establishing the diocesan and
parochial boundaries which exist to this day, calling together the
Councils of Hertford and Hatfield to ensure doctrinal orthodoxy in his
domains, and yet still a curiously neglected figure in the history of the
church in England. The Venerable Bede, however, had words of praise
for him, even if with a spice of cynicism about them, when he called
Theodore 'the first of the Archbishops whom the whole Church
consented to obey'. He earned a more fulsome tribute from the Council
of Rome in 679 which hailed Theodore as 'Archbishop and Philosopher
of the Island of Great Britain'. Other Melkite prelates from the East came
to serve the church in the West: as popes, Theodore I, John V, St Sergius
I, Sisinnius, Constantine I and St Gregory III. In 591 the diocese of Paris
elected Eusebius as archbishop. For our purposes, however, he is a
striking example of the unity of the Church, East and West, in those early
days and a witness to that Chalcedonian orthodoxy for which Melkites
still stand today and which was maintained through all the upheavals
that separate St Theodore from the Eastern Catholics of 1995.

So how best may I summarise what happened between the Eastern
and Western patriarchates during those long centuries? Despite the vast
defections of Christians to Islam, despite all controversies, disputes and
tensions which soured relationships between Rome and Constantinople,
a thread of commonly-shared orthodoxy still bound East and West
together. One wonders, then, what gave rise to that tragic schism
between Christians of East and West which was to occur. I think, like the
late Yves Congar and many others, in terms of a gradual estrangement;
like two sisters, utterly different from each other in many ways though

sharing a common parentage, who find they have become strangers to each other and can no longer live together. They end by drifting apart. Of course the complete ecclesiastical story is vastly more complicated than that, but it seems to me, within the confines of this paper, to be a neat and reasonable explanation of the split in the Church between East and West. A later pope was to refer to the two parts of the Church as the two 'lungs' of the Church, no longer in harmony, in unity, and therefore the body is grossly weakened.

And this estrangement of which I speak was to be the prelude of the second date I have for you, which is –

1054. Strangely enough, perhaps, 1054 is not a date that looms large in Melkite history. The complex problems between East and West in the eleventh century that gave rise to the division in the Church, graphically associated with the furious anathemas which pope and patriarch hurled at one another, was principally a dispute between Pope Leo IX and Michael Cerularios, Patriarch of Constantinople. And it did have the same catastrophic impact elsewhere in the East. In fact it was the then Patriarch of Antioch, Peter III (Melkite, of course) who vainly tried to bring about a reconciliation between the adversaries, but the rift between them had become too deep, and the situation worsened considerably when the crusaders arrived. During the night of 2 June 1098 the Christian crusaders from the West took the city of Antioch, and within a year they had captured Jerusalem, both places in the hands of Arab and Muslim overlords and yet also in the hands of Christian bishops, Melkite ones at that, many of them in full communion with the Pope of Rome who claimed the loyalty of those same crusaders. And those same Latin Crusaders sacked Constantinople in 1204.

For two hundred years a Latin presence prevailed in Byzantine lands. A Latin Empire was set up and Latin patriarchs appointed by Rome to Antioch, Jerusalem and even to Alexandria where no crusader ever set foot. The Melkite patriarchs went into exile, mainly to Constantinople, leaving behind them a resentment towards the Latins that seemed indelible and that led to the Eastern Christian conviction that it was better to be subject to a turban than to a mitre. From upheavals such as these cities like Antioch never recovered, for they lay in ruins. Modern-day Antakya bears no resemblance to the great Antioch of earlier days. The Melkite Patriarchs of Antioch adopted Damascus as the patriarchal seat, and it is still so.

Everything Christian in the Near East was in decline under the suzerainty of Islamic rulers who, although they may have exercised some tolerance of Christians and very often governed with great diplomatic skill, nevertheless isolated those Christians living within the Caliphate from Christians outside, thus serving to widen still further the gap between East and West, and to increase the estrangement. It was in such circumstances that the ill-fated Council of Florence of 1439 took place: a Council which brought about a reunion between East and West which lasted however only a few years, and those few years saw the fall of Constantinople to the Turks in 1453 and the arrival of Ottoman rule in the Middle East set to last until the end of the First World War. From the same city in which sat the Patriarch of Constantinople, the Sultans controlled the affairs of Christian patriarchs and their flocks.

This brings me to the third of my dates for you:
1724. In the years leading up to 1724 I would ask you to note the view of many Melkite historians who consider the close proximity of patriarch and sultan in Constantinople, the New Rome, to be one of the reasons for the increase in power and prestige which deeply affected its relationships both with the other patriarchates in the East as well as with Old Rome in the West. In the previous century the Patriarchate of Antioch had seen a strong movement within it for the restoration of full *communicatio in sacris* with Rome as it had been before the Great Schism; by the turn of the eighteenth century seven bishops of the Antioch Patriarchate had openly declared their support for reunion with Rome. This had not been so with Alexandria and Jerusalem whose patriarchs, normally Greek by birth and often living in wretched conditions in their see cities, were more often than not be found living at the centre of power – Constantinople – and therefore far more likely to adopt New Rome's intransigence towards her sister in the West.

By the time we reach the year 1724 the rift between East and West had hardened to such an extent that when in that year the then Patriarch of Antioch died, there arose a fierce dispute between Rome and Constantinople over the election of his successor. Rome favoured one candidate and Constantinople favoured another. Within Antioch itself, the Catholicising party stood its ground against those who rejected Rome's nomination, provoking a disastrous schism worsened by the traditional rivalry between the cities of Aleppo and Damascus.

The outcome, in a nutshell, was that from 1724 the Melkites of Antioch divided into a Catholic branch and an Orthodox one. They are still divided. From that same year the name 'Melkite' took on a restricted and exclusive meaning referring from now on only to those of the ancient Patriarchates of Alexandria, Antioch and Jerusalem who had re-established communion with the See of Peter in Rome. This remains the present-day usage.

The years following 1724 saw the emergence of what we might call the Uniate position, about which more later, leading to the often-troubled dealings between Rome and those in restored communion with her.

Frequently those troubled dealings centred on the vexed and vexing question of the exercise of due authority, that of the Pope and that of the Patriarchs, that had to await the Second Vatican Council before an improvement could be discerned. Those same years were also the years which saw Western missionary activity in the territories of the Patriarchs along with westernised forms of education fostered by Rome as well as the establishment of specifically Melkite religious orders and congregations, which happily thrive today along with the Benedictine and Carmelite communities which have adopted the Byzantine rite.

I now come to my final date for you:

1962: the year of the opening of the Second Vatican Council and from which date the Eastern Catholic Churches, which include the Melkites, have received increasing attention. The Patriarch of the Melkites in 1962 was Maximos IV who, together with the whole of his delegation, played a crucial role earning for himself the accolade 'the man of the Council', for he caught the eye and the ear of the watching world as well as the attention of the Council Fathers themselves. During the Council he paid a visit to the Ecumenical Patriarch, head of the Orthodox, in the Phanar in Istanbul, having before met him in Jerusalem with Pope Paul VI at an unforgettable moment in renewed contact between Catholics and Orthodox. There in Istanbul Athenagoras told Maximos, in June 1964, 'You represented the East at the Council and there you caused our voice to be heard' – words that have gone down in all the history books.

Before the Council itself opened, Maximos set the scene in a speech he gave in Düsseldorf in 1960, in which he said he would work to awaken a deeper understanding in the West of the great spiritual values of the Eastern Churches and of the possibilities for genuine development of these churches within the framework of the unification of local churches according to the will of Christ. Those were his words. His platform in Germany heralded much that was to appear from Rome in the shape of statements about ecclesiological diversity within unity to be found in a number of conciliar documents. This was seen most significantly in the concept of *ecclesia particularis* – 'particular church' – as described in the Decree on the Eastern Catholic Churches, and set within an organic view of the Church now understood as *ecclesia ecclesiarum*. What is a 'particular church'? It is a group of dioceses which share a discipline, a liturgical usage and a theological and spiritual heritage. How better to describe the Melkite Catholic Church? And let us note in passing that Vatican II preferred to call these particular churches 'Churches' rather than 'Rites'. The Decree I have just referred to is concerned of course solely with the Eastern Catholic Churches. Some will call these churches 'Uniate', and they are distinctive in that while they are in full communion with Rome their canonical, liturgical, theological and spiritual traditions are those of Eastern rather than Western Christianity. Fr Francis A. Sullivan SJ of Rome's Gregorian University writes:

> As distinct from these churches of the eastern rites the churches of the Latin rite together make up the western church, also a particular church. This is the 'Latin Catholic Church', a term that must not be taken as synonymous with 'Roman Catholic' since the latter embraces all the churches in communion with Rome including the eastern Catholic churches.
>
> (*The Church we Believe In*, 1988, p. 50).

This matter of particular churches – a clear green light for the exploration of diversity within unity – is part of the long overdue restoration by Vatican II of the ancient value of the place of the patriarchate within Catholicism. Equally, it is an indication of a new ecclesiology: an 'ecclesiology of communion' or of *koinonia*. Patriarch Maximos IV argued that a revived appreciation of the Eastern tradition of the Church – the Eastern lung – as a plurality of eucharistic communities, could, in his own words,

> harmonize the existence of western patriarchates as juridically self-sufficient and in communion with the See of Rome with the Western tradition of the Church as one Body having the Bishop of Rome as its visible head.
>
> (Descy, *The Melkite Church*, 1993, p. 73).

The implications of this interesting line of thought are still being worked out within the Melkite Church (and presumably elsewhere as well) thirty years later. We ought to recognise that a turning-point has been reached that was going to be echoed in the forthcoming encyclical letter *Ut Unum Sint*. The decrees of Vatican II on ecumenism and the Eastern Catholic Churches make it crystal clear that both Eastern and Western traditions belong to the full Catholic heritage and that neither of them can be ignored since both have the same value and importance.

The Melkite hierarchy, for one, speaks within the Catholic Church for the Eastern tradition: for those churches of apostolic foundation which have emerged, developed and captured whole nations for Christ, creating their own discipline, giving themselves their Eastern order of liturgical prayer, of the sacraments and of the Eucharistic Sacrifice – and all of this without any co-operation at all from the Church of Rome. In short, the expression 'Eastern Catholicism' denotes the Church in its non-Roman aspect. But never let it be thought that *non*-Roman means *anti*-Roman or excluding everything that comes from Rome: far from it. In the East there is the most profound understanding that her bishops are administering a number of apostolic sees whereas the West has only one. Unlike the churches in Ireland, England, Germany and France which owe so much to the Church of Rome in their foundation and development, the churches of the East are what might be called 'Church-sources' in their own right; hence one can but be grateful for the consistent papal teaching that the whole Church would be impoverished if the Eastern tradition were to be swallowed up and lost in the Western one. Pope after pope has spoken or written against the danger of losing the richness of diversity within unity. How about this from Vatican II?

> The individual Churches should not only be preserved in any part of the world but they should also develop, by establishing parishes ... and a hierarchy of their own. All clergy, seminarians and laymen should receive a thorough formation about such Churches.
>
> (*De Ecclesiis Orientalibus Catholicis*, 21 November 1964).

And by 'all clergy etc' was meant those of Western as well as Eastern rite. Pope Pius XI had said something similar in 1928, and even then he was merely reflecting the words of Leo XIII in 1894:

> the preservation of Oriental rites is more important than some may believe. The revered antiquity of these different rites is an eminent ornament of the entire Church and at the same time it makes perceptible the divine unity of the Catholic faith.
>
> (*Orientalium Dignitas*, 30 November 1894).

The Melkite Church has no need to be reminded of these things for she understands them very well indeed, and in these post-conciliar days sees herself as having a clear ecumenical vocation, preventing, on the one hand, the identification of the Catholic Church purely and simply with things Latin, and, on the other, the Eastern Orthodox from continuing to believe that by accepting Petrine primacy, to which the undivided Church bears testimony, they would be giving up the traditions of the East. This living synthesis of both Catholicism and Orthodoxy found in the Eastern Catholic Churches makes these Churches, by their very nature, 'bridge-churches'.

I return now to the vexed question of Uniatism. The description 'Uniate' was first used by the Orthodox opposed to the Union of Brest-Litovsk in 1595 when the Orthodox Metropolitan of Kiev, together with others – bishops and layfolk – were restored to full communion with Rome, thus causing great dismay in Orthodox circles. The word 'Uniate' is largely used, as you may expect, by those who disapprove of reunion with Rome on Rome's terms and who sense treachery all round. Others use the word as a convenient and descriptive expression without necessarily implying anything derogatory or pejorative. Although those to whom it is applied still largely disown a description of themselves which appears to carry a hostile flavour, it is, nevertheless, useful as a means of uncovering the problematical relationships that at times prevail between the Vatican and the Eastern Catholic Churches, despite the often fulsome statements made about those churches by Popes and Council Fathers. Uniatism as understood by those who are highly suspicious of what it entails explains, in part, the criticism that came the way of Patriarch Maximos IV – the man who spoke for all the East – when, at the express request of Pope Paul VI, he accepted a cardinal's hat. That acceptance was not easily given. It needed a special Melkite Synod to discuss it and a transformation by Rome of the nature of the cardinalate into something more than just a Roman domestic institution. After all, what need was there for a Patriarch of an apostolic see to accept the incumbency of a suburban church in Rome? Despite all this, and all the heart-searchings involved, the deepest suspicions of many Orthodox Churches were simply confirmed. The Uniate issue comes up, for instance, whenever the matter of Melkite episcopal jurisdiction in the countries of emigration is under discussion and whenever *ad limina* visits to Rome by Melkite prelates are expected. Melkites nowadays still have to be courageous enough to face the fact that despite the seeming breakthrough for the Eastern Catholic Churches in the processes of Vatican II, there remains a great deal of ambiguity and pain for a bridge-church attempting to bind, reconcile and reassure those at either end of the bridge.

We are all aware of what has happened so recently in the former Communist countries where Byzantine Catholicism, in places officially and at times brutally suppressed and often subjected to enforced absorption into Orthodoxy, has risen from the ashes in the heady freedoms which have come upon religious as well as political life. The outcome is too often a grievous and horrifying breakdown of law and order, and a breakdown too of Christian love and brotherhood. Uniatism is in the firing-line again. And now that the concept of 'sister-churches' has entered the Catholic bloodstream and has transformed its approach to Orthodoxy, the Uniate position is seen in a still more unfavourable light in the context of official theological dialogue between Catholics and Orthodox. We have to accept that Uniatism, now considered to be a stumbling-block rather than a bridge, is to remain one of the most contentious issues in all talk of reunion, even giving rise to a delicate crisis during the official visit to Rome by the Ecumenical Patriarch on St Peter's Day this year. There is thus every sign now that the Uniate way, earlier thought of as a path which could bring the Orthodox back to unity with Rome, has been abandoned as a way forward, as the sister-churches seek to move slowly, ever so slowly, despite the fast-approaching millennium, towards reconciliation and full unity, when the estranged sisters hopefully will find that what is held in common may in the end smooth the path to the rebuilding of the shattered unity.

So, as they say, 'watch this space' for further developments in the

400–year old issue of Uniatism which, in my view and as commonly understood, has become an embarrassment both in Roman ecumenical circles and also in the chiaroscuro of the still-young dialogue between Catholicism and Orthodoxy. In June 1993 the Joint International Commission for the Theological Dialogue between the Roman Catholic Church and the Orthodox Church met in plenary session at the Balamand School of Theology in Lebanon, where it was agreed that the 'form of "missionary apostolate" ... which has been called "uniatism" can no longer be accepted either as a method to be followed or as a model of the unity our Churches are seeking'. Precisely where this leaves the Eastern Catholic Churches who are at the heart of the controversy remains to be seen.

Continuing tension of this kind should not blind us, however, to happier things happening elsewhere. Within the Patriarchate of Antioch itself, the chief seat of the Melkite Catholic Church, not only is charity to be found in abundance, but unity between the churches there is growing as well. In the city of Damascus alone, where three out of the five patriarchs who are styled 'of Antioch' have their headquarters and cathedrals, immense and warm-hearted co-operation takes place regularly in the life of those three Christian communities. In 1987 I myself was present in that same city when the Feast of SS Peter & Paul was solemnly celebrated by the Orthodox patriarchs in the full ceremonial presence of both the Melkite and Syrian Orthodox patriarchs, all three enthroned identically as brothers in Christ. I was given to understand that this was the first time such a thing had happened, and these 'firsts' add up in the end. But the daily lives of those three communities in the Syrian capital have far more than that to show in terms of growing unity in outlook and action. Already great strides have been made in formal agreements between the Greek Orthodox and Syrian Orthodox patriarchs, and exploratory meetings are afoot, at synodical level, between the Melkite and Greek Orthodox patriarchs to pursue the possibility of a local reconciliation of the two Chalcedonian parts of the patriarchate of Antioch. But this is all new, and doubtless fraught with problems, and both sides will recognise that the internal unity of each family, Orthodox and Catholic, will have to be preserved, for who wants to heal a schismatic situation by creating another one? With patriarchs of the calibre of those involved in Damascus at present there is no likelihood of anything but a sober and solid search in theological dialogue and common action in every local sphere, spurred on by the more impatient, towards the fulfilment of the will of the Lord for unity.

I wanted this paper to be more than just a textbook description of what is often thought as exotic, strange, different and puzzling about the Eastern rites and churches by those unfamiliar with them. I wanted it to be an ecclesiological contribution to this conference, although I regret it has not been possible to bypass the movements of history for those who tire of such things. To be of any value to you I thought it more profitable to point you in the direction of an understanding about what has brought the Melkite Catholic Church to its present position in the Catholic and ecumenical spectrum, and particularly to encourage you to investigate, study and wrestle with those ecclesiological models for Christian unity which Vatican II provided and which, in part, impinge on the Melkite Church and the Eastern Christian scene.

So I would ask you to ponder, if you will, the implications of the four dates I have given you. Ponder them, please, for they have shaped the Melkite Church of today.

Ponder on the date 634, when the Church in the Near East began its life of centuries of subjection to hostile and non-Christian rule, hampered by the autonomy of each patriarchate creating differences and rivalries which Islam used to its advantage. The Western patriarchate and the See of Rome, by contrast, stood alone and united against the forces of barbarism in inheriting the mantle of the ancient and civil Rome. The Patriarchate of Antioch has been shaped by the events of 634.

Ponder on the date 1054 and the Great Schism between East and West which set a seal on the growing estrangement as a result of deep differences in theological statement and understanding; of different languages and mutual incomprehension; of differing political structures and economic conditions, and of the barriers raised by Western affluence and Eastern poverty. 'East is east and west is west and never the twain shall meet' wrote Kipling, and so it clearly seemed in the eleventh century, although the lines of communication between Rome and Antioch were never severed completely, for there were Patriarchs of Antioch in those days who continued to look to Rome and a restoration of unity in terms of a re-establishment of the bond of charity – never envisaging a reunion with a Rome that would absorb them with juridical primacy and absolute sovereignty. This too, has shaped the Melkite Church of today.

Ponder on the date 1724 which found a Catholic party in Antioch which many scholars believe was not out to form a new church, but rather wanted to continue the undivided Patriarchate of Antioch whilst adding the See of Rome to their Orthodoxy. But the power struggle by authorities both civil and ecclesiastical, Eastern and Western, together with the legacy of centuries of conflict and suspicion, did their worst, and the patriarchate was torn in two in a tragic schism with which the Melkite Church has to live today.

Ponder on the date 1962 when the Council then just opened was in the end to go beyond post-Tridentine teaching on the nature of the Church and to start talking about sister-churches, particular or local churches, the communion of churches, in a fresh ecclesiology of *koinonia*. It is in the light and spirit and letter of the Second Vatican Council that the Melkite Catholic Church continues its apostolic witness and ministry to its own faithful wherever in the world they may live, and to its co-religionists of both East and West. Time and time again the Melkite leadership has driven home the express teaching of the Council that there is everything to be gained for the whole Church by fostering lawful diversity within the over-arching unity. There is everything to be gained by making sure that those two lungs of the Church, the East and the West, work well and in total harmony. I have heard the present Patriarch preach in places as far apart as Cairo and Paris, and the points he stresses are the points I have just made, to which he adds a clarion call (again an echo of Vatican II) urging the faithful, especially in the western world, to do all in their power, by prayer, study and fellowship, to remain equally faithful to their rite and their church. I am sure that in doing so Maximos V rejoices in the example set by his predecessor thirty-five years ago who said the very same things in that curious prefiguring of the Council of the Church that was yet to come. This is what Maximos IV then had to say, in words with which I close.

> We have a twofold mission to accomplish within the Catholic Church. We must fight to ensure that Latinism and Catholicism are no longer synonymous; that Catholicism remains accessible to every culture, every spirit and every form of organisation compatible with the unity of faith and of love. At the same time, by our example, we must force the Orthodox Church to recognise that a union with the great Church of the West, with the See of Peter, can be achieved without their being compelled to give up Orthodoxy or any of the spiritual treasures of the apostolic and patristic East which is as vital to the Church of the future as to that of the past.
>
> If we remain faithful to this mission we shall succeed in shaping and finding the kind of union that is acceptable to the East as well as to the West, a union that is neither pure autocephaly nor absorption, in principle or in actual fact, but a sharing of the same faith, same sacraments and same organic hierarchy, in a spirit of sincere respect for the spiritual heritage and organization proper to each Church, and all this under the vigilance, both paternal and fraternal, of the successors of the one to whom it was said: 'You are Peter, and upon this rock I will build my Church'.

There spoke the 'man of the Council' who spoke also for the East.

(This paper was given at the ESBVM Conference
Dromantine College, Newry, Co. Down,
in October 1995)

17

Catholic–Orthodox relations in the Patriarchate of Antioch

Archbishop Isidore Battikha

In 1970, Professor Nikos Nissiotis was the first Greek Orthodox theologian to write, against the general Orthodox opinion of the time, that 'maybe the Uniates are not entirely wrong when they think they can serve the cause of *rapprochement* between Orthodoxy and Rome'. And he added that, 'instead of considering the Uniates as apostates, it would be more convenient to see them as a supplementary means at the service of dialogue'.[1]

Ten years ago, a Polish Orthodox theologian, Father Henryk Paprocky, recognized that 'the Melkite episcopate, with its Patriarch Maximos IV, was, in the Second Vatican Council, the voice of the Eastern tradition within Catholicism. More than once the Melkite bishops stated their readiness to resign their episcopal sees, if that would permit the realisation of unity.' He said also that 'there is a need of parallel dialogue between Orthodoxy and the Eastern Church which happens to be under the canonical obedience of Rome. And that has been tried in the Melkite Patriarchate of Antioch'.[2]

Let me recall what I said in Oxford nearly two years ago, speaking about the role of the Melkite Greek Catholic Church as a bridge-church: 'Illuminated by our past experience, we wish that our Church should be a propitious ground where it is possible to test a new vision, a new bridging ecclesiology truly inspired by the Second Vatican Council.'[3]

My wish of only two years ago is now becoming a reality, in these very days.

In fact, as stated by His Beatitude Patriarch Maximos V in his Message to this Congress, that I had the privilege to read yesterday:

> The brotherly contacts between Orthodox and Catholics in the Patriarchate of Antioch have recently increased, first at individual levels, mainly between the two Patriarchs and between several Bishops, and lately at the level of both Holy Synods, in order to restore the unity of the Melkite Patriarchate of Antioch, which existed until the year 1724, and this, in full communion with the Apostolic See of Rome, according to what was the general and canonical rule and use before the year 1054, between the Church of Rome and the Chalcedonian Eastern Churches.

I suppose you do realise that what is happening is a historical event. And, as it is not yet, as far as I know, of public knowledge in Europe, I dare to tell you that this communication I am delivering to the Congress is a real 'first', and I therefore hope that you will allow me to limit myself to the argument of Catholic-Orthodox relations in the Patriarchate of Antioch, and not in the whole Middle East.

By the way, the present situation is very different in countries where our Church has been present for centuries, but which historically are not within the geographical bounds of the Patriarchate of Antioch. I am speaking, for instance of the Patriarchate of Jerusalem, where, for the moment, any *rapprochement* between the local Greek Orthodox Church and Catholics is impossible, or of the Patriarchate of Alexandria, where the dominant denomination is not the Greek Orthodox Church, but the Coptic Orthodox Church, that is to say a non-Chalcedonian Church.

The historical event to which I am referring is the statement made unanimously by the Holy Synod of the Melkite Greek Catholic Church last July 27th, in Raboueh, Lebanon.[4]

In its introduction, it explains the immediate preparation or previous stages of the new situation. Last year, a few months before the July–August meeting of our Holy Synod, Archbishop Emeritus Elias Zoghby of Baalbeck printed, under his own and personal responsibility, and for private distribution, a project for re-unification of the Melkite Patriarchate of Antioch.[5] The Archbishop's argumentation was based upon two main points:

i) I believe in all that is taught by Eastern Orthodoxy;
ii) I am; within the limits recognized by the Eastern Holy Fathers, during the first millennium, before the separation, in communion with the Bishop of Rome, who is the first among the Bishops.

A first Orthodox reaction was received from Metropolitan Archbishop Georges Khodr of Byblos and Batroun, who, after reading the project, wrote, on 20 February 1995: 'I consider that this profession of faith of Archbishop Elias Zoghby states the necessary and sufficient conditions to restore the unity of the Orthodox Churches with Rome.'

Five days later, Greek Catholic Archbishop Cyrille Salim Bustros of Baalbeck (he is Archbishop Zoghby's successor) wrote: 'I agree with His Excellency Archbishop Georges Khodr on the fact that this profession of faith of His Excellency Archbishop Elias Zoghby is sufficient for the realisation of the unity between Eastern Orthodoxy and the Roman Church.'

Later on, nearly all the Archbishops and Bishops of the Melkite Greek Catholic Church gave their agreement and approval to the project, which was also received with the greatest interest by Their Beatitudes Patriarch Maximos V Hakim, Greek Catholic, and Ignatius IV Hazim, Greek Orthodox. During the following months, both Patriarchs met several times to exchange their views about the project and decided to appoint two members each for a four-member Joint Patriarchal and Synodal Commission to study the project. The Commission was formed by Metropolitan Archbishop Georges Khodr and Greek Orthodox Metropolitan Archbishop Elias Aoudé of Beirut, Archbishop Elias Zoghby and Archbishop Cyrille Salim Bustros.

After receiving information about the meetings of the aforesaid Commission, Patriarch Maximos V and the Fathers of the Melkite Greek Catholic Synod stated the following eight points unanimously:

First – The fathers expressed their gratitude to His Beatitude Ignatius IV, the Greek Orthodox Patriarch, and to his Holy Synod, for their interest and 'their brotherly statement about the restoration of the Antiochian unity in the final communiqué of their Holy Synod, which met October 10–22, 1995', adding that they 'share the feelings expressed in the same communiqué'.

In the aforesaid communiqué,[6] the Greek Orthodox Synod Fathers said, after referring to the use of exchanging delegates between both Synods (Greek Orthodox and Greek Catholic) since 1974: 'Together we looked forward to the restoration of the unity of the Patriarchate of Antioch, which will allow us to preserve our common patrimony and worship, patrimony and worship which are the source of our common faith.'

Second – I quote the entire paragraph: 'The Fathers of the Synod yearn unanimously for the day on which Melkite Greek Catholics and Greek Orthodox of the Patriarchate of Antioch will be united within the same Church and the same Patriarchate. And they declare that the restoration of the Antiochian unity does not mean a victory of one Church over the other, nor a conversion of one of them to the other, but the will to put an end to the schism between brothers, which happened in 1724 and which resulted in the existence of two Patriarchates separated the one from the other, and the will to restore together the unity of the Patriarchate of Antioch, as it existed previously to that date.'

Third – The Synod Fathers consider that the restoration of the Antiochian unity is, nowadays, possible, 'due to the progress realised in the last years, by the grace of God, at the level of the communion in the faith, between the Roman Catholic Church and the Orthodox Churches', through the Joint International Commission for theological dialogue, jointly created on November 30, 1979, by Pope John Paul II and Ecumenical Patriarch Dimitrios I in Istanbul.

Here are indicated the three documents of the Commission, which declare 'the unity of faith in the essential dogmas defined by the seven Ecumenical Councils': those published in 1982 ('The Mystery of the Church and of the Eucharist, in the light of the Mystery of the Holy Trinity'), 1987 ('Faith, Sacraments and the Unity of the Church') and 1988 ('The Sacrament of Order in the Sacramental Structure of the Church'), as well as the 1993 Balamand document about 'Uniatism, Method of Union of the Past, and the Present Search for Full Communion'.

Finally, 'the Fathers of the Synod consider that the search for Communion, within the Church of Antioch, must be a contribution to the realisation of the so much desired full Communion between the Roman Catholic Church and the Orthodox Churches, at a world level.'

Fourth – As for the 'role of the Bishop of Rome in the Church and in the Ecumenical Councils', the Synod Fathers fully agree with the Second Vatican Council Decree on Ecumenism, which asks for 'the due consideration to the particular conditions of the birth and the growth of the Eastern Churches, and to the nature of the relations which existed between them and the See of Rome, before the separation'.[7]

They also fully agree with what Pope John Paul II wrote last year in his Encyclical Letter *Ut Unum Sint*: 'The Catholic Church desires nothing less than the full communion between East and West. She finds inspiration for this in the experience of the first millennium.'[8]

Concluding on that point, 'the Fathers of the Synod declare that they take their inspiration, about the Primacy of the Bishop of Rome, from the conception that East and West lived together in the first millennium, in the light of the teachings of the seven Ecumenical Councils. And they consider that the Primacy in itself does not justify the perpetuation of the schism.'

Fifth – In consideration of 'this communion in the essential truths of the faith', the Synod Fathers consider that the *'Communicatio in sacris'* is now 'possible', and they 'admit it', but they add that it is up to both Synods, Melkite Greek Catholic and Greek Orthodox, to fix its bearing and means.

Sixth – Here again I quote the full paragraph: 'The Fathers of the Synod declare that they remain in full communion with the Apostolic Church of Rome and, at the same time, are looking for a dialogue with her, to resolve what is required by the restoration of their communion with the Orthodox Church of Antioch.'

Seventh – the Synod Fathers express their gratitude to the pioneers of Ecumenism, among them Archbishop Elias Zoghby, and to the members of the Joint Patriarchal and Synodal Commission, asking them to continue their efforts to realise the desired restoration, by organising new meetings and associating the faithful of both Churches in their task.

Eighth – They ask their faithful to pray to the Lord with them, so as it may be possible to accomplish the Lord's prayer to His heavenly Father: 'That they may all be one'.[9]

And that is all, for now. I imagine that our statement, when it was transmitted to Rome, at our request, by the Apostolic Nunciature in Syria, must have caused some shock and dismay in the Roman Curia, when it was received there, and certainly has been considered an unexpected move. Until now, we have had no reaction. We hope that it will come soon, and that it will be positive.

Pope John Paul II, in his Apostolic Letter *Orientale Lumen* last year, said:

> I feel the need to increase our common openness to the Spirit who calls us to conversion, to accept and recognize others with fraternal respect, to make fresh, courageous gestures, able to dispel any temptation to turn back. We feel the need to go beyond the degree of communion we have reached.[10]

I think that we are realising precisely one of those 'fresh, courageous gestures' asked for by the Holy Father.

Pope John Paul, in the same Apostolic Letter, writes that

> Today we can co-operate in proclaiming the Kingdom or we can become the upholders of new divisions. May the Lord open our hearts, convert our minds and inspire in us concrete, courageous steps, capable of breaking through clichés, easy resignation or stalemate.'[11]

And that is what we are trying to do: take concrete, courageous steps, capable of breaking through clichés which could consider our move as not conforming to existing codes of canon law.

Again the Holy Father says that

> Today we are conscious – and this has frequently been reasserted – that unity will be achieved how and when the Lord desires, and that it will require the contribution of love's sensitivity and creativity, perhaps even going beyond the forms already tried in history'.[12]

'Perhaps going beyond the forms already tried in history'! Yes, even if some people in the Roman Curia will not agree with our initiative, we are quite sure that the Pope, this Pope, will understand us. As we have said in the third point of our July 27th statement, we want to give 'a contribution to the realisation of the so much desired full Communion between the Roman Catholic Church and the Orthodox Churches'. We are offering a sort of experimentation, geographically limited, of what could be, in the future, the relationship between the Church of Rome and

the Orthodox Churches, if what we are trying to realize, with our Orthodox brethren of the Patriarchate of Antioch, is successful.

Let me read now a last quote of *Orientale Lumen*, when Pope John Paul underlines that the Eastern Catholic Churches

> carry a tragic wound, for they are still kept from full communion with the Eastern Orthodox Churches despite sharing in the heritage of their fathers. A constant, shared conversion is indispensable for them to advance resolutely and energetically towards mutual understanding.[13]

That suffering, that wound was referred to by Patriarch Maximos IV when, in his introduction to the book *L'Eglise Grecque Melkite au Concile*,[14] he wrote:

> The first element of our vocation is Eastern Orthodoxy, with whom we have never lost contact. At no time in our history did we ever consider ourselves a completed community, as if we had reached the end of our evolution; in our thoughts and in our hearts, we have always kept the place of the Absent, of that Orthodoxy from which we came, which we have never denied, but which we sincerely thought we have to achieve through union with Roman Catholicism, a union which we embraced as it was then concretely presented to us. It was only little by little, almost lately, that we have distinguished what was indispensable and therefore permanent in that union, and what was contingent, and therefore worn out.

And what about the Orthodox? What about their answer, what about their acceptance of our full communion with the Church of Rome? We are waiting for their answer, which will be historical too, and which will be decided during the session of the Holy Synod of the Melkite Greek Orthodox Patriarchate of Antioch, due to meet in Damascus within a few days, next October 8th [1996].

We have many reasons of good hope. First of all, we must remember that both Ignatius IV and Maximos V are heirs of the second successor to the Apostle Saint Peter in the See of Antioch, Saint Ignatius 'Bearer of God', who coined that famous sentence about the universal role of the Church of Rome, who 'presides over in the charity',[15] and of Patriarch Peter III, who urged Patriarch Michael Cerularios of Constantinople, in 1054, to be more moderate with the Church of Rome and refused to agree with the excommunication of the Roman Church pronounced by the then Ecumenical Patriarch.[16]

I have already indicated the first Orthodox reaction, last year, to Archbishop Elias Zoghby's project, formulated by the Metropolitan Archbishop of Byblos and Batroun.

Later, there was a letter sent by His Beatitude Patriarch Ignatius IV to Archbishop Elias Zoghby, on 10 August 1995. In that letter, the Orthodox Patriarch said he saw in the Archbishop's project 'a new element of your efforts to look at the See of Antioch as God wants it, and not as the human beings want it, divided without reason and justification', and he added that he had decided to do his 'best to create the broadest interest possible in our Synod on this subject'.

In fact, as indicated in the first point of our statement, the Antiochian Greek Orthodox Synod discussed the project in its session of October last year.

Finally, the day after the publication of our statement in a Lebanese newspaper, the same daily published an interview with an unidentified spokesman of Patriarch Ignatius IV.[17] The spokesman said, first, that

> the project of unification of the two communities is a serious matter, which has been expressed thoroughly, very positively and carefully; it is object of the greatest interest among the leaders of the Orthodox community, and first of all Patriarch Ignatius IV, who wants to realize that true unity practically and solidly as soon as possible.

The spokesman referred then to 'the dialogue between both communities about the importance and necessity of realizing the unity', and especially to the recent and repeated meetings of both Patriarchs, 'who have discussed this vital and constructive project in depth and sincerely; they have expressed their readiness to study the details so as to have them passed from the theoretical to the practical stage'.

The Orthodox source said that the 1724 schism in the Melkite Patriarchate of Antioch was due to conflicts of the past, 'but today the situation has completely changed, and the only question we ask now to ourselves is why this division does continue, as its causes have disappeared'.

The Orthodox spokesman concluded by saying that now

> nobody accepts the dissension and we are running towards unity and understanding, more especially as both Churches do live the same faith, based upon the seven Ecumenical Councils celebrated during the first millennium of the life of the Church;

and for all these reasons the project will be one of the main items of the next October session of the Antiochian Greek Orthodox Holy Synod, which will study it 'very thoroughly and in detail', in Damascus.

So, yes, we have good reasons of hope. And if this hope becomes reality, it will be the first time in history that a 'corporate reunion' of two Churches (to use the words of the Reverend Doctor Bernard Barlow) is agreed, decided and realized by the whole hierarchy of both churches, in this case by their respective Holy Synods.

Remember that, in the Council of Florence (1439), the Patriarchates of Constantinople, Alexandria, Antioch and of Jerusalem were represented only by the Ecumenical Patriarch, Joseph II (who died there), and about twenty Bishops. And, to limit myself to later, and still existing, unions of Greek Catholics, it is to recognize that the Brest–Litovsk Union of 1596, for the Ukrainians, was realized only by a part of the Bishops then under the Metropolitan See of Kiev; that the 1646 Užhorod Union for the Ruthenians and the 1698 Alba Iulia Union for the Rumanians were not signed by any Bishop at all, and that our 1724 union with Rome was in fact a division of the Hierarchy of the Greek Patriarchate of Antioch.

In the 1724 election of the first Melkite Greek Catholic Patriarch of Antioch, Cyril VII, the desire of communion with the Church of Rome was a major element, but not the only one. Paradoxically, for instance, Cyril VII was supported by the Greek Orthodox clergy and faithful of Damascus, while his Greek Orthodox opponent, Sylvester, appointed by the Ecumenical Patriarchate in Istanbul, was supported by the Latin missionaries in Aleppo.[18] Previously, several Bishops of the Antiochian Greek Patriarchate and even some Patriarchs had been Catholic, individually and more or less secretly. Since 1724, and until the end of the first World War, at the beginning of this century, there had been animosity and antagonism between Melkite Catholic and Orthodox clergy and faithful in the Patriarchate of Antioch.

Later on, official relations remained very cold between both clergies. Among the faithful, on the other hand, a feeling of Christian solidarity between the various communities began to prevail in the face of the Muslim majority of our countries.

There was a sad crisis when, in 1949, Pope Pius XII decreed that marriages between Catholics and Orthodox contracted before Orthodox clergy were null and void.[19]

Thanks be to God, after the Second Vatican Council, an atmosphere of openness and mutual esteem between Catholics and Orthodox replaced the former closed and bitter attitude. Meanwhile, there has been an important cultural and spiritual renewal, with ecumenical consequences, of the Orthodox communities of the Church of Antioch.

Among the faithful, the new situation will be considered as a very logical and natural move. Ordinary people, indeed, do not feel the division between Catholics and Orthodox vividly. For them, as I said two years ago in this country,[20]

> the separation between Catholics and Orthodox is merely a quarrel between the hierarchies and does not affect the Christian faith and life. Many Orthodox regularly attend the Divine Liturgy in a Catholic church if that church is

nearer to their home, and only go to the Orthodox church for the official circumstances of baptism, marriage and burial. Holy Communion is given in every church to every Christian faithful who participates in the Divine Liturgy; the only exception regards the clergy and religious, who bear a sign of their determinate dependence ... In the same way, Catholics are accustomed to visit Orthodox shrines. The tradition of pilgrimages remains very much alive and many Catholic parents continue to want their children to be baptised at Orthodox shrines on the occasion of those pilgrimages. Mixed marriages had ceased to be a problem, and the wives consider themselves automatically affiliated to their husband's community.

Nevertheless, there had been a risk of putting an end to all our mutual attempts at *rapprochement*, with the crisis engendered by the 1990 promulgation in Rome of the new *Code of Canons of the Eastern Churches* and its translation into Arabic three years later, as canons 813 to 816 of that *Code* have created new problems about mixed marriages. There was polemical agitation and suspicion which poisoned for a while the good relations between our sister churches. Finally, the storm was calmed down after the Holy Synod of the Melkite Greek Catholic Church, in July 1994, which, while respecting the supreme authority in the Catholic Church, stated that it could not literally apply the legislation in the new *Code of Canons of the Eastern Churches* concerning mixed marriages, 'because the legislation contradicts the new atmosphere presently prevailing in ecumenical matters'. This position was followed later by other Eastern Catholic Churches.[21]

Very recently, without waiting for the Orthodox Holy Synod meeting, we have already taken a significant decision: in Syria, next year, for the first time (although it had been decided previously in some other countries of the Middle East), the great feast of the Resurrection of Christ will be celebrated on the same day by Orthodox and Catholics, according to the 'Julian' computation followed by the Orthodox Churches (instead of the 'Gregorian' computation followed by Western Catholics and Protestants). Thus will end a scandal lasting for centuries, which underlined the lack of mutual understanding before non-Christians.

Before concluding, l should like to say one thing more. At the beginning, I quoted a sentence of Father Paprocky, the Polish Orthodox theologian who, ten years ago, spoke of a 'parallel dialogue' between Orthodoxy and an Eastern Catholic Church which 'has been tried in the Melkite Patriarchate of Antioch'. The project approved last July by our Holy Synod and which will be submitted to the Greek Orthodox Antiochian Holy Synod next month [September 1996], was initially elaborated by Archbishop Elias Zoghby.

The same Archbishop had previously proposed a similar project twice; he then qualified it as a proposal of 'double Communion', that is to say the restoration of communion with the Greek Orthodox Patriarchate of Antioch, without breaking the communion with the Church of Rome. That was the trial Father Paprocky was referring to. In August 1974, Archbishop Zoghby presented his project to our Holy Synod; only one year later, our Holy Synod requested Patriarch Maximos V to submit the project to Rome; the answer was No. In 1981, Archbishop Zoghby developed the project in his book *Tous Schismatiques?*[22] which, four years later, was condemned by Rome as 'incompatible with the Catholic doctrine' in what referred to the 'double Communion' project.[23]

In spite of those two negative reactions in a relatively recent past, we are today rather optimistic because, since those negative reactions, the Catholic–Orthodox theological dialogue has significantly progressed. What was considered impossible only ten years ago is now possible.

Last year, Pope John Paul II, in his Encyclical Letter *Ut Unum Sint*, referred to the requests made to him 'to find a way of exercising the primacy which, while in no way renouncing what is essential to its mission, is nonetheless open to a new situation'.[24] Our hope is that the united Melkite Church of Antioch could offer to His Holiness the Pope and Bishop of Rome the possibility of a new 'way of exercising the primacy'.

On 27 November 1962, Patriarch Maximos IV made an important intervention on ecumenism during the Second Vatican Council; his address, written in French, was immediately translated into Latin and read to the Council Fathers by the then Archbishop of Galilee, now Patriarch Maximos V; the text said, in its last part:

> We, the Orthodox and us, their Byzantine Catholic brethren, form, in peoples of different nationalities, only one family with the same religious mentality, the same Liturgy, the same spiritual history, and many identical reactions. We need to unite ourselves to them as much as they need to unite themselves to us. The time has come in which all Christians must forget their disputes of the past ... The time has come to realize the desire of Christ: 'That they may all be one!'[25]

Our feeling and our situation today may be summarized in one word: hope. Yes, the hope that, in a near future, all the Arab Christians of Byzantine or Chalcedonian tradition, in the Patriarchate of Antioch, will be able, through the Protection of the Holy Theotokos, in communion of faith and charity, to share the same Lord's Chalice, for the glory of the Most Holy Trinity, Father, Son and Holy Spirit, one God.

[We understand that since this paper was delivered, the Orthodox Holy Synod and the Vatican have both approved the 'Zoghby Initiative', and that concrete steps will be taken in two years' time. Deo gratias!]

Notes

1   Nikos Nissiotis, 'Qu'est-ce qui nous sépare encore de l'Eglise catholique romaine?', in *Concilium*, 1970, p. 30, n. 54.
2   *Wiez*, 1986, no. 1; cf. *Le Lien*, Beirut 1987, pp. 72–74, nn. 5–6.
3   Lecture to the Theological Faculty of Oxford University on 24 November 1994; text in *Eastern Churches Journal*, Autumn 1994 (vol. 1, no. 3), pp. 33–39.
4   The statement has been published in Arabic (with the erroneous date of July 29th, instead of 27th) by the Lebanese daily *An-Nahar* of Beirut, 4 September 1996, and in Damascus, Syria, by the Melkite Greek Catholic Patriarchate weekly bulletin, *Batriyarkiyat ar-Roum al-Kathulik*, undated (15 September 1996) special issue.
5   *Orthodoxe uni? Oui! Uniate? Non!* (Jounieh, Lebanon, 18 February 1995).
6   Arabic text in the Lebanese daily *An-Nahar*, October 23, 1995; French extracts in *Le Lien*, 1995, pp. 56–59, n. 6.
7   Decree *Unitatis Redintegratio* 14.
8   *Ut Unum Sint* 61, in *L'Osservatore Romano Weekly Edition in English*, 31 May 1995, p. ix.
9   John 17.21.
10 *Orientale Lumen* 17, in *L'Osservatore Romano Weekly Edition in English*, 3 May 1995, p. v.
11 *Orientale Lumen* 19, ibid. p. vi.
12 *Orientale Lumen* 20, ibid. p. vi.
13 *Orientale Lumen* 21, ibid. p. vi.
14 Beirut, Dar Al-Kalima, 1967, p. vii.
15 *Epistola ad Romanos*.
16 cf. Joseph Nasrallah, *Eglise Melchite et Union des Eglises*, Paris 1976, p. 13.
17 *An-Nahar*, 5 September 1996.
18 cf. Joseph Nasrallah, Sa Béatitude Maximos IV et la succession apostolique du Siège d'Antioche, Paris 1963, pp. 55–58.
19 cf. my lecture on 'The Antioch Ecumenical Paradigm', delivered in Oxford and London, 24 and 28 November 1994 respectively, in *Eastern Churches Journal*, Autumn 1994 (vol. 1, no. 3), p. 43.
20 ibid. pp. 44–46.
21 ibid. pp. 46–48.
22 Beirut, 1981.
23 cf. Elias Zoghby, *Mémoires*, Jounieh (Lebanon), s.d. (1991), pp. 190–228.
24 *Ut Unum Sint* 95, in *L'Osservatore Romano Weekly Edition in English*, 31 May 1995, p. xiii.
25 *L'Eglise Grecque Melkite au Concile*, Beirut 1967, pp. 386–387.

(This paper was given at the Bristol Congress of ESBVM in September 1996)

Mary
and
spirituality

18

A personal approach to Marian spirituality: a Lutheran perspective

Anita J. Baly

Today I would like to share with you my way of incorporating Mary into my own spirituality. I deeply appreciate the support of the American and British Societies that enabled me to attend this conference. I am humbled by that support because I am well aware that many of you are world-class Mariologists and many of you have lifetimes of enjoyment of Mary in prayer. I am a beginner: product of my era, and fruit of the ecumenical seeds so many of you have planted, pruned, and nourished so tenderly. In my contacts with the Society in the United States (and now here), I feel very much at home because I was ecumenical already in the womb: my mother was Catholic, my father Lutheran. I was raised Catholic: my theological formation has been done mostly by Presbyterians and Lutherans. My service as an ordained minister has been in the Lutheran Church, with some work in educational and spirituality ministry and preaching for an Episcopalian congregation. My spiritual direction has been with Catholics recently. For the past two years I taught theology at a Catholic college. I am now visiting faculty in theology at a Presbyterian graduate institution. As a daughter of the Reformation, I hesitate to say this in public, but I will risk this disclosure because I think it is only fair to tell you who I am. There are four saints in my personal pantheon: persons from my past who I know are close to God, to whom I speak on occasion, and on whose help and intercession I rely. They are Jesus, Mary, my mother, and Martin Luther.

As I seek to incorporate Mary into my own spiritual life, I make two assumptions. One is that Mary is valuable for my spiritual life and that our paths converge somewhere. The other assumption is that theology must be linked essentially to Scripture. I try to read Scripture in an historically critical way, faithful to the insights of the Reformation. I believe that it is possible both to honour Mary as a saint and to honour the conclusions of contemporary biblical scholarship. My intent in this paper is to show that such dual honour is not an impossible oxymoron, but instead a potentially nourishing paradox.

In considering Mary, I begin with a question and then move to a two-fold method that may not answer the question but can serve as the question's context. The question is this: Why doesn't Mary appear to me? And that is the question because as I look around the world, I notice that so much serious Marian piety seems to involve appearances. In fact, it seems lately that Mary is appearing in ever-increasing locations and with greater and greater frequency. Even the American town of 1,500 people in which I most recently lived and taught had its Marian visionary. She has been seeing Mary every Thursday evening at about 7:12 p.m. (during the third decade of a Rosary recitation) for months. Hundreds of people now come each week, hoping for a vision. Hundreds more cope with and curse the traffic problems the vision-seekers create. While visions generate enormous theological and practical headaches, wouldn't having one be wonderful and so interesting?

Mary does not appear to me, and I would be beyond amazed if she ever did. Why? Is it because I would hardly welcome the favour, because appearances would violate the structures of my theology, because my piety barely recognizes or even dishonours her, because my cultural conditioning insulates me against such occurrences, because my quest for spiritual experience and development is not serious enough, or because in the post-Enlightenment world such things simply are scientifically impossible? Any one of those reasons could account for the lack of a personal Marian appearance. I suspect that at least most of those reasons apply to me and that taken together their weight must obviate an appearance to me. I believe there are, however, other ways of seeing Mary, other possibilities for encounter, that could enrich – not threaten – my theology and my spiritual life.

It seems to be a commonplace of teaching on prayer or of progressing on the spiritual journey that one needs to begin exactly where one is in time and place and circumstance. Christians would call that an incarnational approach or speak of participating in the sacrament of the present moment. We are an ecumenical society, focused on Mary, meeting today in Norwich, England, because we are celebrating the 600th anniversary of Julian of Norwich. Using the begin-where-you-are spiritual approach, therefore, invites consideration of Julian's reported experience. Mary did appear to her.

Julian saw Mary three times. Jesus showed Mary to Julian: as Mary conceived; as she was in her sorrow at the foot of the cross; and as she is in glory.[1] That is about as much as Julian describes these showings. It is, however, the way in which Julian has these visions that could be instructive for us.

The visions come as Jesus appears to Julian and looks down at his right side. That puts her in mind of Mary's position at the foot of the cross. Then Jesus asks the crucial question: 'Will you see her?'[2] I interpret that question to mean, 'Do you want to see Mary?' At first blush that seems like a very odd question indeed. Why wouldn't Julian want to see Mary? Given the chance, why wouldn't anyone want to see her? The question is odd in precisely the same way that Jesus' question to the blind beggar Bartimaeus was odd. You recall that Bartimaeus was begging at the side of the road when Jesus and a large crowd passed by. He kept shouting 'Jesus, Son of David, have mercy on me!' as the crowd tried to make him be quiet. Jesus, however, attended to him and asked that Bartimaeus be brought to him. When he was, Jesus asked, 'What do you want me to do for you?' (Mark 10.51; Matt. 20.32; Luke 18.41). That, too, was an odd question. Wouldn't *anyone* know that a blind man with the opportunity would ask for his sight?

Jesus' questions in these instances must have had a purpose. Matters like the overcoming of blindness or seeing Mary may not be self-evidently wonderful and seamlessly positive. Perhaps they, too, have their downsides – as most forms of change or growth would. It would seem that Jesus was inviting Bartimaeus and Julian to stop and reflect. Jesus' questions demanded that they clarify their desires and the motivations behind them. They had to assess their readiness to move into futures that would inevitably differ from their pasts. They also had to articulate and affirm their desires in public: in Bartimaeus's case *viva voce* before the crowd; in Julian's through her writing, which would have been as close to the public as an anchoress was expected to get. Moreover, they had to do all this with the degree of honesty, intensity, and reverence that a face-to-face encounter with God implies. The questions are supportive, surely, for they convey respect and freedom. They are also serious and profound and, I daresay, addressed to me.

'Will you see her?' When Julian is asked that question, she says Yes, if it be Jesus' will, and reminds him that she has often prayed for it. She says she expected to see Mary as she was in the body, but theretofore had not seen her. That is Julian's first thought: it is her answer in the earlier Short Text. In that first text, immediately after this answer Jesus shows Mary to her. In her later, edited Long Text Julian records the same response to the same question, but with considerable elaboration and preparation of her readers. This time, before she relates her response, she interprets Jesus' question as meaning something like 'Will you see how I love Mary and, thus, know how you are loved?' She also explains that she had been taught not to yearn to see Mary's bodily presence but instead to desire to see the power of her 'blyssydfulle' soul, that is, her truth, her wisdom, and her charity.

That sort of vision, Julian says, will teach her two things: to know herself and reverently to fear her God. Did someone 'teach' Julian between the two editions that wanting simply to see Mary was theologically misguided? Who knows? In any event, the mature Julian seems intent on explaining that it was not, after all, a vision of the physical Mary that she sought. Julian seems to be communicating that the important 'seeing' or apprehending was of Mary's qualities and virtues, not of her physical or metaphysical body. The early text seems to imply that in her younger days Julian simply sought the vision. In her later days, however, her object had become to seek, use or value experiences to the degree that they could strengthen her own spiritual life. To do that, as she says, experiences must foster her progress in knowing herself and in reverently fearing God.

Immediately after her vision of Mary – in both texts – Julian claims that Jesus then showed himself to her more glorified in her sight than she had ever seen him before. In the short text she explains how seeing Mary helps one to come closer to God: 'In this was I lerede that ilke saule contemplatyfe to whilke es gyffenn to luke and seke god schalle se hire and passe unto god by contemplacionn'.[3] Even in the early period, therefore, it seems that Julian understood the purpose and value of the vision of Mary as the enhancement of her spiritual relationship with God. For Julian, thus, Mary seems to be transparent: Julian's sight of Mary does not stop on her; instead it goes right through her and on to see God. Because her vision has gone through Mary, however, Julian now sees God better than she ever did before. So Mary becomes something of a stained-glass window for Julian. I am reminded here of George Herbert's lines:

> A man that looks on glass
> On it may stay his eye,
> Or, if he pleaseth, through it pass
> And thus the heavens espy.[4]

Julian's vision certainly does not stop with Mary, but goes soaring on through her and beyond her to God.

That, then, is Julian's answer to the question about seeing Mary. Were someone to ask me the same question, my response would be on the same continuum with Julian's. Unlike Julian, I have never prayed for a vision of Mary; and I certainly do not expect such visions to occur. Like Julian, however, I would love to see, to grasp, Mary's essential qualities and virtues. I also appreciate Julian's perception that Mary can be a vehicle for getting closer to Christ, or a window through which to see him better. Such a view comports well with my tradition, my theology and my devotional endeavours. In his commentary on the Magnificat, Martin Luther suggests just this understanding of Marian theology and piety. He wrote:

Whoever . . . would show [Mary] the proper honour must not regard her alone and by herself, but set her in the presence of God and far beneath Him, must there strip her of all honour, and regard her low estate, as she says; he should marvel at the exceedingly abundant grace of God, who regards, embraces, and blesses so poor and despised a mortal ... What do you suppose would please her more than to have you come through her to God this way, and learn from her to put your hope and trust in Him, notwithstanding your despised and lowly estate, in life as well as in death? She does not want you to come to her but through her to God.[5]

Julian, thus, has provided me a helpful lens through which to see Mary better. I agree that 'seeing' Mary's virtues and, I would add, 'seeing' her way of progressing on her own spiritual journey, could help me to attain those ends for which Julian says she valued her vision: knowing myself better and revering God more. To do this today, I believe, no esoteric apparition is required. Some scholars suggest, and I, too, incline to the view, that such apparitions may be at best irrelevant to the spiritual quest and at worst detrimental to it.[6]

More likely to be helpful to me than the seeking of ghostly apparitions would be the effort to discover and to honour those things that are truly essential to Mary's being, character, and journey. I could describe that as an effort to try to see her from God's perspective. Less arrogantly, I prefer to adapt an apt phrase from an American novelist and describe the effort as that of 'seeing Mary real'. Trying to see the real Mary is what this is about. I have been attending to the spiritual quest in earnest for the past four years. The burden of that quest seems to be the effort of coming to an ever-greater acceptance of reality. I'm not sure exactly what the current enthusiasm for seeing, doing and experiencing things in 'virtual reality' means, but I am very sure that when it comes to Marian devotion – or to any other aspect of spirituality – 'virtual' is the kiss of death; real reality – scary and disappointing though it can be – is the path to life. Virtual reality is a game; reality is truth.

That commitment to reality is where the first piece of my method, accepting Julian's guidance, gets me. The other piece of my method is striving faithfully to interpret the biblical texts. From my Lutheran and Reformed formation, I have a clear, and by now almost unconscious, commitment to the principle of scripture alone. For me, 'seeing Mary real' begins – and ends – with the Bible. It is important to emphasize that, because it is not true for all Christians. Last summer I had the opportunity to preach on Mary to a small ecumenical group. I preached on one of the Marian texts and then invited the others present to dialogue about the text. What happened next was that some of the Catholics present began to talk about Mary's meaning for them in ways that had no discernible connection to any biblical texts. That left most of the Protestants bewildered and unable even to follow those comments. I am uncomfortable when theology or spirituality gets divorced completely from the Bible. That is a feeling and a method that I need to honour; that is, when it comes to Mary, I need to start and end with the biblical texts. To be sure, I do not understand the mere words of the Bible to constitute the Word of God. A reader will always interpret the text somehow. Luther's hermeneutical principle, and mine, involves reading the Scriptures through a Christological lens. And at the centre of that lens is the principle of justification by grace through faith. As I read Marian texts, therefore, I keep asking how grace is coming to Mary at each stage of her journey and how she is responding to that grace.

The canonical Scriptures, of course, contain only a few Marian texts. In the Gospel of Mark there are only two pericopes that mention Mary at all; the question of who constitutes Jesus' true family (3.31–35), and the description of Jesus' rejection by his Nazarean kin and neighbours (6.1–6). The Gospel of Matthew contains somewhat modified accounts of those same two incidents (12.46–50 and 13.53–58) and the narratives of Jesus' birth and infancy (Chapters 1 and 2).

Luke–Acts has by far the most extensive treatment of Mary. The Gospel of Luke has a more elaborate birth and infancy narrative than Matthew does. Luke includes the account of the Annunciation, the Visitation, the Magnificat, the Purification in the temple, and the finding of Jesus at age 12 in the Jerusalem temple (Chapters 1 and 2). Referring to Mary, Luke has a gentler account of Jesus' true family (8.19–21), and he so modifies the rejection at Nazareth incident that Mary does not appear in it in Luke's version (4.16–30). Luke has two additional brief references to Mary that are peculiar to his writings. One is the macarism pronounced by a woman in the crowd: '"Happy the womb that bore you and the breasts you sucked!" But [Jesus] said, "Happy, rather, those who hear the word of God and keep it".' (11.27–28). And, finally, there is a single reference to Mary in Acts (1.14), where she is named as belonging to the pre-Pentecost Christian community.

In the Gospel of John, Mary appears twice: at the wedding at Cana (2.1–12) and at the foot of the cross (19.25–27). These appearances are not parallelled in the Synoptics. And that's it! Scholars agree that 'The noncanonical literature, including the apocrypha' – and specifically the *Protevangelium of James* – furnishes very little information about Mary which is not parallelled in the New Testament.'[7]

Following, then, Julian's guidance about seeing Mary 'real' and my own understanding of the essential linkage between the scriptures and God's Word, there are, I think, implications for appropriate and felicitous Marian spirituality. The rest of the paper spells out those implications as

I see them. Specifically, seeing Mary real in the Bible teaches me about God's ways of calling Christians; about the necessity for constant growth; about some ways of conducting the relationship with God; and about the rewards of entering on and continuing the spiritual quest.

Contemplating Mary's spiritual journey can help me with my own journey to the extent that I recognize that Mary can be a model or – as Catholic theology has put it – an *exemplar* for me. If she is a model for me, that simply means that her experiences and ways of dealing with them can illumine my own and teach me something. Mary, to be sure, is unique in that she was Jesus' mother, but she is also altogether human. In the same way you and I, while sharing the common characteristics of humanity, are also unique creatures who are called to fill some particular niche in the Kingdom, some small, peculiar part of God's plan that belongs only to us and to no one else. Filling my own niche is never easy, so any help I can get is to the good. It is worth considering Mary's experience to see whether it can be illuminating, instructive or inspirational for mine.

I learn much about God's ways of calling people to themselves and to God by attending to Mary. I see her call as a paradox. Not everyone expects religious truth to emerge from a process that holds contradictory positions simultaneously and in equal strength. The paradoxical or 'both–and' or dualist or dialogic orientation, however, has had its adherents from Socrates through some medieval mystics and Luther and into Hegel and Kierkegaard and the neo-orthodox tradition. It is my way of knowing.

For me, the paradox in Mary's call is that it is a complete admixture of compulsion and freedom. When the angel Gabriel comes to tell Mary of God's plan for her, her response (Luke 1.38) is usually translated: 'I am the handmaid of the Lord; let it be done to me according to your word'. The rest of that verse reads: 'And the angel left her'. The implication is that the angel was not going to go away until he got Mary's consent – even though the angel's communication is in the form of an announcement, not a question. I understand Mary's consent to become the mother of God as somehow required, expected, desired, or at the very least thought to be fitting. Yet her very way of phrasing her response indicates that Mary knows very well that something else is also going on here. The word that is usually translated as 'handmaid' is actually *doulē*, and that really means 'slave'. Mary does what she does because she *must*; she acts as she is compelled to do.

If Mary is indeed a model for other Christians, if her experience is somehow normative for mine, then perhaps it is true that there is an interplay of compulsion and freedom in my own calls. Christians may well debate how determinative and sovereign is God's election. In Mary's case, however, her consent seems to be involved. It is true that the stories of the calls of the disciples in the Gospels seem pretty cut and dried. Jesus says 'Follow me' to the likes of Peter and Andrew, James and John, and they follow. What we do not know, however, is to how many others Jesus may have addressed the same command who did not obey it, like the rich young man the Synoptics describe. In the same way perhaps it is possible, as a Lutheran minister I know contends, that the reason it took so long for the Son of God to be incarnated in our world is that God had asked many others before Mary to be his mother, but Mary was the first person who said Yes. In any event, I sense myself as being able to make choices when it comes to doing God's will. That is, I can and have avoided doing it for long periods of time. Neither sin nor virtue would make sense without human freedom.

And yet there is a sense of compulsion to the call that the people of God have always acknowledged. I dearly hope that the pull and attraction of God's will for me will always be at least a little stronger than the pull of my own lazy and sinful inclinations to avoid it. Luke seems to speak to this very issue in two places. The first place is in the first chapter of his Gospel. There, just before describing the Annunciation to Mary, Luke describes the angel Gabriel's annunciation to Zechariah about the son he will father who is to be John the Baptist. Because Zechariah and his wife Elizabeth are elderly, Zechariah has the understandable temerity to question the angel's prophecy. 'How can I be sure of this?' he asks (1.18) – and is promptly punished because his faith is imperfect and his obedience slow. Gabriel makes it clear that God's will *shall* be done, and that since Zechariah did not make the proper response to God's invitation – implying that the only correct response is an immediate Yes – Zechariah will lose the power to say anything at all. 'Listen!' says Gabriel, 'Since you have not believed my words, which will come true at the appointed time, you will be silenced and have no power of speech until this has happened' (1.20). And so it was. When the angel comes to Mary, although she asks for clarification, she does not make the same mistake: Mary promptly consents and submits. By juxtaposing Zechariah's and Mary's responses to their annunciations, I think Luke intends to underline for his readers how difficult it can be to submit to God's will. In doing that, he is showing how courageous, faithful and obedient Mary managed to be. No weak little woman she! It is the strength and graciousness of her submission that makes her an attractive model for me.

Another place where Luke treats the human freedom/divine compulsion dialectic, and again seems to emphasize compulsion, is in Acts, as he describes Peter's address to the crowd after the phenomenon of Pentecost. Peter there quotes the prophet Joel's words about the outpouring of the Spirit on the Day of the Lord, but he changes the message slightly. Whereas Joel wrote: 'Even on the slaves, men and women, will I pour out my spirit in those days' (Joel 3.2), Peter says: 'Even on *my slaves*, men and women, in those days, I will pour out my spirit' (Acts 2.18). That 'slaves', *doulous*, is the same word that Mary used to describe herself at the Annunciation. When Peter changes Joel's 'the slaves' to 'my slaves', God's slaves, it is clear that the reference is to the Christian community. Luke seems to be saying that in some sense Christians are in bondage to the Lord. Slavery? To my ears the concept is repugnant and inhuman and very hard to accept. If I am to believe Luke, however, that bondage of which he writes is hardly servile or oppressive or demeaning because it is those very slaves who are bathed in God's own spirit.

If I am correct about this paradoxical interplay of bondage and freedom in our Christian calling, then perhaps Mary, who seems to have experienced both so clearly, may serve as a touchstone of discernment for me. When faced with what I perceive to be God's will, to what extent is my response appropriately discretionary and to what extent am I really constrained by my baptism, ordination, state in life, personal relationships, contracts, and needs to make a living? Which forms of bondage are simply oppressive and which lead to fuller freedom? Contemplating Mary, putting myself in her sandals, may illumine those questions.

Contemplating Mary can also teach me something about the necessity and the inevitability of constant growth in faith, love and hope. That growth seems to be a component of Christian discipleship. If even Mary, blessed as she was, grew in these virtues and *had* to grow in them, then I must need to grow as well. But *did* Mary grow after the Incarnation? Sticking with my two principles of staying with the biblical text and of following Julian's commitment to seeing the real Mary, the answer seems obvious. As Jesus' life unfolds, Mary grows, changes, develops, and matures – and not just a little, but a lot.

Mark's picture of Mary is so 'embarrassing' and on one level so disappointing to Christians that it is very likely to be dead-on accurate.[8] As Jesus goes about preaching and healing, Mark tells us (3.21) that 'When his relatives heard of this, they set out to take charge of him, convinced he was out of his mind'. It is true that the term 'relatives' is general and does not allude specifically to Mary or to any other given individual. Just ten verses later, however, we hear that Jesus' 'mother and brothers' arrived and sent him a message that they were outside asking for him. Surely this mother and these brothers are the same relatives just mentioned, the kin who thought Jesus was crazy.

In Mark 3.31–35, it is irrefutable that Mary is on the scene and is about to be rejected and rebuked sharply by her son. Jesus replied, 'Who are my mother and my brothers?' And looking round at those sitting in a circle about him, he said, 'Here are my mother and my brothers. Anyone who does the will of God, that person is my brother and sister and mother.' That was surely good news for the people sitting in the circle, but must have been painful news indeed for the woman outside who bore Jesus, changed his diapers, taught and nurtured him. Other interpretations may be possible here, but I believe that Jesus is saying that his true family are those who do the will of God and that his mother and brothers do not. That interpretation is consistent with their wanting to, as we say in the Southern United States, make him hush and get him home before he embarrassed the family any further. The evidence that this misunderstanding of Jesus and his work, this internal family struggle, was a continuing thing is Jesus' remark later in Mark that, 'A prophet is only despised in his own country, among his own relations and in his own house' (6.4). For Mark, thus, it seems clear that at the time of the public ministry, Mary did not know what Jesus was about and did not support what she saw him doing nor, perhaps, affirm his way of being.

Matthew – who has Joseph's dream about Jesus' identity, but no annunciation to Mary – relates these same two Marcan episodes from Jesus' life but softens them somewhat. In the incident about Jesus' true family, Matthew does not include the introductory comment that Jesus' relatives thought he was out of his mind. And he alters the comment about the prophet to read that such is 'only despised in his own country and in his own house', not referring specifically to 'relations' (13.57). If not Jesus' closest relatives, however – including his mother – just who would have been in his own house? And why does the Son of Man eventually have nowhere to lay his head (Matt. 8.20)? The fact that these are difficult questions to answer lends additional support to the view that the tensions were such that Jesus could not live at home. Why not? It is possible that his mother and other relatives did not understand his strangeness to be divine, and condemned it.

Luke has the full annunciation and expanded birth and infancy narratives. Luke's description of the incident about Jesus' true family is very similar to Matthew's account. And his citation of the comment about the prophet is downsized radically to 'No prophet is ever accepted in his own country' (4.24). Nonetheless, according to Luke, 'everyone' in Jesus' hometown synagogue was so enraged by his teachings that they wanted to throw him over a cliff (4.28–30). Just who would the 'everyone' in the hometown congregation include? Although Luke is consistent and careful not to say it, his account implies that even Mary did not understand Jesus.

Even John's unique account of Mary and Jesus at the wedding at Cana raises real questions about Mary's estimation of Jesus. While it is true that in John's view Mary believes that Jesus has water-changing powers that are at least magical, it is very doubtful that she understood anything more. Otherwise she would hardly have persisted with her wine-procurement process after Jesus' sharp comment calling her 'woman', and stating that his hour had not come (2.4). In Jesus' other direct address to Mary in John's Gospel, when she is at the foot of the cross, he again calls her 'woman'. The term is not negative, but it seems to me to lack endearment and a fitting recognition of the relationship. From Jesus' perspective such matters may have been trivial indeed. From Mary's human female perspective, however, I hear pain at that mode of address. I cannot speak for mothers, but I can tell you that if one of my students addressed me as 'woman', I would be inclined to take offence.

Despite this lack of understanding and perhaps even hostility toward Jesus' mission, in the end Mary makes it into the post-resurrection/pre-Pentecostal Christian community. There she joins with the apostles, Jesus' brothers, and several other women in continuous prayer (Acts 1.14). So somehow, by the grace of God, Mary changes. She moves from the immaturity and limited spiritual consciousness that produced disbelief or flawed belief, imperfect trust, unfriendly action, and perhaps weak hope (could that be what her absence from Calvary, according to the Synoptics, means?). She moves from that existential position into the fullness of mature, conscious Christian faith, hope, and charity. And once again I, so prone to immaturity in Christian faith and discipleship, so conscious of the need for growth and change, see in Mary an accessible sister-companion. If Mary does not change and grow, she is of no use to me as a model. I believe, however, that Mary has been where I am, and I rejoice in that conviction. It tells me that the Christian spiritual journey is a process and a progress, whether the pilgrim is full-of-grace she or full-of-grace me. The spiritual world is not one of powerful giants and inept pygmies. Contemplating Mary seems to affirm that spiritual growth is an equal-opportunity pursuit. If once-unwed, pregnant, teenaged girls – surely the bottom of the social heap – can march into the fullness of God's Kingdom, it must be a large, open, welcoming kingdom indeed. If the Kingdom can embrace Mary, it can also embrace me.

Should anyone arrive into the kingdom, I believe what she finds enthroned there is simply the sovereign and inscrutable will of God. The way to remain in that kingdom is through discipleship, that is, submission to God's will, in faith. Jesus said: 'It is not those who say to me, "Lord, Lord", who will enter the kingdom of heaven, but the person who does the will of my Father in heaven' (Matt. 7.21). As Mary submits so completely at the Annunciation, she becomes the model disciple, the new Abraham. She gives herself over, soul and body, to she knows not what, and thereby manifests the promise to Abraham: 'I will bless you and make your name so famous that it will be used as a blessing' (Gen. 12.2).[9] Like Abraham, Mary gives herself over to living out her faith, but she does it in her own way. Whereas Abraham went out into the world in faith, Mary came inward in faith. It is like a story Muslims tell: 'The mystic Rabia was in her house one day when her friend said, "Come out and behold what God has made". Rabia answered, "Come in and behold the Maker".'[10]

I doubt whether many people find it easy to believe that the divine is within them. I certainly find that news difficult, demanding, and painful. If I accept that divinity is within me, then I have a responsibility to my Lord and his Kingdom: I have to do the work myself of being a guardian, a nourisher, and an evangelist. In my own existential situation, that means being a loving, diligent, faithful, inspiring, and exacting teacher. While in one sense I take that in my stride because it is my present call, my preparation, and my gift, in another sense I find it daunting because I am well aware of how far short of the mark I fall.

Mary seems to be able to acknowledge and to sit with the enormous contradictions of her situation. She is pregnant and unwed, yet she knows that the baby in her womb is to save the world. As I see it, she does not try to suppress the paradox. Instead, she lets those two realities converse with each other. In this way, she is saved from both pride and despair. While aware of her own weaknesses, she is able to celebrate the full reality of God's gracious gift to her. The recognition of her 'low estate' may be the very thing that prompts her to celebrate God's grace to her as strongly as she does celebrate it.

It is, I believe, the affirmation of the paradox that allows Mary to accept Elizabeth's wondrous greeting to her: 'Of all women you are the most blessed, and blessed is the fruit of your womb' (Luke 1.42). It is, I believe, the affirmation of the paradox that would have made it appropriate for Mary to say: 'From this day forward all generations will call me blessed, for the Almighty has done great things for me' (Luke 1.48). The profound humility bespoken here awes me because I see that Mary accepts the fullness of her responsibilities, the entirety of her vocation, with no excuses. That is such a grown-up thing to do. I suspect that it is ever thus with any true disciple, and, please God, could some day be true of me. That is because Mary exemplifies what can some day be true of each of us. As Luther said: Mary sang the Magnificat 'not for herself alone but for us all, to sing it after her'.[11] As a true disciple, Mary points always and only to the being and work of the divinity within her. Luther understood that as he suggested that we address Mary thus:

O Blessed Virgin, Mother of God, you were nothing and all despised; yet God in His grace regarded you and worked such great things in you. You were worthy of none of them, but the rich and abundant grace of God was upon you, far above any merit of yours. Hail to you! Blessed are you, from thenceforth and forever, in finding such a God.[12]

It is not Mary herself whom we honour and revere, nor do I take pride in my own accomplishments. In both cases, if there is any glory due, it is solely to the grace of God. Both Luther and Julian so teach, as does St. Paul:

Through our Lord Jesus Christ, by faith we are judged righteous and at peace with God, since it is by faith and through Jesus that we have entered this state of grace in which we can boast about looking forward to God's glory (Rom. 5.1–2).

Mary is not only full of God's grace, however; she is also full of her own human limitations. She is not the complete and perfect disciple all the time. That is good news for me, because I am certainly not. Mary makes a wonderful beginning and reaches discipleship again at the last. In between, she is on a very human, zigzag journey during what we know of her in Jesus' growing-up years and public ministry. How true to human experience that is. Most of us are glorious idealists when we are young. That is probably the best time to decide to live the gospel, get married, get ordained, enter the convent, go off to do missionary work or join the army. Most of those things most of us for long hesitate to do, once experience turns us stodgy and cautious, and we realize that all pastures have muddy bare spots, and that none is any greener than the adjacent ones. Those early commitments, however, provide a kind of elastic frame in which we can wriggle and writhe until we finally assume our place in the picture, and rest. I think that is how early enthusiastic commitment worked for Mary; and I think that is how it is coming to work for me.

Not even Mary was spared the labour pains that coming to full, conscious discipleship entails. It has been suggested that this is the real meaning of the sword that Simeon prophesies will pierce her soul (Luke 2.35). Mary, too, is not to be spared the tests, the discernment, the perils, and the suffering of the process of coming to discipleship.[13] No disciple is so spared.

If, however, Mary does come to full discipleship, that must mean that her fundamental disposition was correct more or less throughout the process; she was on the right path. In her case that path seems to involve prayer and self-giving. In what is really a small amount of text devoted to Mary, Luke tells us three times that Mary was at prayer or pondering things in her heart (Luke 2.19, 51; Acts 1.14). Besides those three instances, the Magnificat is a prayer. Clearly the point is that Mary was at prayer very often. I think prayer is the ground of the spiritual life. Public prayer and the eucharist are necessary, of course, but what I really mean here is, first, some form of meditation, like centering prayer, that gets the self more or less out of the way so that God can be heard. Mary's pondering in her heart could be this sort of prayer.

A second necessary form of prayer has to do with disposing myself to submit to God and obey. As Kierkegaard said and Gordon Wakefield once reminded the Society: 'True prayer is a struggle with God, and man emerges victorious when God is the victor'.[14] Mary's way of submitting immediately to the angel's demands bespeaks prayer of this submissive, obedient, vocation-centered sort. Her prayer, thus, exemplifies normative biblical prayer. Ralph A. Keifer expresses this well, saying that in the Bible:

> Where we are given portrayals of people actually engaged seriously in the business of prayer, the heart of the matter is neither praise nor petition, but obedience ... the obedience of those who wrestle with living the mission they sense has been laid upon them ... of being given a task that the bearers sense will shape their whole life and demand the attention of their whole heart, without them wholly wishing it could be that way, and without them having any sense of adequacy to do it. 'Let this cup pass from me' is much more characteristic of biblical prayer at its very heart than [is] 'Praise the Lord'.[15]

If true biblical prayer has to do with disposing oneself to live faithfully to one's vocation and, thus, to fulfil God's will, Mary's response at the Annunciation manifests it.

One additional way Mary teaches me about relating to God is through self-giving. She gives her will, and importantly her body, over to the bearing and nurturing of the divinity within her. She is, moreover, privileged to give herself to God with little apparent reward. After that first flush of joy and delight at bearing the saviour of the world, mostly what she seems to me to reap is her son ignoring or insulting her in public. I believe that at death I, too, will have the opportunity to give myself wholly to God, and the self as I experience it now will no longer be there to receive any possible return. That prospect is so far beyond my experience that it is terrifying. I can see how the petition in the 'Hail Mary' prayer to 'pray for us sinners now and at the hour of our death' is useful here. The prayers of one who is as proficient at self-giving as she, are so authentic that they are bound to be heard.

Although Mary gives herself with no immediate assurance of a return, I believe that Mary actually does receive a magnificent reward. She is finally taken into the glory in God, I would prefer to say, though others may say she is assumed into heaven. Here, admittedly, my method falters, and sheer intuition, hope, and faith take over. That is because, as Donald G. Dawe told the Society, 'Scripture does not contain an explicit witness to the dogma of the Assumption', though one can, as Dawe indicates, undergird theologically the foundation of the dogma through an appeal to the *sensus plenior* of such pericopes as the Annunciation and the Magnificat.[16] Instances of assumption of others do appear in both the canonical Old and New Testaments, though those assumed are in all cases Old Testament people. In the Letter of Jude, there is a description of the archangel Michael and the devil fighting over the corpse of Moses (v. 9). While Mary's Assumption cannot be derived from scripture, I believe that Mary is taken into the fullness of God's glory. Maybe I believe that simply because I need that to be so, to know that the Yes of a loving God finally triumphs over God's No. As Dawe said: 'Mary is the expression of the proleptic nature of the Kingdom. She is the sign of hope living amidst the people of God to embody the full salvation for which they long.'[17] I think that Mary longed for that full salvation; I know that I long for it; and I believe that we shall both be satisfied. The Bible tells me so, as in John 10.10: Jesus said, 'I have come that they may have life and have it to the full'. And once again, because I see that fullness realized in Mary, I dare to hope for it for myself.

Scripture, thus, and Julian of Norwich, show me Mary in a way that empowers me to continue my own journey. I will always welcome seeing such a Mary, who is to my mind realistic, authentic, and imitable. She turns out to be such a good model for my own spiritual journey, that in a sense, perhaps, she serves as a kind of talisman. Among my own four saints at the beginning of this talk, I included my mother. My mother died last year. As I thought back later, the last gift she gave me seemed odd to me at the time, and, to tell you the truth, not all that welcome. On my birthday, about three weeks before her death, she had sent me two Marian medals. Attached to one was a handwritten note that said, 'Wear this close to your heart, and she will protect you'. That made little sense to me at the time and had even less appeal because I understood it as a fruit of a piety that robbed Mary of her humanity and robbed me of a sister-companion. Now I see it differently. The Mary I am coming to know as a sister traveller and companion for my own spiritual journey has the potential – as a model – to empower, inspire, goad, and, yes, in that sense, to protect me on that journey.

Notes

1 Short Text: ch. xiii; Long Text: ch. 25, Revelation 11. Citations to Julian are from *A Book of Showings to the Anchoress Julian of Norwich*, Parts I (Short text, ST) and II (Long text, LT), eds. Edmund Colledge OSA and James Walsh SJ (Toronto, Pontifical Institute of Mediaeval Studies, 1978).
2 ibid. LT: ch. 25, 1.5; ST: ch. xiii, 1.10.
3 ST, ch. xiii.
4 'The Elixir'.
5 Martin Luther, *The Magnificat, Luther's Works*, v. 21 (St Louis, Concordia, 1956), p. 152.
6 See Jean-Hervé Nicolas, 'Les Apparitions Mariales dans la Vie du Chrétien,' *Mater Fidei et Fidelium* (Marian Library Studies) (Dayton, University of Dayton, 1985–1991), pp. 673–83, in which the author concludes that apparitions are a private matter between the individual seer and God, and that the rest of the Christian community is best off treating them as such, because it is true both that Christians need in principle to remain open to messages from heaven and that apparitions are not verifiable. See also Nicholas Perry and Loreto Echeverria, *Under the Heel of Mary* (London, Routledge, 1988), an historical study that claims that from the earliest days of the Church until now and into the foreseeable future, Marian apparitions are 'at the service of manipulative power (p. 313), particularly of the right-wing sort' (p. 3 and *passim*).
7 *Mary in the New Testament*, ed. Raymond E. Brown et al. (Philadelphia, Fortress, 1978), pp. 257, 260.
8 See John Macquarrie, *Mary for All Christians* (Grand Rapids, Eerdmans, 1990), pp. 33–35.
9 *Redemptoris Mater* (Washington, DC, US Catholic Conference, 1987), relates Mary to Abraham in ch. 14.
10 Ira Friedlander, *The Whirling Dervishes* (New York, Macmillan, 1975), p. 19.
11 Luther, p. 306.
12 ibid. p. 322.
13 Brown et al. pp. 154–57.
14 'Intercession,' *Mary's Place in Christian Dialogue* (Middlegreen, England, St Paul Publications, 1982), pp. 263–70, 269.
15 *The Mass in Time of Doubt* (Washington, DC, Pastoral Press, 1983), p. 20.
16 'The Assumption of the Blessed Virgin in Ecumenical Perspective,' in *Mary and Ecumenism* (*The Way* Supplement, no. 45, June 1982) p. 44.
17 ibid. p. 48.

(This paper was given at the ESBVM Congress
at Norwich in July 1994)

19

Julian of Norwich and the Blessed Virgin Mary

John P.H. Clark

It is a happy occasion that this Congress of the ESBVM should be taking place in Norwich, the place where one of the most creative English female theologians lived. Thomas Merton ranked Julian of Norwich beside Cardinal Newman as a theologian. Julian is a profoundly faithful daughter of the Church, deeply rooted in the tradition, who as a wise scribe brings out of her treasure things old and new.

Julian is known for her *Revelations of Divine Love*, based on the disclosure which was made to her at the age of thirty in May 1373.[1] In the texts which we have, Julian is described as an anchoress. She was still alive in 1413,[2] and there is mention of the anchoress attached to St Julian's Church in Norwich in a will of 1415;[3] this anchoress is taken to be Julian, rather than a successor.

We do not know where she came from, nor her baptismal name; anchorites and anchoresses commonly took the name of the church to which they were attached. It has been suggested that she may have been a nun of the Benedictine convent of Carrow in Norwich who subsequently became an anchoress, but this is simply speculation. We do not, indeed, know whether she was already an anchoress when she received her Revelations, or whether she became one in consequence of them. Sister Benedicta Ward has pointed to Julian's profound compassion with those in suffering, and has suggested the possibility that she may have been a housewife who was bereaved of her husband and children in one of the successive outbreaks of the Black Death which continued from time to time after the disastrous year of 1349.[4] We simply do not know. As an anchoress, Julian clearly had a reputation as a spiritual guide, and Margery Kempe, the idiosyncratic but surely heroic housewife of Lynn, mentions her in her *Book* as one of those with whom she took counsel.

The *Revelations* have come to us in two forms: the relatively simple Short Text, and the Long Text, which is built around the material in the Short Text but contains very much more theological reflection, including the teaching on the motherhood of God in Christ for which Julian is famous. The image of God as 'mother' is not in itself new; there are passages in the Wisdom literature of the Bible, and indeed in the Gospels, which provide a basis for it, and the image crops up in the

Church Fathers of East and West, including Augustine.[5] But Julian is remarkable for the way in which she works out a profoundly Trinitarian theology which includes the 'motherhood' image, centred on Christ, to whom in Augustinian theology 'Wisdom' is commonly appropriated.

The Long Text also includes Julian's exposition of the Lord and the Servant, which is so important for her understanding of the Atonement and is bound up with her searching questions as to the scope of salvation. This is not found in the Short Text; Julian says that this Revelation did form part of the original revelations that were given to her, but that it was too difficult to be included in her first draft of her work; it was only, she says, twenty years after the event that the meaning of this revelation was given to her.[6] Because of this statement, it has been commonly assumed until recently that the Short Text was written quite soon after the event, while the completion of the Long Text might be placed in or relatively soon after 1393. Professor Nicholas Watson has now proposed a longer time-scale for Julian's literary work.[7] It may well be that the Short Text did take longer to compose than had been supposed, but I am not totally convinced that Julian was still at work on the Long Text right into her old age.

Julian's visions place her within a whole genre of mediaeval visionaries, not least from Germany and the Low Countries. Christina of Markyate (fl. 1142 – 1155) is one such figure from England, though her visions are only an incidental feature in her life.[8] The *Revelations* of Elizabeth of Hungary (d. 1231)[9] and of Mechtilde of Hackeborn (d.(?) 1299)[10] are found in English in fifteenth-century manuscripts. There is also of course St Bridget of Sweden (*c.* 1303 – 1373), whose *Revelations* were known to Margery Kempe of King's Lynn[11], and are found in English again in various fifteenth-century manuscripts, in different versions[12]. But while Julian may be seen within such a wider movement, her visions are a point of departure for a very personal and creative theological reflection.

Estimates of Julian's learning have varied. Fathers Colledge and Walsh, the editors of the standard edition of her *Revelations*, have seen her as a distinctly learned woman, but by no means all of the sources and analogues that they have adduced have convinced other people. While some general antecedents may be found in the Cistercian tradition, and in the devotion to the Sacred Humanity of Christ as this was fostered especially by the Franciscans, the particular analogues which the learned editors have drawn with William of St Thierry are not compelling. On the other hand, I find their argument that she could read Latin[13] convincing, and she was familiar, clearly, with some of the commonplaces of monastic and scholastic theology, which she is fully capable of developing and applying in ways which are new and yet fully compatible with the received tradition; for instance, it has been shown that her exposition of the Lord and the Servant owes much to a passage in Augustine's *De Trinitate* on the sending in time of the second Person of the Trinity, which was familiar to mediaeval theologians generally and specifically to those of Julian's day.[14] Norwich had considerable theological resources, and apart from the Benedictine Cathedral Priory there were houses of all four learned mendicant Orders there in Julian's day, of which the Austin Friars were closest geographically to St Julian's Church. No doubt Julian had competent spiritual advisers. Julian's teaching on the Motherhood of Christ, together with her affective (but still intellectually and spiritually tough) theology, and her by-passing of any interpretation of the Atonement which might lend support to a 'juridical' understanding, in favour of one which emphasises God's timeless compassion for his creation expressed in the profound cost of Christ's saving work performed in time, have naturally made her a key person for those with feminist concerns in theology. Late twentieth-century issues can hardly have been consciously present to Julian, but no doubt it is very proper to turn to Julian – and to others – for principles which may be applied to present-day concerns, just as Julian herself saw the tradition which she inherited as dynamic and alive rather than static.

But in any case, any feminist theology which fails to take very seriously the place of Mary in the pattern of salvation, in intimate association with and yet subordinate to Christ, does less than justice to the resources of the Christian tradition. Moreover, the place accorded to Mary is a corollary of the whole understanding of grace as an intrinsic principle of supernatural life, of the real effect of Christ's redeeming love within the soul, and also of the Church as the Body of Christ in which as brothers and sisters of Christ we have Mary as the mother of grace. The debate about the ordination of women, at the level at which it has been commonly conducted, has left these issues largely untouched, but they will certainly need to be addressed. As well as, and in conjunction with, her doctrine of the motherhood of God in Christ, Julian has a very positive emphasis on the place of Mary, This is already established in its essentials in the Short Text, but added nuances are given in the Long Text.

Julian's Revelations, sixteen in all, were given to her by God in response to her desire for three graces: to have 'mind' of the Passion of Christ; to have bodily sickness, and to have three wounds.[15] Two points should be made here. First, while the Cross is central to Julian, it is not to be separated from the Incarnation and from the Resurrection. The constant liturgical emphasis of the Church in keeping these three elements of the mystery of Christ in balance is much in evidence. Secondly, Julian's desire to share in Christ's Passion is not a 'private' matter. Her whole emphasis, as befits one who is, or was to become an anchoress, is strongly ecclesial. The Revelations were given to her not simply for her own benefit, but for the benefit of the 'even-Christians' to whom she constantly refers.[16] Her own assurance of salvation is seen by her as representative of all those who are on the way to salvation with her. Moreover, her powerful emphasis on the 'cosmic' Christ leads her to reflect on the point at which the Passion of Christ touches not only those who are 'friends' of Christ, but also, as an additional passage in the Long Text declares, those who are unbelievers – she instances Pilate and St Denis of France – Dionysius the Areopagite. The Passion touches also the inanimate creation.[17]

As the priest holds the Crucifix before the young Julian and gives her the last rites, she receives her first Revelation. Already in the Short Text at this early point Julian speaks of God's (or Christ's) 'homely loving', and goes on to picture this in almost 'motherly' terms:

> He is our clothing, for love enwraps us and envelops us, embraces us and guides us; [he] hovers over us, for tender love, that he may never leave us.[18]

The image of God's creation as 'a little thing, the quantity of a hazel-nut', with the Trinitarian disclosure of God as 'Maker', 'Lover', 'Keeper', follows in the Short Text, and then the first showing of Mary.[19] In the Long Text, the showing of Mary is placed before the image of the hazel-nut and its accompanying Trinitarian statement.[20]

In either case, there is a certain implied association between the tender and almost motherly care of God for his creation, and the person of Mary, mother of the Redeemer, who herself owes to God every grace which she has. We shall notice later one of the expansions in the Long Text where Julian will develop further the relationship – and the distinction – between the uncreated motherhood of God in Christ, and the created motherhood of Mary.[21]

Already in the Short Text the link between God's saving action in Christ and the mother of Christ is clear. Julian asks who is to grant her that union in the spirit with God for which she longs? 'In truth, Himself, by his mercy and his grace, because he has made me for this and blessedly restored me thereto'.[22] This passage is only partially marked in the Long Text. At this point, Julian passes at once, in the Short Text, to the vision that was given her of Mary's receptivity and obedience at the Annunciation – that receptivity which, humanly speaking, opens the door to the Incarnation:

> *In this* [italics mine], God brought our Lady to my understanding. I saw her spiritually, in bodily likeness, a simple maiden and humble, young of age, in

the stature that she was when she conceived. Also God shewed me in part the wisdom and the truth of her soul, wherein I understood the reverent beholding wherewith she beheld her God that is her Maker, marvelling with great reverence that he that was her Maker would be born of her who was a simple creature of His making. And this wisdom [and] truth, this knowing the greatness of her Maker and the littleness of herself that is made, made her to say humbly to the angel Gabriel: 'Lo me here, God's handmaiden' (Luke 1.38). In this sight I saw truly that she is greater than all that God made beneath her in worthiness and in fullness of grace. For above her is nothing that is made but the blessed Manhood of Christ. This little thing that is made, that is beneath our Lady, Saint Mary, God shewed it to me as little as if it had been a hazel nut.[23]

The second passage, with the significant omission of the last sentence, does occur in the Long Text, including the opening words 'In this', but it is now in a different context, following a discussion of preservation in the face of temptations.[24] The final sentence in the Short Text does not alter the doctrinal balance; it does no more than repeat in essence what is said in the preceding sentence, common to both texts. But its omission in the Long Text is because the total passage has been moved in the Long Text from its proper context in conjunction with the 'hazel-nut' passage. The shift of context in the Long Text means that what is supposed to be the connecting link, 'In this', now loses its force.

As herself a contemplative, Julian sees Mary's faith, love and obedience as a contemplative act – hence her reference to 'the reverent beholding wherewith she beheld her God ...' It is this act which, in opening the way to the Incarnation, contains the germ of all the saving possibilities that this brings for the future Church, and indeed for all creation. Mary's assent to her vocation has a universal significance.

The truth and wisdom of Mary's soul, her acknowledgement of her creaturely status, together with confidence in God and readiness to fulfil his purpose, may be contrasted – though Julian does not bring this out – with the self-exaltation which is of Adam's pride and so of his Fall. Julian would have been familiar with the picture of Mary as the second Eve, reflecting Christ as the second Adam. But the reference to truth and wisdom contains further possibilities for reflection, which Julian will again bring out in a later passage in the Long Text.

In Augustinian theology Power, Wisdom and Love (or Goodness) are appropriated to the three Persons of the Trinity – to the Father, the Son and the Holy Spirit respectively.[25] Man's soul, made in the image of God, is a created trinity, in which the three faculties of *memoria* (awareness), *intelligentia* (understanding), and *voluntas* (will), answer to the Uncreated Trinity.[26]

Julian is familiar with the commonplaces of Augustinian theology, including especially the theology of Trinitarian appropriation. She refers repeatedly to God as Power, Wisdom, and Love (or Goodness). In a chapter in the Long Text where she is developing points that arise from the Revelations, she recalls something of the common appropriations to the Persons of the Trinity, but substitutes Truth for Power, and relates this to the Revelation of Mary's obedience. Julian distinguishes between the Uncreated Truth, Wisdom and Love in God, and created truth, wisdom and love in the human soul, more especially in the soul of Mary:

> God showed in all the Revelations often that man works evermore his will and his worship lastingly, without any stinting. And what this work is, was showed in the first, and that in a marvellous example: for it was showed in the working of the soul of our blessed Lady, Saint Mary: that is, in the working of Truth and Wisdom ...
> Truth sees God, and Wisdom beholds God, and of these two comes the third; that is, a holy marvellous delight in God: which is Love. Where Truth and Wisdom are truly, there is Love truly, coming from them both. And all of God's making: for He is endless sovereign Truth, endless sovereign Wisdom, endless sovereign Love, unmade; and man's soul is a creature in God which has the same properties made ... [27]

The Eighth Revelation is concerned with our sharing in the Passion of Christ. Julian gives vivid physical details of the reality of our Redeemer's suffering. In the Short Text, in a passage which is not matched in the Long Text, Julian describes the suffering of her own mother as she saw her own daughter apparently at the point of death.[28] This deepens Julian's own sense of suffering with Christ. As Julian is taken out of herself, made forgetful of herself, in love for Christ in his sufferings, so she is led to think of the sufferings of Mary, who is the supreme lover of Christ. From Mary, Julian is led to consider all those who loved Christ and suffered with him, albeit less than did his mother, and even the sense in which inanimate creatures shared in the Passion:

> Here I felt truly that I loved Christ so much above myself that I thought it had been a great ease to me to have died bodily. Herein I saw a part of the Compassion of our Lady, Saint Mary, for Christ and she were so oned in love that the greatness of her love was the cause of the greatness of her pain. For in so much as she loved Him more than all others, her pain surpassed all others' pain; and so all His disciples and all His true lovers suffered pains greater than those of their own bodily dying ... Here I saw a great oneing between Christ and us, for when He was in pain we were in pain: all creatures that might suffer pain suffered with Him, and they who knew Him not had this for their pain, that all creatures, sun and moon, withdrew their service ... [29]

Just as Mary is central to the mystery of the Incarnation, and just as she shares intimately in the Passion, so she shares in the Resurrection, and in its consequences, which follow directly upon the Passion of Christ. The Tenth Revelation is of the wounded side of Christ,[30] but this leads directly to the Eleventh Revelation, of Mary who stood beside the wounded side of Christ at the Cross, and who now shares in the joy of the Resurrection. Not only should all Christians share with Christ in the pain of the Cross and in the victory of his Resurrection, but also, because of the mutual love between Jesus and Mary, they should share with Jesus in the joy that he has in his mother's glorification, which is a corollary of his own:

> With the same gladness Christ looked down at His right-hand side and brought to my mind where our Lady stood in the time of his Passion ...
> Often I had prayed (to see her) ... Jesus, when he said this word, showed me a spiritual sight of her: just as I had before seen her little and simple, right so he showed her then high and noble and glorious, and pleasing to Him above all creatures. Thus He wills that it be known that all those who like in Him should like in her, and she in Him. And in that word: 'Wilt thou see her?', I thought I had the greatest liking that he could have given me, with the spiritual showing that he gave me of her.[31]

Generally Julian says that Christ deliberately refrained from giving her a vision of the state of any particular departed person. But an exception is made in the case of Mary, precisely because of the intimate union that exists between herself and her Son, so that to see Mary is to see her participation in the work of Christ and his work in her. Julian emphasises how the Revelations of Mary are bound up with the three principal aspects of the mystery of Christ:

> For our Lord granted me no special showing but that of our Lady, Saint Mary, and He showed her me three times. The first time was at the moment of her conceiving Him; the second time, as she was in her sorrow under the cross; and the third time, as she is now – in liking, worship and joy.[32]

From the sight of Mary in glory, Julian is led to see Christ in his own enhanced glory. She takes this as a sign that the vision of Mary is an integral element in the progress of contemplative souls – a vision of Mary which points beyond her to Christ, and to God revealed in Christ:

> After this our Lord showed Himself to me more glorified, as to my sight, than I saw Him before; and in this showing I was taught that every contemplative soul to whom it is given to behold and feel God, shall see her and pass to God by contemplation.[33]

The equivalent passage in the Long Text omits the specific Marian reference in this last paragraph, preferring to speak simply of finding rest in Christ.[34] But the point remains, that the vision of Mary is bound up especially with the Incarnation, Passion and Resurrection of Christ, and that Mary points us to closer union with Christ.

While Julian would have been familiar with the liturgical observance of Mary's Assumption, she is more concerned to speak of Mary's present state of glorification rather than of the event as such of her Assumption. All that Mary was in her earthly life is now glorified. When Julian spoke earlier of the created world as the 'hazel-nut' 'beneath' the Mary of the Annunciation, it is already this present state of glorification which is implied, though the dignity of Mary within God's purpose at the moment of the Annunciation was veiled. For that matter, as she pictures the glorified Christ, Julian does not formally distinguish between Christ's Resurrection and Ascension, though the Christ who is seated in the City which is the human soul, who makes this City his 'homeliest home'[35] is implicitly the Ascended Christ.

Other passages in the Long Text which have no parallel in the Short Text indicate continuing reflection on the role of Mary. The vision of the Lord and the Servant is stated to have been part of the original Revelations, although its subject-matter was too difficult for it to be included in the original, Short Text. In this vision, a Servant stands before his Lord, eager to do his Lord's will. Setting out, in his eagerness he falls into a deep valley and is badly hurt, so that he cannot raise himself. The Lord looks on him with pity and compassion rather than with blame, because it was the Servant's good-will which was the occasion of his falling. At the same time the Lord looks on the servant with joy, seeing that the Servant's fall and distress will be the occasion of his being raised to greater dignity and joy than he had before the fall.[36]

The Servant is a composite figure, holding together Adam and Christ, who in the Lord's (God the Father's) sight are seen as one, in a single moment. The Servant's fall represents both the fall of Adam, and the 'fall' of Christ into the womb of Mary in the Incarnation, with the purpose of restoring Adam who represents humanity. As already mentioned, Julian is here giving a new application to Augustine's familiar teaching on the sending of God the Son into the world as the disclosure within time and history of the life of the Holy Trinity:[37]

> Adam fell from life to death, into the valley of this wretched world, and after that into hell; God's Son fell with Adam, into the valley of the Maiden's womb, who was the fairest daughter of Adam; and for this end; to excuse Adam from blame in heaven and in earth; and mightily He fetched him out of hell.[38]

Apart from the debt to Augustine, Julian is here, as so often, recalling the Liturgy; we think at once of the *Te Deum*: 'When thou tookest upon thee to deliver man, thou didst not abhor the Virgin's womb'.

The debate as to whether Mary was immaculately conceived, or whether she inherited the taint of Adam's sin at her conception but was sanctified in the womb, had been going on for a long time by the time that Julian wrote her Long Text in the 1390s. In general, in England the view of Duns Scotus, who took it that it was both possible and fitting for Christ to have redeemed his Mother from original sin in a preventive and so in a more radical sense than if she had actually contracted it, had gained ground, and was held by most of the religious Orders apart from the Dominicans, who after a spell in which at least one Cambridge Dominican theologian had embraced the Immaculate Conception[39] had reverted to the older perspective, especially in deference to their great doctor Saint Thomas Aquinas. Julian is a contemplative rather than an academic theologian, and she is not concerned to discuss this point, any more than, say, Richard Rolle, Walter Hilton, or the unknown but probably Carthusian author of the *Cloud of Unknowing* are. If we were to press words to their logical implications, we might argue that when Julian speaks of Mary as the 'fairest daughter of Adam' she means that Mary is the holiest of God's creatures – free, indeed, as was universally accepted, from actual sin – but still subject to the taint of Adam's original sin. But Julian may equally have meant simply that Mary is the fairest of all those who are Adam's daughters by descent, without attempting to define further.

In fact, the fluctuations in the doctrine concerning Mary's sinlessness have been bound up with varying understandings of the nature of original sin and of grace, and especially regarding the transmission of Adam's guilt (*reatus*)[40] to his descendants. While Julian is firmly if somewhat idiosyncratically within the parameters of orthodoxy where sin and redemption is concerned, she is deliberately silent on any question of original sin as conveying an inherited guilt apart from actual sin, as the whole tone of her discussion of the Lord and the Servant makes clear. (There is a contrast here with, for instance, the compassionate and pastoral but theologically severely Augustinian Walter Hilton.) Therefore it is in the highest degree unlikely that Julian would have wanted to discuss the theological rationale of Mary's sinlessness in such terms – not out of any hesitation regarding the pre-eminent holiness of Mary, full of grace, but because Julian would not have been at home with the category of imputed guilt apart from actual sin.

We have seen that already in the account of the First Revelation in the Short Text, Julian has used language of God (or of Christ) which is not out of keeping with the image of Christ as mother, as she speaks of

God's love in the creation and conservation of the world as well as in its redemption. It is from chapter 48 onwards of the Long Text that Julian develops explicitly the image of Christ as Mother, within a closely integrated Trinitarian theology. Developing a point that she has made lightly in the Short Text, she now makes a clear distinction between mercy and grace as aspects of God's remedy for sin, appropriating Mercy to the Motherhood of God (introduced here for the first time), and Grace to the Lordship of God: 'Mercy is a pitiful property, which belongs to motherhood in tender love; and grace is a worshipful property which belongs to royal lordship in the same love.'[41] A little further on, Julian elaborates her own variation on the traditional Augustinian appropriations pertaining to Trinitarian theology. It is as the Wisdom of God, *Sapientia Dei*, that Christ specifically may be called Mother, while the Lordship of God is ascribed to the Holy Spirit, *Bonitas Dei*: 'The almighty truth of the Trinity is our Father ... And the deep wisdom of the Trinity is our Mother ... and the high Goodness of the Trinity is our Lord.'[42]

In the Incarnation, Christ united himself to our common humanity when he took flesh in Mary's womb, and raised our humanity to a supernatural level (potentially at least), by uniting our *sensualité* – our body of flesh and blood with its senses and emotions – to our *substance* – the essential humanity of each of us as this exists in the mind of God. Mary is indeed the mother of all Christians – but Mary's motherhood at a deeper level derives from the Motherhood of Christ her Son:

> For in that same time that God united himself to our body in the Virgin's womb he took our *sensualité*; in which taking He, having us all enclosed in Himself, united it to our *substance*; in which union he was perfect man ... Thus our Lady is our Mother in whom we are all enclosed, and of her born in Christ, for she that is Mother of our Saviour is mother of all that are saved in our Saviour; and our Saviour is our very Mother in whom we are endlessly born, and never shall come out of him.[43]

'Enclosed' ('beclosyd') echoes something of the passage quoted earlier from the very beginning of the Short Text: 'He is our clothing, for love; he enwraps us and envelops us ...'. 'Born' could mean either 'carried' or else 'brought to birth'. Perhaps, since Julian is speaking of an on-going process rather than of a single act, 'carried' should be preferred.

Julian sums up her theology of Trinitarian appropriation, as this is disclosed in God's action towards us:

> I beheld the working of all the Blessed Trinity ... I saw ... the property of the Fatherhood, and the property of the Motherhood, and the property of the Lordship in one God ... All our life is in three; in the first we have our being,

in the second we have our increasing, and in the third we have our fulfilling. The first is nature ('kynde'), the second is mercy, the third is grace.[44]

So Christ is called 'our mother of mercy' through the assumption of our *sensualité*.[45] Julian will have been familiar with the title given to Mary in the *Salve Regina: Mater misericordiae*. She will have known that this Marian reference is simultaneously a reference to Christ – that Mary is the mother of Christ's mercy. The way will be open to representing further the union and interaction of the Mother and the Son.

Julian takes it that since Christ as the second Person of the Trinity is active with the Father (and the Holy Spirit) in creation, his 'motherhood' belongs not only to the order of redemption, but to that of creation: 'We have our being of Him, where the ground of motherhood begins.'[46] And, succinctly: 'Thus Jesu is our very mother by nature ("in kynd") of our first making, and he is our mother in grace by assuming our created nature ("by takyng of oure kynde made").[47]

Once again, as Julian expounds the orders of creation and redemption, of nature and grace, she turns to the First Revelation, of Mary at the Annunciation. She is saying in effect that the natural order is taken up into the supernatural, the order of creation into the order of redemption which both restores and enhances it. In order to become our Mother in the fullest sense, not only in the order of creation but also in that of redemption, Christ is born of his human Mother, Mary. In the following passage Julian is surely making use of the multiplicity of meanings available in Middle English, where 'kind' as an adjective can mean both 'kind' in its modern sense, and also 'natural', just as 'gracious' conveys not only its common modern meaning, but also points to 'grace' as distinct from 'nature':

> Our kind Mother, our gracious Mother, because he would all wholly become our Mother in all things, he took the ground of his works full low and full mildly in the Maiden's womb. And that he showed in the first [showing], where he brought that humble Maid before the eye of my understanding in the simple stature as she was when she conceived. That is to say: our high God is sovereign Wisdom of all: in this low place he arrayed and prepared himself full ready in our poor flesh, himself to do the service and the office of motherhood in all things.[48]

Julian's Marian devotion is an extension of her devotion to our Lord, as she sees the Incarnation as the essential starting-point of Christ's saving work. Her emphasis on the place of Mary in conjunction with the Mysteries of the Incarnation, Passion and Resurrection, draws on biblical and pictorial material – the sort of visual aids which would have been to hand in the churches which she knew – and has obvious roots in the liturgical, and para-liturgical, observance of the Church: with Christmas, Good Friday and Easter in reference to our Lord, and beside this to the Marian observances of the Annunciation, Compassion and Assumption.

This pattern is closely matched in the Joyful, Sorrowful and Glorious Mysteries of the Rosary of our Lady as these are prayed today. But the modern Rosary has its origins more particularly in fifteenth-century Germany, in the movement associated with the Carthusians Adolph of Essen and Dominic of Prussia.[49] An earlier antecedent, and one which Julian is overwhelmingly likely to have known in some form, is the meditation known as the Joys of Mary. The number of Joys varied, but from the thirteenth century five was the commonest number in England; this includes the Incarnation, the Resurrection consequent upon the Passion, and the Assumption.[50]

Above all Julian emphasises the value of Mary's contemplative obedience. It is this, under God, which makes possible the Incarnation and Redemption. So for Julian, for whom the Christian life is so profoundly a life of union with her fellow-Christians, union with Christ leads her to union with Mary. Julian's life of contemplative prayer reaches out to include all Christians, and seeks also more widely, within the mind of the Church, to embrace all of God's creation within the Redemption wrought by Christ.

Notes

1   These are available in numerous editions. Page references are to the standard edition by E. Colledge and J. Walsh, *A Book of Showings to the Anchoress Julian of Norwich*, Texts and Studies, 35 (2 vols.), (Pontifical Institute of Mediaeval Studies, Toronto, 1978) which contains both the Short and Long Texts. The editors' choice of MS Paris B.N. Fonds Anglais 40 as the base-text for the Long Text has been far from receiving universal support, and reference must also be made to *Julian of Norwich: A Revelation of Love*, ed. Marion Glasscoe (University of Exeter 1976 and subsequent revisions), which is an edition of the Long Text based on MS British Library, Sloane 2499, collated with the Paris MS.

For quotations from the Short Text, I have made use of *A Shewing of God's Love*, the modernised version by Sister Anna Maria Reynolds, (London 1958), with occasional adjustments. For quotations from the Long Text, I have made my own modernised version from the Colledge/Walsh edition, referring also to Miss Glasscoe's text and indicating any disputed points. Colledge and Walsh have also produced a modern-language version of the Long Text in the *Classics of Western Spirituality* series, (Paulist Press 1978).

The old edition of the Long Text by Grace Warrack, (London 1901), based on MS Sloane, keeps much of the flavour of Julian's English, but its modernisations are sometimes unsatisfactory.

Studies of Julian are numerous. A very convincing theological study is Margaret Ann Palliser OP, *Christ, Our Mother of Mercy* (Berlin/New York 1992). There is also Grace M. Jantzen, *Julian of Norwich: Mystic and Theologian* (Paulist Press 1987); Joan M. Nuth, *Wisdom's Daughter: The Theology of Julian of Norwich* (New York 1991). Brant Pelphrey, *Love was his Meaning: The Theology and Mysticism of Julian of Norwich* (Salzburg 1982), is written with great love for Julian and has many valuable insights, but does not do justice to the Latin theological tradition in which Julian was nourished. An older study, E.I. Watkin, *On Julian of Norwich*, most recently reprinted with his *In Defence of Margery Kempe* (Exeter 1979), is still worth reading.

Ritamary Bradley, *Julian's Way: A Practical Commentary on Julian of Norwich* (London 1992), is the fruit of long and profound reflection, and has very much greater theological depth than the modest title suggests. The place of Mary in Julian's theology is given proper prominence.

Paul Molinari SJ, *Julian of Norwich: The Teaching of a Fourteenth-Century English Mystic* (London 1958), is an important assessment of the theological status of Julian's visions.

Roland Maisonneuve, *L'Univers Visionnaire de Julian of Norwich* (Paris 1987), is a profound and creative treatment of Julian's language and symbolism.

Among articles: J.P.H. Clark, 'Fiducia in Julian of Norwich', *Downside Review* 99 (1981), pp. 97–108; 214–229; 'Nature, Grace and the Trinity in Julian of Norwich', *Downside Review* 100 (1982), pp. 203–220; 'Predestination in Christ according to Julian of Norwich', *Downside Review* 100 (1982); the last superseded by 'Time and Eternity in Julian of Norwich', *Downside Review* 109 (1991), pp. 259–276; Marion Glasscoe, 'Time of Passion: Latent Relationships between Liturgy and Meditation in two Middle English Mystics', in *Langland, the Mystics, and the Medieval English Religious Tradition: Essays in Honour of S.S. Hussey*, edited by Helen Phillips (Woodbridge, Suffolk, 1990), pp. 141–160.

2   Colophon of MS B.L. Add. 37790, f. 97 r, the unique manuscript of the Short Text, given in *A Book of Showings*, p. 201.

3   *A Book Of Showings*, pp. 33f.

4   Benedicta Ward SLG, 'Julian the Solitary', in *Julian Reconsidered*, by Kenneth Leech and Sr Benedicta SLG (Fairacres, Oxford, 1988).

5   See e.g. Kari Børresen, 'Christ notre Mère: La Théologie de Julienne de Norwich', in *Das Menschenbild des Nikolaus von Kues und der Christliche Humanismus* (Cusanus-Gesellschaft, Mainz, 1978), pp. 320–329.

Also Ritamary Bradley, 'Patristic Background of the Motherhood Similitude in Julian of Norwich', *Christian Scholars' Review* 8 (1978), pp. 101–113. Sr Ritamary refers on pp. 103–104 to instances of 'female' imagery for God or Christ in Augustine, with reference both to the spirit of God 'hovering over the waters at creation' (Gen. 1) and to Matthew 23.37, where Christ likens himself to a hen in her care for her young – *De Gen. ad Litt.* 1.18.36 (*PL* 34.260). Other references from the *Enarrationes in Psalmos* are also given.

6   Long Text, ch. 51, in *A Book of Showings*, ed. Colledge/Walsh, pp. 520–521; ed. Glasscoe, p. 56.

7   N. Watson, 'The Composition of Julian's *Revelations of Love*', *Medium Aevum* 68 (1993), pp. 637–683.

8 *The Life of Christina of Markyate, a Twelfth-Century Recluse*, ed. C.H. Talbot (Oxford 1959).

9 An edition is in preparation: *The Two Middle English Versions of the Revelations of Elizabeth of Hungary*, in *Middle English Texts* (Heidelberg, 1994/5) ed. Sarah McNamer.

10 *The Booke of Gostlye Grace of Mechtild of Hackeborn*, ed. Theresa A. Halligan (Pontifical Institute of Mediaeval Studies, Toronto 1979).

11 *The Book of Margery Kempe*, ed. S.B. Meech and Hope Emily Allen, Early English Text Society, Ordinary Series 212 (1940), p. 143 and other references to St Bridget in the index.

12 *The Revelations of Saint Birgitta*, ed. W.P. Cumming, Early English Text Society, Ordinary Series 178 (1929).
The Liber Celestis of St Bridget of Sweden, ed. R. Ellis, Vol. 1, Early English Text Society, Ordinary Series 291 (1987).

13 See further E. Colledge and J. Walsh, 'Editing Julian of Norwich's *Revelations*: A Progress Report', *Mediaeval Studies* 38 (1976), pp. 404–427, esp. pp. 409 ff.

14 Clark, 'Time and Eternity'.

15 Short Text, ch. 1, ed. Colledge/Walsh, p. 201; Long Text, ch. 2, ed. Colledge/Walsh, p. 285; ed. Glasscoe, p. 2.

16 Short Text, ch. 6, ed. Colledge/Walsh, p. 219; similarly Long Text, ch. 8, ed. Colledge/ Walsh p. 319; ed. Glasscoe, p. 10. The Short Text has: 'All that I say of myself I mean in the person of all my fellow-Christians.' Both the Paris and Sloane MSS have 'saw' in the corresponding passage in the Long Text.

17 Short Text, ch. 10, ed. Colledge/Walsh, pp. 235–236; cf. Long Text, ch. 18, ed. Colledge/ Walsh, pp. 367–369; ed. Glasscoe, p. 21.

18 Short Text, ch. 4, ed. Colledge/Walsh, p. 212; Long Text, ch. 5, ed. Colledge/Walsh, p. 299; ed. Glasscoe, p. 5. The second 'he' is supplied editorially, and does not occur at this point in either the Short or the Long Text. In the Long Text, the whole passage begins: 'He is our clothing, that for love ...'

19 Short Text, ch. 4, ed. Colledge/Walsh, pp. 212–214.

20 Long Text, ch. 4, ed. Colledge/Walsh, pp. 297–8; ed. Glasscoe, p. 5; ch. 5, pp. 299–300; p. 5.

21 Long Text, ch. 60.

22 Short Text, ch. 4, ed. Colledge/Walsh, p. 213. Contrast the Long Text, ch. 5, ed. Colledge/Walsh, p. 300; ed. Glasscoe, p. 5.

23 Short Text, ch. 4, ed. Colledge/Walsh, pp. 213–214; Long Text, ch. 4, ed. Colledge/Walsh, pp. 297–298; ed. Glasscoe, p. 5. The Short Text has 'wisdom of truth', but I have corrected this from the Long Text.

24 Long Text, ch. 4, ed. Colledge/Walsh, pp. 296–297; ed. Glasscoe, pp. 4–5.

25 e.g. St Thomas, *Summa Theologiae* 1, q. 39 a 8, building on the use made of Augustine's *De Trinitate* by Hugh of St Victor, *De Sacramentis*, and Peter Lombard, *Sententiae*.

26 Peter Lombard, *Sententiae*, 1, dist. 3, cap. 2, citing Augustine, *De Trinitate* 10.11.18.

27 Long Text, ch. 44, ed. Colledge/Walsh, pp. 483–484; ed. Glasscoe, p. 47.

28 Short Text, ch. 10, ed. Colledge/Walsh, p. 234.

29 Short Text, ch. 10, ed. Colledge/Walsh, pp. 235–236; cf. Long Text, chs. 17–18, ed. Colledge/Walsh, pp. 365–367; ed. Glasscoe, p. 20–21.
30 Short Text, ch. 13, ed. Colledge/Walsh, p. 242; Long Text, ed. Colledge/Walsh pp. 394–6; ed. Glasscoe, p. 26.
31 Short Text, ch. 13, ed. Colledge/Walsh, p. 242; Long Text, ed. Colledge/Walsh, pp. 398–400; ed. Glasscoe, p. 27.
32 Short Text, ch. 13, ed. Colledge/Walsh, pp. 242–243; Long Text, ch. 25, ed. Colledge/Walsh, p. 401; ed. Glasscoe, pp. 27–28.
33 Short Text, ch. 13, ed. Colledge/Walsh, p. 243.
34 Long Text, ch. 26, ed. Colledge /Walsh, p. 402; ed. Glasscoe, p. 28.
35 Short Text, ch. 22, ed. Colledge/Walsh, p. 268; Long Text, ch. 68, pp. 639–641.
36 Long Text, ch. 51, ed. Colledge/Walsh, pp. 513–518; ed. Glasscoe, pp. 54–55.
37 See above, note 8.
38 Long Text, ch. 51, ed. Colledge/Walsh, pp. 533–534; ed. Glasscoe, pp. 58–59.
39 S.L. Forte, 'Thomas Hopeman, O.P.', *Archivum Fratrum Praedicatorum* 25 (1955), pp. 311–344.
40 Augustinian doctrine on this point is transmitted through e.g. Peter Lombard, *Sententiae* 2, dist. 32.
41 Long Text, ch. 48, ed. Colledge/Walsh, p. 502; ed. Glasscoe, p. 51.
42 Long Text, ch. 54, ed. Colledge/Walsh, p. 563; ed. Glasscoe, p. 65.
43 Long Text, ch. 57, ed. Colledge/Walsh, pp. 579–580; ed. Glasscoe, p. 69. Where the Paris MS has 'are saved', the Sloane MS has 'shall be saved'.
44 Long Text, ch. 58, ed. Colledge/Walsh, pp. 583–585; ed. Glasscoe, pp. 70–71.
45 Long Text, ch. 58, ed. Colledge/Walsh, pp. 586, 587; ed. Glasscoe, p. 71. Colledge/ Walsh, p. 586/44 has 'oure moder of mercy' whereas Glasscoe (using MS Sloane) has 'our moder in mercy'. Colledge/Walsh, p. 586/49–50 have 'oure moder in mercy', matched exactly in Glasscoe. Colledge/Walsh, p. 587/56–57 has 'oure moder of mercy', and this time 'of' is matched in Glasscoe.
46 Long Text, ch. 59, ed. Colledge/Walsh, p. 589; ed. Glasscoe, p. 72.
47 Long Text, ch. 59, ed. Colledge/Walsh, p. 592; ed. Glasscoe, p. 72.
48 Long Text, ch. 60, ed. Colledge/Walsh, pp. 594–595; ed. Glasscoe, p. 73.
49 K.J. Klinkhammer, *Adolf von Essen und seine Werke. Der Rosenkranz in der geschichtlichen Situation seiner Entstehung und in seinem bleibenden Anliegen* (Frankfurt/Main 1972).
50 Orientation in A. Wilmart, 'Les Méditations d'Etienne de Salley sur les Joies de la Vierge Marie', in *Auteurs Spirituels et Textes Dévots du Moyen Age Latin* (Paris 1932), pp. 317–360, esp. pp. 326–336.

(This paper was given at the ESBVM Congress at Norwich in July 1994)

20

Mary, Mary, quite contrary:
a meditation on Mary
in natural religion and psychology

Emma Shackle

I. Natural religion, psychology, and Mary

In this meditation I shall be looking at the 'left-handed spirituality' of Christianity in order to reach a better appreciation of the humanity of both Mary and Jesus. Under the heading of 'left-handed spirituality' or 'esoteric mysticism', to use a recent phrase by R.A. Gilbert, we can class mysticisms of descent and return such as are found in some types of gnosticism, hermetic philosophy, shamanism, spiritual alchemy, and the journeys to the underworld or Hades found in Greek mystery religions, especially the celebrations of the myth of Demeter and Persephone at Eleusis. There is a case for including the recent visionary experiences of Adrienne van Speyr, relating to the Holy Saturday experience, the 'descent into hell', among these mysticisms of descents.

They are to be contrasted with those mysticisms of ascent that, typically, value spirit above matter, and see the way as upwards via ladders or climbing up mountains. My suggestion is that, just as men tend to identify or be identified with the world of spirit, women tend to identify with and be identified with the world of matter. Hence there has been a history of an overvaluation of mysticisms of ascent and an overly suspicious attitude to mysticisms of descent in the Church.

The Greek Tri-partite Universe
To understand these mysticisms we need to rehabilitate the tri-partite universe of Olympus, Earth and the Underworld which forms the background both of Greek Myths and Christian Mystery. Hugo Rahner, in a book with this title, discussed the connections between these universes and brought his understanding of the symbolism of the Fathers to the world of alchemical mysticism explored by Carl Jung in the interests of understanding the process of individuation.

The Underworld has too often been equated with the world of the demonic or the Christian Hell. One of my theses in this talk is that an acknowledgement of the positive significance of all three realms is demanded if we are to understand the humanity of both Jesus and Mary.

Jung spoke of the reality of the experience both of the Christ archetype and its chthonic opposite, the spirit Mercurius. According to him the 'Mercurius–lapis'

> formulates an aspect of the self which stands apart, bound to nature, and at odds with the Christian spirit. It represents all those things which have been eliminated from the Christian model. But since they possess living reality they cannot express themselves otherwise than in dark Hermetic symbols.
>
> (Jung, p. 241)

Perhaps there is also an opposite to the conventional depictions of Mary.

In Christian thinking about Jesus and Mary we have had a stress on the heavenly and the earthly rather than the realm of the Underworld or unconscious. Grace builds on nature; spirit is more important than matter, soul than body, theology than psychology, holiness than wholeness. The process of divinization matters more than the process of humanization. Pagan gods and goddesses are seen as demonic rather than as an integral part of what used to be called 'natural religion'.

The Semantic Differential and Binary Thinking

When reading theology, I am constantly reminded of the work of Osgood Suci and of Tannenbaum in experimental psychology on what is known as the semantic differential. Osgood and his colleagues have demonstrated how much binary thinking is based on three factors: the evaluative factor, i.e good–bad; the potency factor, i.e. strong–weak; and the activity factor, i.e. active–passive.

We can easily see from this the extent to which male theologians tend to class *spirit* as good, strong, active, and, of course, masculine, while *matter* is classed as bad, weak, passive and feminine; and how much this type of unconscious thinking has affected theological reasoning. Hirn, a Finnish aesthetician, has demonstrated the extent to which the whole aesthetic culture of the Catholic Church is based on the contrasts between spirit and matter, active and passive, masculine and feminine, seed and earth, 'overshadowing' and receptive womb, divinity and sacred shrine.

All these are androcentric ways of appreciating the mystery of the Incarnation, dependent on male perspectives and primitive biological ideas. For balance and wholeness they must be re-imaged from 'female' perspectives.

My major field of interest is the psychology of religion. When I teach psychology to committed Catholics, in a range of institutions, I have become aware of the extent to which there are strong gender differences in their response. Theologically-trained males tend to be suspicious of psychology unless they are aware of their own psychological problems; religiously-committed females love psychology because it helps them to understand how they might better express their religious commitment in practical terms.

It could be argued that the academic discipline of theology as presently constituted in western and Christian universities is not complete if it does not contain courses in psychology and the social sciences. However, the useful binary distinction between 'orthodox' and 'heretical' can be used as a defence against the difficult task of becoming literate in the social sciences.

Psychologists are more interested in whether religion is 'functional' or 'dysfunctional'; 'appropriate' or 'inappropriate'. The Jesuit psychologist of religion, André Godin, has developed a theory of religious maturity which, if true, would show, how 'natural religiousness' militates against the correct appreciation of Christian religious concepts. If this is true – and its truth or falsity cannot be ascertained without recourse to empirical research – we would expect children and adults to wind a devious course in their way towards religious maturity. What psychologists of religion call the 'quest' dimension in religion, and lack of premature closure, appear to be an important component of religious maturity.

Another point of worry for theologians about psychologists is their apparent conviction that there are severe limitations on human freedom.

Virtually the whole of empirical psychology, from behaviourism to psychoanalysis, is concerned with the causal understanding and prediction of human behaviour, and thus with the limits on human freedom. However, there are paradoxes about human freedom brought out by such notions as 'reflexivity'. One such paradox concerns the fact that psychological 'laws' are not deterministic in the sense that an effect will always follow from a cause. Psychologists who know how they are likely to behave in a certain situation are then able to choose not to behave in this way. Knowledge brings the possibility of freedom.

Much psychology can be construed as being concerned with what neo-Thomist theologians used to call 'natural' as opposed to 'revealed' religion. My argument is that Mary is a key figure in the rehabilitation of natural religion, natural theology, and psychology, not only within a Christian context, but also within the patriarchal religions of the children of Abraham. The reason for this is that as a woman she is more rooted in nature than the male Jesus. Thus if we have to take not only the Christ but also the Hermes–Mercurius archetypes to appreciate the wholeness of Jesus, so much more do we have to look at those aspects of Mary which root her in nature and female humanity, rather than those which set her apart from other women. One way of doing this is to look at the figure I have named 'Mary, Mary, quite contrary'.

II. 'O Maria, Maria, valde contraria'

'O Maria, Maria, valde contraria, quomodo crescit hortulus tuus?'

This is a Latin version by Charles Lamb of the first two lines of the English nursery rhyme:

'Mary, Mary, quite contrary, how does your garden grow?'

Iona and Peter Opie, the editors of the *Oxford Dictionary of Nursery Rhymes* tell us that it has religious roots, and may refer to Mary, Queen of Scots. The Opies declare, however, that 'Catholic writers feel it to be a lament for the persecution of the Roman Church; Protestant writers declare it is a lament at the reinstatement of the Roman Church'.

A look at 'Mary, Mary, quite contrary' involves looking at the shadow side of Mary. For a believer, this shadow side relates not so much to Mary herself as to the misuse that has been made of her image. Feminist theologians have been quick to point out how Mary has been used to control women and keep them in their 'proper' sphere of *Kinder, Kirche, und Küche*. Certain sorts of devotion to Mary are often found in practice to be linked to a system of fixed gender roles and assumptions that women should know their proper place. The implicit model in the minds of many male clerics of the Roman Catholic Church seems to be of a Church run by a male clerical élite (the masters) who are in the business of feeding the male laity (the children). The women and children are identified with the dogs under the table; any attempt by them to speak is heard as barking. Perhaps this parable was at the back of Samuel Johnson's mind when he said, 'A woman's preaching is like a dog's walking on his hinder legs. It is not done well; but you are surprised to find it done at all' (Johnson: *Oxford Dictionary of Quotations*).

There is another understanding of Mary's shadow, which is not evil and controlling but benign and mysterious. The survival of the cults of the Black Madonna make some acknowledgement of this side of Mary.

However, my method is not to start from Mary and move into reflections about modern women, but to start from contemporary psychology as a critique of current images of Mary. I take my cue from George Tavard, in his *Woman in Christian Tradition*, who states after a complex and fascinating reflection that

a theological reflection on woman should not take as its chief focus the feminine image of the Virgin Mary, even though this image has long been close to centrality in the faith of large numbers of Christians. The Virgin Mary ought to come within the scope of our study only insofar as she is a woman and thus participates in the general study of womanhood ...'

(Tavard, p. 187)

If this is true then the same thing is true of the concept of the family. So I shall start with what I tend to call the 'hole–y' holy family, at least as when represented on Italian holy cards. The family represented there is idealized, and has little relationship to current views of the family as a context in which violence is so common as to be called normal. Psychologists are better-trained than theologians to consider the extent to which the behaviour of Jesus and Mary, let alone Joseph, might be in various senses subject to psychological laws. The idealized conception of the holy family is clearly full of holes and must be relegated to the graveyard of kitsch.

The mystery of the Incarnation cannot be plumbed to the depths, but the idea that it is inappropriate to try and understand it in the terms of what is best in current psychology as well as current theology cannot be defended.

Those who take the findings of psychoanalysis seriously would posit that the inner life of a Jesus who 'had no human father' would be turbulent and disturbed. If he was brought up in a household where his putative father had no sexual intercourse with his wife, the mother of Jesus, Jesus' need for an understanding of his origins would be even more intense. The idea that there would be no tension between the historical Jesus and his mother, if such were indeed the circumstances of his birth, is not only contrary to all clinical experience, but is belied by the Gospels themselves. The tensions between Mary and Joseph over her pregnancy are recorded by Matthew. The stressful nature of his birth in a strange town would leave a mark upon the family. The massacre of the Innocents would be likely to create guilt in Jesus about his survival. The problems that Jesus' parents had with him as a child are manifest in Luke's account of his strange disappearance without giving notice of absence, and of their finding of him in the Temple. Like many a child who is unsure of his real parentage he may have assumed himself (correctly) to be in a special relationship to the Divine.

III. Contrariness

Let us move then to further discussion of the notion of contrariness as a clue to where we find the image of the contrary Mary. Here we might ponder on these words of Jung about Hermes–Mercurius:

> Hesitantly, as in a dream, the introspective brooding of the centuries gradually put together the figure of Mercurius and created a symbol which, according to all the psychological rules, stands in a compensatory relationship to Christ. It is not meant to take his place, nor is it identical with him, for then indeed it could replace him. It owes its existence to the law of compensation, and its object is to throw a bridge across the abyss separating

the two psychological worlds by presenting a subtle compensatory counterpoint to the Christ image.

(Jung, p. 245)

There is one discourse of contrariness known to many ex-convent schoolgirls, such as Germaine Greer, Marina Warner, and Antonia White. It is not exclusive to Catholicism and it is often judged to be blasphemous. It uses the devices of parody and irony to mock the religion of the establishment. The most recent example of this genre is Salman Rushdie's *The Satanic Verses*. It is difficult for many to believe that this 'mocking' discourse is not irreligious but it is in fact often profoundly religious, bringing in astringency to combat sentimentality, truth to combat hypocrisy.

If we can conceive of discourse about Mary as a choral symphony made up of different instruments and voices, we can see this contrary voice as forming part of the counterpoint. It has a function similar to that of the chorus of demons in Newman's *The Dream of Gerontius*. Another metaphor might be that of the grit that is needed if the oyster is to produce a pearl.

The major poet of Marian contrariness in English literature is Algernon Charles Swinburne, who was brought up in Anglo-Catholic circles and knew John Henry Newman, but lost his faith at Oxford.

In his poem 'Dolores', an invocation to a prostitute modelled on devotion to *Notre Dame des Sept Douleurs*, he parodies the Litany of Our Lady of Loreto with such lines as 'O garden where all men may dwell', and he has a recurring invocation to 'Our Lady of Pain'.

'Dolores' is a far less mature work than his 'Hymn to Proserpine' published in the same volume. This hymn is set after the time of the proclamation in Rome of the Christian faith, and is headed by the words 'Vicisti Galilaee', which were attributed to Julian the Apostate on his deathbed by his Christian opponents.

Most dabblers in English literature have heard the lines:

Thou hast conquered, O pale Galilean; the world has grown grey from
thy breath.

However, few know of the explicit (and unfavourable) contrast between Mary and Proserpina that is made later in the poem.

Yet thy kingdom shall pass, Galilean, thy dead shall go down to thee dead.

writes Swinburne, and goes on as follows:

Of the maiden thy mother men sing as a goddess with grace clad around;
Thou art throned where another was king; where another was queen she is
crowned.

Yea, once we had sight of another: but now she is queen, say these.
Not as thine, not as thine was our mother, a blossom of flowering seas,
Clothed round with the world's desire as with raiment, and fair as the foam,
And fleeter than kindled fire, and a goddess, and mother of Rome.
For thine came pale and a maiden, and sister to sorrow; but ours,
Her deep hair heavily laden with odour and colour of flowers,
White rose of the rose-white water, a silver splendour, a flame,
Bent down unto us that besought her, and earth grew sweet with her name.
For thine came weeping, a slave among slaves, and rejected; but she
Came flushed from the full-flushed wave, and imperial, her foot on the sea.
And the wonderful waters knew her, the winds and the viewless ways.
And the roses grew rosier, and bluer the sea-blue stream of the bays.
Ye are fallen, our lords, by what token? we wist that ye should not fall.
Ye were all so fair that are broken; and one more fair than ye all.
But I turn to her still, having seen she shall surely abide in the end;
Goddess and maiden and queen, be near me now and befriend.

Swinburne is describing the annual return of the colourful Proserpina or Persephone from Hades through the Sicilian fountain of Cyane. He writes of her further in 'The Garden of Proserpina'.

IV. Mary and the return of the goddesses

The theme of the return of the pagan gods and goddesses is found in the literature of depth psychology, the New Age movement, and feminist theology. It is particularly dear to my heart since I am the sort that wept at the banishment of the gods and goddesses that I found in the myth and poetry of my childhood. Milton in his ode 'On the Morning of Christ's Nativity' linked this departure explicitly with the birth of Christ and spoke of:

'A voice of weeping heard and loud lament'

This theme is also found in the legends in the Everyman *A Child's Book of Saints* by William Canton, published in 1898.

In the chapter 'The Ancient Gods Pursuing,' Canton tells of the journeys of St Hilary and his companions who overturned the shrines of the ancient gods, broke their images, cut down their sacred trees, and defiled their wells of healing. They arrived at midsummer on the feast of St John at the house of the Lady Pelagia. She entertained them royally and asked them three questions. To the third 'What is the distance between heaven and earth?' a voice in Hilary answered 'Who can tell us more certainly than Lucifer who fell from heaven?' At this point the Lady Pelagia rose and the voice cried out that he was to breathe on her in the name of Christ.

And the Bishop rising, breathed on the white lovely face the breath of the holy name; and in an instant the starry eyes were darkened, and the spirit and flower of life perished in her sweet body; and the companions saw no longer the Lady Pelagia, but in her stead a statue of white marble. At a glance Hilary knew it for a statue of the goddess whom men in Rome called Venus and in Greece Aphrodite, and with a shudder he remembered that another of her names was Pelagia, Lady of the Sea. But, swifter even than that thought, it seemed as though the statue was smitten by an invisible hand, for it reeled and fell, shattered to fragments .....'

(Canton, p. 42)

Who would not wish that Hilary and his companions had been of that school of thought that built on the ancient religion, preserved the images, and blessed the sacred trees and sacred wells?

Today the goddesses and gods are back with us. An important Jungian text by Jennifer and Roger Woolger attempts to acquaint modern women with 'The Goddess Within.' In so doing they define 'goddess' as

a psychological description of a complex female character type that we intuitively recognize both in ourselves and in the women around us, as well as in the images and icons that are everywhere in our culture.

(Woolger, p. 7)

They develop the female typology of Jung's colleague, Toni Wolff, and suggest that women (and men) need to come to terms with the goddess within, who can be imaged in terms of six Greek goddesses, viz. Athena, Aphrodite, Persephone, Artemis, Demeter and Hera or, in their Latin forms, Minerva, Venus, Proserpina, Diana, Ceres and Juno. They use the image of the goddess wheel to help put ourselves in touch with these powerful archetypes.

Another Jungian, Robert Grinnell, in his *Alchemy in a Modern Woman* suggests that the current move of women into the 'masculine' realm of Logos and away from the 'feminine' realm of Eros has necessitated a development of complex processes that can be described in the language of alchemy. The new theme is that of the development of the 'glorified body' and a new impetus for mysticisms of descent or mysticisms of matter, as opposed to mysticisms of ascent or mysticisms of spirit.

These processes bring with them a new reaching into the depths of the unconscious for ancient rituals. The new woman

performs heroic tasks. But these tasks differ from those of a masculine hero in that they have something of the character of ancient ceremonials and rituals rather than raiding expeditions; her voyages are more like seasonal migrations or sacred embassies; processionals outward and return, which become circumambulations illustrating a fundamental circulation of psychic energy.

(Grinnell, p. 36)

So what have these notions of the contrary Mary and the changes in women's consciousness today have to do with our understanding of Mary the woman?

Taking my cue from Jung and Tavard, I would assert that Mary, like modern women, may now at last be reconnected to her female humanity. She need no longer be seen only in opposition to Eve, Proserpina and Aphrodite, but also in a new relationship to these feminine depths and heights. The contrary Mary is also a symbol of the *prima materia* on which the alchemical work is performed. Then Mary the woman and contrary Mary can be seen in relationship to what might be termed the traditional Mary of the Christian Church, with titles ranging from '*Theotokos*' to 'The Immaculate Conception', making up a triple Goddess.

V. 'My Eros is crucified'

It is no wonder that it has taken so long for Aphrodite to have any status in the Christian religious universe. If Aphrodite returns, we have to face the problem of the place of sexuality in religion. The worship of a celibate Jew and his virgin-mother has tended to make the question of Eros a difficult one for Christians. I have already suggested that the displacement of erotic imagery into the discussion of the relationship of Christ and his Church may have been a way of avoiding this problem.

Ignatius of Antioch made the famous assertion 'My Eros is crucified'. Is it not true to say that the Eros of both Mary and Jesus was in some sense crucified?

One important feature of Gestalt psychology is its insistence on the human need for form. We can see this principle operating in the need to complete the sacred texts when they fail to answer our questions. The legendary material on the human ancestry of Jesus in the *Protevangelium* is a case in point.

We do have a Gospel in which Jesus is identified with Logos, but we do not have one in which he is identified with Eros. My suggestion is that we find traces of this missing gospel in literary sources.

Let us first look at the myth of Eros. A psychologist is bound to be interested in this myth since the major female character is Psyche. The classical source is *The Golden Ass* of Lucius Apuleius. The Jungian analytical psychologist, Erich Neumann, wrote a major psychological study of it: *Amor and Psyche: The Psychic Development of the Feminine* and C.S. Lewis used it in his novel *Till We Have Faces*.

One of the interesting things about this myth is the light it sheds on the Venus or Aphrodite, the mother of Amor or Eros, as a potential mother-in-law. Venus is jealous of the beautiful Psyche: when she is cast forth into the world after lighting the lamp to look at her bridegroom,

Venus gives her three 'impossible' tasks to perform. The third and final task is to go to Hades to collect a casket of beauty ointment from Persephone for Venus–Aphrodite. Heedless of the command not to open the box, Psyche opens it and falls into a deep sleep, from which she is rescued by Eros.

Neumann interprets this as follows:

> Through Psyche's sacrifice and death the divine lover is changed from a wounded boy to a man and a savior, because in Psyche he finds something that exists only in the earthly human middle zone between heaven and the underworld: the feminine mystery of rebirth through love. In no goddess can Eros experience and know the miracle that befalls him through the human Psyche, the phenomenon of a love which is conscious, which, stronger than death, anointed with divine beauty, is willing to die, to receive the beloved as the bridegroom of death.
>
> (Neumann, p. 125)

Neumann argues that Psyche fulfils the masculine aspects of herself in doing the three tasks, but reunites herself with her feminine centre when she seeks the beauty unguent for herself and thus wins the forgiveness of Aphrodite–Persephone (the Terrible Mother).

In a footnote Neumann speaks of the 'trinitarian duality' of Zeus who 'in his highest stage of manifestation as winged Eros possesses the character both of Son and Holy Ghost', and sees the figure of Psyche as 'analogous to Mary'. He points out that he was engaged in writing this book in 1950 when the dogma of the Assumption was proclaimed.

Needless to say there have been later interpretations from a more feminist angle. Christine Downing writes:

> The beauty to which Persephone but not Aphrodite has access is the beauty that comes with an intimate, inner knowledge of death ...

She goes on to say:

> I imagine a Psyche who, putting on this beauty ointment, discovers that the real aim of her journey all along has been not the reunion with Eros, not her own divinization, but the meeting with Persephone, and the discovery that *they* are sisters, sister doubles, one immortal, one mortal.
>
> (Downing, p. 51)

My interest is less in the sisters than in the theme of the mother-in-law. For me one understanding of the Aphrodite–Persephone figure is in the problems that arise about Mary if a Christian woman, say Mary Magdalene, is imagined within an erotic, even a legitimate erotic, relationship with Jesus, as in *Jesus Christ Superstar*. Mary then turns either into the disapproving mother-in-law Aphrodite, or into the frightening Persephone to be confronted 'at the hour of our death'. Despite this, the language of the 'bride of Christ' has always been a major theme in Roman Catholic writing about nuns.

Thus Arthur Devine, an English Passionist, in his book published in 1889 on *Convent Life or The Duties of Sisters Dedicated in Religion to the Service of God* quotes from a text entitled the *Divina Paraninfa* where 'Our Blessed Lady speaks to the Novice on the day of her Profession' (Devine, p. 74). She says, 'Behold then, my child, you have arrived at the happy time when you are to be bound in ties of love to my divine Son, your Spouse ...' Clearly this document must be judged in the context of its day (and the time when the quoted text was written) but I doubt if I am the only one who finds the question of religious Eros in Christianity both puzzling and disturbing.

The sexuality and playfulness of the Hindu Krishna are not easily linked to the historical Jesus. However, there is no problem in relating these missing aspects to the elusive and poly-sexual Hermes–Mercurius. Equally, it seems more appropriate to put eroticism not so much in the individual relationship of Jesus to a professed nun but rather in the realm of the archetypal.

My assertion would be that Jesus had no bride and that he is not married to the Church. As a man his Eros was not fulfilled. The marriage of Christ and his Church is an archetypal union analogous to the alchemical union of Sol and Luna, or the marriage of Eros and Psyche, or the marriage forced on Persephone by Hades, the dark brother of Zeus. In the latter cases the identification for Mary that becomes salient is that with the great goddesses of Olympus and the Underworld, viz. Aphrodite and Persephone. Mary can be seen as a symbol of the Church, but this identification has its own limitations and 'shadow'. The four 'marks' of the Church – one, holy, Catholic, and apostolic, – are 'marks' of the true Christian insofar as he or she is a true member of the Church.

VI. Mary and Gnostic Sophia

Much has been made of Mary's *'Fiat'*, her assent to God's Will for her. The contrary story is surely that of the Gnostic Sophia of the Valentinians whose masculine counterpart was 'What has been Willed.' Here I quote extensively from Elaine Pagels' rendering of this story from her *Adam, Eve, and the Serpent*. Pagels sees this story as expressing the conviction of the Valentinians that 'it is wisdom to live in harmony with what [the Father] has willed'.

> But Wisdom belied her name and acted foolishly. Because she longed to know the Father, she rejected her place in the scheme of things, severed her relationship with What-has-been-willed, and plunged herself into a desperate search to understand the nature of her divine Source. As Irenaeus told her

story, 'when she could not achieve her purpose, both because of the enormous depth and the incomprehensible nature of the Father, she stretched herself forward, and was in danger of being absorbed into His sweetness and dissolved into His absolute essence, until she encountered the Power that sustains and preserves all things, called "the Limit" ... the power by whom, they say, she was restored and supported. Then, having with great difficulty been brought back to herself, she became convinced that the Father is incomprehensible.'

(Irenaeus, quoted in Pagels, p. 75)

The Father then sent Christ and the Holy Spirit to reveal that

although none but the primal Mind could possibly comprehend God, all other beings, too, come from him ... When wisdom was restored to her place within the divine being, she left her sufferings behind her. Followers of Ptolemy said that these sufferings – the fear, confusion, grief and ignorance she suffered in her search for God – had to be excluded from the divine being. Yet Wisdom joined herself with Christ to recover the residual spiritual energy left in these experiences. Together she and Christ set out to transform these sufferings: they turned her fear into water, her grief into air, her confusion into earth, and her ignorance into fire. Then they used the elements of suffering to create the present universe.

(Pagels, p. 75)

Such a view of the creation of the universe is compatible with left-handed Christian spirituality. It is not surprising that Jungians find gnostic myths throw light on the sufferings of their clients.

The Christian woman who is trapped in a relationship in which she or her children are maltreated by her partner may find that the myth of the Gnostic Sophia is a much better guide to the way to freedom and dignity than the mythical treatments of Mary's *'fiat'* so dear to the heart of those Christians, whether male or female, clerical or lay, who want their universe to be tidy, and women to be subservient to men.

In the preface of a recent biography of Cornelia Connelly, the American foundress of the Society of the Holy Child Jesus, written by Radegunde Flaxman, Rosemary Haughton makes an important point about the misuse of 'obedience' in religious life.

Cornelia was called a 'bold' woman, and it was not intended as a compliment. This was a woman whose passionate inner conviction burned through the polite hypocrisy of so much religion of her time and ours, and through the smothering false piety which demanded she give up her integrity in the name of a spurious concept of obedience ... Cornelia strenuously sought to be obedient wherever she felt ... obedience was due, yet refused to be manipulated. As a woman of her time she accepted the fact of a woman's subordination, but something bright and unquenchable in her would not let her betray her integrity for acceptability or a spurious kind of 'peace'.

(Haughton, p. xii)

The Gospel Mary who did not hesitate to ask questions of God was surely a 'bold' woman. The Gnostic Sophia was also bold in the extremity of her love.

VII. Mary's garden

Let us return finally to the garden of Mary, Mary, quite contrary. What does grow in it, and where is it to be located? The rhyme tells us that the garden contains not only silver bells and cockle shells but also pretty maids all in a row.

> *Campanulae ibi sunt argenteae*
> *Necnon cochleae formosaeque puellae*
> *Omnes recto in ordine dispositae*

The pretty maids rule out the possibility that this particular garden is to be found on Mount Athos. Given our identification of Mary, Mary, quite contrary, with Persephone, it seems that one strong candidate is the Garden of Proserpina. There are two 'Victorian' poems by Antonia Byatt that feature in her novel *Possession*, and express perennial male and female attitudes towards this garden.

Byatt's male vision of Proserpina's garden as written by her character Randolph Henry Ash in 1861, is suitably romantic:

> These things are there. The garden and the tree,
> The serpent at its root, the fruit of gold,
> The woman in the shadow of the boughs,
> The running water and the grassy space.

(Byatt, p. 1)

This archetypal garden leads into the paradisal garden of Eve. The tree of Paradise is often identified with the cross of Christ. (The cross and Adam's tree stood in one place.) However, it is often forgotten that the Garden of Eden contained two trees, the Tree of the Knowledge of Good and Evil, and the Tree of Life. According to Bernoulli this latter tree is identified in gnostic literature with the alchemical tree, 'the tree of mercury, of living silver' (Bernoulli, p. 338). Apart from the link with the silver bells, we are left wondering whether one or both trees formed the cross of Christ. Perhaps that cross had its roots in both Earth and Hades.

Byatt's female version of the garden (in the words of her character Christabel LaMotte) is astringent and down-to-earth, and set at Golgotha, the place of the skull.

Our Lady – bearing – Pain
She bore what the Cross bears
She bears and bears again –
As the Stone – bears – its scars.

(Byatt, p. 381)

Coda

The argument of this paper is that the proper place of both Mary the woman, and of women in the Church, will only be appreciated if the study of what used to be termed 'natural religion' is taken more seriously by Christian theologians (and theologians in other patriarchal religions). Some Fathers of the Church tended to equate natural religion with both the demonic and the feminine. Others, like Clement of Alexandria, saw the 'pagan mysteries' as a prelude and a stepping stone to the revelation of God in Jesus Christ. The mistake that appears to have been made was to jettison 'natural religion' in favour of 'supernatural' religion, to the detriment of both. The neglect of what is good in non-Christian religion and humanistic philosophy and psychology has been one of the causes of sexism in the Christian churches.

My suggestion is that it is urgent for theologians, both male and female, to think about the relationship of the Church to Hermetic philosophy in its present-day manifestations, both in analytic psychology and in the New Age movement. The task of evangelization in contemporary society is impossible and counter-productive if catechists and missionaries are not well-informed about both the theory and practice of religious education in the widest sense, and the findings of the disciplines of psychology and sociology of religion. In addition, if they are not to become prey to wishful thinking and guilty of sins of omission, they must learn to use the methods of the social sciences to evaluate the effects of their initiatives.

References

Bernoulli, Rudolf, 'Spiritual Development in Alchemy' in Campbell, Joseph (ed) *Spiritual Disciplines* (Routledge Kegan Paul 1960).

Byatt, A.S., *Possession: A Romance* (Vintage Books, 1990).

Canton, William, *A Child's Book of Saints* (Everyman, 1906).

Devine, A., *Convent Life* (London, 1889).

Downing, Christine, *Psyche's Sisters* (Harper & Row, 1988).

Gilbert, R.A., *Elements of Mysticism* (Element Books, 1991).

Grinnell, Robert, *Alchemy in a Modern Woman* (Spring Publications, 1973).

Haughton, Rosemary, in Flaxman, Radegunde, *A Woman Styled Bold* (Darton, Longman and Todd, 1991).

Hirn, Yrjo, *The Sacred Shrine* (Faber and Faber, 1958).

Jung, C.G., *Alchemical Studies* (Routledge Kegan Paul, 1967).

Neumann, Erich, *Amor and Psyche* (Bollingen, 1956).

Opie, Iona and Peter, eds., *The Oxford Dictionary of Nursery Rhymes* (Clarendon Press, Oxford, 1951).

Pagels, Elaine, *Adam, Eve, and the Serpent* (Penguin Books, 1988).

Rahner, Hugo, *Greek Myths and Christian Mystery* (Burns & Oates, 1963).

Swinburne, Algernon Charles, *Selected Poems* (Carcanet Press, 1987).

Tavard, George, *Woman in Christian Tradition* (Notre Dame Press, 1973).

Woolger, Jennifer and Roger, *The Goddess Within* (Rider, 1990).

Wulff, David, *Psychology of Religion* (Wiley, 1991).

(This paper was given at the ESBVM Congress at Winchester in July 1991)

21

Mary, intercessor on our behalf, one with us in the communion of saints, and witness to what we may become in Christ: a personal ecumenical journey

Ross Mackenzie

(This paper was originally scheduled under the assigned title of 'My ecumenical journey and its value in my spiritual life')

I am deeply grateful to Joe Farrelly [Associate General Secretary of ESBVM] for all that he means to this Society. I also place the highest value on the worthy manner in which he has continued and adorned the pioneering work of Martin Gillett. (Let Martin's blessed memory remain fresh in this Congress and in the life of the Society!) Joe, however, is Irish; I in origin am Scottish. My Calvinistic family held it as an article of faith that all sin is addictive, and that the terminal point of that addiction is having a swollen head. So, Joe, I would never choose as a title for any talk, 'My Ecumenical Journey and its Value in My Life'. The firm conviction of Granny Anderson, in whose house I grew to adulthood, would be curtly phrased: '*Your* ecumenical journey? You're not that important, Ross Mackenzie.'

Yet, in truth, I am grateful to Joe for the title. For it allows me, honouring still my grandmother's admonitions against pride, to reflect at least on journeying. From the first, God's people have been wanderers and wayfarers – 'strangers and pilgrims'. 'Leave your country', the Lord said to Abram and Sarai, 'and go to the land I will show you'. So they went, 'looking for a place to call their own' (Heb. 11.14). They heard a nagging, inner voice, telling them to get up and move from where it was comfortable, from a first place called home to another place that would come to be called home: and that by God's call. The journey of faith always and inevitably involves some such displacement. For the God whom we worship, the God who is good and who loves humankind, was, after all, the displaced God: for the Word who from the beginning was with God became flesh and roughed it here with us, 'mantled in mist', as we are in Auden's phrase, 'and remote from the happy' (W.H. Auden, *Age of Anxiety*, p. 104).

If this divine displacement is the core of the gospel of the incarnate Word, then is our story not constantly to be one of moving on? Of

pilgrimage? Of moving on from the early place where we feel at home
to another place that we make home – and doing so in response to God's
call? Is our story not one of moving from the family rituals and traditions
that formed us to new rituals and customs that we come to make our
own?

Disregarding, then, my grandmother's strictures, I invite you to come
with me in imagination to the four places, for me holy places, where I
have found – and this is my preferred title for this address – the joyful
mystery of 'Mary, intercessor on our behalf; one with us in the
communion of saints; and witness to what we may become in Christ'.

St Giles' Cathedral: Mary as intercessor on our behalf

I invite you to come in imagination first to St Giles' Cathedral,
Edinburgh. The name, 'Cathedral,' is a courtesy title now. The origins of
St Giles' lie somewhere in the 1100s. I was ordained in that church as a
minister of word and sacraments, according to the ordination rites of the
Church of Scotland.

A word about how that church thinks of itself. The Church of
Scotland is one of the Reformed family of churches, so it is Protestant.
Yet all the early Scottish reformers thought of themselves as in continuity
with the Church Catholic from the beginning. The church – to use the
curious phrase of the Scots Confession – is 'Fra' Adam'. They meant (to
use the language of the Confession) that 'there has been, now is, and to
the end of the world will be, one Kirk'. That means: one company and
multitude of men and women who rightly worship and embrace God by
true faith in Christ Jesus. So to be reformed means that the church is
renewed only as it constantly returns to the waters of life that have
nurtured it from the beginning.

Every Sunday in St Giles' we heard ancient words made fresh in the
celebration of Holy Communion.

> Therefore with angels and archangels and all the company of heaven, we laud
> and magnify Thy holy name, evermore praising Thee and saying, 'Holy, holy,
> holy ...'

With *all the company of heaven*! That must then mean that in this
celebration of the Lord's Supper we were one with all those who had
ever come to St Giles' in generations before us: with working men,
leaving the closes of the High Street for their daily labour with hands
calloused and bones sore; one with the children, unshod, dribbly-nosed
and ill-clad, who scampered in the alleys like rabbits; and one with the
women you could see daily sweeping clean their tenement stairs. For
centuries, in feast and famine, they had all come. Hadn't they all prayed

often too to the Mother of God, who also swept the stairs at Nazareth? 'Hail Mary, fu' o' grace,' they would have said in the native Doric, 'pray for us sinners ...'

It was a little touch, that glimpse of praying to Mary in heaven, that glimpse of Mary praying for us. It was like gossamer, so gently brushing the skin that you don't notice the lure of the eternal seeping through the material, the eternal glory dipping into the kirk where John Knox had thundered out his reforming message.

The little touch was the question: What could it mean to ask Mary to pray on our behalf? As a good Calvinist, I was intellectually clear about one thing: that Jesus Christ is the only mediator between God and ourselves. But the heart has reasons of its own the mind knows nothing of. Then do the dead pray for us? The question kept coming back. Are the dead – intercessors? (I'm not sure I yet like the Latin word. Go-betweens? Friends who stand by us and love us for always? That's getting close.) Do the people I have known and loved pray for me, in that great and widening circle that now includes my father, my mother, my sister Maureen; dear friend, Joan, who died of cancer; Watt, my fishing buddy in Florida; Mrs Randolph, who baked Christmas puddings for our family every year?

Does Mary stand by us and love us for always? Do our beloved dead pray for us? Do they remember us?

In the fall of 1989, I received a telephone call from Scotland. My brother informed me that my 92-year-old mother had suffered a heart attack and a stroke. I reached the hospital in which she was a patient in Inverness within two days. Her children were all present. I had to leave within a few days: as it turned out, she died a week later. I knew when I saw her on my last day that it would be for the last time. Before I left, we held hands and prayed an old childhood prayer she had taught me. Almost her last words were: 'Ross, dear son, I'll keep praying for you all'.

If she, could that not much more be Mary, who was drawing me to herself, ineluctably? When I knelt in St Giles' to pray day by day, diffidently, I realized that I was one in a long line of folk who had come in from the High Street to pray. I didn't like saying, 'Hail Mary'! Saying 'Hail' sounded to me like a gladiator greeting Caesar in the Colosseum. 'Hello, Mary,' sounded a little too informal. So in between the formal private prayers appropriate to the dusty dignity of St Giles', I sometimes prayed as my Mother taught me in childhood, but changing the words of her prayer: 'Gentle Mary, meek and mild...'

To pray that Mary remember us means simply asking that we come closer and closer to Christ and find her God and ours. For she always points beyond herself, with the bidding: 'Do whatever Jesus tells you to do.' To be aware that Mary is praying for us is to become increasingly conscious that the energising powers of her own love are stirring us up and making us ready to receive what God yearns to give us by way of grace and blessing.

Iona: Mary in the communion of saints

The second holy place to which I invite you is the bleakly beautiful Island of Iona.

Two names will inevitably be associated in any history of Iona. The first is that of Columba, who landed on the island in 563 with twelve companions. Iona was his base of operations for thirty-five years. From Iona missionaries, teachers, agriculturalists, musicians, and healers, as well as priests, brought the gospel of Christ and Celtic culture to the Picts of Scotland, and to the English from Northumbria to East Anglia. The second name associated with Iona is that of George MacLeod, founder of the Iona Community. He landed on the island with his twelve companions in 1938.

The two men, separated by 1400 years, were remarkably alike: experienced in war and lovers of peace; aristocrats who had the common touch. They shared three common convictions. First, the world is disintegrating for loss of community. Second, the gospel is about rebuilding the beloved community, through Christ the Master Carpenter. Third, only in the shared life of this community will people come to understand the covenantal nature of faith.

On Iona, ministers and craftsmen worked in teams. Since ministers like me knew little about stonemasonry or carpentry, we were left to hew wood and draw water or cut the grass in the Reilig Odhrain, the sacred place of sepulchre for monarchs, prelates, and Lords of the Isles. We called that job 'trimming the toenails of the Scottish kings'.

In the cloisters of the restored Abbey is a bronze statue of the Blessed Virgin Mary, one of three cast by Jacob Lipschitz, an Orthodox Jew. Against the prevailing anti-Catholic currents of his time, George MacLeod refused to take No for an answer until the statue stood in the most public and central place of the community's life.

The people of the Celtic Church have always had Mary in their midst from the birthing of the babies to the lambing, to the cutting of the peat, and the lighting of the family fire. Think of some of the songs from the *Carmina Gadelica* that express this confidence: late, to be sure, the songs are, but they give expression to the soul of the Gaelic spirituality of the Highlands and Islands:

> Mary, the fair and tender,
> Be nigh the hearth ...

Or this:

> May Mary give blessing
> To the house that is here ...

Or this:

> The peace of Mary be yours in the grazing,
> And may you return home safe-guarded.

Or this rune of the well:

> The shelter of Mary Mother
> Be nigh my hands and feet
> To go out to the well.

Or this prayer:

> O! in my heart and soul always
> May the blessed Virgin Mary
> And the fragrant Branch of Glory dwell.

To have Mary in our midst – Mary, daughter of Israel, gift of the Jews – to have her as one with us in the Communion of Saints is to experience the companionship of one who shares our faith in every part of life. 'Think of the dead,' Columba said, 'as if they were your own particular friends.' To think of the dead as friends, as those with whom we are still in relationship, is to know that they are still in a real, if intangible, way bound up with us in our joys and struggles on earth.

A church, a community of people that thus senses Mary's presence in the whole round of its life has an integrity, a wholeness, a feeling for the sanctity of the whole of life that became colourless and less familial when it was announced after the time of John Knox that such idolatry was henceforth to be abolished and only the unadulterated word of God to be preached. 'The religion that had sweetened their labours and sufferings,' writes Orkney poet George Mackay Brown, 'was a creed now of terror and hellfire' (*An Orkney Tapestry*, p. 38). Marian spirituality was another kind of fire in the Celtic tradition: like the aurora borealis, a streamer of light in the night sky of the northern hemisphere.

South India: Mary as witness to what we may become in Christ

The third holy place to which I will take you in imagination is Kerala, in South India.

The tradition of the Malankara Orthodox Church of India is that in the year 52, St Thomas the Apostle landed on an island near Cranganore in what is now Kerala State. From the fruit of his early missionary work there the Syrian Christians of Kerala, the most ancient Christian community in India, have grown into a position of respect and equality among the Orthodox family of churches.

When I taught on the faculty of the Orthodox Church there, my host, Father Thomas, frequently invited me to visit congregations throughout the state. I frequently spoke or preached in these congregations. Once, hearing more laughter than I thought was right for a fairly conservative sermon, I asked Father Thomas if he had, indeed, been translating my sermon. 'Oh, yes', he replied with a twinkle in his eyes, 'word for word. Of course, I added just a little spice to make it more interesting.'

On the twenty-fifth anniversary of his ordination, Father Thomas was at a celebration of the Holy Qurbana in the village church. It was the church where he had been baptized and confirmed, where he had received first communion, and where he had been ordained to the priesthood. It was a Marian feast. Without prior notice, Father Thomas invited me to preach on the gospel text of the day, John 2.

The waiting congregation sat on the earthen floor, his own mother among them. My poor sermon went in this fashion:

> Mary had given him birth for such a ministry as this. Mary is the one who notices what is lacking in the community, where there should be joy. She is the one who brings the needs of the friends she loves to her son. She is the one who, where there is want, helps to bring the good measure that runs over. She is the one who brings another future to us that the gloom of the present failure keeps us from seeing.

In a white Orthodox church, dedicated to St Mary, and in the mountain country of South India, I learned more of what it means to believe that Mary is the witness to what we may become in Christ and through Christ.

To bid Mary stand beside us, naming her as Ever-Virgin in our greeting, is to remember, as the Apostle Paul teaches us, that we are already in the new creation. It is a new creation, for as the first creation came about by the will of God alone, the new creation in Christ involved this woman's Yes also. To invoke her as *Theotokos*, Mother of him who is God, is to bear our witness as the Church of Jesus Christ that this people, named for her Son, seek as their ministry to notice and provide what is lacking in the community around it. (Think of the desolations of our modern inner cities, and reflect on what ministry in the name of Christ can mean there.) This people who call Mary blessed pray to have their eyes open to the sadness of the 'mantled in mist, and remote from the happy'. This people who see Mary as the one on whom the Spirit descended remember afresh at every time of worship that the Spirit has come for the healing of the nations, and of the cities, and of the villages, and of the broken homes of our world.

The statue of the Virgin by Jacob Lipschitz is entitled, 'The Descent of the Spirit'. The inscription on the canopy at the back reads: 'Jacob Lipschitz, a Jew faithful to the religion of his ancestors, has made this Virgin for a good understanding of the people on earth, *that the Spirit may reign'*. The beautiful conjunction of Mary and the Spirit is so typically Eastern. To have Mary in our midst is to be alert to the continual coming of the Spirit to our world. As we stand at the edge of a new millennium, we seek the transformation of the old landscapes of conflict into a scene of fruitfulness and peace. A people to whom Mary is dear will be those who, where there is want, help to bring the good measure that runs over, who seek to bring a better social and political programme that the pessimism of the present keeps us from achieving.

Pentecost, 1996

To bring the record of a pilgrimage to a close, I take you to Staten Island, New York. On Pentecost Sunday this year, I took part in a celebration of the Holy Qurbana of the Malankara Orthodox Church in a borrowed Catholic church on the island. There are over 50,000 Orthodox Indians now resident in the United States and Canada. The church is small. It is strongly Indian. The Metropolitan of the church is Bishop Makarios, whom I introduced to you earlier as Father Thomas. He longs for his church to become not simply an exotic eastern flower, planted in a western soil, but authentically part and parcel of the new country to which his people have come.

At that service I was received by anointing with holy *muron* as a member of that church, and ordained as a deacon. I have left my country, but I have found a land that God has shown me.

That itself is of less import for me than to speak in closing rather of two realities that bring us to the centre of why this Society exists.

One is to ask ourselves constantly what it means to find the place where we truly belong, a place to call truly our own. I have no mood to ask any one to take a long road to Orthodoxy. The Church, G.K. Chesterton said, 'is a house with a hundred gates: and no two enter at exactly the same angle'. For most of us, I imagine, T.S. Eliot has said it well:

> ... the end of all our exploring
> Will be to arrive where we started
> And know the place for the first time.

The gift of this Society has been just that for those of us who explored the riches of Marian spirituality. We returned to our starting-point, but as all pilgrims, changed, and knowing our old tradition in a new way.

The other reality is to find ways – and this Society is one – to declare in speech, song, and prayer that we are grateful for God's gift of Mary.

I come through my father's people from Ross in the north of Scotland, where a Gaelic saying is still handed on: *An da mhaireann, goal na mathar agus gradh Dhe*. It means 'the immortal twain, the mother's love and the love of God'. If Mary's love for her Son never ceases – from cradle to cross and for ever – her love will not cease either for those who come to her through her Son or for those whom her Son gives to her. Using the words of the Holy Qurbana of the Malankara Orthodox Church, let us therefore bless

> her who is worthy to be blessed and glorified of all the generations of the earth, the holy, the exalted, the glorious and Ever-virgin Mary, Mother of God.

(This paper was given at the Bristol Congress of ESBVM in September 1996)

22

Why should he send his Mother? some theological reflections on Marian apparitions

Richard Rutt

Our Lady spoke to Sister Mary Anne of Jesus in the chapel of the Convent of the Immaculate Conception at Quito (Ecuador) and told her that in the difficult days of the 20th century faith and morals would increasingly be destroyed, there would be disastrous loss of religious and priestly vocations, youth would be ever more corrupted, and the Church would be racked with heresy and secularization – until, after a fearful catastrophe, she would be renewed. The date was 2 February 1634.

Some may feel this story has the ring of divine truth; others may hear psychological echoes and find reasons why Sister Mary Anne should have thought of the 20th century. These are the two extremes of catholic attitudes to Marian apparitions: one believing, one sceptical. Neither has the blessing of the Church – and yet both have it, while neither likes to think that the other has it. The problems are fundamentally spiritual.

In proposing to reflect on them theologically, I do not pretend to offer a theological synthesis or exhaustive treatment. I have not burrowed deeply into the enormous mass of published papers on the subject. I have read only a small part of the vast output of the indefatigable Fr René Laurentin, the investigator of apparitions. I speak as a priest trying to look pastorally at what I shall claim is primarily a lay interest; and I know well that today's preoccupation with Marian apparitions must be tempered by recall of Christ's words, 'Blessed are they who have not seen, yet have believed' – that we need balance in our perspective. And I will hint at an ecumenical setting.

A pastoral question

Although the subject is most often presented as doctrinal, the Church usually treats it as fundamentally pastoral. Contrary to widely held ideas, the Holy See does not solemnly authenticate apparitions: decisions of that kind are left to local bishops. This procedure distances the whole question from the universal *magisterium*, for local bishops cannot make dogmatic decisions. Further distancing of papal authority from the whole subject came in 1966 through the repeal of the old Canons (1399.5 and 2318) that forbade the publication of unauthorized accounts of apparitions. Since then specialist publishing houses have arisen and an enormous literature has boomed, much of it poor, some of it good; but all of it showing how the Church is reacting and what her needs are.

The traditional way for a bishop to approve an apparition was essentially a declaration that the story was not harmful to the faith and morals of Christians. This meant that the story might be told and pilgrimages were allowed. The supernatural nature of the event was usually confirmed, but the faithful were not bidden to believe the story. Even under the old canons, the Church was effectively showing pastoral care rather than making a historical or doctrinal judgment.

In examining an apparition story, the bishop's investigation proceeded on the assumption that the story was likely to be false. Witnesses such as St Bernadette and the Fatima children were examined like witnesses in a court of law, in a juridical process that could be fierce. The outcome of the process was always phrased in cautious terms, and even when the decision was favourable, the pilgrims' subsequent verdict would have greater power. Guadalupe, Lourdes and Fatima have vast pilgrimages and quite different standing from La Salette, Beauraing, Banneux and Betania, – all of which have been approved. On the other hand Rue du Bac 1830 was never formally approved, but has attained a world-wide importance.

The diocesan process can still be negative. At Medjugorje, Bishop Zanic disapproves, but leaves the question juridically in the air. Medjugorje has a sad problem of obedience unresolved (about which our Lady seems reticent), but pilgrimages from all over the world ignore the bishop and continue to multiply. Things are happier at San Nicolas in Argentina, where our Lady is said to have appeared to a working-class housewife from 1983 to 1990. The diocesan has issued no juridical statement, but has clearly satisfied himself that the story is wholesome. Since 1986 he has responded to the devotion of the laity by frequently visiting the place and presiding at celebrations. He preaches on our Lady, but not on the apparitions, and asks his priests to do the same. He is backed by the Bishops' Conference. As a result he has a much-needed new urban church, a new diocesan congregation of religious sisters and a great outburst of devotion. Fr Laurentin regards Bishop Castagna's response as a model for imitation by others.

Another aspect of the older treatment of apparitions is also essentially pastoral, though it is formally a matter of liturgical legality. Though the 1830 apparitions in the Rue du Bac were never formally judged, Rome did something ambivalent by authorizing a liturgical celebration. Several other apparitions have received similar authority for liturgical commemoration, at first locally, and, following the perceptions of the faithful, later universally. Thus Guadalupe remains in the liturgy of the Americas, Lourdes in the universal calendar (from 1910, but optional since 1969). Fatima is not celebrated outside Portugal – unless the optional commemoration of the Immaculate Heart of Mary is regarded as a Fatima feast. (Note that Roman approval for liturgical celebration of the Heart of Mary dates from the late 18th century, but for the epithet 'Immaculate' only from 1944.)

Popes have tacitly approved apparition stories: Leo XIII, Pius XII and John XXIII of Lourdes, Pius XII of Fatima. The age of peripatetic popes took Paul VI and John Paul II to Fatima, and John Paul II has shown much affection for the Fatima cultus. Thus popes were seen tacitly accepting and following the devotion of the people, and there has been no claim that they were exercising a theological function of the papacy in doing so. They responded personally to the apparition reports, and, perhaps more importantly, to the phenomena of pilgrimages. There is a pastoral element in each of the stories. In the light of these, the prudent reluctance of the Pope to approve Medjugorje, one of the most popular pilgrimage centres in the world, is the more striking. The Medjugorje problem too is essentially pastoral.

The question of Mariophanies (Jean Guitton's word is convenient, if barbarous) presents itself everywhere in practical pastoral form. Many priests are uncomfortable with apparition accounts. Apparitions in themselves seem to conflict with modern theological methods and definitions, even to conflict with a biblical theology – though there are plentiful apparitions and visions in the Bible. The laity sometimes complain that 'our priests won't talk about apparitions'; and some priests admit their puzzlement. Not that there is any lack of literature on the subject. There is more than anyone could ever read in an ever-increasing mass of devotional and prophetic publications, but it tends to concentrate on questions of When, Where, What happened in detail, and What was said – establishing the credibility of the event before giving a journalistic account of our Lady's message. Much less has been written about what an apparition really is, or why it should happen. Pastoral reaction needs this essentially theological motivation.

Apparition or vision

The very vocabulary of the subject deserves careful handling. Is an apparition different from a vision? In practice, our Lady's appearances are called apparitions; and in the popular mind an *apparition* connotes a real visit, while a *vision* is an impression of a visit.

The so-called apparition of St Michael on Monte Gargano about AD 495 is clearly not in the same category as our Lady at Lourdes in 1858, because St Michael has no bodily form and our Lady has. Indeed our Lady alone of all saints now has a bodily form, because she alone has been assumed into heaven; her apparitions may be of the same nature as our Lord's resurrection appearances. After his ascension the Lord will never again appear on earth in bodily form until the Second Coming, because of his promised perpetual presence in word and sacrament and his gift of the Holy Spirit; nor will he anticipate his glorious Advent. (One notes that St Margaret Mary is usually said to have witnessed not apparitions of the Sacred Heart of Jesus, but visions.) These reasons would not apply to his Mother. Here we have what may sound like the groundwork of an attractive explanation of Mary's apparitions; but we must bear in mind that in the enormous catalogue of what might be called collectively our Lady's interventions (in order to cover locutions and visions as well as apparitions) it will be impossible to distinguish all those that were true as apparitions from those which were true in some other sense. The evidence is both too complex and too patchy.

Following St Augustine, visions are traditionally distinguished as corporeal, imaginative, and spiritual or intellectual. *Corporeal visions*, in which the person seen is objectively present, are presumably only possible for persons with resurrection bodies (Rahner pp. 41ff and 58–9). They are practically impossible to prove; but in respect of our Lady they are at least theoretically possible. *Imaginative visions* are those in which the appearance is only in the mind of the witness, without objective bodily presence, though the witness's memory is of a visible or audible presence. (Notice that 'imaginative' here does not refer to creative or resourceful thinking, as in an imaginative story or imaginative solution to a problem; nor does it mean 'imaginary'. It is a technical term of psychology, meaning the presentation of an image to the mind.) This is the commonest sort of vision (Rahner p. 38). *Spiritual or intellectual visions* are purely spiritual and have no pictorial qualities. The mystic tradition of the Catholic Church, represented by St Teresa and St John of the Cross, esteems the three kinds in reverse order, giving highest regard to spiritual visions.

There is, however, another distinction (Rahner p. 17) we might bear in mind, even though it deserves further debate: between a *mystical* vision, which is part of the personal spiritual growth of the witness (like the visions of St Gemma Galgani, of which she was so distrustful), and a *prophetic* vision, which gives the witness a mission or a message for the Church or world (like the visions of St Margaret Mary Alacoque). Modern Mariophanies are nearly always prophetic, as though Mary does not favour individuals, but, as Mother of the Church, appears for all

Christ's children. Yet there are elements in Mariophanies that are personal and should not be taken as intended for the whole Church, such as the Fatima children's prayer, 'O my Jesus', that is now so regrettably and widely inserted into public recitation of the Rosary. Meanwhile, the whole question of secrets in apparition accounts deserves more investigation, though we have not time to do it justice here. (Karl Rahner's idea that secrets express the fundamental duty of silence about visions suggests one line of thought).

Apart from the word 'apparition' others that deserve reflection are 'visionary' and 'seer', applied to those who see apparitions. *Visionary* suggests a person detached from normal experience in a way that is opposed to the way in which St Bernadette, to name but one, thought of her own experience. *Seer* is a synonym in English for 'prophet'. I prefer to call the recipients of apparitions 'witnesses', a cooler and less weighted term.

Psychology

The natural direction of thought today, even among the devout, must be towards understanding the witnesses' perceptions. There is no reason to see this as either reductionism or rationalism. Though in this as in every other aspect of the subject we must constantly remind ourselves that Mariophanies are not an homogeneous collection of phenomena, we must at least accept that perception is a psychological event. Would-be Freudian attempts to explain apparitions as a version of the Oedipus pattern in which a depressed sexuality finds relief in maternal fantasy are not promising. Jungian and New Age explanations are even less satisfying; while taking refuge in talk of *miracula* merely shifts the question. The French priest-psychologist Marc Oraison says apparitions are perceptions that are received as exterior, but are truly interior – in technical terms, hallucinations. The degree to which they ought to be described as pathological requires examination.

Theological study of mental pathology is a developing science. If there is a pathological element in an apparition, that is not of itself a reason for believing that the apparition is not a gift from God. Believing that St Joan of Arc displayed classic symptoms of schizophrenia does not mean that one cannot accept her as a saint whose holiness came from God. Catholics have long accepted that physical suffering can, under God's providence, help spiritual growth; so also can mental suffering. Earlier this year [1996] Fr Duncan Campbell of the Dominican church in Leicester was taken by surprise when a member of his choir gave him a dramatic written account of the sufferings he endured as a schizophrenic. He wanted others to know about them and to recognize them as a gift from God. 'Care in the community' as a way of treating those who suffer from mental illness is faulty, but it has brought many people a closer understanding of the real condition of the sufferers and it has led to greater distrust of drugs in their treatment. Either psychotherapy or spiritual care is proving to be the better response.

Certainly all must admit that the visible qualities of Mariophanies and the words attributed to Mary are normally identified as consonant with, even part of, the mental furniture of the witnesses. In the Ukraine, Mary appears as an icon of the Mother of God, in Ireland as a missal card – though we must remember that the witnesses often claim that they do not at first recognize her. When she speaks, they know who she is. (We recall Mary Magdalene in the garden on the first Easter morning.)

Karl Rahner, examining the objectivity of visions in his book, *Visions and Prophecies*, does not make a special case of Mariophanies, but begins by granting that an appearance of the glorified body of Mary could be granted by God: the rest of his book assumes that this gift is extremely unlikely.

He gives much attention to the reliability of witnesses. Indeed, one should, for there is every reason to be wary. Few will admit that their memories are unreliable, though it is doubtful whether any of us has an infallible memory. Sometimes it is hard to discern whether a vision is false or the witness is unreliable. Memories such as those that Lucia dos Santos produced as much as forty years after the event at Fatima must be regarded with special care. Even accounts given soon after an apparition may be dubious (Rahner p. 71). According to Lucia, the angel of Fatima spoke of men offering the soul and divinity of Christ, as well as his Body and Blood, to the Father. When told that this was theologically impossible, she replied 'the angel may just not have studied any theology'. If a reported vision contradicts revealed truth, there must be an error in either the vision or the account.

As to the credibility of Mariophanies, theologians make distinctions between different kinds of faith. Without resorting to technical terms, any Christian can distinguish divine or catholic faith from human faith. The saving faith a Christian has in God, itself a gift of God, is vastly different from human faith in the truth of an historical event. Faith in an apparition or the words reported from an apparition can only be faith of a purely human order. It may nevertheless be a gift of God, though personal, not covenanted to all people. It follows – and Rahner (pp. 10–12) quotes ancient and consistent authority for this – that no harm is done even though a genuine vision be rejected, approved liturgical observances notwithstanding. Pope Benedict XIV (1675–1740–1753) allowed that Catholics might dissent from the Church's official judgement on a vision, provided that charity and good order were not imperilled by tactless expression of that dissent (as appears to have happened very recently at Guadalupe when Abbot Schulenberg spoke unadvisedly). The faith in which we are baptized does not include Lourdes or any other Mariophany.

It is perhaps worth mentioning that these remarks about faith apply *a fortiori* to miraculous signs that are said to accompany Mariophanies in order to validate them. One may reasonably believe in an apparition but not in its attendant 'miracles'. It is salutary to recall that not all the great crowd present at Fatima on the day of the miracle of the sun saw anything unusual in the skies (Rahner p. 82 n. 108 and 84). The authenticity of Fatima does not depend on such signs. But the matter of so-called confirmatory miracles is too complex to be discussed further now.

Mary is sent

Common parlance tells of our Lady as though she appears of her own volition. I have deliberately spoken of her as being sent. As a saint in eternal glory her will must be so united to the Will of God, and so far beyond the space-time continuum, that she can appear only if God wills it; and since God's will is prior to ours in all things good, it is better to speak of her as being sent by God. There is much more for Mariology to say, defining what God has confided to Mary's maternal love, but we know that any true apparition must be according to his Will: that Mary moves when moved by God; and that what she says will always be an amplification of what she said to the servants at Cana; 'Whatever he says, do it.'

Eschatology

St Louis Grignon de Montfort (1673–1716), that startling French home missionary whose writings have been attracting more attention among Mariologists since he was canonized fifty years ago, was convinced that our Lady would have a special and glorious role in the Last Days. This may be one reason why eschatological messages are prominent in the popular view of Marian apparitions; but there is a widespread sense among devout Christians that the world is rushing to its end. We are acutely aware that the end of the world is an immediate issue, if only because we know that one or two women or men could in short order make decisions that would destroy the earth as a habitable planet. The approach of the second millennial year favours this emphasis.

The place of Mary in the Last Times was dealt with extensively by a series of essays in *Etudes Mariales* ten years ago. One may note that the time and the hour are hidden even from the Son of God (Mark 13.32;

Matt. 24.36), although Mary's role as Mother of the Church gives a reason for associating her with the doctrine of the Second Coming. The Ratzinger report reminds us that all we need to know on the subject is in the New Testament; and the relevant sections of *Lumen Gentium* are a corrective to false perspectives. The Church has always been aware that she is already in the Last Days and must always live in preparation for the immediate return of the Lord. Insofar as we do not live in that constant expectation, we are unfaithful. We note gratefully that the reform of the Latin rite has emphasized the eschatological element in the eucharist, although apologists have become more embarrassed about the doctrine of the Second Coming and we are told that preachers are less willing to tackle it than once they were.

What Marian apocalyptic and eschatological messages seem to do is to supply the laity with instruction on the Parousia at a time when the teaching Church is not satisfying this need. The messages must be taken as admonitory rather than sensational, comforting rather than frightening – as the appropriate passages of the Gospels are. Our daily proclamation of the Parousia in the Latin rite is in the mode of joyful hope; and the note of joy is essential. If we exert ourselves to pray in that mode, we find that another part of the typical Marian apparition message, the part about penitence, also takes a new focus. The pastoral response to fears of the end of time should be an affirmation of forgiveness and joy.

The Last Days theme is also allied to the strong sense of Mary's glory and loveliness that is typical of apparition accounts. As Mother of the Church and type of the Church, she foreshadows the eternal glory of the Church; and Fr Koehler has called attention to St Anselm's meditation on her as 'Mother of all the re-created' – Second Eve and Mother of the New Creation. The glory of her perceived appearances is as much a promise as any of the reported messages.

Prophetic mission

Fr Koehler, attempting to discern a single message in Mariophanies, finds it is: 'I am suppliant and loving omnipotence; pray and repent (or be converted), especially by means of pilgrimage.' This message makes the apparition prophetic, giving the witnesses a task to carry out. Koehler says it came in this form to the poor and simple of the 19th century, commissioning them to proclaim both the urgency and the glory of the Gospel. Rahner (p. 84) compliments this with a touching phrase. He speaks of 'little doors' in theology that may be opened by visions and apparitions, doors that lead to loftier portals. He insists that one must not stop at a little door. One must enter and go further. An apparition of our

Lady is never an end itself. It opens a way – penance, or prayer, or pilgrimage or whatever – a way in the life of her Son.

Apparitions and the laity

Yves Chiron lists some 350 reported apparitions between 1900 and 1993. Fr O'Carroll gives even more. Hierzenberger and Nedomansky give a select list since the beginning of the Church. The full number is, of course, unknowable. There is not much to be gained from comparing the data of thousands of apparitions, recorded without a firm database and often without sifting of evidence. Yet one striking element emerges; the witnesses of apparitions during the last two centuries are overwhelmingly lay. Priests and bishops are rarely witnesses of apparitions, though like Fr Gobbi of the Marian Movement for Priests they may receive locutions and spiritual visions. Could this mean merely that the minds of theologically uneducated laypeople are more liable to the psychological conditions required for witnessing apparitions? Or should it recall us to that idea now usually attributed to Cardinal Newman: that the laity is given true faith by God and is to be consulted by the *magisterium* in making dogmatic decisions?

This idea is attractive to intellectuals who believe that the lay majority favours ordaining women to the priesthood, abolishing clerical celibacy, and other policies supported by mass opinion surveys in Austria and elsewhere. In truth, we have no agreement about how the laity are to be consulted in matters of belief, or which laypeople are qualified to advise. Pius XII nevertheless thought he knew the lay mind when he defined the Assumption of Mary in 1950, and I have not seen any suggestion that he was wrong. Pilgrimage statistics in the 1990s could be said to show that the laity has high regard for Mariophanies. I wonder whether many of the radical intellectuals to whom I have referred would think this an authentic expression of the belief of the laity, something that should commit the whole Church.

But perhaps that is not the most fruitful way of considering lay devotion to Mariophanies. There is another aspect. René Laurentin (p. 91) suggests that there has been a serious reduction in the 'nutrients of popular religion' in the Catholic Church since Vatican II. The attempt to substitute a heightened appreciation of Holy Scripture, of liturgical piety, and of coinherence in the Communion of Saints has achieved much since the Council. This sort of spirituality, however, which has long existed also in the Church of England, is essentially theological and clerical. To live by it needs an imaginative intellectual ability. The Church of England itself regrets (though perhaps too much) that it has not found a spiritual response in the poor. The Roman Catholic Church seems once to have had more response than it has now – few layfolk read Vatican II documents with zest, and theological élitism afflicts those teachers who fear it most. Clerically-inspired worship has created a vacuum that has been filled by charismatic manifestations in all the churches; and while the parish priest in his homily expounds the relevance for today of St Paul's problems at Corinth or of Jeremiah's disintegrating loincloth, some of the congregation sit quietly fingering those Medjugorje rosaries whose chains have turned to gold.

There, then, is a reason for treating Mariophanies with respect. They answer a need. That could be a reason why he would send his mother.

Tailpiece

I have a tailpiece, glimmer of an ecumenical perspective.

Bruno Cornacchiolo was a City of Rome tramways worker and a violently anti-clerical member of an Adventist sect, aged 34. On Sunday afternoon 12 April 1947 he took his three little children for an outing to a wilderness near the Cistercian Abbey of Tre Fontane, where the three springs – long since capped – mark the traditional site of St Paul's martyrdom. It was a popular place for strolling outside the city walls and had gained an unsavoury reputation during the immediate post-war period from its use by American soldiers and local girls; but on a sunny afternoon the children played among the bushes while Bruno sat under a tree putting finishing touches to a talk he was to give denouncing the doctrine of papacy and the Immaculate Conception.

Four-year-old Gianfranco wandered off after his ball and got lost. Carlo and Isola interrupted Bruno and got him to help them find their little brother. He was found in a grubby grotto where some garbage had been thrown, kneeling on the ground and murmuring 'Beautiful lady!' Bruno saw her too, standing on a shelf of the soft rock, dressed in the green, pink and white of Our Lady of Guadalupe (though he did not recognize that) and carrying a Bible. She said she was the Virgin of Revelation, who dwelt in the Divine Trinity. 'You have been persecuting me. *Ora basta!* – Stop it!' she said, with colloquial bluntness. The rest of her message was much as one might expect, except that she concluded by telling him to get people to pray for the unity of Christians.

The phrase 'Unity of Christians' was not very common in Rome in 1947, though it was used in connection with the story of Sister (now Blessed) Maria Gabriella of the monastery of Grottaferrata a few miles away, where the nuns had responded to Paul Couturier's call for prayer. Everything else about the story is typical of modern Mariophanies, save that adult male witnesses are not very common; the ecumenical element is striking. In 1987, for the 40th anniversary of the apparition, Bruno wrote a message calling Mary 'Ecumenical Mother, Mother of Peace'.

A little shrine now stands on the site, which grows in popularity as a place of pilgrimage, served by Conventual Franciscans. Ecclesiastical authority has made no declaration about authenticity, but the people come. It has the atmosphere Eliot described at Little Gidding:

> ... You are here to kneel
> Where prayer has been valid.

Principal works consulted

Bavaud, Georges, and others, *Maria e la fine dei tempi*, Rome 1994, (originally 'Marie et le fin des temps: I Approche biblique; II Approche patristique; III Approche historico-théologique' in *Etudes Mariales* 1984–1986, Paris 1984–87).

Chiron, Yves, *Enquête sur les apparitions de la Vierge*, Perrin/Mame 1995.

Hierzenberger, Gottfried, and Nedomansky, Otto, *Tutte le apparizioni della Madonna in 2000 anni di storia*, Casale Monferrato 1996 (originally *Erscheinungen und Botschaften der Gottesmütter Maria ...*).

Koehler, Théodore: see the last paper in Bavaud, Georges, above.

Laurentin, René, *Pilgrimages, sanctuaries, icons, apparitions: an historical and scriptural account*, Milford, Ohio 1994 (lectures originally given at the International Marian Research Institute, Dayton, Ohio).

Rahner, Karl, *Visions and Prophecies*, London 1963 (originally *Visionen und Prophezeiungen*, Freiburg 1963).

(This paper was given at the Bristol Congress of ESBVM
in September 1996)

23

Apparitions of our Lady.

Michael O'Carroll CSSp

By way of introduction to a vast subject, let me recount two narratives I have heard which are relevant. In Manila, one evening after a lecture, I met one of the most respected women in that mighty country, Aurora Aquino, mother of the martyred Benigno Ninoy. I had heard from a Canadian missionary that while in prison, where he was held unjustly, he had gone through a spiritual transformation. His mother told me how it happened. Entirely bereft, all his belongings taken, he suddenly saw our Lady in his cell: 'Why do I have to suffer all this?' he cried out. The reply, unexpected, changed his life. 'But Benigno, think of all we have given you.'

Some years later Manila was in its moment of crisis. The tyrant was rigging the elections to keep out Cory Aquino. Fidel Ramos, a Methodist, then Deputy Chief of Staff of the army, revolted with the Minister for Defence, Ponce Enrile, and a small group. They had no hope. But Ramos on the telephone asked Cardinal Sin to come to their help, adding, 'I believe the Blessed Virgin Mary can save us'. The Cardinal appealed to the citizens over Radio Veritas (operating dangerously, thanks to a courageous girl – June Keightley, now Castro), to go into the streets to separate the armies. The crunch came when the regular soldiers were ordered to fire on the massed citizens. Then those in the front line saw before them a globe of light, from which a Lady stepped out with the words, 'I am the Queen of this country: do not kill my children!' The soldiers refused to obey military orders; the colonel in charge of a group of official helicopter-gunships had a spiritual experience and changed sides, followed by all except one. The crisis was over.

Now I had heard the story of the soldiers from the Cardinal. Fr René Laurentin wanted to check it, so we asked him to repeat the narrative. He did so, and added, 'I was not there: these boys came to see me after the crisis, and that's their story. Why should they invent such a thing?'

I would just add one other personal reminiscence. In September 1971 I attended the annual session of the French Society of Marian Studies; one of the speakers was Professor Paul Evdokimov, a Russian Orthodox from the St Serge Institute in Paris, a specialist on icons. At the meeting, where apparitions were being discussed, the chairman turned to him and said, 'I suppose, M. Evdokimov, in your communion you do not deal with this problem'. 'On the contrary,' was the reply; 'I consider apparitions a sign of divine tenderness'. He then explained that in their churches it was sometimes the icon that blazed with light, thus manifesting the Presence. At the present time two icons in Orthodox churches, one in Pittsburgh, the other in Copenhagen, are exuding oil: I have had utterly reliable testimony on this. And there have been apparitions to members of the Coptic Church in Zeitoun (approved with minimal delay) and Shoubra, both near Cairo.

But to turn strictly to our subject. We shall deal with apparitions which have had or are having an impact in the life of the Church. The first of these is Our Lady of Guadalupe (1531), which I personally think the most important in the history of the modern church; we then come forward to the nineteenth century, which yields the Miraculous Medal (1830), La Salette (1847), Lourdes (1858), Pellevoisin (1870), and Knock (1879).

The first notable apparition in the present century is Fatima. The story is well known and continues within the life of the Church. We will look at this in some detail, as we have on it the scholarship of one of the greatest Marian theologians of modern times, Fr Joaquin Maria Alonso, a Claretian, whose monumental work did not appear during his life; it runs to 20 volumes of meticulous erudition. He did for Fatima, which had its experts already, what René Laurentin did for Lourdes – 20 volumes also – and as the same writer is doing annually for Medjugorje.

There is at the present time a vast panorama of reported apparitions, occurring or brought to appraisal in the 1980s. Between Fatima and this amazing manifestation we meet the apparitions at Beauraing (1932) and Banneux (1933), both already approved, and Garabandal, still subject to review, but with increasing favour. I list some of the best known recent alleged apparitions: Akita, Japan (1973), approved 1981; Betania, Venezuela (1976), approved 1987; Cuapa, Nicaragua (1980); Medjugorje (1981); Kibeho, Africa, 1981; San Nicolas, Argentina (1983); Mount Melleray, Ireland (1984); Naju, South Korea (1985); Souphanieh, Syria (1986); Cuenca, Ecuador (1988); Scottsdale, Arizona (1988); Mayfield, Ireland (1988). This list is not complete, but it shows that there is a widespread phenomenon which commands our attention.

We have not the time or interest to analyse all these alleged happenings. We should perhaps profitably consider the general position in regard to apparitions, and apply these to two, Fatima and Medjugorje.

In the factual order the story of apparitions in the Catholic Church is, at times, disgraceful. Visionaries have been persecuted by members of the clergy, treated almost as enemies of the Church. A visionary who was given the choice of signing an official retraction or leaving her convent, and who to her honour refused to sign a falsehood, was banished from her community. I have met her. She told me that five bishops had signed a statement that she was a fraud: four of them had never met her. Today, thirty years later, she is practically reinstated.

I could quote other instances, such as one known to me who because she alleges that she has visions, is refused Holy Communion in her parish church: I assure you I do not exaggerate. Conchita Gonzales of Garabandal was for a while excommunicated; the visionary at Dozulé in France, not directly related to apparitions of our Lady, was denied Holy Communion in her church. Joan of Arc was burned at the stake as a witch on the order of the bishop, Cauchon; the English merely lit the fire. Today her statue is in every French church: his name is one of disgrace. Remember that the bishop was a former rector of the Sorbonne University, prestigious then; he was supported by many theologians.

You will hear the cry for prudence in dealing with alleged apparitions. It is scarcely prudence in its strict sense that is meant, but caution, or something worse. Prudence is needed through the whole of life: supernatural prudence in the Christian life. It is discernment that is required in judging claims to special graces. It is to be regretted that future priests do not have mystical theology as part of their seminary course. They come to think of it·as freakish, irrelevant. It is an integral part of the sacred discipline. Look at the superb contribution made to the subject by the Anglican theologian, Evelyn Underhill; I had to study her writings for the *Dictionnaire de Spiritualité* and was profoundly impressed.

Before addressing the essential problems I may just mention contacts I have had with individual visionaries. This is in no way privileged, as there are so many at the present time. In 1940 I met the last surviving witness of Knock, Pat Beirne, a gruff old gentleman, but as a witness straight as a die. He was living in relative poverty; this enhanced his testimony for me: it was rock-solid. In a very passing way, with Belgian friends I met Mariette Beco, the visionary of Banneux in the Belgian Ardennes. I spoke at some length to Teresina, the visionary of Lipa in the Philippines, and with Conchita Gonzales of Garabandal, married to an Irish-American and living in New York. I spoke briefly also to Patricia Talbot of Cuenca, and I have met the Considine sisters more than once. I was present a number of times during the apparitions in Medjugorje, and was also present during special happenings in Scottsdale, Arizona.

How to decide on the authenticity of an apparition? Each one must be judged in itself. There is no point is making global assertions such as 'There are too many of them: they cannot all be genuine', or 'Why is it always to young girls? Or when there is a group of visionaries, why are there always more girls than boys?' Broadly these questions proceed from a truth of fact, though at Guadalupe it was Juan Diego, at Schio today it is Roberto Barone, and at Tre Fontane it was Bruno Cornacchiolo. Nonetheless the feminine factor dominates.

Here then are the criteria, standards which must be applied: sufficient information; orthodox doctrine, that is, conformity with the teaching of the Church; transparency, which means direction of the visionary to God, not preoccupation with himself or herself; signs of divine action, such as miracles of healing or conversion; good fruits, which is the test given by the Master himself; acceptance by the *sensus fidelium*; attitude of the church authority.

Each of these tests has to be applied without any previous commitment save to truth. For instance, it would be wrong to begin with the previous notion that there are too many apparitions, or that only saints get these special graces. To have sufficient information means that the witness is a normal human being and truthful; in one word, reliable. Whatever is said must conform to church doctrine – that is, authentic doctrine, not the opinion of any individual or coterie. When St Catherine Labouré gave her message, 'O Mary, conceived without sin, pray for us who have recourse to thee', the Immaculate Conception was not a dogma of faith. But already, after centuries of controversy, the obstacles to a definition had been overcome, and on 8 December 1661 Alexander VII by the bull *Sollicitudo Omnium Ecclesiarum* had shown the preference of the Holy See for the doctrine. His text remarkably resembles *Ineffabilis Deus*, by which Pius IX defined the doctrine.

The other criteria do not present any special problem. Judging the verdict of the *sensus fidelium* brings us into one of the paradoxes of church life. People are occasionally told that they must not accept a particular apparition until the Church has pronounced. But the people know instinctively that they will not get a church ruling if they do not manifest their interest and belief. There would be no church pronouncement if there had been no prior manifestation of public interest and belief. If this devotional interest dies out there is no need for an intervention by the church authority.

What is the importance to be attached to such a pronouncement? No-one claims that it is infallible. There have been too many mistakes. It is a guideline to future behaviour and is generally in two stages: first, permission to have liturgical celebration on the scene of the apparition, and then formal declaration of authenticity. This is more a permission to act on belief in the supernatural event than formal teaching about it. The Church is careful not to give the same importance to private revelations as to the public revelation entrusted to it in Sacred Scripture and Sacred Tradition.

Just as the Pope does not issue a binding dogmatic statement without previous consultation and expert advice, which procedure is also adopted by a General Council (witness Vatican II), so a bishop will generally establish a commission to examine and evaluate evidence relevant to an alleged apparition. Not all the cases where this procedure has been adopted are wholly edifying: commission members were chosen at times because they were known to favour an opinion, usually negative, favoured by the bishop. Without anticipating what I have to say about Medjugorje, I record my regret that on neither of the two commissions, diocesan and national, was the outstanding expert of all time, Fr René Laurentin, invited to serve. He had given in writing abundant evidence of exhaustive research on the subject itself.

The church authority must take account of the *sensus fidelium*, which is a concerted expression of faith by the body of the faithful. It was Newman, the great intellectual, who saw the importance of consulting the body of the faithful on matters of doctrine; I suggest that his idea, now supported by Vatican II, can apply to the matter we are considering, all important factors being carefully considered. We are not talking about opinion polls, or dogma by plebiscite.

Perhaps we may now look at two well-known apparitions or series of apparitions, Fatima in 1916, and Medjugorje from 1981 to the present time. You know the story of Fatima. After visitations from an angel in the year 1916, on the 13th of each month from May to October 1917 three children, Lucia, Francisco and Jacinta saw our Lady and received messages from her. On the last day, a spectacular solar phenomenon was witnessed by thousands of people, as had been foretold: the sun was seen spinning in the heavens and moving downwards towards the earth. The content of the messages I am not giving completely. I note that Russia, which in that year was embarking on the Marxist phase of its history, was mentioned as a special object of prayer, and that a particular form of piety towards our Lady, already known to Catholics and esteemed by Newman, prayer and consecration to her Immaculate Heart, is very prominent.

Eventually the world heard of three secrets entrusted to the children. Two were secrets to them, though perhaps they would not appear so to everyone: the existence of hell, and the importance of devotion to the Immaculate Heart – though the promise that special consecration of Russia would be called for one day and lead to its conversion was a secret. The third secret of Fatima is a debating point among Catholics – I should remind you that the events of 1917, and the shrine, have strong worldwide support within the Church. The apparitions have been declared genuine; there have been three papal pilgrimages, with millions of pilgrims annually. Sister Lucia, in her 88th year, is a Carmelite nun in Coimbra, very much a focus of respect. I shall spare you the details of the controversy within the Catholic body on the consecration. As the trustee of the message, Lucia supports those who believe that it has been truly and properly made.

Medjugorje! Since 1981 this Croatian village has become the centre of a spiritual revolution of vast dimensions. Some facts will illustrate the phenomenon. Some years ago it was estimated that ten million pilgrims from the five continents had gone there; 20,000 priests, over 100 bishops. On the spot very many conversions have been recorded: a feature is the number of those seeking the Sacrament of Penance; at times 150 confessors are in demand. Miracles of healing have been reported: 570 dossiers await investigation. Throughout the Church there has been a proliferation of books and regular periodicals reporting what would instruct, explain or edify.

Still more striking is the number of prayer groups deriving directly from belief in Medjugorje. Austria reports 500, but three Australian cities, Sydney, Melbourne and Brisbane have 6000.

What has the Church done in face of all this attention to messages initially received from two boys and three girls? The bishop of the diocese, Mostar, was at first favourable, then changed his opinion. He set up a diocesan commission, and wrote to a friend in France that it would render a negative judgement. But on orders from Rome the competence was transferred to a national commission. This body rendered judgement on 27/28 November 1991. The hierarchy issued a statement saying that they could not say that the messages were supernatural in origin. They did not say that they were not supernatural; they just withheld a firm affirmation. In technical theological terms it is the difference between *non constat de supernaturalitate* and *constat de non supernaturalitate*: the difference between 'I have no proof that you have money in the bank' and 'You have no money in the bank'.

There the position rests. The bishops did undertake to help in pastoral care for the pilgrims who have continued going there despite war. Devotees of Medjugorje have shown their true Christian spirit by organising gigantic aid and relief programmes, none proportionately greater than that directed, planned and effected by Kay Barry in Ireland –I met immense gratitude to her some months ago in that war-stricken country.

Returning to the general theme of present-day Marian apparitions, there are two questions which I leave to your reflection: Are there recurring ideas in the different apparitions which would help us understand the overall purpose of such supernatural interventions? And, taking account of the fact that there are cases calling for reserve as regards authenticity, and one or two almost certainly fraudulent, does this subject present a problem for the movement towards Christian unity?

The second question first: I suggest that the mutual respect which we have for the traditions and practice of our different communions may enable us to overcome, or rather to solve, any problem which arises. As to the content of messages associated with one intervention or another, one may say that certain ideas recur: the need for conversion; the call to prayer, penance, occasionally fasting; attention is drawn to the evil in the world due to decline in faith and fervour; the mercy of God who is so willing to forgive those who repent; promise of a peaceful future after chastisement.

Finally, I can scarcely leave you curious about the Third Secret of Fatima. It was sent to Rome by Sister Lucia and has been read by the Popes and, apparently, some others. It has not been published, though this publication was permissible after 1960. Have we any means of guessing its content? Well, an Italian priest, Don Luigi Bianchi, wrote a book about it. He gave the text to a Vatican prelate who had read the document containing the 'secret'. He asked frankly, would this prelate change anything in his book? 'Nothing', was the reply. Don Luigi maintains in his book that the secret is to do with the general apostasy in the Church in our time. Quite a number of other writers have defended the same thesis. But then our individual reactions, especially in an ecumenical context, will depend upon our personal beliefs, experience, background, hopes and fears.

(This paper was given at the ESBVM Conference at Dromantine College, Newry, in October 1995)

Mary
in
literature

24

The Blessed Virgin Mary
in some modern poets

Gordon S. Wakefield

My title promises a consideration of modern poets, but I want to begin in the seventeenth century with George Herbert. What historians call the 'modern' period extended from around 1450 to 1950, so perhaps he may count under the title. But my reason for including him is that in his poem,'To all Angels and Saints', he speaks for many who would crave the assistance of the saints in prayer, Mary above all, but who are restrained because of their Protestant principles.

George Herbert has been claimed by Anglo-Catholics. He was the Anglican *par excellence*, though the term was not then invented. He was an apostle of the middle way between what a more forthright divine called 'the meretricious gaudiness of Rome and the squalid sluttery of fanatic conventicles'. In his poem 'The British Church', which should be 'The English Church', he describes 'the lady of the hill' who

> Hath kiss'd so long her painted shrines,
> That ev'n her face by kissing shines,
> > For her reward.

And the shy maiden of the valley

> While she avoids her neighbour's pride,
> She wholly goes on th' other side
> > And nothing wears.

What the Oxford Movement made us forget is that seventeenth-century adherents of *Ecclesia Anglicana* insisted on their Protestantism. Archbishop Laud called himself a Protestant on the scaffold. George Herbert's theology was Calvinist tempered by Martin Luther, to whom his religious experience was akin in what seems to have been its *Anfechtung*, turmoil and desolation of spirit. Scripture was Herbert's supreme authority, the very word of God. Therefore though he has a real devotion to Mary, to angels and saints, he tells them:

> Not out of envie or maliciousnesse
> Do I forbear to crave your speciall aid;
> > I would address
> My vows to thee most gladly, blessed Maid,
> And Mother of my God, in my distresse.

Thou art the holy mine, whence came the gold,
The great restorative for all decay
         In young and old;
Thou art the cabinet where the jewell lay:
Chiefly to thee I would my soul unfold.

But now (alas!) I dare not; for our King,
Whom we all joyntly do adore and praise,
         Bids no such thing:
And where his pleasure no injunction layes,
('Tis your own case) ye never move a wing.

All worship is prerogative, and a flower
Of his rich crown, from whom lyes no appeal
         At the last houre:
Therefore we dare not from his garland steal,
To make a posie for inferiour power.

Although then others court you, if ye know
What's done on earth, we shall not fare the worse,
         Who do not so;
Since we are ever ready to disburse,
If any one our Master's hand can show.

This raises many questions for our day and the Society. There is a certain religious temperament which is allured by Mary, and this irrespective of denomination. I have known Methodists who were ill at ease with denunciations of Marian devotion, while some Catholics are embarrassed by its excesses and do not give prominence to the Lord's mother in their worship. As all the world knows, the Second Vatican Council did not accord Mary a separate Constitution, but included her in that on the Church. Feminist and liberation theologies have discovered the Mary of Magnificat. Theirs is a very different devotion from what has been traditional since the Middle Ages, which has regarded Mary almost as a goddess and an intercessor with Christ. She is the Mary of feminism and revolution.

Herbert's poem raises the whole question of the authority of Scripture. Does its silence about prayer to Mary and the Saints, its emphatic insistence on the sole mediatorship of Christ, mean that subsequent developments are in error? Or is Scripture the foundation document of Christianity, but, as George Every once pointed out in a discussion at Oscott, too fragmentary to constitute an irrefragable rule for all time? (I bypass feminist objections to Scripture as from a patriarchal society and male-dominated, and the strictures of Robert Carroll, who believes it outlawed by its unedifying episodes.)

It was Newman, of course, who gave us from his own wrestlings a study of development. And we must recognise with him that 'In a higher world it is otherwise, but here below to live is to change and to be perfect is to have changed often'. My radical students cherished those words, not realising where they led Newman!

Certain considerations are important:

i)   As Christianity advanced into the world, it was bound to assimilate ideas from non-Scriptural cultures and philosophies, both in order to acquire a grammar, as the fashionable jargon has it, in which to commend itself to them, and to discover in the wealth of its own resources what it was capable of becoming in an expanding universe.

ii)   Mary as *theotokos*, God-bearer, was a necessary figure in the fight against Arianism in the fourth century, though the title emphasises her human nature, not her semi-divine station.

iii)   Much spirituality arises out of human need and becomes enshrined in official dogmas by popular demand. This was what was said in 1950 when the dogma of the Assumption was promulgated. We are always being told, in Protestantism at any rate, that there is too great a gulf between the *magisterium*, particularly the theologians, and ordinary people. The Church must be *vulgar*. And yet that way may lie heresy and superstition. There must be some control. An issue today not unconnected with Mariology is the relation of Christianity and paganism. Is the religion of Nature wholly wrong? After all, Romanesque religion attempted to baptise much paganism into Christ, as any visit to one of its churches or cathedrals shows. Think of the Green Man and the associations with the Virgin, particularly at Ely and Exeter. The women ordinands who danced around the decorated pillars at Hereford Cathedral were expressing something of the faith which the pillars represent. Creation Spirituality and the New Age movement would applaud. Classic Protestantism, the New Testament, and parts of the Old, would not. And the cult of the goddess is receiving new sympathy from feminist theology. This cannot be ignored, though it demands the most rigorous examination. It calls for a Balthasar or a Torrance. For the moment it throws one back on George Herbert's caution. I recall what C.S. Lewis wrote in his posthumous *Letters to Malcolm: Chiefly on Prayer*:

> While Christendom is divided about the rationality and even the lawfulness of praying *to* the saints, we are all agreed about praying *with* them. 'With angels and archangels and all the company of heaven.'

I do not forget, however, Maurice Nédoncelle's sadly neglected *The Nature and Use of Prayer* (1962), and the consideration in Part One of 'Prayer from Man to Man' which considers prayer as belonging to 'the domain of the vocative'. We pray to one another. The requests may conceal our real desire, which is 'bonding', union with one another, heart speaking to heart, to which our petitions are an appeal. Is not prayer to Mary and the Saints a wish for union with them in the worship and service of the Blessed Trinity?

Catholic doctrine would consider Mary as a special case. True, in the first chapter of Acts, she is named with the praying women and Jesus' family as Pentecost is awaited, and not given undue prominence, much less veneration. Her uniqueness is established by later theology because of her distinctive and indispensable role in the Incarnation. And that is the presupposition of the next poem.

I now turn to Gerard Manley Hopkins, the Jesuit priest. He died in 1889, but is an authentic modern poet, not simply because his works were not as a whole given to the world until 1918, but because in his sprung rhythm and idiosyncratic compound words as well as his unconventional and at times colloquial language, he effected a revolution from which modern poetry, although he is beyond imitation, cannot escape. Tennyson is no more. We are here in another dimension from Herbert's devotion disciplined by Scripture and the creeds.

Hopkins's poem,'The Blessed Virgin Compared to the Air we Breathe' may be called by the bedevilled term 'mystical', in that it presumes a unity between nature and sense experience and God. It is certainly not pagan. In his commentary on 'Contemplation for Obtaining Love' from Ignatius Loyola's *Spiritual Exercises* Hopkins wrote:

> Suppose God shewed us in a vision the whole world enclosed first in a drop of water, allowing everything to be seen in its native colours; then the same in a drop of Christ's blood, by which everything whatever was turned scarlet, keeping nevertheless mounted in the scarlet its own colour too.

The drop of Christ's blood becomes the world in itself, dipped in Christ's blood but retaining its own identity. In the poem

> This air, which by life's law,
> My lung must draw and draw
> Now but to breathe its praise,
> Minds me in many ways
> Of her who not only
> Gave God's infinity
> Dwindled to infancy
> Welcome in womb and breast,
> Birth, milk, and all the rest
> But mothers each new grace
> That does now reach our race –

Mary Immaculate,
Merely a woman, yet
Whose presence, power is
Great as no goddess's
Was deemèd, dreamèd; who
This one work has to do –
Let all God's glory through,
God's glory which would go
Through her and from her flow
Off, and in no way but so.

I say that we are wound
With mercy round and round
As if with air: the same
Is Mary, more by name.
She, wild web, wondrous robe,
Mantles the guilty globe,
Since God has let dispense
Her prayers his providence:
Nay, more than almoner,
The sweet alms' self is her,
And men are meant to share
Her life as life does air.

If I have understood,
She holds high motherhood
Towards all our ghostly good
And plays in grace her part
About man's beating heart,
Laying, like air's fine flood,
The deathdance in his blood;
Yet no part but what will
Be Christ our Saviour still.
Of her flesh he took flesh:
He does take fresh and fresh,
Though much the mystery how,
Not flesh but spirit now
And makes, O marvellous!
New Nazareths in us,
Where she shall yet conceive
Him, morning, noon, and eve;
New Bethlems, and he born
There, evening, noon, and morn –
Bethlem or Nazareth,
Men here may draw like breath
More Christ and baffle death;
Who, born so, comes to be
New self and nobler me

> In each one and each one
> More makes, when all is done,
> Both God's and Mary's Son.

Because she bore the Incarnate God, Mary bears us who are born again in him, not once for all in one dramatic moment of conversion, but continually, like each breath of air.

Then Hopkins looks to the azure, heavenward. He thinks of the pure air of the blue heaven, which mediates the face of the sun, lest the earth be obliterated, burnt to a cinder. So Mary makes it possible for the burning rays of the Divine being not to consume us utterly, but to be our light and warmth in our earthly lives.

> So God was god of old:
> A mother came to mould
> Those limbs like ours which are
> What must make our daystar
> Much dearer to mankind;
> Whose glory bare would blind
> Or less would win man's mind.
> Through her we may see him,
> Made sweeter, not made dim,
> And her hand leaves his light
> Sifted to suit our sight.

Mary, then, may be the atmosphere of our lives, the spiritual air we breathe, pure and soul-converting. Through her we live in the life of the God of whom no mortal eye can bear the sight.

This Mariology is derived from her part in the Incarnation. She is no goddess, 'merely a woman', yet it is through her that we live our regenerate lives. She is the mother, in whose embraces the little Christ in us may grow.

Some may think that Hopkins transfers to Mary what belongs to Christ, or to the Holy Spirit who is his breath. Is not the Spirit our air? And are we not saved from the sentimentality into which both Marian and Jesus piety may drift if we remember that? Yet the Holy Spirit in Christian understanding is the particular gift to Christians in consequence of the Incarnation and the glory through the cross. And whereas the Holy Spirit is difficult for some and may seem impersonal – wind, breath, fire, dove – Mary takes us back to the mother and the child in the lowly manger, to the tender homeliness of the gospel and to the mother watching her Son die a hideous death. And here is the relation of faith to nature. The creation, the world around us, is an analogy of God's being and activity, a 'book who runs may read', as in Keble's hymn. A long and ecumenical tradition of Christian spirituality found in Bonaventure, and surprisingly in the radical reformer Thomas Muntzer, teaches us so to live in the world of physical reality that every sight and sound, act, incident, experience is sacramental of life in Christ.

The other two poems I have chosen are both concerned with Jesus and Mary in their human lives.

First, there is the cradle song 'At the Manger' from W.H. Auden's *For the Time Being: A Christmas Oratorio* in memory of his mother, set to music by Benjamin Britten at the time of their co-operation in the United States during the second world war. This lullaby does not presume the courtly stable, the angel's song, the joy of the Christ child's birth. As for John Donne, and later for Dag Hammarskjöld, Christmas Day and Good Friday are but the morning and the evening of one and the same day. Mary sings of the premonitions of sorrows to come:

O shut your bright eyes that mine must endanger
With their watchfulness; protected by its shade
Escape from my care: what can you discover
From my tender look but how to be afraid?
Love can but confirm the more it would deny.
    Close your bright eye.

Sleep. What have you learned from the womb that bore you
But an anxiety your Father cannot feel?
Sleep. What will the flesh that I gave do for you,
Or my mother love, but tempt you from His will?
Why was I chosen to teach His Son to weep?
    Little One, sleep.

Dream. In human dreams earth ascends to Heaven
Where no one need pray nor ever feel alone.
In your first few hours of life here, O have you
Chosen already what death must be your own?
How soon will you start on the Sorrowful Way?
    Dream while you may.

Here Mary is the Mother of Sorrows, who, in spite of the archangel's salutation, has given birth for her son to die. It is from her, the human mother, that Jesus will learn human anxiety, take on himself those fears and griefs which the impassible God cannot share. The sword is already piercing Mary's soul. Her motherhood is as much a means of danger to Christ as a protection because she has brought him into this world, while her very love may seek to deter him from what his Father, God, demands.

The poem would almost justify the conviction of some Puritans that Christmas should be a fast, not a feast, since the Son of God came into a world of so much suffering and sin. It is well to remember that this is the perennial state of the world in time, though that is not difficult since every news bulletin tells us so. We cannot expect otherwise. But Christians believe that Christ, because he is the Incarnate God, bore the whole burden of the world's sin and pain and griefs beyond our understanding. If we are to know a more than ephemeral joy in what is passing away and touched with pain, compounded by the tragedies of the world, it is in the Holy Eucharist, thanksgiving only in the context of his Passion, of what he bore for us from Bethlehem to Calvary. And yet like Jesus according to Mary in the song, we must learn to take what repose we can and ascend to heaven if only in our dreams. 'Dream while you may.' Jesus knew joy in his earthly life, and sometimes we have to shut out the world's problems and anxieties, else we should not survive for what God may intend as the supreme moment of our sacrifice, our part with Christ.

Thom Gunn is a poet, educated at Cambridge, who has lived in the United States these many years. I liked what he wrote some years ago in a symposium about his Cambridge life. Latterly his poetry has been preoccupied with homosexuality and Aids. He seems to be very much with and for the gays, since he is confessedly one himself. He enters into their conditions, which seem to him to be a consequence of humanity. Sympathetic, I am yet made uncomfortable by this, which may show that I am a case for the psychoanalyst, but is not relevant to our subject now.

'Jesus and his Mother', an earlier poem, strikes me as very fine. Like Auden's lullaby, it is true to what we read in the gospels in its understanding that the relationship between Jesus and his mother could not have been an easy one. It does not surround the home at Nazareth with an aura of heaven, except that the unique vocation of Mary's son in the divine will, his ultimate heavenly origin, could have made life there more difficult, not at all a paradise. It is good to break free of pious idealism.

> My only son, more God's than mine,
> Stay in this garden ripe with pears.
> The yielding of their substance wears
> A modest and contented shine:
> And when they weep with age, not brine
> But lazy syrup are their tears.
> 'I am my own and not my own.'

He seemed much like another man,
That silent foreigner who trod
Outside my door with lily rod:
How could I know what I began
Meeting the eyes more furious than
The eyes of Joseph, those of God?
I was my own and not my own.

And who are these twelve labouring men?
I do not understand your words:
I taught you speech, we named the birds,
You marked their big migrations then
Like any child. So turn again
To silence from the place of crowds.
'I am my own and not my own.'

Why are you sullen when I speak?
Here are your tools, the saw and knife
And hammer on your bench. Your life
Is measured here in week and week
Planed as the furniture you make,
And I will teach you like a wife
To be my own and all my own.

Who like an arrogant wind blown
Where he may please, needs no content?
Yet I remember how you went
To speak with scholars in furred gown.
I hear an outcry in the town;
Who carried that dark instrument?
'One all his own and not his own.'

Treading the green and nimble sward
I stare at a strange shadow thrown.
Are you the boy I bore alone
No doctor near to cut the cord?
I cannot reach to call you Lord,
Answer me as my only son.
'I am my own and not my own.'

There are many allusions there to what the early traditions tell us about Jesus, the apocryphal story of his naming the birds, his work as a carpenter, his discussion with the scholars in the temple at the age of twelve, the call of the disciples and the shadow of the cross. It gets behind reverential imagination, the stained glass, the pious legends, to what may well have been the bewildering reality of the two natures, the two loyalties to heavenly Father and to human mother, and the Divine will. Mary is no goddess here; just a puzzled mother, who, as the synoptists imply, longs to have her son to herself as all mothers do, and yet is aware that she also is caught up in a unique vocation from the birth of a child outside marriage onwards. 'I was my own and not my own'.

To conclude: these poems all make us understand that any devotion to Mary must follow from her relation to Christ and the mystery of the Incarnation. This is a divine event which includes all nature in its vaster scope, which itself is as the air we breathe. For the Church, it is the Incarnation and not the world which writes the agenda. But Mary's is also a human story, complicated, not made more simple, by God's part in it. There are many vicissitudes: joy but also sorrow; obedience, but also misunderstanding and bewilderment. There is no clear path through human life, unambiguous, certain and sure. There are no signposts other than those of faith. This is apparent both in the Incarnate life and in Mary's. Yet, if we are so inclined, we may enter through her into the union of the Word and nature and humanity in Christ and find various consolations, whether we think of her as our mother too, making the new birth possible every day of our lives, through the one she bore; or as the mediatrix of the Mediator, since he who reconciles all things to God was conceived in his incarnate life in her womb; or as the woman who knew the agonies as well as the joys of childbirth, and suffered with her son, not least because he was at once man and God.

Marian devotion is not mandatory for Christians, but some may find that it brings them nearer to God in Christ as he was in the strange historic events of our redemption. It is not a means of elevating one woman into high heaven while leaving others in a submissive and subordinate role on earth. Much less does it see Mary as the compassionate mother who may turn away the wrath of her Son as he does that of his Father. Marian devotion may grow wild and need to be pruned by Scripture and the fundamental truths of Christian belief. It must always be, like Mary herself, the handmaiden of faith in the one unique Trinity, Father, Son and Holy Spirit, to whom be the glory for ever and ever.

(This paper was given at the ESBVM Congress
at Norwich in July 1994)

THE ECUMENICAL SOCIETY OF THE BLESSED VIRGIN MARY
Registered Charity no. 282748

If you would like to know more about the activities of our Society and how to become a member, please write to:

Membership Secretary (Peter Holm)
24 Frobisher Court
Sydenham Rise
Forest Hill
London SE23 3XH

Details of previous collections of papers (*Mary's Place in Christian Dialogue*, *Mary and the Churches*, *Mary in Doctrine and Devotion*), and of our numerous occasional pamphlets, may be obtained from:

Publications Secretary ESBVM
11 Drove Acre Road
Oxford OX4 3DF